Elbert Hubbard

ELBERT HUBBARD'S SCRAP BOOK

CONTAINING THE INSPIRED
AND INSPIRING SELECTIONS
GATHERED DURING A LIFE
TIME OF DISCRIMINATING
READING FOR HIS OWN USE

A FIREBIRD PRESS BOOK

PELICAN PUBLISHING COMPANY
Gretna 1998

Manufactured in the United States of America
Published by Pelican Publishing Company, Inc.
1000 Burmaster Street, Gretna, Louisiana 70053

FOREWORD

WHEN Elbert Hubbard was storing up in his Scrap Book the fruits of other men's genius, he did not contemplate a volume for publication ❧ He was merely gathering spiritual provisions for his own refreshment and delectation ❧ ❧

To glance at the pages of his Scrap Book is to realize how far and wide he pursued the quest, into what scented rose gardens of Poetry, and up what steep slopes of Thought. To Alpine Valleys of classical literature it led him, and through forests and swamps of contemporary writing. For him it was the quest that mattered, it was the quest he loved ❧ ❧

The Reader will remember Keats' dream of "a very pleasant life."

> " I had an idea that a Man might pass a very pleasant life in this manner: Let him on a certain day read a certain page of full Poesy or distilled Prose, and let him wander with it, and muse upon it, and reflect from it, and dream upon it: until it becomes stale—But when will it do so? Never— When a man has arrived at a certain ripeness in intellect any one grand and spiritual passage serves him as a starting-post towards all the 'two-and-thirty Palaces.' How happy is such a voyage of conception, what delicious, diligent indolence!"

Elbert Hubbard's lifelong labor has placed in all our hands the power to realize Keats' dream. Here in Hubbard's Scrap Book the Reader will find " full Poesy " and " distilled Prose," of a pleasing savor to the tongue and a strangely nourishing relish to the intelligence.

Let the reader browse but a moment and—to use Keats' image—he will find the sails of his soul set for one of those high voyages of the spirit which give to life its most exalted meaning, and bring back as cargo the thrice-tried gold of ecstasy and vision.

What inspired Elbert Hubbard should set other pulses to beating. What stimulated and uplifted him should furnish others with strength for the struggle against the eroding sameness of the workaday world. Such at least is the purpose to which the book is dedicated; such is the pious hope of Elbert Hubbard's literary executors.

THE PUBLISHERS.

THERE is an ancient legend which tells us that when a man first achieved a most notable deed he wished to explain to his tribe what he had done. As soon as he began to speak, however, he was smitten with dumbness, he lacked words, and sat down. Then there arose—according to the story—a masterless man, one who had taken no part in the action of his fellow, who had no special virtues, but afflicted—that is the phrase—with the magic of the necessary words. He saw, he told, he described the merits of the notable deed in such a fashion, we are assured, that the words " became alive and walked up and down in the hearts of all his hearers." Thereupon, the tribe seeing that the words were certainly alive, and fearing lest the man with the words would hand down untrue tales about them to their children, they took and killed him. But later they saw that the magic was in the words, not in the man.

—*Kipling*

PROVIDENCE—AN APOLOGUE

HE other evening I was a little late in going down to dinner, and this was the reason: I noticed a number of dead bees lying on the floor of the lookout where I am accustomed to work—a sight that I encounter every spring. The poor things had come in through the open window. When the windows were closed they found themselves prisoners. Unable to see the transparent obstacle, they had hurled themselves against the glass panes on all sides, east, north, south and west, until at last they fell to the floor exhausted, and died. But, yesterday, I noticed among the bees, a great drone, much stronger than the bees, who was far from being dead, who, in fact, was very much alive and was dashing himself against the panes with all his might, like the great beast that he was. "Ah! my fine friend," said I, "it would have been an evil day for you had I not come to the rescue. You would have been done for, my fine fellow; before nightfall you would be lying dead, and on coming up-stairs, in the evening with my lamp, I would have found your poor little corpse among those of the other bees." Come, now, like the Emperor Titus I shall mark the day by a good deed: let us save the insect's life. Perhaps in the eyes of God a drone is as valuable as a man, and without any doubt it is more valuable than a prince.

I threw open the window, and, by means of a napkin, began chasing the insect toward it; but the drone persisted in flying in the opposite direction. I then tried to capture it by throwing the napkin over it. When the drone saw that I wished to capture it, it lost its head completely; it bounded furiously against the glass panes, as though it would smash them, took a fresh start, and dashed itself again and again against the glass. Finally it flew the whole length of the apartment, maddened and desperate. " Ah, you tyrant!" it buzzed. " Despot! you would deprive me of liberty! Cruel executioner, why do you not leave me alone? I am happy, and why do you persecute me?"

After trying very hard, I brought it down and, in seizing it with the napkin, I involuntarily hurt it. Oh, how it tried to avenge itself! It darted out its sting; its little nervous body, contracted by my fingers, strained itself with all its strength in an attempt to sting me. But I ignored its protestations, and, stretching my hand out the window, opened the napkin. For a moment the drone seemed stunned, astonished; then it calmly took flight out into the infinite.

Well, you see how I saved the drone. I was *its Providence.* But (and here is the moral of my story) do we not, stupid drones that we are, conduct ourselves in the same manner toward the providence of God? We have our petty and absurd projects, our small and narrow views, our rash designs, whose accomplishment is either impossible or injurious to ourselves. Seeing no farther than our noses and with our eyes fixed on our immediate aim, we plunge ahead in our blind infatuation, like madmen. We would succeed, we would triumph; that is to say, we would break our heads against an invisible obstacle.

And when God, who sees all and who wishes to save us, upsets our designs, we stupidly complain againstHim, we accuse His Providence.We do not comprehend that in punishing us, in overturning our plans and causing us suffering, He is doing all this to deliver us, to open the Infinite to us.—*Victor Hugo.*

IT is not possible to have the true pictures or statues of Cyrus, Alexander, Cæsar, no, nor of the kings or great personages of much later years; for the originals can not last, and the copies can not but leese of the life and truth. But the images of men's wits and knowledges remain in books, exempted from the wrong of time, and capable of perpetual renovation ᴥ Neither are they fitly to be called images, because they generate still, and cast their seeds in the minds of others, provoking and causing infinite actions and opinions in succeeding ages: so that, if the invention of the ship was thought so noble, which carrieth riches and commodities from place to place, and consociateth the most remote regions in participation of their fruits, how much more are letters to be magnified, which as ships, pass through the vast sea of time, and make ages so distant to participate of the wisdom, illuminations, and inventions the one of the other?—Francis Bacon.

ᴥ ᴥ

IT is the Indian summer. The rising sun blazes through the misty air like a conflagration. A yellowish, smoky haze fills the atmosphere, and a filmy mist lies like a silver lining on the sky. The wind is soft and low. It wafts to us the odor of forest leaves, that hang wilted on the dripping branches, or drop into the stream. Their gorgeous tints are gone, as if the autumnal rains had washed them out. Orange, yellow and scarlet, all are changed to one melancholy russet hue ᴥ The birds, too, have taken wing, and have left their roofless dwellings. Not the whistle of a robin, not the twitter of an eavesdropping swallow, not the carol of one sweet, familiar voice. All gone. Only the dismal cawing of a crow, as he sits and curses that the harvest is over; or the chit-chat of an idle squirrel, the noisy denizen of a hollow tree, the mendicant friar of a large parish, the absolute monarch of a dozen acorns.
—Longfellow.

ᴥ ᴥ

WHAT moods, what passions, what nights of despair and gathering storms of anger, what sudden cruelties and amazing tendernesses are buried and hidden and implied in every love story! What a waste is there of exquisite things! So each spring sees a million glorious beginnings, a sunlit heaven in every opening leaf, warm perfection in every stirring egg, hope and fear and beauty beyond computation in every forest tree; and in the autumn before the snows come they have all gone—of all that incalculable abundance of life, of all that hope and adventure, excitement and deliciousness, there is scarcely more to be found than a soiled twig, a dirty seed, a dead leaf, black mould, or a rotting feather.
—H. G. Wells.

ᴥ ᴥ

Speech is the index of the mind.—Seneca.

Serene, I fold my hands and wait,
Nor care for wind nor tide nor sea:
I rave no more 'gainst time or fate,
For, lo! my own shall come to me.

I stay my haste, I make delays:
For what avails this eager pace?
I stand amid the eternal ways,
And what is mine shall know my face.

Asleep, awake, by night or day,
The friends I seek are seeking me;
No wind can drive my bark astray,
Nor change the tide of destiny.

What matter if I stand alone?
I wait with joy the coming years:
My heart shall reap where it has sown,
And garner up the fruit of tears.

The waters know their own, and draw
The brook that springs in yonder heights.
So flows the good with equal law
Unto the soul of pure delights.

The stars come nightly to the sky,
The tidal wave unto the sea;
Nor time nor space, nor deep nor high,
Can keep my own away from me.

"Waiting," by John Burroughs

HE tradition of the stage is a tradition of villains and heroes. Shakespeare was a devout believer in the existence of the true villain—the man whose terrible secret is that his fundamental moral impulses are by some freak of nature inverted, so that not only are love, pity, and honor loathsome to him, and the affectation of them which society imposes on him a constant source of disgust, but cruelty, destruction, and perfidy are his most luxurious passions. This is a totally different phenomenon from the survivals of the ape and tiger in the normal man. The average normal man is covetous, lazy, selfish; but he is not malevolent, nor capable of saying to himself, " Evil: be thou my good." He only does wrong as a means to an end, which he always represents to himself as a right end. The case is exactly reversed with a villain; and it is my melancholy duty to add that we sometimes find it hard to avoid a cynical suspicion that the balance of social advantage is on the side of gifted villainy, since we see the able villain, Mephistopheles-like, doing a huge amount of good in order to win the power to do a little daring evil, out of which he is as likely as not to be cheated in the end; whilst your normal respectable man will countenance, connive at, and grovel his way through all sorts of meanness, baseness, servility, and cruel indifference to suffering in order to enjoy a miserable tuppence worth of social position, piety, comfort, and domestic affection, of which he, too, is often ironically defrauded by Fate.—George Bernard Shaw.

War
I do abhor;
And yet how sweet
The sound along the marching street
Of drum or fife, and I forget
Broken old mothers, and the whole
Dark butchering without a soul.

Without a soul—save this bright treat
Of heady music, sweet as hell;
And even my peace-abiding feet
Go marching with the marching street,
For yonder goes the fife,
And what care I for human Life!
The tears fill my astonished eyes,
And my full heart is like to break,
And yet it is embannered lies,
A dream those drummers make.

Oh, it is wickedness to clothe
Yon hideous, grinning thing that stalks
Hidden in music like a queen
That in a garden of glory walks,
Till good men love the thing they loathe;
Art, thou hast many infamies,
But not an infamy like this.
O, snap the fife and still the drum,
And show the monster as she is.

"The Illusions of War," *by Richard Le Gallienne*

I WAS passing along the street when a beggar, a decrepit old man, stopped me. ¶ Swollen, tearful eyes, blue lips, bristling rags, unclean sores. . . . . Oh, how horribly had poverty gnawed that unhappy being! He stretched out to me a red, bloated, dirty hand. . . He moaned, he bellowed for help.

I began to rummage in all my pockets . . Neither purse, nor watch, nor even handkerchief did I find . . . I had taken nothing with me.

And the beggar still waited . . .and extended his hand, which swayed and trembled feebly.

Bewildered, confused, I shook that dirty, tremulous hand heartily . . . . " Blame me not, brother; I have nothing, brother."

¶ The beggar man fixed his swollen eyes upon me; his blue lips smiled—and in his turn he pressed my cold fingers.
" Never mind, brother," he mumbled.
" Thanks for this also, brother.—This also is an alms, brother."
I understood that I had received an alms from my brother.—" The Beggar Man," by Turgenef.

Drudgery is as necessary to call out the treasurers of the mind as harrowing and planting those of the earth.
—Margaret Fuller.

TO make my readers realize what a philosopher is, I can only say that *I* am a philosopher. If you ask incredulously, "How, then, are your articles so interesting?" I reply that there is nothing so interesting as philosophy, provided its materials are not spurious.

For instance, take my own materials—humanity and the fine arts. Any studious, timorously ambitious bookworm can run away from the world with a few shelves full of history, essays, descriptions, and criticisms, and, having pieced an illusory humanity and art out of the effects produced by his library upon his imagination, build some silly systematization of his worthless ideas over the abyss of his own nescience. Such a philosopher is as dull and dry as you please; it is he who brings his profession into disrepute, especially when he talks much about art, and so persuades people to read him. Without having looked at more than fifty pictures in his life, or made up his mind on the smallest point about one of the fifty, he will audaciously take it upon himself to explain the development of painting from Zeuxis and Apelles to Raphael and Michelangelo ✺ ✺

As to the way he will go on about music, of which he always has an awe-stricken conceit, it spoils my temper to think of it, especially when one remembers that musical composition is taught (a monstrous pretension) in this country by people who *read* scores, and never by any chance listen to performances.

Now, the right way to go to work—strange as it may appear—is to look at pictures until you have acquired the power of seeing them. If you look at several thousand good pictures every year, and form some sort of practical judgment about every one of them—were it only that it is not worth troubling over—then at the end of five years or so you will, if you have a wise eye, be able to see what is actually in a picture, and not what you think is in it. Similarly, if you listen critically to music every day for a number of years, you will, if you have a wise ear, acquire the power of hearing music. And so on with all the arts ✺ ✺

When we come to humanity it is still the same: only by intercourse with men and women can we learn anything about it. This involves an active life, not a contemplative one; for, unless you do something in the world, you can have no real business to transact with men; and unless you love and are loved, you can have no intimate relations with them. And you must transact business, wirepull politics, discuss religion, give and receive hate, love, and friendship with all sorts of people before you can acquire the sense of humanity.

If you are to acquire the sense sufficiently to be a philosopher, you must do all these things unconditionally. You must not say that you will be a gentleman and limit your intercourse to this class or that class; or that you will be a virtuous person and generalize about the affections from a single instance—unless, indeed, you have the rare happiness to stumble at first upon an all-enlightening instance. You must have no convictions, because as Nietzsche puts it, " convictions are prisons." Thus, I blush to add, you can not be a philosopher and a good man, though you may be a philosopher and a great one.

You will say, perhaps, that if this be so, there should be no philosophers; and perhaps you are right; but though I make you this handsome concession, I do not defer to you to the extent of ceasing to exist.

After all, if you insist on the hangman, whose pursuits are far from elevating, you may very well tolerate the philosopher, even if philosophy involves philandering; or, to put it another way, if, in spite of your hangman, you tolerate murder within the sphere of war, it may be necessary to tolerate comparatively venial irregularities within the sphere of philosophy ✺ ✺

It is the price of progress; and, after all, it is the philosopher, and not you, who will burn for it.

—George Bernard Shaw.

HE summits of the Alps. . . . A whole chain of steep cliffs . . . The very heart of the mountains.

Overhead a bright, mute, pale-green sky. A hard, cruel frost; firm, sparkling snow; from beneath the snow project grim blocks of ice-bound, wind-worn cliffs.

Two huge masses, two giants rise aloft, one on each side of the horizon: the Jungfrau and the Finsteraarhorn.

And the Jungfrau says to its neighbor: "What news hast thou to tell? Thou canst see better.—What is going on there below?"

Several thousand years pass by like one minute. And the Finsteraarhorn rumbles in reply: "Dense clouds veil the earth . . . Wait!"

More thousands of years elapse, as it were one minute.

"Well, what now?" inquires the Jungfrau. "Now I can see; down yonder, below, everything is still the same: party-colored, tiny. The waters gleam blue; the forests are black; heaps of stones piled up shine gray. Around them small beetles are still bustling,—thou knowest, those two-legged beetles who have as yet been unable to defile either thou or me."

"Men?"

"Yes, men."

Thousands of years pass, as it were one minute

"Well, and what now?" asks the Jungfrau

"I seem to see fewer of the little beetles," thunders the Finsteraarhorn. "Things have become clearer down below; the waters have contracted; the forests have grown thinner."

More thousands of years pass, as it were one minute.

"What dost thou see?" says the Jungfrau

"Things seem to have grown clearer round us, close at hand," replies the Finsteraarhorn; "well, and yonder, far away, in the valleys there is still a spot, and something is moving."

"And now?" inquires the Jungfrau, after other thousands of years, which are as one minute.

"Now it is well," replies the Finsteraarhorn; "it is clean everywhere, quite white, wherever one looks . . .

"Everywhere is our snow, level snow and ice. Everything is congealed. It is well now, and calm."

"Good," said the Jungfrau.—"But thou and I have chattered enough, old fellow. It is time to sleep."

"It is time!"

The huge mountains slumber; the green, clear heaven slumbers over the earth which has grown dumb forever.—"A Conversation," based on the fact that never yet has human foot trod either the Jungfrau or the Finsteraarhorn, by Turgenef

E said, "I see." And they said: "He's crazy; crucify him." He still said: "I see." And they said: "He's an extremist." And they tolerated him. And he continued to say: "I see." And they said: "He's eccentric." And they rather liked him, but smiled at him. And he stubbornly said again: "I see." And they said: "There's something in what he says." And they gave him half an ear. But he said as if he'd never said it before: "I see." And at last they were awake; and they gathered about him and built a temple in his name. And yet he only said: "I see." And they wanted to do something for him. "What can we do to express to you our regret?" He only smiled. He touched them with the ends of his fingers and kissed them. What could they do for him? "Nothing more than you have done," he answered. And what was that? they wanted to know. "You see," he said, "that's reward enough; you see, you see."—'The Prophet," by Horace Traubel.

REMBRANDT belongs to the breed of artists which can have no posterity. His place is with the Michelangelos, the Shakespeares, the Beethovens. An artistic Prometheus, he stole the celestial fire, and with it put life into what was inert, and expressed the immaterial and evasive sides of nature in his breathing forms.—Emile Michel.

TEP by step my investigation of blindness led me into the industrial world. And what a world it is! I must face unflinchingly a world of facts—a world of misery and degradation, of blindness, crookedness, and sin, a world struggling against the elements, against the unknown, against itself. How reconcile this world of fact with the bright world of my imagining? ✎ My darkness had been filled with the light of intelligence, and, behold, the outer day-lit world was stumbling and groping in social blindness. At first I was most unhappy; but deeper study restored my confidence ✎ By learning the sufferings and burdens of men, I became aware as never before of the life-power that has survived the forces of darkness—the power which, though never completely victorious, is continuously conquering. The very fact that we are still here carrying on the contest against the hosts of annihilation proves that on the whole the battle has gone for humanity. The world's great heart has proved equal to the prodigious undertaking which God set it. Rebuffed, but always persevering; self-reproached, but ever regaining faith; undaunted, tenacious, the heart of man labors towards immeasurably distant goals. Discouraged not by difficulties without, or the anguish of ages within, the heart listens to a secret voice that whispers: "Be not dismayed; in the future lies the Promised Land."
—Helen Keller.

✎ ✎

Man is the merriest species of the creation; all above or below him are serious.
—Addison.

Life! we 've been long together
Through pleasant and through
cloudy weather;
'T is hard to part when friends
are dear—
Perhaps 't will cost a sigh, a
tear;
Then steal away, give little
warning,
Choose thine own time;
Say not Good-Night—but in
some brighter clime
Bid me Good-Morning.

"Life," by Anna Letitia Barbauld

HERE has arisen in society a figure which is certainly the most mournful, and in some respects the most awful, upon which the eye of the moralist can dwell. That unhappy being whose very name is a shame to speak; who counterfeits with a cold heart the transports of affection, and submits herself as the passive instrument of lust; who is scorned and insulted as the vilest of her sex and doomed, for the most part, to disease and abject wretchedness and an early death, appears in every age as the perpetual symbol of the degradation and sinfulness of man ✎

✐ Herself the supreme type of vice, she is ultimately the most efficient guardian of virtue.

✐ But for her, the unchallenged purity of countless happy homes would be polluted, and not a few who, in the pride of their untempted chastity, think of her with an indignant shudder, would have known the agony of remorse and despair.

On that one degraded and ignoble form are concentrated the passions that might have filled the world with shame. She remains, while creeds and civilizations rise and fall, the eternal priestess of humanity, blasted for the sins of the people.—William E. H. Lecky.

✎ ✎

IN the Twentieth Century war will be dead, the scaffold will be dead, hatred will be dead, frontier boundaries will be dead, dogmas will be dead; man will live. He will possess something higher than all these—a great country, the whole earth, and a great hope, the whole heaven.—Victor Hugo.

✎ ✎

If you have knowledge, let others light their candles at it.—Margaret Fuller.

NEW era is dawning on the world. We are beginning to believe in the religion of usefulness ❧ ❧
The men who felled the forests, cultivated the earth, spanned the rivers with bridges of steel, built the railways and canals, the great ships, invented the locomotives and engines, supplying the countless wants of civilization; the men who invented the telegraphs and cables, and freighted the electric spark with thought and love; the men who invented the looms and spindles that clothe the world, the inventors of printing and the great presses that fill the earth with poetry, fiction and fact, that save and keep all knowledge for the children yet to be; the inventors of all the wonderful machines that deftly mold from wood and steel the things we use; the men who explored the heavens and traced the orbits of the stars—who have read the story of the world in mountain range and billowed sea; the men who have lengthened life and conquered pain; the great philosophers and naturalists who have filled the world with light; the great poets whose thoughts have charmed the soul, the great painters and sculptors who have made the canvas speak, the marble live; the great orators who have swayed the world, the composers who have given their souls to sound, the captains of industry, the producers, the soldiers who have battled for the right— these are our Christs, apostles and saints. The books filled with the facts of Nature are our sacred scriptures, and the force that is in every atom and in every star— in everything that lives and grows—is the only possible god.—R. G. Ingersoll.

The golden poppy is God's gold,
The gold that lifts, nor weighs us down,
The gold that knows no miser's hold,
The gold that banks not in the town,
But singing, laughing, freely spills
Its hoard far up the happy hills;
Far up, far down, at every turn—
What beggar has not gold to burn!

" The California Poppy," *by Joaquin Miller*

ORATORY offers the acme of human delight; it offers the nectar that Jupiter sips; it offers the draft that intoxicates the gods, the divine felicity of lifting up and swaying mankind. There is nothing greater on this earth. 'T is the breath of the Eternal—the kiss of the Immortal ❧ ❧
Oratory is far above houses and lands, offices and emoluments, possessions and power.
While it may secure all of these it must not for a moment be classed with them. These things offer nothing that is worthy of a high ambition. Enjoyed to their fullest, they leave you hard, wrinkled and miserable. Get all they can give and the hand will be empty, the mind hungry, and the soul shriveled ❧ ❧
Oratory is an individual accomplishment, and no vicissitudes of fortune can wrest it from the owner. It points the martyr's path to the future; it guides the reaper's hand in the present, and it turns the face of ambition toward the delectable hills of achievement. One great speech made to an intelligent audience in favor of the rights of man will compensate for a life of labor, will crown a career with glory, and give a joy that is born of the divinities. There is no true orator who is not also a hero.
—John P. Altgeld.

❧ ❧

NO one has success until he has the abounding life. This is made up of the many-fold activity of energy, enthusiasm and gladness. It is to spring to meet the day with a thrill at being alive. It is to go forth to meet the morning in an ecstasy of joy. It is to realize the oneness of humanity in true spiritual sympathy.—Lillian Whiting.

UKA:—Treat every one with friendliness—injure no one. *Natasha:*—How good you are, grandfather! How is it that you are so good?

Luka:—I am good, you say. Nyah—if it is true, all right. But you see, my girl— there must be some one to be good. We must have pity on mankind. Christ, remember, had pity for us all and so taught us. Have pity when there is still time, believe me, that is right. I was once for example, employed as a watchman, at a country place which belonged to an engineer, not far from the city of Tomsk, in Siberia. The house stood in the middle of the forest, an out-of-the-way location; and it was winter and I was all alone in the country house. It was beautiful there —magnificent! And once—I heard them scrambling up!

Natasha:—Thieves?

Luka:—Yes. They crept higher, and I took my rifle and went outside. I looked up—two men, opening a window, and so busy that they did not see anything of me at all. I cried to them: Hey, there, get out of that! And would you think it, they fell on me with a hand ax! I warned them. Halt, I cried, or else I fire! Then I aimed first at one and then at the other. They fell on their knees saying, Pardon us! I was pretty hot—on account of the hand ax, you remember. You devils, I cried, I told you to clear out and you did n't! And now, I said, one of you go into the brush and get a switch. It was done. And now, I commanded, one of you stretch out on the ground, and the other thrash him. And so they whipped each other at my command. And when they had each had a sound beating, they said to me: Grandfather, said they, for the sake of Christ give us a piece of bread. We have n't a bite in our bodies. They, my daughter, were the thieves who had fallen upon me with the hand ax. Yes, they were a pair of splendid fellows. I said to them, If you had asked for bread! Then they answered: We had gotten past that. We had asked and asked, and nobody would give us anything. Endurance was worn out. Nyah— and so they remained with me the whole

winter. One of them, Stephen by name, liked to take the rifle and go into the woods. And the other, Jakoff, was constantly ill, always coughing. The three of us watched the place, and when spring came, they said, Farewell, grandfather, and went away—to Russia.

Natasha:—Were they convicts, escaping?

Luka:—They were fugitives—they had left their colony. A pair of splendid fellows. If I had not had pity on them— who knows what would have happened? They might have killed me? Then they would be taken to court again—put in prison, sent back to Siberia—why all that? You can learn nothing good in prison, nor in Siberia. But a man, what can he not learn!—Maxim Gorky.

TWO contrary laws stand today opposed: one a law of blood and death, which, inventing daily new means of combat, obliges the nations to be ever prepared for battle; the other a law of peace, of labor, of salvation, which strives to deliver man from the scourges which assail him. One looks only for violent conquest; the other for the relief of suffering humanity. The one would sacrifice hundreds of thousands of lives to the ambition of a single individual; the other places a single human life above all victories. The law of which we are the instruments essays even in the midst of carnage to heal the wounds caused by the law of war.—Louis Pasteur, at the opening of Pasteur Institute.

DO not waste your time on Social Questions. What is the matter with the poor is Poverty. What is the matter with the Rich is Uselessness.
—George Bernard Shaw.

Who shall put his finger on the work of justice and say, " It is there"? Justice is like the kingdom of God: it is not without us as a fact; it is within us as a great yearning.—George Eliot.

THE Age of Romance has not ceased; it never ceases; it does not, if we will think of it, so much as very sensibly decline.—Carlyle.

H, God, here in my dressing room, with the door shut, I am alone with Thee.

I am glad I know the great spirit that stands silently by, here, as in every place where a human heart is beating!

Can not an actor be God's man? Can not I, whose business it is to play, be as conscientious as those in authority or peril or solemn function? ❧ ❧

Convention classes me and my fellows among the loose and thoughtless.

So Thou art my secret. I triumph inwardly to find Thy presence and taste the mystic joy of Thy friendship, while the world suspects not.

❧ Thou washest my heart clean as the Priest's. Thou givest me a holy ambition to do my work well, that I also may be a devout craftsman ❧

Thou teachest me subtle ways to resist despair, to master my passions, to heal unworthy weakness; the rare medicine of Thy presence is for me, too, as well as for the cloistered monk or meditating scholar. ❧ Teach me to be great among the many who are content to be called great. ❧ Reveal to me the satisfaction of virtue, the inner rewards of loyalty, helpfulness, and self-control. Let me be an unusual person because of that simplicity of heart and that lovableness of nature that I learn from Thee.

❧ May I also touch the infinite and share the divine current that thrills all high souls. Save me from the bogs of pettiness, from egotism, self-pity, envy, and all the corrosives that mar life.

I do not serve in the temple; mine is no solemn office nor critical station; but I thank Thee that the river of God flows through the streets of the city and whosoever will may drink.

Make me to achieve a better success in my role before the ever present audience of the angels than I hope to have when I play my part upon the mimic stage. Ever, in all junctures, in hours of lightness as in stress or trial, God of my soul, help me to play the man. Amen!—" The Actor's Prayer," by Dr. Frank Crane.

❧ ❧

What is this mystery that men call
* death?*
My friend before me lies; in all save
* breath*
He seems the same as yesterday. His
* face*
So like to life, so calm, bears not a trace
Of that great change which all of us so
* dread.*
I gaze on him and say: He is not dead,
But sleeps; and soon he will arise and
* take*
Me by the hand. I know he will awake
And smile on me as he did yesterday;
And he will have some gentle word to say,
Some kindly deed to do; for loving
* thought*
Was warp and woof of which his life
* was wrought.*
He is not dead. Such souls forever live
In boundless measure of the love they
* give.*

" Mystery," by Jerome B. Bell

WHAT is the law of nature? Is it to know that my security and that of my family, all my amusements and pleasures, are purchased at the expense of misery, deprivation, and suffering to thousands of human beings—by the terror of the gallows; by the misfortune of thousands stifling within prison walls; by the fears inspired by millions of soldiers and guardians of civilization, torn from their homes and besotted by discipline, to protect our pleasures with loaded revolvers against the possible interference of the famishing! Is it to purchase every fragment of bread that I put in my mouth and the mouths of my children by the numberless privations that are necessary to procure my abundance? Or is it to be certain that my piece of bread only belongs to me when I know that every one else has a share, and that no one starves while I eat?—Leo Tolstoy.

❧ ❧

CONVICTION brings a silent, indefinable beauty into faces made of the commonest human clay; the devout worshiper at any shrine reflects something of its golden glow, even as the glory of a noble love shines like a sort of light from a woman's face.—Balzac.

THE place to take the true measure of a man is not in the darkest place or in the amen corner, nor the cornfield, but by his own fireside. There he lays aside his mask and you may learn whether he is an imp or an angel, cur or king, hero or humbug. I care not what the world says of him: whether it crowns him boss or pelts him with bad eggs. I care not a copper what his reputation or religion may be: if his babies dread his homecoming and his better half swallows her heart every time she has to ask him for a five-dollar bill, he is a fraud of the first water, even though he prays night and morning until he is black in the face and howls hallelujah until he shakes the eternal hills. But if his children rush to the front door to meet him and love's sunshine illuminates the face of his wife every time she hears his footfall, you can take it for granted that he is pure, for his home is a heaven—and the humbug never gets that near the great white throne of God. He may be a rank atheist and red-flag anarchist, a Mormon and a mugwump; he may buy votes in blocks of five, and bet on the elections; he may deal 'em from the bottom of the deck and drink beer until he can't tell a silver dollar from a circular saw, and still be an infinitely better man than the cowardly little humbug who is all suavity in society but who makes home a hell, who vents upon the helpless heads of his wife and children an ill nature he would inflict on his fellow men but dares not. I can forgive much in that fellow mortal who would rather make men swear than women weep; who would rather have the hate of the whole world than the contempt of his wife; who would rather call anger to the eyes of a king than fear to the face of a child.— "A Man's Real Measure," by W. C. Brann.

❧ ❧

THE present position which we, the educated and well-to-do classes, occupy, is that of the Old Man of the Sea, riding on the poor man's back; only, unlike the Old Man of the Sea, we are very sorry for the poor man, very sorry; and we will do almost anything for the poor man's relief. We will not only supply him with food sufficient to keep him on his legs, but we will teach and instruct him and point out to him the beauties of the landscape; we will discourse sweet music to him and give him abundance of good advice. ❡ Yes, we will do almost anything for the poor man, anything but get off his back.—Leo Tolstoy.

❧ ❧

List to that bird! His song—what poet pens it?
Brigand of birds, he 's stolen every note!
Prince though of thieves—hark! how the rascal spends it!
Pours the whole forest from one tiny throat!

" The Mockingbird,"
by Ednah Proctor (Clarke) Hayes

IF you succeed in life, you must do it in spite of the efforts of others to pull you down. There is nothing in the idea that people are willing to help those who help themselves. People are willing to help a man who can't help himself, but as soon as a man is able to help himself, and does it, they join in making his life as uncomfortable as possible.
—E. W. Howe.

❧ ❧

I HAVE told you of the man who always put on his spectacles when about to eat cherries, in order that the fruit might look larger and more tempting. In like manner I always make the most of my enjoyments, and, though I do not cast my eyes away from troubles, I pack them into as small a compass as I can for myself, and never let them annoy others.—Robert Southey.

❧ ❧

Come, follow me, and leave the world to its babblings.—Dante.

HE millionaire is a new kind of man—many of them. It is almost as if a new sort of human nature had been produced—rolled up on us by the sheer development and fruitfulness, and heating up, and pouring over, and expansion of the earth. Great elemental forces silently working out the destiny of man have seized these men, touched their eyes with vision. They are rich by revelations, by habits of great seeing and great daring. They are idealists. They have really used their souls in getting their success, their mastery over matter, and it is by discovering other men's souls, and picking out the men who had them, and gathering them around them, that the success has been kept. Many of them are rich by some mighty, silent, sudden service they have done to a whole planet at once. They have not had time to lose their souls. There is a sense in which they might be called The Innocents of Riches—some of them.

—Gerald Stanley Lee.

When a bit of sunshine hits ye,

After passing of a cloud,

When a fit of laughter gits ye

And ye'r spine is feelin' proud,

Don't forget to up and fling it

At a soul that's feelin' blue,

For the minit that ye sling it

It 's a boomerang to you.

"The Boomerang," *by Capt. Jack Crawford*

MEN are tattooed with their special beliefs like so many South Sea Islanders; but a real human heart with divine love in it beats with the same glow under all the patterns of all earth's thousand tribes.—O. W. Holmes.

EXCEPT a living man there is nothing more wonderful than a book! a message to us from the dead—from human souls we never saw, who lived, perhaps thousands of miles away. And yet these, in those little sheets of paper, speak to us, arouse us, terrify us, teach us, comfort us, open their hearts to us as brothers.—Charles Kingsley.

EDUCATION does not mean teaching people what they do not know. It means teaching them to behave as they do not behave. It is not teaching the youth the shapes of letters and the tricks of numbers, and then leaving them to turn their arithmetic to roguery, and their literature to lust. It means, on the contrary, training them into the perfect exercise and kingly continence of their bodies and souls. It is a painful, continual and difficult work to be done by kindness, by watching, by warning, by precept, and by praise, but above all—by example

—John Ruskin

SAD will be the day for every man when he becomes absolutely contented with the life that he is living, with the thoughts that he is thinking, with the deeds that he is doing, when there is not forever beating at the doors of his soul some great desire to do something larger, which he knows that he was meant and made to do because he is still, in spite of all, the child of God.

—Phillips Brooks.

DIE when I may, I want it said of me by those who knew me best, that I always plucked a thistle and planted a flower where I thought a flower would grow.—Abraham Lincoln.

THAT we should do unto others as we would have them do unto us—that we should respect the rights of others as scrupulously as we would have our rights respected—is not a mere counsel of perfection to individuals—but it is the law to which we must conform social institutions and national policy, if we would secure the blessings and abundance of peace.—Henry George.

OOKING more and more like an orchid, Yetta stood the real one, the blood mounting to her cheeks, and waited for the storm to pass. "I'm not going to talk about this strike," she said when she could make herself heard. "It's over. I want to tell you about the next one—and the next. I wish very much I could make you understand about the strikes that are coming. . . .

"Perhaps there's some of you never thought much about strikes till now. Well. There's been strikes all the time. I don't believe there's ever been a year when there was n't dozens here in New York. When we began, the skirt-finishers was out. They lost their strike. They went hungry just the way we did, but nobody helped them. And they're worse now than ever. There ain't no difference between one strike and another. Perhaps they are striking for more pay or recognition or closed shops. But the next strike 'll be just like ours. It 'll be people fighting so they won't be so much slaves like they was before.

"The Chairman said perhaps I'd tell you about my experience. There ain't nothing to tell except everybody has been awful kind to me. It's fine to have people so kind to me. But I'd rather if they'd try to understand what this strike business means to all of us workers —this strike we've won and the ones that are coming . . . .

"I come out of the workhouse today, and they tell me a lady wants to give me money to study, she wants to have me go to college like I was a rich girl. It's very kind. I want to study. I ain't been to school none since I was fifteen. I guess I can't even talk English very good. I'd like to go to college. And I used to see pictures in the papers of beautiful rich women, and of course it would be fine to have clothes like that. But being in a strike, seeing all the people suffer, seeing all the cruelty—it makes things look different ✀ ✀

"The Chairman told you something out of the Christian Bible. Well, we Jews have got a story too—perhaps it's in your Bible—about Moses and his people in Egypt. He'd been brought up by a rich Egyptian lady—a princess—just like he was her son. But as long as he tried to be an Egyptian he was n't no good. And God spoke to him one day out of a bush on fire. I don't remember just the words of the story, but God said: 'Moses, you're a Jew. You ain't got no business with the Egyptians. Take off those fine clothes and go back to your own people and help them escape from bondage.' Well. Of course, I ain't like Moses, and God has never talked to me. But it seems to me sort of as if—during this strike—I'd seen a *Blazing Bush.* Anyhow I've seen my people in bondage. And I don't want to go to college and be a lady. I guess the kind princess could n't understand why Moses wanted to be a poor Jew instead of a rich Egyptian. But if you can understand, if you can understand why I'm going to stay with my own people, you'll understand all I've been trying to say ✀ ✀

"We're a people in bondage. There's lots of people who's kind to us. I guess the princess was n't the only Egyptian lady that was kind to the Jews. But kindness ain't what people want who are in bondage. Kindness won't never make us free. And God don't send any more prophets nowadays. We've got to escape all by ourselves. And when you read in the papers that there's a strike—it don't matter whether it's street-car conductors or lace-makers, whether it's Eyetalians or Polacks or Jews or Americans, whether it's here or in Chicago—it's my People— the People in Bondage who are starting out for the Promised Land."

She stopped a moment, and a strange look came over her face—a look of communication with some distant spirit. When she spoke again, her words were unintelligible to most of the audience. Some of the Jewish vest-makers understood. And the Rev. Dunham Denning, who was a famous scholar, understood. But even those who did not were held spellbound by the swinging sonorous cadence. She stopped abruptly.

"It's Hebrew," she explained. "It's what my father taught me when I was a little girl. It's about the Promised Land—I can't say it in good English—I——"

"Unless I've forgotten my Hebrew," the Reverend Chairman said, stepping forward, "Miss Rayefsky has been repeating God's words to Moses, the Lawgiver, as recorded in the third chapter of Exodus. I think it's the seventh verse: 'And the Lord said, I have surely seen the affliction of my people which are in Egypt, and have heard their cry by reason of their taskmasters; for I know their sorrows;

"'And I am come down to deliver them out of the hand of the Egyptians and to bring them up out of that land unto a good land and a large, unto a land flowing with milk and honey.'"

"Yes. That's it," Yetta said. "Well that's what strikes mean. We're fighting, fighting, for the old promises."

—"Comrade Yetta," by Albert Edwards.

I am part of the sea and stars
And the winds of the South and North,
Of mountain and moon and Mars,
And the ages sent me forth!

Blind Homer, the splendor of Greece,
Sang the songs I sang ere he fell;
She whom men called Beatrice,
Saw me in the depths of hell.

I was hanged at dawn for a crime—
Flesh dies, but the soul knows no death;
I piped to great Shakespeare's chime
The witches' song in Macbeth.

All, all who have suffered and won,
Who have struggled and failed and died,
Am I, with work still undone,
And a spear-mark in my side.

I am part of the sea and stars
And the winds of the South and North,
Of mountains and moon and Mars,
And the ages sent me forth!
    "Kinship," *by Edward H. S. Terry*

HERE are two ways of being happy: We may either diminish our wants or augment our means—either will do—the result is the same; and it is for each man to decide for himself, and do that which happens to be the easiest.

If you are idle or sick or poor, however hard it may be to diminish your wants, it will be harder to augment your means.

If you are active and prosperous or young or in good health, it may be easier for you to augment your means than to diminish your wants.

But if you are wise, you will do both at the same time, young or old, rich or poor, sick or well; and if you are very wise you will do both in such a way as to augment the general happiness of society.—Franklin.

TO judge human nature rightly, a man may sometimes have a very small experience, provided he has a very large heart.—Bulwer-Lytton.

ALL higher motives, ideals, conceptions, sentiments in a man are of no account if they do not come forward to strengthen him for the better discharge of the duties which devolve upon him in the ordinary affairs of life.
    —Henry Ward Beecher.

THE soul is a fire that darts its rays through all the senses; it is in this fire that existence consists; all the observations and all the efforts of philosophers ought to turn towards this me, the center and moving power of our sentiments and our ideas.—Madame De Stael.

A GREAT deal of the joy of life consists in doing perfectly, or at least to the best of one's ability, everything which he attempts to do. There is a sense of satisfaction, a pride in surveying such a work—a work which is rounded, full, exact, complete in all its parts—which the superficial man, who leaves his work in a slovenly, slipshod, half-finished condition, can never know. It is this conscientious completeness which turns work into art. The smallest thing, well done, becomes artistic.
    —William Mathews.

E are taught, many of us, from our youth onwards, that competition is essential to the health and progress of the race. Or, as Herbert Spencer puts it, " Society flourishes by the antagonism of its atoms."

But the obvious golden truth is that co-operation is good and competition bad, and that society flourishes by the mutual aid of human beings. I say that is obvious, and so it is. And it is so well known that in all great military or commercial enterprises individualism has to be subordinated to collective action. We do not believe that a house divided against itself shall stand; we believe that it shall fall ✤ ✤ We know that a State divided by internal feuds and torn by faction fighting can not hold its own against a united people. We know that in a cricket or football team, a regiment, a ship's crew, a school. the " antagonism of the atoms " would mean defeat and failure. We know that a society composed of antagonistic atoms would not be a society at all, and could not exist as a society. We know that if men are to found and govern cities, to build bridges and make roads, to establish universities, to sail ships and sink mines, and create educational systems, and policies and religions, they must work together and not against one another. Surely these things are as obvious as the fact that there could be no hive unless the bees worked as a colony and on the lines of mutual aid.
—Robert Blatchford.

✤ ✤

Your sole contribution to the sum of things is yourself.—Frank Crane.

There is something in the Autumn that
  is native to my blood,
Touch of manner, hint of mood;
And my heart is like a rhyme,
With the yellow and the purple and the
  crimson keeping time.

The scarlet of the maples can shake me
  like a cry
Of bugles going by.
And my lonely spirit thrills
To see the frosty asters like smoke
  upon the hills.

There is something in October sets the
  gipsy blood astir;
We must follow her,
When from every hill aflame,
She calls and calls each vagabond by
  name.
  " An Autumn Song," *by Bliss Carman*

OH, if they would only let you work. Would n't it be fine just to be able to work? Do you know the real thing that puts people in their little hospital cots with nervous prostration is not working, but trying to work and not being allowed to. Work never hurt anybody. But this thing of being in the middle of a letter and then rising to shake hands with a man who knew you when you were a boy, and then sitting down and trying to catch the thread of that letter again—that 's what gives one general debility.
—SaundersNorvell.

✤ ✤

I CAN no more understand that any serious injury can come to my moral nature from disbelief in Samson than from disbelief in Jack the Giant-Killer ✤ I care as little for Goliath as for the giant Blunderbore. I am glad that children should amuse themselves with nursery stories, but it is shocking that they should be ordered to believe in them as solid facts, and then be told that such superstition is essential to morality.
—Sir Leslie Stephen.

✤ ✤

NO civilization is complete which does not include the dumb and defenseless of God's creatures within the sphere of charity and mercy.—Queen Victoria.

✤ ✤

AS good almost kill a man as kill a good book; who kills a man kills a reasonable creature, God's image, but he who destroys a good book kills reason itself.—John Milton.

✤ ✤

Success or failure in business is caused more by mental attitude even than by mental capacities.—Walter Dill Scott.

IT is undeniable that the great quest of humanity is happiness. But was the world created to be happy? How many are truly happy? I 've studied people in all classes and conditions, and everywhere I have found, when you get below the surface, that it is mostly the insincere individual who says, ''I am happy.'' Nearly everybody wants something he has n't got, and as things are constructed, what he wants is money— more money than he has in his pocket ❧ ❧ | But after all, money can buy only a few things Why should any one envy the captains of industry? Their lives are made up of those vast, incessant worries from which the average individual is happily spared. Worry, worry, that is the evil of life ❧ ❧

For each and every joyful thing,
For twilight swallows on the wing,
For all that nest and all that sing,—

For fountains cool that laugh and leap,
For rivers running to the deep,
For happy, care-forgetting sleep,—

For stars that pierce the sombre dark,
For morn, awaking with the lark,
For life new-stirring 'neath the bark,—

For sunshine and the blessed rain,
For budding grove and blossomy lane,
For the sweet silence of the plain,—

For bounty springing from the sod,
For every step by beauty trod,—
For each dear gift of joy, thank God!
" For Joy," by Florence Earle Coates

What do I consider the nearest approximation to happiness of which the present human nature is capable? Why, living on a farm which is one's own, far from the hectic, artificial conditions of the city—a farm where one gets directly from one's own soil what one needs to sustain life, with a garden in front and a healthy, normal family to contribute those small domestic joys which relieve a man from business strain.—Edison.

❧ ❧

I AM not so lost in lexicography as to forget that words are the daughters of earth, and that things are the sons of heaven.—Samuel Johnson.

❧ ❧

There exists no cure for a heart wounded with the sword of separation.
—Hitopadesa.

THE great voice of America does not come from the seats of learning. It comes in a murmur from the hills and woods and farms and factories and the mills, rolling and gaining volume until it comes to us from the homes of common men. Do these murmurs echo in the corridors of the universities? I have not heard them. The universities would make men forget their common origins, forget their universal sympathies, and join a class—and no class can ever serve America. I have dedicated every power there is in me to bring the colleges that I have anything to do with to an absolutely democratic regeneration in spirit, and I shall not be satisfied until America shall know that the men in the colleges are saturated with the same thought, the same sympathy, that pulses through the whole great body politic.—Woodrow Wilson.

❧ ❧

THE man who has not anything to boast of but his illustrious ancestors is like a potato—the only good belonging to him is underground.
—Sir Thomas Overbury.

❧ ❧

A MAN without mirth is like a wagon without springs, in which one is caused disagreeably to jolt by every pebble over which it runs.
—Henry Ward Beecher.

❧ ❧

AMERICA has furnished to the world the character of Washington, and if our American institutions had done nothing else, that alone would have entitled them to the respect of mankind.
—Daniel Webster.

OUR world is pervaded and deeply moved by the power of ideals. There is no perfect statesman, or poet, or artist, but the virtues of many persons in each one of these great pursuits become detached, and like star-dust, they form a new and perfect star in the expanse of thought. The orator that stands before us in our moments of reflection and dream is not Cicero, or Burke, or Webster, but always some nameless one with a wisdom, a language and a presence better than were found in those actual incarnations.

Our statesman is not Alfred, nor Napoleon, nor even Washington, but he is some yet mightier being with an infinite power and unknown name, his features not yet fully visible, as though he had not yet emerged from the shadows of old forums and the lonely columns of ruined states. All around our hearts stand these final shapes of the powerful, the perfect and the sublime—the aggregations of long ages of thought and admiration. ¶ Our earth is great not only because of what it has, but also because of what lies within its reach.

The quest after ideals is the central reason of life. This pursuit abandoned, life need not run along any longer. The pitcher is broken at the fountain. The idealists are creating a human world after the pattern shown them in the Mount. Each art stands as a monument to a host of idealists who in their own day perhaps toiled hopelessly and amid the sneers of those who were only the children of dust. Music, now so infinite in extent and sweetness, is such a monument. The first rude harps are broken and lost; dead the hands that smote them; but the art is here with no enchantment lost. We do not know the names of those singers. Like us they were pilgrims.

They had to pass into the beyond, but they left an art which the world loves. It was so of liberty, temperance, justice and all the higher forms of human life. . . . . Some speak of ideals as being only girls' dreams. On the opposite, high ideals are lifelike portraits seen in advance. Only the greatest minds living in an age of tyranny could see in prophecy the portrait of a free people. Instead of being a romantic dream an ideal is often a long mathematical calculation by an intellect as logical as that of Euclid. Idealism is not the ravings of a maniac, but it is the calm geometry of life. Ideals try our faith, as though to show us that nothing is too good to be true. In noble ideals there is something aggressive. They are not aggressive like an army with gun and spear, but aggressive like the sun which coaxes a June out of a winter. All great truths are persistent. Each form of right is a growing form. All high ideals will be realized. This one perceives who takes a long view—the triumph of ideality over apathy, indolence and dust. There is nothing in history, dark as much of it is, to check the belief that man will at last be overcome by his highest ideals *&*

—David Swing.

I AM aware that many object to the severity of my language; but is there not cause for severity? I will be as harsh as Truth, and as uncompromising as Justice. On this subject I do not wish to think, or speak, or write, with moderation. No! No! Tell a man whose house is on fire to give a moderate alarm; tell him to moderately rescue his wife from the hands of the ravisher; tell the mother to gradually extricate her babe from the fire into which it has fallen—but urge me not to use moderation in a cause like the present. I am in earnest—I will not equivocate—I will not excuse—I will not retreat a single inch—and I will be heard. The apathy of the people is enough to make every statue leap from its pedestal and hasten the resurrection of the dead.

—William Lloyd Garrison.

WE live in deeds, not years; in thoughts, not breaths;
In feelings, not in figures on a dial.
We should count time by heart-throbs.
   He most lives
Who thinks most, feels the noblest, acts the best.—Philip James Bailey.

A MAN'S Thanksgiving: God of commonsense, I give Thee thanks for the heavy blows of pain that drive me back from perilous ways into harmony with the laws of my being; for stinging whips of hunger and cold that urge to bitter strivings and glorious achievement; for steepness and roughness of the way and staunch virtues gained by climbing over jagged rocks of hardship and stumbling through dark and pathless sloughs of discouragement; for the acid blight of failure that has burned out of me all thought of easy victory and toughened my sinews for fiercer battles and greater triumphs; for mistakes I have made, and the priceless lessons I have learned from them; for disillusion and disappointment that have cleared my vision and spurred my desire; for strong appetites and passions and the power they give when under pressure and control; for my imperfections that give me the keen delight of striving toward perfection.

God of common good and human brotherhood, I give Thee thanks for siren songs of temptation that lure and entangle and the understanding of other men they reveal; for the weaknesses and failings of my neighbors and the joy of lending a helping hand; for my own shortcomings, sorrows and loneliness, that give me a deeper sympathy for others; for ingratitude and misunderstanding and the gladness of service without other reward than self-expression.—Arthur W. Newcomb.

Ye stars! which are the poetry of heaven,
If in your bright leaves we would read the fate
Of men and empires—'t is to be forgiven
That in our aspirations to be great
Our destinies o'erleap their mortal state,
And claim a kindred with you; for ye are
A beauty and a mystery, and create
In us such love and reverence from afar,
That fortune, fame, power, life, have named themselves a star.

"Stars," by Lord Byron

A LTHOUGH imitation is one of the great instruments used by Providence in bringing our nature toward its perfection, yet if men gave themselves up to imitation entirely, and each followed the other, and so on in an eternal circle, it is easy to see that there could never be any improvement among them. Men must remain as brutes do, the same at the end that they are at this day, and that they were at the beginning of the world. To prevent this, God has implanted in man, a sense of ambition, and a satisfaction arising from the contemplation of his excelling his fellows in something deemed valuable among them. It is this passion that drives men to all the ways we see in use of signalizing themselves, and that tends to make whatever excites in a man the idea of this distinction so very pleasant. It has been so strong as to make very miserable men take comfort that they were supreme in misery; where we can not distinguish ourselves by something excellent, we take complacency in some singular infirmity, folly or defect.

—Edmund Burke.

THE first and best victory is to conquer self; to be conquered by self is, of all things, the most shameful and vile.—Plato.

THE only way in which one human being can properly attempt to influence another is the encouraging him to think for himself, instead of endeavoring to instil ready-made opinions into his head.—Sir Leslie Stephen.

HAT we have a right to expect of the American boy is that he shall turn out to be a good American man. The boy can best become a good man by being a good boy—not a goody-goody boy, but just a plain good boy. I do not mean that he must love only the negative virtues; I mean that he must love the positive virtues also. "Good," in the largest sense, should include whatever is fine, straight forward, clean, brave, and manly. The best boys I know—the best men I know—are good at their studies or their business, fearless and stalwart, hated and feared by all that is wicked and depraved, incapable of submitting to wrongdoing, and equally incapable of being aught but tender to the weak and helpless. Of course the effect that a thoroughly manly, thoroughly straight and upright boy can have upon the companions of his own age, and upon those who are younger, is incalculable. If he is not thoroughly manly, then they will not respect him, and his good qualities will count for but little; while, of course, if he is mean, cruel or wicked, then his physical strength and force of mind merely make him so much the more objectionable a member of society. He can not do good work if he is not strong and does not try with his whole heart and soul to count in any contest; and his strength will be a curse to himself and to every one else if he does not have a thorough command over himself and over his own evil passions, and if he does not use his strength on the side of decency, justice and fair dealing. In short, in life, as in a football-game, the principle to follow is: Hit the line hard; don't foul and don't shirk, but hit the line hard.—" The American Boy," by Theodore Roosevelt.

Out of the night that covers me,
Black as the Pit from pole to pole,
I thank whatever gods may be
For my unconquerable soul.

In the fell clutch of circumstance
I have not winced nor cried aloud.
Under the bludgeonings of chance
My head is bloody, but unbowed.

Beyond this place of wrath and tears
Looms but the Horror of the Shade,
And yet the menace of the years
Finds, and shall find, me unafraid.

It matters not how strait the gate,
How charged with punishments the scroll,
I am the master of my fate:
I am the captain of my soul.

" Invictus," *by W. E. Henley*

IN the beginning, men went forth each day—some to do battle, some to the chase; others, again, to dig and to delve in the field—all that they might gain and live, or lose and die. Until there was found among them one, differing from the rest, whose pursuits attracted him not, and so he staid by the tents with the women, and traced strange devices with a burnt stick upon a gourd. This man, who took no joy in the ways of his brethren—who cared not for conquest, and fretted in the field—this designer of quaint patterns—this deviser of the beautiful — who perceived in Nature about him curious curvings, as faces are seen in the fire—this dreamer apart, was the first artist. ¶ We have then but to wait—until, with the mark of the gods upon him—there come among us again the chosen—who shall continue what has gone before. Satisfied that, even were he never to appear, the story of the beautiful is already complete—hewn in the marbles of the Parthenon—and broidered, with the birds, upon the fan of Hokusai—at the foot of Fuji-Yama.
—J. McNeill Whistler.

THERE is but one virtue: to help human beings to free and beautiful life; but one sin: to do them indifferent or cruel hurt; the love of humanity is the whole of morality. This is Goodness, this is Humanism, this is the Social Conscience.—J. William Lloyd.

NO man has earned the right to intellectual ambition until he has learned to lay his course by a star which he has never seen—to dig by the divining-rod for springs which he may never reach. In saying this, I point to that which will make your study heroic. For I say to you in all sadness of conviction, that to think great thoughts you must be heroes as well as idealists. Only when you have worked alone— when you have felt around you a black gulf of solitude more isolating than that which surrounds the dying man, and in hope and in despair have trusted to your own unshaken will— then only will you have achieved. Thus only can you gain the secret isolated joy of the thinker, who knows that, long after he is dead and forgotten, men who never heard of him will be moving to the measure of his thought— the subtile rapture of a postponed power, which the world knows not because it has no external trappings, but which to his prophetic vision is more real than that which commands an army. And if this joy should not be yours,—still it is only thus that you can know that you have done what it lay in you to do,—can say that you have lived, and be ready for the end.—Oliver Wendell Holmes.

❧ ❧

AN enlightened mind is not hoodwinked; it is not shut up in a gloomy prison till it thinks the walls of its own dungeon the limits of the universe, and the reach of its own chain the outer verge of intelligence.
—Henry Wadsworth Longfellow.

God, we don't like to complain—
We know that the mine is no lark—
But—there's the pools from the rain:
But—there's the cold and the dark.

God, You don't know what it is—
You, in Your well-lighted sky,
Watch the meteors whizz;
Warm, with the sun always by.

God, if You had but the moon
Stuck in Your cap for a lamp,
Even You'd tire of it soon,
Down in the dark and the damp.

Nothing but blackness above,
And nothing that moves but the cars—
God, if You wish for our love,
Fling us a handful of stars!

"Caliban in the Coal Mines," *by Louis Untermeyer*

SELFISHNESS is not living as one wishes to live; it is asking others to live as one wishes to live. And unselfishness is letting other people's lives alone, not interfering with them. Selfishness always aims at creating around it an absolute uniformity of type. Unselfishness recognizes infinite variety of type as a delightful thing, accepts it, acquiesces in it, enjoys it.—Oscar Wilde.

❧ ❧

THE tree which moves some to tears of joy is in the eyes of others only a green thing which stands in the way. Some see Nature all ridicule and deformity, and by these I shall not regulate my proportions; and some scarce see Nature at all. But to the eyes of the man of imagination Nature is Imagination itself. As a man is, so he sees.—William Blake.

❧ ❧

THE plant is an animal confined in a wooden case; and Nature, like Sycorax, holds thousands of "delicate Ariels" imprisoned in every oak. She is jealous of letting us know this; and among the higher and more conspicuous forms of plants reveals it only by such obscure manifestations as the shrinking of the Sensitive Plant, the sudden clasp of the Dionea, or still more slightly, by the phenomena of the cyclosis.—Huxley.

❧ ❧

ALL truth is safe and nothing else is safe; and he who keeps back the truth, or withholds it from men, from motives of expediency, is either a coward or a criminal, or both.—Max Müller.

❧ ❧

Never leave that till tomorrow which you can do today.—Franklin.

BE courteous to all, but intimate with few; and let those few be well tried before you give them your confidence. True friendship is a plant of slow growth, and must undergo and withstand the shocks of adversity before it is entitled to the appellation. Let your heart feel for the affections and distresses of every one, and let your hand give in proportion to your purse; remembering always the estimation of the widow's mite, that it is not every one that asketh that deserveth charity; all however, are worthy of the inquiry, or the deserving may suffer.

Do not conceive that fine clothes make fine men, any more than fine feathers make fine birds. A plain, genteel dress is more admired, obtains more credit, than lace and embroidery, in the eyes of the judicious and sensible.—George Washington in a letter to his nephew, Bushrod Washington, 1783.

THE names of the Periclean Age are high. There is a higher one yet, that of Pericles. Statesman, orator, philosopher, soldier, artist, poet and lover, Pericles was so great that, another Zeus, he was called the Olympian. If to him Egeria came, would it not, a poet somewhere asked, be uncivil to depict her as less than he? It would be not only uncivil but untrue.

Said Themistocles, " You see that boy of mine? Though but five, he governs the universe. Yes, for he rules his mother, his mother rules me, I rule Athens and Athens the world." After Themistocles it was Pericles' turn to govern and be ruled

His sovereign was Aspasia.

—Edgar Saltus.

TO me it seems as if when God conceived the world, that was poetry; He formed it, and that was sculpture; He varied and colored it, and that was painting; and then, crowning all, He peopled it with living beings, and that was the grand divine, eternal drama.

—Charlotte Cushman.

COMMERCE is a game of skill, which every man can not play, which few men can play well. The right merchant is one who has the just average of faculties we call commonsense; a man of strong affinity for facts, who makes up his decision on what he has seen. He is thoroughly persuaded of the truths of arithmetic. There is always a reason, in the man, for his good or bad fortune; and so, in making money. Men talk as if there were some magic about this, and believe in magic, in all parts of life. He knows that all goes on the old road, pound for pound, cent for cent—for every effect a perfect cause—and that good luck is another name for tenacity of purpose.—Emerson.

TO be honest, to be kind, to earn a little, and to spend a little less, to make upon the whole a family happier for his presence, to renounce when that shall be necessary and not to be embittered, to keep a few friends, but these without capitulation; above all, on the same condition, to keep friends with himself; here is a task for all a man has of fortitude and delicacy.

—Robert Louis Stevenson.

GOD is to be our father, yet we are far from being fathers to our own children. We presume to have insight into divine things, and yet we neglect as unworthy of notice those human relations which are a key to the divine.

—Friedrich Froebel.

A BAD man is wretched amidst every earthly advantage; a good man—troubled on every side, yet not distressed; perplexed, but not in despair; persecuted, but not forsaken; cast down, but not destroyed.—Plato.

I LOVE children. They do not prattle of yesterday: their interests are all of today and the tomorrows—I love children.—Richard Mansfield.

God gave man an upright countenance to survey the heavens, and to look upward to the stars.—Ovid.

THE faculty to dream was not given to mock us. There is a reality back of it. There is a divinity behind our legitimate desires.

By the desires that have divinity in them, we do not refer to the things that we want but do not need; we do not refer to the desires that turn to Dead Sea fruit on our lips or to ashes when eaten, but to the legitimate desires of the soul for the realization of those ideals, the longing for full, complete self-expression, the time and opportunity for the weaving of the pattern shown in the moment of our highest transfiguration.

A man will remain a rag-picker as long as he has only the vision of the ragpicker &o &o

Our mental attitude, our heart's desire, is our perpetual prayer which Nature answers. She takes it for granted that we desire what we are headed toward, and she helps us to it. People little realize that their desires are their perpetual prayers—not head prayers, but heart prayers—and that they are granted.

Most people do not half realize how sacred a thing a legitimate ambition is. What is this eternal urge within us which is trying to push us on and on, up and up? It is the urge, the push in the great force within us, which is perpetually prodding us to do our best and refuses to accept our second best.

—Orison Swett Marden.

&o &o

Things printed can never be stopped; they are like babies baptized, they have a soul from that moment, and go on forever.—Meredith.

Leaf after leaf drops off, flower after flower,

Some in the chill, some in the warmer hour:

Alive they flourish, and alive they fall,

And Earth who nourished them receives them all.

Should we, her wiser sons, be less content

To sink into her lap when life is spent?

"Leaf After Leaf Drops Off,"
by Walter Savage Landor

IT is a curious reflection that the ordinary private person who collects objects of a modest luxury has nothing about him so old as his books. If a wave of the rod made everything around him disappear that did not exist a century ago, he would suddenly find himself with one or two sticks of furniture perhaps, but otherwise alone with his books. Let the work of another century pass, and certainly nothing would be left but these little brown volumes—so many caskets full of tenderness and passion, disappointed ambition, fruitless hope, self-torturing envy, conceit, aware, in maddening, lucid moments, of its own folly &o
—Edmund Gosse

&o &o

MY share of the work of the world may be limited, but the fact that it is work makes it precious. Darwin could work only half an hour at a time; yet in many diligent half-hours he laid anew the foundations of philosophy.

Green, the historian, tells us that the world is moved not only by the mighty shoves of the heroes, but also by the aggregate of the tiny pushes of each honest worker.—Helen Keller.

&o &o

THE character and qualifications of the leader are reflected in the men he selects, develops and gathers around him. Show me the leader and I will know his men. Show me the men and I will know their leader. Therefore, to have loyal, efficient employees—be a loyal and efficient employer.—Arthur W. Newcomb.

&o &o

Of all kinds of pride I hold national pride the most foolish; it ruined Greece; it ruined Judea and Rome.—Herder.

E have reached Cascade Creek at last; and a beautiful grove of pine trees, beneath whose shade a clear stream, whose waters are free from the nauseous taste of alkali, furnishes a delightful place to camp. Now, dismounting and seeing that your horse is well cared for, while the men are unloading the packmules and pitching the tents, walk up that trail winding up the hillside, follow it for a little among the solemn pines, and then pass out from the tree shadows and take your stand upon that farther rock, clinging to it well meanwhile and being very sure of your footing, for your head will swim and grow dizzy, and there opens before you one of the most stupendous scenes of Nature, the Lower Falls of the Grand Canyon of the Yellowstone so so

And now where shall I begin, and how shall I, in any wise, describe this tremendous sight; its overpowering grandeur, and at the same time, its inexpressible beauty?

Look yonder! Those are the Lower Falls of the Yellowstone. They are not the grandest in the world, but there are none more beautiful. There is not the breadth and dash of Niagara, nor is there the enormous depth of leap of some of the waterfalls of Yosemite.

But there is a majesty of its own kind, and beauty, too. On either side are vast pinnacles of sculptured rock. There, where the rock opens for the river, its waters are compressed from a width of two hundred feet, between the Upper and Lower Falls, to less than one hundred feet where it takes the plunge. The shelf of rock over which it leaps is absolutely level. The water seems to wait a moment on its verge, then it passes with a single bound, three hundred and fifty feet below.

It is a sheer, unbroken, compact, shining mass of silver foam. But your eyes are all the while distracted from the fall itself, great and beautiful as it is, to its marvelous setting; to the surprising, overmastering canyon into which the river leaps, and through which it flows, dwindling to but a foamy ribbon there in its appalling depths. As you cling here to this jutting rock, the falls are already many hundred feet below you. The falls unroll their whiteness down amid the canyon gloom so so

These rocky sides are almost perpendicular; indeed, in many places the boiling springs have gouged them out so as to leave overhanging cliffs and tables at the top. Take a stone and throw it over; you have to wait long before you hear it strike. Nothing more awful have I ever seen than the yawning of that chasm; and the stillness, solemn as midnight, profound as death. The water dashing there as in a kind of agony, against those rocks, you can not hear.

❡ The mighty distance lays the finger of silence on its white lips. You are oppressed by a sense of danger. It is as though the vastness would soon force you from the rock to which you cling. The silence, the sheer depth, the gloom, burden you. It is a relief to feel the firm earth beneath your feet again, as you carefully crawl back from your perching-place so so

But this is not all, nor is the half yet told. As soon as you can stand it, go out on that jutting rock again and mark the sculpturing of God upon those vast and

With fingers weary and worn,
With eyelids heavy and red,
A woman sat, in unwomanly rags,
Plying her needle and thread,—
Stitch! stitch! stitch!
In poverty, hunger, and dirt;
And still with a voice of dolorous pitch
She sang the "Song of the Shirt!"

" Work—work—work
Till the brain begins to swim!
Work—work—work
Till the eyes are heavy and dim!
Seam, and gusset, and band,—
Band, and gusset, and seam,—
Till over the buttons I fall asleep,
And sew them on in a dream!

(Continued on next page)

solemn walls. By dash of wind and wave, by forces of the frost, by file of snow-plunge and glacier, and the mountain-torrents, by the hot breath of the balmy Spring, those walls have been cut into the most various and surprising shapes. I have seen the " Middle Ages" castles along the Rhine; there those castles are reproduced exactly. I have seen the soaring summits of the great cathedral-spires in the country beyond the sea; there they stand in prototype, only loftier and more sublime ᴊ ᴊ And then, of course and almost beyond all else, you are fascinated by the magnificence and utter opulence of color ᴊ Those are not simply gray and heavy depths, and reaches, and domes, and pinnacles of solid rock. ❡ The whole gorge flames ᴊ It is as though rainbows had fallen out of the sky and hung themselves there like glorious banners. The underlying color is the clearest yellow; this flushes onward into orange. Down at the base the deepest mosses unroll their draperies of the most vivid green; browns, sweet and soft, do their blending; white rocks stand spectral; turrets of rock shoot up as crimson as though they were drenched with blood ᴊ ᴊ
It is as if the most glorious sunset you ever saw had been caught and held upon that resplendent, awful gorge.
Throughout nearly all the hours of that afternoon until the sunset shadows came, and afterwards among the moonbeams, I waited there, clinging to that rock, jutting out into that overpowering, gorgeous chasm. I was appalled and fascinated, afraid and yet compelled to cling there. It was an epoch in my life.

—Doctor Wayland Hoyt

"O Men, with sisters dear!
O Men, with mothers and wives!
It is not linen you 're wearing out,
But human creatures' lives.
Stitch—stitch—stitch
In poverty, hunger, and dirt,—
Sewing at once, with a double thread,
A shroud as well as a Shirt!

" But why do I talk of Death—
That phantom of grisly bone!
I hardly fear his terrible shape,
It seems so like my own—
It seems so like my own
Because of the fasts I keep:
O God! that bread should be so dear,
And flesh and blood so cheap!"

"The Song of the Shirt," by Thomas Hood

I T is nothing to give pension and cottage to the widow who has lost her son; it is nothing to give food and medicine to the workman who has broken his arm, or the decrepit woman wasting in sickness. But it is something to use your time and strength to war with the waywardness and thoughtlessness of mankind· to keep the erring workman in your service till you have made him an unerring one, and to direct your fellow-merchant to the opportunity which his judgment would have lost ᴊ

—John Ruskin.

S O long as we love, we serve. So long as we are loved by others I would almost say we are indispensable; and no man is useless while he has a friend.

—R. L. Stevenson.

T HE men whom I have seen succeed best in life have always been cheerful and hopeful men, who went about their business with a smile on their faces, and took the changes and chances of this mortal life like men, facing rough and smooth alike as it came.—Chas. Kingsley.

I T is easy in the world to live after the world's opinions; it is easy in solitude to live after our own; but the Great Man is he who in the midst of the crowd keeps with perfect sweetness the independence of solitude.—Emerson.

H E who is silent is forgotten; he who abstains is taken at his word; he who does not advance falls back; he who stops is overwhelmed, distanced, crushed; he who ceases to grow greater becomes smaller; he who leaves off, gives up; the stationary condition is the beginning of the end.—Amiel.

YOUNG men, life is before you. Two voices are calling you—one coming out from the swamps of selfishness and force, where success means death; and the other from the hilltops of justice and progress, where even failure brings glory. Two lights are seen in your horizon—one the fast fading marsh light of power, and the other the slowly rising sun of human brotherhood. Two ways lie open for you—one leading to an even lower and lower plain, where are heard the cries of despair and the curses of the poor, where manhood shrivels and possession rots down the possessor; and the other leading to the highlands of the morning, where are heard the glad shouts of humanity and where honest effort is rewarded with immortality.

—John P. Altgeld.

ALL works of taste must bear a price in proportion to the skill, taste, time, expense and risk attending their invention and manufacture.

Those things called dear are, when justly estimated, the cheapest: they are attended with much less profit to the Artist than those which everybody calls cheap

Beautiful forms and compositions are not made by chance, nor can they ever, in any material, be made at small expense. ⊄ A composition for cheapness and not excellence of workmanship is the most frequent and certain cause of the rapid decay and entire destruction of arts and manufacturers.—Josiah Wedgwood.

IT is an instinct with me personally to attack every idea which has been full grown for ten years, especially if it claims to be the foundation of all human society. I am prepared to back human society against any idea, positive or negative, that can be brought into the field against it.—George Bernard Shaw.

I LIVE on the sunny side of the street; shady folks live on the other. I have always preferred the sunshine and have tried to put other people there, if only for an hour or two at a time.

—Marshall P. Wilder.

I LOVE you for what you are, but I love you yet more for what you are going to be.

I love you not so much for your realities as for your ideals. I pray for your desires that they may be great, rather than for your satisfactions, which may be so hazardously little.

A satisfied flower is one whose petals are about to fall. The most beautiful rose is one hardly more than a bud wherein the pangs and ecstacies of desire are working for larger and finer growth. ⊄ Not always shall you be what you are now

You are going forward toward something great. I am on the way with you and therefore I love you.

—Carl Sandburg.

YOU can dissolve everything in the world, even a great fortune, into atoms. And the fundamental principles which govern the handling of postage-stamps and of millions of dollars are exactly the same. They are the common law of business, and the whole practice of commerce is founded on them. They are so simple that a fool can't learn them; so hard that a lazy man won't.

—Philip D. Armour.

TO look fearlessly upon life; to accept the laws of nature, not with meek resignation, but as her sons, who dare to search and question; to have peace and confidence within our souls—these are the beliefs that make for happiness.

—Maeterlinck.

NOTHING is easier than fault-finding; no talent, no self-denial, no brains, no character are required to set up in the grumbling business.

—Robert West.

FEAR not that thy life shall come to an end, but rather fear that it shall never have a beginning.

—Cardinal Newman.

Be sure that religion cannot be right that a man is the worse for having.

—William Penn.

IN supplying the men for the carnage of a battlefield, women have not merely lost actually more blood, and gone through a more acute anguish and weariness, in the months of bearing and in the final agony of childbirth, than has been experienced by the men who cover it; but, in the months of rearing that follow, the women of the race go through a long, patiently endured strain which no knapsacked soldier on his longest march has ever more than equalled; while, even in the matter of death, in all civilized societies, the probability that the average woman will die in childbirth is immeasurably greater than the probability that the average male will die in battle. ¶ There is, perhaps, no woman, whether she have borne children, or be merely potentially a child-bearer, who could look down upon a battlefield covered with slain, but the thought would rise in her, "So many mother's sons! So many young bodies brought into the world to lie there! So many months of weariness and pain while bones and muscles were shaped within! So many hours of anguish and struggle that breath might be! So many baby mouths drawing life at women's breasts;—all this, that men might lie with glazed eyeballs, and swollen faces, and fixed, blue, unclosed mouths, and great limbs tossed—this, that an acre of ground might be manured with human flesh, that next year's grasses or poppies or karoo bushes may spring up greener and redder, where they have lain, or that the sand of a plain may have the glint of white bones!" And we cry, "Without an inexorable cause, this must not be!" No woman who is a woman says of a human body, "It is nothing!"—Olive Schreiner.

I met her on the Umbrian Hills,
Her hair unbound, her feet
unshod;
As one whom secret glory fills
She walked—alone with God.

I met her in the city street;
Oh, changed was her aspect
then!
With heavy eyes and weary feet
She walked alone—with men.

"The Lady Poverty," by Evelyn Underhill

CONSCIENTIOUSNESS has in many outgrown that stage in which the sense of a compelling power is joined with rectitude of action. The truly honest man, here and there to be found, is not only without thought of legal, religious, or social compulsion, when he discharges an equitable claim on him; but he is without thought of self-compulsion. He does the right thing with a simple feeling of satisfaction in doing it, and is indeed impatient if anything prevents him from having the satisfaction of doing it.
—Herbert Spencer.

I AM homesick. ¶ Homesick for the home I never have seen.
For the land where I shall look horizontally into the eyes of my fellows.
The land where men rise only to lift.
¶ The land where equality leaves men to differ as they will.
The land where freedom is breathed in the air and courses in the blood.
Where there is nothing over a man between him and the sky. Where the obligations of love are sought for as prizes,
And where they vary as the moon.
That land is my true country.
I am here by some sad cosmic mistake,
And I am homesick.—Ernest Crosby.

WHEN men are rightly occupied, their amusement grows out of their work, as the color petals out of a fruitful flower; when they are faithfully helpful and compassionate, all their emotions are steady, deep, perpetual and vivifying to the soul as is the natural pulse to the body.—John Ruskin.

E have talked much of the brotherhood to come; but brotherhood has always been the fact of our life, long before it became a modern and insipid sentiment. Only we have been brothers in slavery and torment, brothers in ignorance and its perdition, brothers in disease and war and want, brothers in prostitution and hypocrisy. What happens to one of us sooner or later happens to all; we have always been unescapably involved in a common destiny. The world constantly tends to the level of the downmost man in it; and that downmost man is the world's real ruler, hugging it close to his bosom, dragging it down to his death. You do not think so, but it is true, and it ought to be true. For if there were some way by which some of us could get free apart from others, if there were some way by which some of us could have heaven while others had hell, if there were some way by which part of the world could escape some form of the blight and peril and misery of disinherited labor, then would our world indeed be lost and damned; but since men have never been able to separate themselves from one another's woes and wrongs, since history is fairly stricken with the lesson that we can not escape brotherhood of some kind, since the whole of life is teaching us that we are hourly choosing between brotherhood in suffering and brotherhood in good, it remains for us to choose the brotherhood of a co-operative world, with all its fruits thereof—the fruits of love and liberty.—George D. Herron.

ᴴHE worst of errors is to believe that any one religion has the monopoly of goodness. For every man, that religion is good which makes him gentle, upright and kind. But to govern mankind is a difficult task. The ideal is very high and the earth is very low. Outside the sterile province of philosophy, what we meet at every step is unreason, folly and passion. The wise men of antiquity succeeded in winning to themselves some little authority only by impostures, which gave them a hold upon the imagination, in their lack of physical force.
—Ernest Renan.

ᴵT is a truly sublime spectacle when in the stillness of the night, in an unclouded sky, the stars, like the world's choir, rise and set, and as it were divide existence into two portions,—the one, belonging to the earthly, is silent in the perfect stillness of night; whilst the other alone comes forth in sublimity, pomp, and majesty. Viewed in this light, the starry heavens truly exercise a moral influence over us; and who can readily stray into the paths of immorality if he has been accustomed to live amidst such thoughts and feelings, and frequently to dwell upon them? How are we entranced by the simple splendors of this wonderful drama of nature!—Wilhelm von Humboldt.

Human nature craves novelty.—Pliny.

Men! whose boast it is that ye
Come of fathers brave and free,
If there breathe on earth a slave,
Are ye truly free and brave?
If ye do not feel the chain
When it works a brother's pain,
Are ye not base slaves indeed,
Slaves unworthy to be freed!

Is true Freedom but to break
Fetters for our own dear sake,
And, with leathern hearts, forget
That we owe mankind a debt?
No! True Freedom is to share
All the chains our brothers wear,
And, with heart and hand, to be
Earnest to make others free!

They are slaves who fear to speak
For the fallen and the weak;
They are slaves who will not choose
Hatred, scoffing and abuse,
Rather in silence shrink
From the truth they needs must think:
They are slaves who dare not be
In the right with two or three.
" Freedom," by James Russell Lowell

HAT, speaking in quite unofficial language, is the net purport and upshot of war? To my own knowledge, for example, there dwell and toil, in the British village of Dumdrudge, usually some five hundred souls. From these, by certain " Natural Enemies" of the French, there are successfully selected, during the French war, say thirty able-bodied men: Dumdrudge, at her own expense, has suckled and nursed them: she has, not without difficulty and sorrow, fed them up to manhood, and even trained them to crafts, so that one can weave, another build, another hammer, and the weakest can stand under thirty stone avoir-dupois. Nevertheless, amid much weeping and swearing, they are selected; all dressed in red, and shipped away, at the public charges, some two thousand miles, or say, only, to the south of Spain; and fed there till wanted. And now to that same spot, in the south of Spain, are thirty similar French artisans, from a French Dumdrudge, in like manner wending; till at length, after infinite effort, the two parties come into actual juxtaposition, and Thirty stands fronting Thirty, each with a gun in his hand. Straightway the word " Fire!" is given and they blow the souls out of one another, and in place of sixty brisk useful craftsmen, the world has sixty dead carcasses, which it must bury, and anew shed tears for. Had these men any quarrel? Busy as the Devil is, not the smallest! They lived far enough apart; were the entirest strangers; nay, in so wide a Universe, there was even, unconsciously, by Commerce, some mutual helpfulness between them. How then? Simpleton! their Governors had fallen out; and, instead of shooting one another, had the cunning to make these poor blockheads shoot.—Alas, so is it in Deutschland, and hitherto in all other lands; still as of old, " what deviltry soever Kings do, the Greeks must pay the piper!"—In that fiction of the English Smollett, it is true, the final Cessation of War is perhaps prophetically shadowed forth; where the two Natural Enemies, in person, take each a Tobacco-pipe, filled with Brimstone; light the same, and smoke in one another's faces, till the weaker give in: but from such predicted Peace-Era, what blood-filled, trenches, and contentious centuries, may still divide us!—Carlyle.

Or ever the knightly years were gone
With the old world to the grave,
I was a King in Babylon
And you were a Christian Slave.

I saw, I took, I cast you by,
I bent and broke your pride.
You loved me well, or I heard them lie,
But your longing was denied.
Surely I knew that by and by
You cursed your gods and died.

And a myriad suns have set and shone
Since then upon the grave
Decreed by the King in Babylon
To her that had been his Slave.

The pride I trampled in now my scathe,
For it tramples me again.
The old resentment lasts like death,
For you love, yet you refrain.
I break my heart on your hard unfaith,
And I break my heart in vain.

Yet not for an hour do I wish undone
The deed beyond the grave,
When I was a King in Babylon
And you were a Virgin Slave.

" Or Ever the Knightly Years Were Gone,"
by William Ernest Henley

IGOTRY has no head and can not think, no heart and can not feel. When she moves it is in wrath; when she pauses it is amid ruin. Her prayers are curses, her God is a demon, her communion is death, her vengeance is eternity, her decalogue written in the blood of her victims, and if she stops for a moment in her infernal flight it is upon a kindred rock to whet her vulture fang for a more sanguinary desolation.—Daniel O'Connell.

AS far back as we know anything about civilization, the cultivation of the soil has been the first and most important industry in any thriving State. It will always be. Herodotus, the father of history, tells the story of the human race in the Valley of the Euphrates

He says that with poor cultivation those who tilled the soil there got a yield of fiftyfold, with fair cultivation one hundredfold, and with good cultivation two hundredfold. That was the garden of the world in its day. Its great cities, Babylon and Nineveh, where are they? Piles of desert sand mark where they stood. In place of the millions that overran the world, there are a few wandering Arabs feeding half-starved sheep and goats. The Promised Land—the Land of Canaan itself—to which the Children of Israel were brought up from Egypt, what is it now?

A land overflowing with milk and honey? Today it has neither milk nor honey. It is a barren waste of desert, peopled by scattered robber bands. A provision of Providence fertilized the soil of the valley of the Nile by overflowing it every year. From the earliest records that history gives, Egypt has been a land of remarkable crops; and today the land thus fertilized by overflow is yielding more abundantly than ever.

It is made clear by every process of logic and by the proof of historic fact that the wealth of a nation, the character of its people, the quality and permanence of its institutions are all dependent upon sound and sufficient agricultural foundation.
C Not armies or navies or commerce or diversity of manufacture or anything other than the farm is the anchor which will hold through the storms of time that sweep all else away.—James J. Hill.

AS man advanced gradually in intellectual power, and was enabled to trace the more remote consequences of his actions; as he acquired sufficient knowledge to reject baneful customs and superstitions; as he regarded more and more, not only the welfare, but the happiness of his fellowmen; as from habit, following beneficial experience, his sympathies became more tender and widely diffused, extending to men of all races, and finally to the lower animals, so would the standard of his morality rise higher and higher.

Looking to future generations, there is no cause to fear that the social instincts will grow weaker, and we may expect that virtuous habits will grow stronger. The struggle between our higher and lower impulses will be less severe, and virtue will be triumphant.
—Charles Darwin.

OH! Unseen Power that rules and controls the destinies of the children of earth: teach me the symphony of life so that my nature may be in tune with Thine.
C Reveal to me the joy of being loving, self-sacrificing and charitable.
Teach me to know and play life's game with courage, fortitude and confidence.
C Endow me with wisdom to guard my tongue and temper, and learn with patience the art of ruling my own life for its highest good, with due regard for the privacy, rights and limitations of other lives

Help me to strive for the highest legitimate reward of merit, ambition, and opportunity in my activities, ever ready to extend a kindly helping hand to those who need encouragement and succor in the struggle.

Enable me to give a smile instead of a frown, a cheerful, kindly word instead of harshness and bitterness.

Make me sympathetic in sorrow, realizing that there are hidden woes in every life no matter how exalted or lowly.
C If in life's battle I am wounded or tottering, pour into my wounds the balm of hope, and imbue me with courage undaunted to arise and continue the strife.
C Keep me humble in every relation of life, not unduly egotistical, nor liable to the serious sin of self-depreciation.

In success keep me meek.

In sorrow, may my soul be uplifted by the thought that if there were no shadow, there would be no sunshine, and that everything in life must have its antithesis.

Grant that I may be a true, loyal friend, a genial companion with the broad honest charity born of an intimate knowledge of my own shortcomings.

If I win, crown me with the laurels fitting to be worn by a victor, and if I fall, may it be with my face to the foe, fighting manfully, and falling, fling to the host behind,—play up, play up, and play the game.—" The Optimist's Prayer," by William J. Robinson.

ᴥ ᴥ

THE bells will peal, long-haired men will dress in golden sacks to pray for successful slaughter. And the old story will begin again, the awful customary acts.

The editors of the daily Press will begin virulently to stir men up to hatred and man-slaughter in the name of patriotism, happy in the receipt of an increased income. Manufacturers, merchants, contractors for military stores, will hurry joyously about their business, in the hope of double receipts.

All sorts of Government officials will buzz about, foreseeing a possibility of purloining something more than usual. The military authorities will hurry hither and thither, drawing double pay and rations, and with the expectation of receiving for the slaughter of other men various silly little ornaments which they so highly prize, as ribbons, crosses, orders, and stars. Idle ladies and gentlemen will make a great fuss, entering their names in advance for the Red Cross Society, and ready to bind up the wounds of those whom their husbands and brothers will mutilate; and they will imagine that in so doing they are performing a most Christian work *ᴥ* And, smothering despair within their souls by songs, licentiousness, and

The crest and crowning of all good,
Life's final star, is Brotherhood;
For it will bring again to earth
Her long-lost Poesy and Mirth:
Will send new light on every face,
A kingly power upon the race.
And till it comes, we men are slaves,
And travel downward to the dust of graves.

Come, clear the way, then, clear the way:
Blind creeds and kings have had their
*   day.*
Break the dead branches from the path:
Our hope is in the aftermath—
Our hope is in heroic men,
Star-led to build the world again.
To this event the ages ran:
Make way for Brotherhood—make way
*   for Man!*

" Brotherhood," *by Edwin Markham*

wine, men will trail along, torn from peaceful labor, from their wives, mothers and children—hundreds of thousands of simple-minded, good-natured men with murderous weapons in their hands—anywhere they may be driven.

They will march, freeze, hunger, suffer sickness, and die from it, or finally come to some place where they will be slain by thousands or kill thousands themselves with no reason; men whom they have never seen before, and who neither have done nor could do them any mischief.

And when the number of sick, wounded and killed becomes so great that there are not hands enough left to pick them up, and when the air is so infected with the putrefying scent of the " food for powder" that even the authorities find it disagreeable, a truce will be made, the wounded will be picked up anyhow, the sick will be brought in and huddled together in heaps, the killed will be covered with earth and lime, and once more the crowd of deluded men will be led on and on till those who have devised the project, weary of it, or till those who thought to find it profitable receive their spoil. And so once more men will be made savage, fierce and brutal, and love will wane in the world, and the Christianizing of mankind, which has already begun, will lapse for scores and for hundreds of years *ᴥ ᴥ*

And so the men who reaped profit from it all will assert that since there has been a war there must needs have been one, and that other wars must follow, and they will again prepare future generations for a continuance of slaughter, depraving them from their birth.—Leo Tolstoy.

IN a sinless and painless world the moral element would be lacking; the goodness would have no more significance in our conscious life than that load of atmosphere which we are always carrying about with us.

We are thus brought to a striking conclusion, the essential soundness of which can not be gainsaid. In a happy world there must be pain and sorrow, and in a moral world the knowledge of evil is indispensable. The stern necessity of this has been proved to inhere in the innermost constitution of the human soul. It is part and parcel of the universe ∽ To him who is disposed to cavil at the world which God has in such wise created, we may fairly put the question whether the prospect of escape from its ills would ever induce him to put off this human consciousness, and accept some form of existence unknown and inconceivable! The alternative is clear: on the one hand a world with sin and suffering, on the other hand an unthinkable world in which conscious life does not involve contrast. We do not find that evil has been interpolated into the universe from without; we find that, on the contrary, it is an indispensable part of the dramatic whole. God is the creator of evil, and from the eternal scheme of things diabolism is forever excluded. Ormuzd and Ahriman have had their day and perished, along with the doctrine of special creation and other fancies of the untutored mind. From our present standpoint we may fairly ask, what would have been the worth of that primitive innocence portrayed in the myth of the Garden of Eden, had it ever been realized in the life of men? What would have been the moral value or significance of a race of human beings ignorant of sin, and doing beneficent acts with no more consciousness or volition than the deftly contrived machine that picks up raw material at one end, and turns out some finished product at the other? Clearly, for strong and resolute men and women, an Eden would be at best but a fool's paradise.—Fiske.

A silence there expectant, meaning,
 And then a voice clear-pitched and
  tense;
A thousand hearers, forward-leaning,
 Were in the thrall of eloquence.

He saw the graves of heroes sleeping,
 He saw men's eyes suffused and dim;
A triumph great, a nation weeping,
 Found true expression there in him.

Not often in a nation's story,
 Such words supreme, such manhood
  fine;
He gave that day our grief and glory
 The dignity of things divine.

(Concluded on next page)

DO-NOTHING days may be the busiest ones ∽ They are the days in which we absorb; while on the do-much days we try to make others absorb from us whatever we have in overplus: ribbons, wisdom or cheese. If we oftener eased the strain on our eyes and minds, we should be enriched by impressions that in our usual attent and mastering attitude we refuse to heed. Americans ought to have a wholesome laziness preached to them, after three centuries of urging to gain and work, and several patriotic citizens make examples of themselves, for the public benefit, by refraining from toil.

—Charles M. Skinner.

GOVERN the lips as they were palace-doors, the king within; tranquil and fair and courteous be all words which from that presence win.

—Sir Edwin Arnold.

A MAN asked to define the essential characteristics of a gentleman—using the term in its widest sense—would presumably reply, " The will to put himself in the place of others; the horror of forcing others into positions from which he would himself recoil; the power to do what seems to him to be right, without considering what others may say or think."—John Galsworthy.

ET me do my work each day; and if the darkened hours of despair overcome me, may I not forget the strength that comforted me in the desolation of other times. May I still remember the bright hours that found me walking over the silent hills of my childhood, or dreaming on the margin of the quiet river, when a light glowed within me, and I promised my early God to have courage amid the tempests of the changing years ◄► Spare me from bitterness and from the sharp passions of unguarded moments. May I not forget that poverty and riches are of the spirit. Though the world know me not, may my thoughts and actions be such as shall keep me friendly with myself. Lift my eyes from the earth, and let me not forget the uses of the stars. Forbid that I should judge others, lest I condemn myself. Let me not follow the clamor of the world, but walk calmly in my path. Give me a few friends who will love me for what I am; and keep ever burning before my vagrant steps the kindly light of hope. And though age and infirmity overtake me, and I come not within sight of the castle of my dreams, teach me still to be thankful for life, and for time's olden memories that are good and sweet; and may the evening's twilight find me gentle still.

—Max Ehrmann.

◄► ◄►

READING is to the mind what exercise is to the body. As by the one, health is preserved, strengthened and invigorated: by the other, virtue (which is the health of the mind) is kept alive, cherished and confirmed.—Addison.

Brief, so brief—the words were falling
  Ere men had time to note and weigh;
As if again the gods were calling
  From some Homeric yesterday.

No impulse this, no actor speaking
  Of thoughts which came by happy
    chance;
The man, the place, were God's own
    seeking;
  The words are our inheritance.

A pause, a hush, a wonder growing;
  A prophet's vision, understood;
In that strange spell of his bestowing,
  They dreamed, with him, of Brotherhood.

" Abraham Lincoln at Gettysburg,"
      by Harrison D. Mason

MEN will have, and must have, their pleasures. Social reformers and temperance agitators could not make a greater mistake than by following the example of the Puritans and tabuing all pleasures. They ought to distinguish between those that have a tendency to excess and vice, and those that are harmless and ennobling, encouraging the latter in every possible way. And first among those that should be encouraged is music, because it is always ennobling, and can be enjoyed simultaneously by the greatest number. Its effect is well described in Margaret Fuller's private journal: " I felt raised above all care, all pain, all fear, and every taint of vulgarity was washed out of the world." That is precisely wherein the moral power of music lies; for vulgarity is the twin sister of vice.

—Henry T. Finck.

◄► ◄►

FORSOOTH, brothers, fellowship is heaven, and the lack of fellowship is hell; fellowship is life and the lack of fellowship is death; and the deeds that ye do upon the earth, it is for fellowship's sake that ye do them. Therefore, I bid you not dwell in hell, but in heaven— upon earth, which is a part of heaven and forsooth no foul part.

—William Morris.

◄► ◄►

GIVE me the money that has been spent in war, and I will clothe every man, woman and child in an attire of which kings and queens would be proud. I will build a schoolhouse in every valley over the whole earth. I will crown every hillside with a place of worship consecrated to the gospel of peace.

—Charles Sumner.

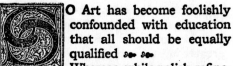

S O Art has become foolishly confounded with education that all should be equally qualified ✌ ✌

Whereas, while polish, refinement, culture and breeding are in no way arguments for artistic results, it is also no reproach to the most finished scholar or greatest gentleman in the land that he be absolutely without eye for painting or ear for music—that in his heart he prefer the popular print to the scratch of Rembrandt's needle, or the songs of the hall to Beethoven's C minor symphony. Let him have but the wit to say so, and not feel the admission a proof of inferiority.

❡ Art happens—no hovel is safe from it, no Prince may depend upon it, the vastest intelligence can not bring it about, and puny efforts to make it universal end in quaint comedy, and coarse farce. This is as it should be—and all attempts to make it otherwise are due to the eloquence of the ignorant, the zeal of the conceited.—Whistler.

✌ ✌

IT is idle to think that, by means of words, any real communication can ever pass from one man to another. The moment that we have something to say to each other, we are compelled to hold our peace: and if at such times we do not listen to the urgent commands of silence, invisible though they be, we shall have suffered an eternal loss that all the treasures of human wisdom can not make good; for we shall have let slip the opportunity of listening to another soul, and of giving existence, be it only for an instant, to our own. And again, I doubt whether anything in the world can beautify a soul more spontaneously, more naturally, than the knowledge that somewhere in its neighborhood exists a pure and noble being whom it can unreservedly love. When the soul has veritably drawn near to such a being, beauty is no longer a lovely, lifeless thing that one exhibits to the stranger, for it suddenly takes unto itself an imperious existence, and its activity becomes so natural as to be henceforth irresistible.—Maeterlinck.

IT is the prime secret of the Open Road that you are to pass nothing, reject nothing, despise nothing upon this earth. As you travel, many things both great and small will come to your attention; you are to regard all with open eyes and a heart of simplicity. Believe that everything belongs somewhere; each thing has its fitting and luminous place within this mosaic of human life. The Road is not open to those who withdraw the skirts of intolerance or lift the chin of pride. Rejecting the least of those who are called common or unclean, it is (curiously) you yourself that you reject ✌ ✌

If you despise that which is ugly you do not know that which is beautiful.

—David Grayson.

✌ ✌

IN its heart the world cares for little but play; but in its life it does hardly anything but work, for the world has forgotten that the reason of its work is—play. The natural man works that he may play—works that he may love and dream, and know while he may the wonders and joys of the strange and lovely world which for a short space he is allowed to inhabit; the unnatural man plays that he may work. So unnatural indeed have we become that not only have we forgotten our dreams, but we have actually grown ashamed of them.

❡ Proverbially there is nothing of which an Englishman is so much ashamed as his emotions. To suspect him of sentiment is to imply insult, to surprise him in tears is to commit a mortal offense. Laughter he still retains, but too often for the unworthy purpose of laughing at other people's emotions, and ridiculing beautiful things he no longer understands. England indeed is the Siberia of emotions. Let us all escape from Siberia.

—Richard Le Gallienne.

✌ ✌

THE law should be loved a little because it is felt to be just; feared a little because it is severe; hated a little because it is to a certain degree out of sympathy with the prevalent temper of the day; and respected because it is felt to be a necessity.—Emile Fourget.

HE love of dirt is among the earliest of passions, as it is the latest. Mud-pies gratify one of our first and best instincts. So long as we are dirty we are pure. Fondness for the ground comes back to a man after he has run the round of pleasure and business, eaten dirt, and sown wild-oats, drifted about the world and taken the wind of all its moods. The love of digging in the ground (or of looking on while he pays another to dig) is as sure to come back to him as he is sure, at last, to go under the ground and stay there. To own a bit of ground, to scratch it with a hoe, to plant seeds, and watch their renewal of life—this is the commonest delight of the race, the most satisfactory thing a man can do. When Cicero writes of the pleasures of old age, that of agriculture is chief among them

To dig in the mellow soil—to dig moderately, for all pleasure should be taken sparingly—is a great thing. One gets strength out of the ground as often as one touches it with a hoe. Antæus was no doubt an agriculturist; and such a prize-fighter as Hercules could n't do anything with him till he got him to lay down his spade and quit the soil. It is not simply potatoes and beets and corn and cucumbers that one raises in his well-hoed garden; it is the average of human life. There is life in the ground; it goes into the seeds; and it also, when it is stirred up, goes into the man who stirs it. The hot sun on his back as he bends to his shovel and hoe, or contemplatively rakes the warm and fragrant loam, is better than much medicine. The buds are coming out on the bushes round about; the blossoms of the fruit-trees begin to show; the blood is running up the grape-vines in streams; you can smell the wild-flowers on the near bank; and the birds are flying and glancing and singing everywhere.

To the open kitchen-door comes the busy housewife to shake a white something, and stands a moment to look, quite transfixed by the delightful sights and sounds. Hoeing in the garden on a bright, soft May day, when you are not obliged to, is nearly equal to the delight of going trouting

Blessed be agriculture!—if one does not have too much of it. All literature is fragrant with it, in a gentlemanly way. At the foot of the charming, olive-covered hills of Tivoli, Horace had a sunny farm: it was in sight of Hadrian's villa, who did landscape-gardening on an extensive scale, and probably did not get half as much comfort from it as Horace did from his more simply tilled acres. We trust that Horace did a little hoeing and farming himself, and that his verse is not all fraudulent sentiment. In order to enjoy agriculture you do not want too much of it, and you want to be poor enough to have a little inducement to work moderately yourself. Hoe while it is Spring and enjoy the best anticipations. It is not much matter if things do not turn out well.

—Charles Dudley Warner.

The night has a thousand eyes,
And the day but one,
Yet the light of the bright world
dies
With the dying sun.

The mind has a thousand eyes,
And the heart but one,
Yet the light of a whole life dies
When its love is done.

—Francis W. Bourdillon

WE have committed the Golden Rule to memory; let us now commit it to life

We have preached Brotherhood for centuries; we now need to find a material basis for brotherhood. Government must be made the organ of Fraternity—a working-form for comrade-love.

Think on this—work for this.

—Edwin Markham.

IN these days, much of the profit and sometimes the whole of success depend upon utilizing the odds and ends, the so-called "by-products."

❆ The by-product is something apart from the main article manufactured, and yet something that has an actual value of its own. For instance, in the manufacture of gas there are many by-products; these are obtained from the coal as the latter is made into lighting-gas. And these by-products, including the coke from the coal, actually suffice to pay the cost of the gas.

All kinds of big businesses have their by-products, their little odds and ends that pay well. In Mr. Armour's enormous meat-factory, for instance, there are endless by-products, from the pigtails which are dried and sold as a delicacy, to the hair of animals made into a powerful, valuable kind of rope.

If Mr. Armour neglected making the hair rope, or selling the pigtails, it would make a big difference in his dividends ✐

The point for the reader is this: The individual man does not manufacture, as a rule. But we are, all of us, dealers in time ✐ ✐

Time is the one thing we possess. Our success depends upon the use of our time, and its by-product, the odd moment ✐ ✐

Each of us has a regular day's work that he does in a routine, more or less mechanical, way. He does his clerking, his writing, his typewriting, or whatever it may be, so many hours per day. And that ends it.

But what about the by-product, the odd moments? Do you know that the men that have made great successes in this world are the men that have used wisely those odd moments? ❆ Thomas A. Edison, for instance, was hammering away at a telegraph-key when he was telegraph-operator on a small salary. He did n't neglect the by-product, the odd moments. He thought, and planned, and tried between messages. And he worked out, as a by-product of his telegraph job, all the inventions that have given him millions, and given to the inhabitants of the world thousands of millions' worth of dollars in new ideas.

Benjamin Franklin in his story of his life shows an endless number of such efforts along the lines using the odd moments. In a hundred different ways he managed to make the extra hours useful and productive.

And this I hate—not men, nor flag nor race,
But only War with its wild, grinning face.
God strike it till its eyes be blind as night,
And all its members tremble with affright!
Oh, let it hear in its death agony
The wail of mothers for their best-loved ones,
And on its head
Descend the venomed curses of its sons
Who followed her, deluded, where its guns
Had dyed the daisies red.

(Concluded on next page)

What a man does in his odd moments is not only apt to bring him profit; it is apt also to increase his mental activity ✐ The mind craves a change, and it often does well the unusual thing, out of the routine ✐ ✐

" Letting well enough alone" is a foolish motto in the life of a man who wants to get ahead. In the first place, nothing is " well enough," if you can do better ✐ No matter how well you are doing, do better. There is an old Spanish proverb which says, " Enjoy the little you have while the fool is hunting for more." ✐ The energetic American ought to turn this proverb upside down and make it read, " While the fool is enjoying the little he has, I will hunt for more."

The way to hunt for more is to utilize your odd moments.

Every minute that you save by making it useful, more profitable, is so much added to your life and its possibilities. Every minute lost is a neglected by-product—once gone, you will never get it back.

Think of the odd quarter of an hour in the morning before breakfast, the odd half-hour after breakfast, remember the chance to read, or figure, or think with concentration on your own career, that comes now and again in the day. All of these opportunities are the by-products of your daily existence.

Use them, and you may find what many of the greatest concerns have found, that the real profit is in the utilization of the by-products. ❡ Among the aimless, unsuccessful or worthless, you often hear talk about "killing time." ❧ The man who is always killing time is really killing his own chances in life; while the man who is destined to success is the man who makes time live by making it useful.—Arthur Brisbane.

❧ ❧

All these I hate—war and its panoply,
The lie that hides its ghastly mockery,
That makes its glories out of women's
*   tears,*
The toil of peasants through the
*   burdened years,*
The legacy of long disease that preys
On bone and body in the after-days.
*   God's curses pour,*
Until it shrivel with its votaries
And die away in its own fiery seas,
*   That nevermore*
Its dreadful call of murder may be heard;
A thing accursed in very deed and word
*   From blood-drenched shore to shore!*

"The Hymn of Hate," *by Joseph Dana Miller*

WHAT is the good of prescribing to art the roads that it must follow ❧ To do so is to doubt art, which develops normally according to the laws of Nature, and must be exclusively occupied in responding to human needs. Art has always shown itself faithful to Nature, and has marched with social progress. The ideal of beauty can not perish in a healthy society; we must then give liberty to art, and leave her to herself. Have confidence in her; she will reach her end, and if she strays from the way she will soon reach it again; society itself will be the guide. No single artist, not Shakespeare himself, can prescribe to art her roads and aims.—Dostoievski.

❧ ❧

I BELIEVE emphatically in religion. God made religion, and man made theology, just as God made the country and man the town. I have the largest sympathy for religion, and the largest contempt I am capable of for a mis-leading theology. Do not feed children on a maudlin sentimentalism or dogmatic religion; give them Nature. Let their souls drink in all that is pure and sweet. Rear them, if possible, amid pleasant surroundings. If they come into the world with souls groping in darkness, let them see and feel the light. Do not terrify them in early life with the fear of an after-world. Never was a child made more noble and good by a fear of Hell ❧ Let Nature teach them the lessons of good and proper living, combined with an abundance of well-balanced nourishment. Those children will grow to be the best men and women. Put the best in them by contact with the best outside. They will absorb it as a plant absorbs the sunshine and the dew.
—Luther Burbank.

❧ ❧

ABOVE the indistinguishable roar of the many feet I feel the presence of the sun, of the immense forces of the universe, and beyond these the sense of the eternal now, of the immortal. Full aware that all has failed, yet, side by side with the sadness of that knowledge, there lives on in me an unquenchable belief, thought burning like the sun, that there is yet something to be found, something real, something to give each separate personality sunshine and flowers in its own existence now. Something to shape this million-handed labor to an end and outcome, leaving accumulated sunshine and flowers to those who shall succeed. It must be dragged forth by might of thought from the immense forces of the universe.—Richard Jeffries.

❧ ❧

There is a chord in every heart that has a sigh in it if touched aright.—Ouida.

THERE is one beautiful sight in the East End, and only one, and it is the children dancing in the street when the organ-grinder goes his round. It is fascinating to watch them, the new-born, the next generation, swaying and stepping, with pretty little mimicries and graceful inventions all their own, with muscles that move swiftly and easily, and bodies that leap airily, weaving rhythms never taught in dancing school.

I have talked with these children, here, there, and everywhere, and they struck me as being bright as other children, and in many ways even brighter. They have most active little imaginations. Their capacity for projecting themselves into the realm of romance and fantasy is remarkable. A joyous life is romping in their blood. They delight in music, and motion, and color, and very often they betray a startling beauty of face and form under their filth and rags.

But there is a Pied Piper of London Town who steals them all away. They disappear. One never sees them again, or anything that suggests them. You may look for them in vain among the generation of grown-ups. Here you will find stunted forms, ugly faces, and blunt and stolid minds. Grace, beauty, imagination, all the resiliency of mind and muscle, are gone. Sometimes, however, you may see a woman, not necessarily old, but twisted and deformed out of all womanhood, bloated and drunken, lift her draggled skirts and execute a few grotesque and lumbering steps upon the pavement. It is a hint that she was once one of those children who danced to the organ-grinder. Those grotesque and lumbering steps are all that is left of the promise of childhood. In the befogged recesses of her brain has arisen a fleeting memory that she was once a girl. The crowd closes in. Little girls are dancing beside her, about her, with the pretty graces she dimly recollects, but can no more than parody with her body. Then she pants for breath, exhausted, and stumbles out through the circle. But the little girls dance on.

The children of the Ghetto possess all the qualities which make for noble manhood and womanhood; but the Ghetto itself, like an infuriated tigress turning on its young, turns upon and destroys all these qualities, blots out the light and laughter, and moulds those it does not kill into sodden and forlorn creatures, uncouth, degraded, and wretched below the beasts of the field.—Jack London.

WHEN we succeed in adjusting our social structure in such a way as to enable us to solve social questions as fast as they become really pressing, they will no longer force their way into the theater. Had Ibsen, for instance, had any reason to believe that the abuses to which he called attention in his prose plays would have been adequately attended to without his interference, he would no doubt have gladly left them alone. The same exigency drove William Morris in England from his tapestries, his epics, and his masterpieces of printing, to try and bring his fellow-citizens to their senses by the summary process of shouting at them in the streets and in Trafalgar Square. John Ruskin's writing began with *Modern Painters,* Carlyle began with literary studies of German culture and the like; both were driven to become revolutionary pamphleteers. If people are rotting and starving in all directions, and nobody else has the heart or brains to make a disturbance about it, the great writers must.
—George Bernard Shaw.

EVERY one now believes that there is in a man an animating, ruling, characteristic essence, or spirit, which is himself. This spirit, dull or bright, petty or grand, pure or foul, looks out of the eyes, sounds in the voice, and appears in the manners of each individual. It is what we call personality.
–Chas. W. Eliot.

Sleep hath its own world, a boundary between the things misnamed death and existence.—Byron.

Reason is the life of the law.—Coke.

DON'T know what I would do if I had only "two minutes to live," or what message I should give to the world. If I really thought I had only that time to live, I should like to take time to think up a fine and noble message so that my last words might have the dignity of those we have read about, which probably were n't last words at all.

However, I think if I had the power to do what I wish to do for humanity, I would give to every person the ability to put himself into the place of every other person in the world.

¶ In this way he would have that education, that culture which comes of the highest quality of imagination, and that quality, I take it, has been most perfectly exemplified in the poets and saviors of the race, in that they were able to feel and suffer what others were feeling and suffering, and when we come to a time when we realize just what the other fellow is suffering we will be moved by the desire to help him, and when we are moved by the desire to help him we come to a time when we see that this help must be administered intelligently, and ultimately we realize that it is the denial of equality, the denial of liberty, political and economic, in the world which is the cause of most of its suffering. If we had a world made up of people possessing this quality of imagination, this kind of culture, we would soon do away with the causes of involuntary poverty, and to do away with involuntary poverty would mean to do away with practically all the crime and vice and most of the suffering in the world.
—Brand Whitlock.

So he died for his faith. That is fine,
* More than most of us do.*
But, say, can you add to that line
* That he lived for it, too?*
In his death he bore witness at last
* As a martyr to the truth.*
Did his life do the same in the past,
* From the days of his youth?*
It is easy to die. Men have died
* For a wish or a whim—*
From bravado or passion or pride,
* Was it harder for him?*
But to live—every day to live out
* All the truth that he dreamt,*
While his friends met his conduct with
*   doubt*
* And the world with contempt.*
Was it thus that he plodded ahead,
* Never turning aside?*
Then we'll talk of the life that he lived.
* Never mind how he died.*

"Life and Death," *by Ernest Crosby*

WE beseech Thee, Lord, to behold us with favor, folk of many families and nations, gathered together in the peace of this roof; weak men and women, subsisting under the covert of Thy patience. Be patient still; suffer us yet awhile longer — with our broken purposes of good, with our idle endeavors against evil — suffer us awhile longer to endure, and (if it may be) help us do better. Bless to us our extraordinary mercies; if the day come when these must be taken, have us play the man under affliction. Be with our friends; be with ourselves. Go with each of us to rest; if any awake, temper to them the dark hours of watching; and when the day returns to us, our sun and comforter, call us up with morning faces and with morning hearts —eager to labor—eager to be happy, if happiness shall be our portion—and if the day be marked for sorrow—strong to endure it.—"An Evening Prayer," by Robert Louis Stevenson.

WHEN I would beget content and increase confidence in the power and wisdom and providence of Almighty God, I will walk the meadows by some gliding stream, and there contemplate the lilies that take no care, and those very many other little living creatures that are not only created, but fed (man knows not how) by the goodness of the God of Nature, and therefore trust in Him.—Izaak Walton.

HAVE no special regard for Satan, but I can at least claim that I have no prejudice against him. It may even be that I have been a little in his favor, on account of his not having a fair show. All religions issue Bibles against him, but we never hear his side. We have none but the evidence for the prosecution, and yet we have rendered the verdict. To my mind this is irregular. It is un-English, it is un-American.

Of course, Satan has some kind of a case, it goes without saying. It may be a poor one, but that is nothing; that can be said about any of us. As soon as I can get at the facts I will undertake his rehabilitation myself, if I can find an impolite publisher. It is a thing which we ought to do for anybody who is under a cloud ✆ ✆ We may not pay him reverence, for that would be indiscreet; but we can at least respect his talents. A person who has for untold centuries maintained the imposing position of spiritual head of four-fifths of the human race, and political head of the whole of it, must be granted the possession of executive abilities of the loftiest order. In his large presence the other popes and politicians shrink to midgets for the microscope. I would like to see him. I would rather see him and shake him by the tail than any other member of the European Concert.

—Mark Twain.

It is portentous, and a thing of state
That here at midnight, in our little town
A mourning figure walks, and will not
   rest,
Near the old court-house pacing up and
   down.

Or by his homestead, or in shadowed
   yards
He lingers where his children used to
   play,
Or through the market, on the well-
   worn stones
He stalks until the dawn-stars burn
   away.

A bronzed, lank man! His suit of
   ancient black,
A famous high top-hat and plain worn
   shawl
Make him the quaint great figure that
   men love,
The prairie-lawyer, master of us all.

He can not sleep upon his hillside now.
He is among us:—as in times before!
And we who toss and lie awake for long
Breathe deep, and start, to see him
   pass the door.

(Concluded on next page)

THE so-called artistic temperament explains the failure of innumerable talented men and women who never get over the frontier line of accomplishment. Symptoms of the artistic temperament should be fought to the death.

Work, work, whether you want to or not. I throw away a whole day's work sometimes, but the simple effort of turning it out has kept my steam up and prevented me from lagging behind. You can not work an hour at anything without learning something. ⁋ The matter of giving life to the pages of a novel is the result of industrious study of human beings. Writing is the result of thinking about things to write about and studying the details of contemporaneous life, so that you may set them down, not imaginatively but accurately. — David Graham Phillips.

✆ ✆

IF we are tempted to make war upon another nation, we shall remember that we are seeking to destroy an element of our own culture, and possibly its most important element. As long as war is regarded as wicked, it will always have its fascination. When it is looked upon as vulgar, it will cease to be popular.

—Oscar Wilde.

✆ ✆

YOU can not force the growth of human life and civilization, any more than you can force these slow-growing trees. That is the economy of Almighty God, that all good growth is slow growth.—Gaynor.

HAT distinguishes war is, not that man is slain, but that he is slain, spoiled, crushed by the cruelty, the injustice, the treachery, the murderous hand of man.

The evil is moral evil. War is the concentration of all human crimes. Here is its distinguishing, accursed brand. Under its standard gather violence, malignity, rage, fraud, perfidy, rapacity and lust. If it only slew men, it would do little. It turns man into a beast of prey. Here is the evil of war that man, made to be the brother, becomes the deadly foe of his kind; that man, whose duty it is to mitigate suffering, makes the infliction of his suffering his study and end; that man, whose office it is to avert and heal the wounds which come from Nature's powers, makes researches into Nature's laws, and arms himself with her most awful forces, that he may become the destroyer of his race. Nor is this all. There is also found in war a cold-hearted indifference to human miseries and wrongs, perhaps more shocking than the bad passions it calls forth. To my mind, this contempt of human nature is singularly offensive. To hate expresses something like respect. But in war, man treats his brother as nothing worth; sweeps away human multitudes as insects; tramples them down as grass; mocks at the rights, and does not deign a thought to their woes.
—William Ellery Channing.

His head is bowed. He thinks on men
  and kings.
Yea, when the sick world cries, how
  can he sleep?
Too many peasants fight, they know
  not why,
Too many homesteads in black terror weep.

The sins of all the war-lords burn his heart.
He sees the dreadnaughts scouring
  every main.
He carries on his shawl-wrapped
  shoulders now
The bitterness, the folly and the pain.

He can not rest until a spirit-dawn
Shall come; the shining hope of Europe
  free;
The league of sober folk, the Workers'
  Earth,
Bring long peace to Cornland, Alp and Sea.

It breaks his heart that kings must murder
  still,
That all his hours of travail here for men
Seem yet in vain. And who will bring
  white peace
That he may sleep upon his hill again?
" Abraham Lincoln Walks at Midnight,"
by Vachel Lindsay

NOW the universal heart of man blesses flowers! They are wreathed round the cradle, the marriage-altar and the tomb. The Persian in the Far East delights in their perfume, and writes his love in nosegays; while the Indian child of the Far West claps his hands with glee as he gathers the abundant blossoms —the illuminated scriptures of the prairies. The Cupid of the ancient Hindoos tipped his arrows with flowers, and orange-flowers are a bridal crown with us, a nation of yesterday. Flowers garlanded the Grecian altar, and hung in votive wreath before the Christian shrine. All these are appropriate uses. Flowers should deck the brow of the youthful bride, for they are in themselves a lovely type of marriage. They should twine round the tomb, for their perpetually renewed beauty is a symbol of the resurrection. They should festoon the altar, for their fragrance and their beauty ascend in perpetual worship before the Most High.—L. M. Child.

WHEN you get into a tight place and everything goes against you, till it seems as though you could not hold on a minute longer, never give up then, for that is just the place and time that the tide will turn.—Harriet Beecher Stowe.

DESPISE not any man, and do not spurn anything; for there is no man that has not his hour, nor is there anything that has not its place.—Rabbi Ben Azai.

THE majesty of suffering labor is no longer dumb: it speaks now with a million tongues, and it asks the nations not to increase the ills which crush down the workers by an added burden of mistrust and hate, by wars and the expectation of wars.

Gentlemen, you may ask how and when and in what form this longing for international concord will express itself to some purpose .... I can only answer you by a parable which I gleaned by fragments from the legends of Merlin, the magician, from the *Arabian Nights,* and from a book that is still unread.

Once upon a time there was an enchanted forest. It had been stripped of all verdure, it was wild and forbidding. The trees, tossed by the bitter winter wind that never ceased, struck one another with a sound as of breaking swords. When at last, after a long series of freezing nights and sunless days that seemed like nights, all living things trembled with the first call of spring, the trees became afraid of the sap that began to move within them. And the solitary and bitter spirit that had its dwelling within the hard bark of each of them said very low, with a shudder that came up from the deepest roots: " Have a care! If thou art the first to risk yielding to the wooing of the new season, if thou art the first to turn thy lance-like buds into blossoms and leaves, their delicate raiment will be torn by the rough blows of the trees that have been slower to put forth leaves and flowers."

And the proud and melancholy spirit that was shut up within the great Druidical oak spoke to its tree with peculiar insistence: " And wilt thou, too, seek to join the universal love-feast, thou whose noble branches have been broken by the storm? "

Thus, in the enchanted forest, mutual distrust drove back the sap, and prolonged the death-like winter even after the call of spring.

What happened at last? By what mysterious influence was the grim charm broken? Did some tree find the courage to act alone, like those April poplars that break into a shower of verdure, and give from afar the signal for a renewal of all life? Or did a warmer and more life-giving beam start the sap moving in all the trees at once? For lo! in a single day the whole forest burst forth into a magnificent flowering of joy and peace.

—Jean Leon Jaurès.

I JOIN with you most cordially in rejoicing at the return of peace. I hope it will be lasting, and that mankind will at length, as they call themselves reasonable creatures, have reason enough to settle their differences without cutting throats; for, in my opinion, there never was a good war or a bad peace. What past additions to the conveniences and comforts of life might mankind have acquired, if the money spent in wars had been employed in works of utility! What an extension of agriculture, even to the tops of the mountains; what rivers rendered navigable, or joined by canals; what bridges, aqueducts, new roads, and other public works, edifices and improvements, rendering England a complete paradise, might not have been obtained by spending those millions in doing good, which in the last war have been spent in doing mischief—in bringing misery into thousands of families and destroying the lives of so many working people, who might have performed the useful labors.

—Franklin.

IT is a glorious privilege to live, to know, to act, to listen, to behold, to love. To look up at the blue summer sky; to see the sun sink slowly beyond the line of the horizon; to watch the worlds come twinkling into view, first one by one, and the myriads that no man can count, and lo! the universe is white with them; and you and I are here.—Marco Morrow.

BELIEVE me, every man has his secret sorrows, which the world knows not; and oftentimes we call a man cold when he is only sad.—Longfellow.

GE, that lessens the enjoyment of life, increases our desire of living. Those dangers which, in the vigor of youth, we had learned to despise, assume new terrors as we grow old. Our caution increasing as our years increase, fear becomes at last the prevailing passion of the mind, and the small remainder of life is taken up in useless efforts to keep off our end, or provide for a continued existence ∞ Whence, then, is this increased love of life, which grows upon us with our years? Whence comes it that we thus make greater efforts to preserve our existence at a period when it becomes scarce worth the keeping? Is it that Nature, attentive to the preservation of mankind, increases our wishes to live, while she lessens our enjoyments; and, as she robs the senses of every pleasure, equips imagination in the spoil? Life would be insupportable to an old man, who loaded with infirmities, feared death no more than when in the vigor of manhood: the numberless calamities of decaying Nature, and the consciousness of surviving every pleasure would at once induce him with his own hand to terminate the scene of misery: but happily the contempt of death forsakes him at a time when it could only be prejudicial, and life acquires an imaginary value in proportion as its real value is no more.

—Oliver Goldsmith.

He who would do some great thing in this short life must apply himself to work with such a concentration of his forces as, to idle spectators, who live only to amuse themselves, looks like insanity.

—Parkman.

The streets are full of human toys,
*   Wound up for threescore years;*
Their springs are hungers, hopes and
*   joys,*
*   And jealousies and fears.*

They move their eyes, their lips, their
*   hands;*
*   They are marvellously dressed;*
And here my body stirs or stands,
*   A plaything like the rest.*

The toys are played with till they fall,
*   Worn out and thrown away.*
Why were they ever made at all!
Who sits to watch the play!
   " Playthings," by Robert Louis Stevenson

WHAT if I differ from some in religious apprehensions? Am I therefore incompatible with human societies? I know not any unfit for political society but those who maintain principles subversive of industry, fidelity, justice and obedience. Five things are requisite for a good officer; ability, clean hands, dispatch, patience and impartiality.

—William Penn.

A STRONG life is like that of a ship of war which has its own place in the fleet and can share in its strength and discipline, but can also go forth alone to the solitude of the infinite sea. We ought to belong to society, to have our place in it and yet be capable of a complete individual existence outside of it.

—P. G. Hamerton.

HAPPINESS in this world, when it comes, comes incidentally. Make it the object of pursuit, and it leads us a wild-goose chase, and is never attained. Follow some other object, and very possibly we may find that we have caught happiness without dreaming of it; but likely enough it is gone the moment we say to ourselves, " Here it is!" like the chest of gold that treasure-seekers find.

—Nathaniel Hawthorne.

FOR those who seek Truth and would follow her; for those who recognize Justice and would stand for her, success is not the only thing. Success! Why, Falsehood has often that to give; and Injustice often has that to give. Must not Truth and Justice have something to give that is their own by proper right—theirs in essence, and not by accident? That they have, and not here and now, every one who has felt their exaltation knows.—Henry George.

HEN we say a man or a woman we know is a thorough-bred, we pay to him or her the greatest compliment of which we are capable. There is not in the vocabulary of pleasant terms a stronger word.

Visit a stock-farm, the home of high-grade horses or cattle, and you will see that the physical signs of the thoroughbred are fine eyes and an erect bearing. These are the symbols of a high, generous spirit ∞ ∞

The keeper of the stock-farm will tell you that a thoroughbred never whines. One illustrated this to me by swinging a dog around by the tail. The creature was in pain, but no sound escaped him. "You see," said the keeper, "they never complain. It ain't in 'em. Same way when a stable burns. It ain't the best horses that scream when they're burnin'. It 's the worst."

All this is quite as true of the human thoroughbred. The visible signs of the invisible spirit are the eyes that are steady and shoulders that are straight. No burden except possibly the weight of many years bends his shoulders, and his eyes meet yours in honest fashion, because he neither fears, nor has been shamed, at the bar of his own soul.
❡ He never complains. He keeps his troubles to himself, having discovered, as thoroughbreds do, that to tell troubles is to multiply them, and to lock them in the breast is to diminish and finally end them. He never talks about what Fate has done to him. He knows he is master of his own destiny. He never bewails the treatment he has received from another, for he knows no one can do him lasting harm except himself.—Ada Patterson.

∞ ∞

HE fact is, that civilization requires slaves. The Greeks were quite right there. Unless there are slaves to do the ugly, horrible, uninteresting work, culture and contemplation become almost impossible. Human slavery is wrong, insecure, and demoralizing. On mechanical slavery, on the slavery of the machine, the future of the world depends.—Oscar Wilde.

ODAY is your day and mine, the only day we have, the day in which we play our part. What our part may signify in the great whole we may not understand; but we are here to play it, and now is our time. This we know: it is a part of action, not of whining. It is a part of love, not cynicism. It is for us to express love in terms of human helpfulness.—David Starr Jordan.

∞ ∞

HE perfect historian is he in whose work the character and spirit of an age is exhibited in miniature. He relates no fact, he attributes no expression to his characters, which is not authenticated by sufficient testimony ∞ By judicious selection, rejection and arrangement, he gives to truth those attractions which have been usurped by fiction. In his narrative a due subordination is observed: some transactions are prominent; others retire. But the scale on which he represents them is increased or diminished not according to the dignity of the persons concerned in them, but according to the degree in which they elucidate the condition of society and the nature of man. He shows us the court, the camp and the senate. But he shows us also the nation. He considers no anecdote, no peculiarity of manner, no familiar saying, as too significant for his notice which is not too insignificant to illustrate the operation of laws, of religion, and of education, and to mark the progress of the human mind. Men will not merely be described, but will be made intimately known to us.
—Macaulay.

∞ ∞

HE ideal life is in our blood and never will be still. Sad will be the day for any man when he becomes contented with the thoughts he is thinking and the deeds he is doing,—where there is not forever beating at the doors of his soul some great desire to do something larger, which he knows that he was meant and made to do.
—Phillips Brooks.

∞ ∞

He jests at scars that never felt a wound.
—Shakespeare.

E rejoined the Colors on Friday. On Monday we are to move out. Today, being Sunday, is full dress Church Parade ◆ ◆

I slept badly last night, and am feeling uneasy and limp.

And now we are sitting close-packed in church ◆ ◆

The organ is playing a voluntary. ❦ I am leaning back and straining my ears for the sounds in the dim twilight of the building ◆ ◆

Childhood's days rise before my eyes again. I am watching a little solemn-faced boy sitting crouched in a corner and listening to the divine service ◆ The priest is standing in front of the altar, and is intoning the Exhortation devoutly. The choir in the gallery is chanting the responses. The organ thunders out and floods through the building majestically. I am rapt in an ecstasy of sweet terror, for the Lord God is coming down upon us. He is standing before me and touching my body, so that I have to close my eyes in a terror of shuddering ecstacy. . . .

That is long, long ago, and is all past and done with, as youth itself is past and done with. . . .

Strange! After all these years of doubt and unbelief, at this moment of lucid consciousness, the atmosphere of devoutness, long since dead, possesses me, and thrills me so passionately that I can hardly resist it. This is the same heavy twilight—these are the same yearning angel voices—the same fearful sense of rapture— ◆ ◆

I pull myself together, and sit bolt upright on the hard wooden pew.

In the main and the side aisles below, and in the galleries above, nothing but soldiers in uniform, and all, with level faces, turned toward the altar, toward that pale man in his long, dignified black gown, toward that sonorous, unctuous mouth, from whose lips flows the name of God ◆ ◆

Look! He is now stretching forth his hands. We incline our heads. He is pronouncing the Benediction over us in a voice that echoes from the tomb. He is blessing us in the name of God, the Merciful. He is blessing our rifles that they may not fail us; he is blessing the wire-drawn guns on their patent recoilless carriages; he is blessing every precious cartridge, lest a single bullet be wasted, lest any pass idly through the air; that each one may account for a hundred human beings, may shatter a hundred human beings simultaneously.

Father in Heaven! Thou art gazing down at us in such terrible silence. Dost Thou shudder at these sons of men? Thou poor and slight God! Thou couldst only rain Thy paltry pitch and sulphur on Sodom and Gomorrah. But we, Thy children, whom Thou hast created, we are going to exterminate them by high-pressure machinery, and butcher whole cities in factories. Here we stand, and while we stretch our hands to Thy Son in prayer, and cry Hosannah! we are hurling shells and shrapnel in the face of Thy Image, and shooting the Son of Man down from His Cross like a target at the rifle-butts.

❦ And now the Holy Communion is being celebrated. The organ is playing mysteriously from afar off, and the flesh and blood of the Redeemer is mingling with our flesh and blood.

There He is hanging on the Cross above me, and gazing down upon me.

How pale those cheeks look! And those eyes are the eyes as of one dead! Who was this Christ Who is to aid us, and Whose blood we drink? What was it they once taught us at school? Didst Thou not

Under the wide and starry sky
Dig the grave and let me lie;
Glad did I live and gladly die,
And I laid me down with a will.

This be the verse you grave for me:
Here he lies where he longed to be;
Home is the sailor, home from sea,
And the hunter home from the hill.

"*Requiem,*" *by Robert Louis Stevenson*

love mankind? And didst Thou not die for the whole human race? Stretch out Thine arms toward me. There is something I would fain ask of Thee. . . . Ah! they have nailed Thy arms to the Cross, so that Thou canst not stretch out a finger toward us.

Shuddering, I fix my eyes on the corpse-like face and see that He died long ago, that He is nothing more than wood, nothing other than a puppet. Christ, it is no longer Thee to whom we pray. Look there! Look there! It is he. The new patron saint of a Christian State! Look there! It is he, the great Genghis Khan. Of him we know that he swept through the history of the world with fire and sword, and piled up pyramids of skulls. Yes, that is he. Let us heap up mountains of human heads, and pile up heaps of human entrails. Great Genghis Khan! Thou, our patron saint! Do thou bless us! Pray to thy blood-drenched father seated above the skies of Asia, that he may sweep with us through the clouds; that he may strike down the accursed nation till it writhes in its blood, till it never can rise again. A red mist swims before my eyes. Of a sudden I see nothing but blood before me. The heavens have opened, and the red flood pours in through the windows. Blood wells up on the altar. The walls run blood from the ceiling to the floor, and— God the Father steps out of the blood. Every scale of his skin stands erect, his beard and hair drip blood. A giant of blood stands before me. He seats himself backward on the altar, and is laughing from thick, coarse lips—there sits the King of Dahomey, and he butchers his slaves. The black executioner raises his sword and whirls it above my head. Another moment and my head will roll down on the floor—another moment and the red jet will spurt from my neck . . . . . Murderers, murderers! None other than murderers! Lord God in Heaven! Then—

The church door opens creaking—

Light, air, the blue of heaven, burst in. I draw a breath of relief. We have risen to our feet, and at length pass out of the twilight into the open air.

My knees are still trembling under me. ❡ We fall into line, and in our hob-nailed boots tramp in step down the street toward the barracks. When I see my mates marching beside me in their matter-of-fact and stolid way, I feel ashamed, and call myself a wretched coward. What a weak-nerved, hysterical breed, that can no longer look at blood without fainting! You neurasthenic offspring of your sturdy peasant forebears, who shouted for joy when they went out to fight! ❧ ❧

I pull myself together and throw my head back.

I never was a coward, and eye for eye I have always looked my man in the face, and will so do this time, too, happen what may.—Wilhelm Lamszus.

❧ ❧

KNOWLEDGE is essential to conquest; only according to our ignorance are we helpless. Thought creates character. Character can dominate conditions. Will creates circumstances and environment.—Annie Besant.

❧ ❧

IT is assumed that labor is available only in connection with capital; that nobody labors unless somebody else, owning capital, somehow by the use of it, induces him to labor. This assumed, it is next considered whether it is best that capital shall hire laborers, and thus induce them to work by their own consent, or buy them and drive them to do it without their consent. Having proceeded so far, it is naturally concluded all laborers are either hired laborers or what we call slaves.

Now, there is no such relation between capital and labor as here assumed. . . . Labor is prior to and independent of capital. Capital is only the fruit of labor, could never have existed if labor had not first existed. Labor is the superior of capital, and deserves much the higher consideration.—Abraham Lincoln.

❧ ❧

To be seventy years young is sometimes far more cheerful and hopeful than to be forty years old.

—Oliver Wendell Holmes.

F we were to single out the men who from the beginning of our Colonial state until the present time have most eminently contributed to fostering and securing religious freedom, who have made this country of ours the haven of refuge from ecclesiastical tyranny and persecution, who have set an example more puissant than army or navy for freeing the conscience of men from civil interference, and have leavened the mass of intolerance wherever the name of America is known, I would mention first the Baptist, Roger Williams, who maintained the principle that the civil powers have no right to meddle in matters of conscience, and who founded a State with that principle as its keystone. I would mention second the Catholic, Lord Baltimore, the proprietor of Maryland, to whom belongs the credit of having established liberty in matters of worship which was second only to Rhode Island. I would name third the Quaker, William Penn, whose golden motto was, " We must yield the liberties we demand." Fourth on the list is Thomas Jefferson, that " arch-infidel," as he has been termed by some religious writers, who overthrew the established church in his own State, and then, with prophetic statesmanship, made it impossible for any church to establish itself under our national Constitution or in any way to abridge the rights of conscience.—Oscar S. Straus.

I LIKE to be beholden to the great metropolitan English speech, the sea which receives tributaries from every region under heaven. I should as soon think of swimming across the Charles River when I wish to go to Boston, as of reading all my books in originals, when I have them rendered for me in my mother tongue.—Emerson.

THAT night there was an unusual atmosphere in her corner. She had a newly tallied cap on her head and her little Sunday shawl over her shoulders. Her candle was burning and the hearth stones had an extra coat of whitewash.

She drew me up close beside her and told me a story.

" Once, a long, long time ago, God, feelin' tired, went to sleep an' had a nice wee nap on His throne. His head was in His han's an' a wee white cloud came down an' covered Him up. Purty soon He wakes up an' says He:

" ' Where 's Michael? '

" ' Here I am, Father! ' said Michael.

" ' Michael, me boy,' says God, ' I want a chariot and a charioteer! '

" ' Right ye are!' says he. Up comes the purtiest chariot in the city of Heaven an' the finest charioteer.

" ' Me boy,' says God, ' take a million tons of th' choicest seeds of th' flowers of Heaven an' take a trip around th' world wi' them. Scatter them,' says He, 'be th' roadsides an' th' wild places of th' earth where my poor live.'

" ' Aye,' says the charioteer, ' that's jist like Ye, Father. It's th' purtiest job of m' afther-life an' I 'll do it finely.'

" 'It 's jist come t' Me in a dream,' says th' Father, ' that the rich have all the flowers down there and the poor have nown at all."

At this point I got in some questions about God's language and the kind of flowers

" Well, dear," she said, " He spakes Irish t' Irish people, an' the charioteer was an Irishman."

" Maybe it was a woman!" I ventured. ¶ " Aye, but there's no difference up there."

" Th' flowers," she said, " were primroses, buttercups, an' daisies, an' th' flowers that be handy t' th' poor, an' from that day to this there 's been flowers a-plenty for all of us everywhere!"— " My Lady of the Chimney-Corner," by Alexander Irvine.

IT is well for a man to respect his own vocation whatever it is, and to think himself bound to uphold it, and to claim for it the respect it deserves.
—Charles Dickens.

The religions of the world are the ejaculations of a few imaginative men.
—Emerson.

SUNDOWN is the hour for many strange effects in light and shade—enough to make a colorist go delirious—long spokes of molten silver sent horizontally through the trees (now in their brightest, tenderest green), each leaf and branch of endless foliage a lit-up miracle, then lying all prone on the youthful-ripe, interminable grass, and giving the blades not only aggregate but individual splendor, in ways unknown to any other hour. ❡ I have particular spots where I get these effects in their perfection. One broad splash lies on the water, with many a rippling twinkle, offset by the rapidly deepening black-green murky-transparent shadows behind, and at intervals all along the banks. These, with great shafts of horizontal fire thrown among the trees and along the grass as the sun lowers, give effects more peculiar, more and more superb, unearthly, rich and dazzling.
—Walt Whitman.

Preach about yesterday, Preacher!
The time so far away:
When the hand of Deity smote and
slew,
And the heathen plagued the stiff-
necked Jew;
Or when the Man of Sorrow came,
And blessed the people who cursed His
name—
Preach about yesterday, Preacher,
Not about today!

Preach about tomorrow, Preacher!
Beyond this world's decay:
Of the sheepfold Paradise we priced
When we pinned our faith to Jesus
Christ;
Of those hot depths that shall receive
The goats who would not so believe—
Preach about tomorrow, Preacher,
Not about today!

(Concluded on next page)

IF I had my life to live over again, I would have made a rule to read some poetry and listen to some music at least once a week; for perhaps the parts of my brain now atrophied would thus have been kept active through use. ❡ The loss of these tastes is a loss of happiness, and may possibly be injurious to the intellect, and more probably to the moral character, by enfeebling the emotional part of our nature.—Darwin.

Better late than never.—Dionysius.

WHAT gives Anatole France his lasting hold over his hearers is not his cleverness, but himself—the fact that this savant who bears the heavy load of three cultures, nay, who is in himself a whole little culture—this sage, to whom the whole life of the earth is but an ephemeral eruption on its surface, and who consequently regards all human endeavor as finally vain—this thinker, who can see everything from innumerable sides and might have come to the conclusion that things being bad at the best, the existing state of matters was probably as good as the untried: that this man should proclaim himself a son of the Revolution, side with the workingman, acknowledge his belief in liberty, throw away his load and draw his sword—this is what moves a popular audience, this is what plain people can understand and can prize. It has shown them that behind the author there dwells a man—behind the great author a brave man.—Georg Brandes.

LOVE is the river of life in this world. Think not that ye know it who stand at the little tinkling rill, the first small fountain.
Not until you have gone through the rocky gorges, and not lost the stream; not until you have gone through the meadow, and the stream has widened and deepened until fleets could ride on its bosom; not until beyond the meadow you have come to the unfathomable ocean, and poured your treasures into its depths—not until then can you know what love is.
—Henry Ward Beecher.

IFE seems a perpetual succession of events, to which man submits. We never know from which direction the sudden blow will come. Misery and happiness enter and make their exits, like unexpected guests. Their laws, their orbits, their principle of gravitation, are beyond man's grasp. Virtue conducts not to happiness; nor crime to retribution; conscience has one logic, fate another, and neither coincide. Nothing is foreseen. We live confusedly and from hand to mouth. Conscience is the straight line, life is the whirlwind which creates over man's head either black chaos or the blue sky. Fate does not practise the art of gradations ৯ Her wheel turns sometimes so fast that we can scarcely distinguish the interval between one revolution and another, or the link between yesterday and today.
—Victor Hugo.

৯ ৯

Great spenders are bad lenders.—Franklin

৯ ৯

EACH and every man ought to interest himself in public affairs. There is no happiness in mere dollars. After they are acquired, one can use but a very moderate amount. It is given a man to eat so much, to wear so much, and to have so much shelter, and more he can not use. When money has supplied these, its mission, so far as the individual is concerned, is fulfilled, and man must look still further and higher. It is only in wide public affairs, where money is a moving force toward the general welfare, that the possessor of it can possibly find pleasure, and that

only in constantly doing more ৯ The greatest good a man can do is to cultivate himself, develop his powers, in order that he may be of greater service to humanity.—Marshall Field.

৯ ৯

WE must learn that any person who will not accept what he knows to be truth, for the very love of truth alone, is very definitely undermining his mental integrity. It will be observed that the mind of such a person gradually stops growing, for, being constantly hedged in and cropped here and there, it soon learns to respect artificial fences more than freedom for growth. ❡ You have not been a very close observer of such men if you have not seen them shrivel, become commonplace, mean, without influence, without friends and without the enthusiasm of youth and growth, like a tree covered with fungus, the foliage diseased, the life gone out of the heart with dry rot, and indelibly marked for destruction—dead, but not yet handed over to the undertaker.
—Luther Burbank.

৯ ৯

MAN is incomprehensible without Nature, and Nature is incomprehensible apart from man. For the delicate loveliness of the flower is as much in the human eye as in its own fragile petals, and the splendor of the heavens as much in the imagination that kindles at the touch of their glory as in the shining of countless worlds.
—Hamilton Wright Mabie.

৯ ৯

I would rather be sick than idle.—Seneca.

Preach about the old sins, Preacher!
And the old virtues, too:
You must not steal nor take man's life,
You must not covet your neighbor's wife,
And woman must cling at every cost
To her one virtue, or she is lost—
Preach about the old sins, Preacher!
Not about the new!

Preach about the other man, Preacher!
The man we all can see!
The man of oaths, the man of strife,
The man who drinks and beats his wife,
Who helps his mates to fret and shirk
When all they need is to keep at work—
Preach about the other man, Preacher!
Not about me!

"To the Preacher,"
by Charlotte Perkins Gilman

EOPLE say to me, " Well, Lyeff Nikolaevitch, as far as preaching goes, you preach; but how about your practice? "

The question is a perfectly natural one; it is always put to me, and it always shuts my mouth. " You preach," it is said, " but how do you live? "

I can only reply that I do not preach, passionately as I desire to do so.

I might preach through my actions, but my actions are bad. That which I say is not preaching; it is only my attempt to find out the meaning and the significance of life.

People often say to me, " If you think that there is no reasonable life outside the teachings of Christ, and if you love a reasonable life, why do you not fulfil the Christian precepts? " I am guilty and blameworthy and contemptible because I do not fulfil them: but at the same time I say—not in justification, but in explanation, of my inconsistency— " Compare my previous life with the life I am now living, and you will see that I am trying to fulfil. I have not, it is true, fulfilled one eighty-thousandth part, and I am to blame for it; but it is not because I do not wish to fulfil all, but because I am unable. Teach me how to extricate myself from the meshes of temptation in which I am entangled— help me—and I will fulfil all. Condemn me if you choose—I do that myself— but condemn Me, and not the path which I am following, and which I point out to those who ask me where, in my opinion, the path is."—Leo Tolstoy.

⁂

HERE is no place where humor counts for more in a commercial way than in advertising. If you can only land your shot under a man's funny bone you have done the deadly work and can interest him in whatever you have to offer. The necessity of saying things tersely and compactly, as the advertising writer must always say them, is a cardinal point in the training of the humorist, and for this reason I believe that the writing of advertisements is one of the best courses of instruction through which the man ambitious to shine as a professional humorist can pass.

—George Ade.

⁂

HERE have I come from, where did you pick me up? " the baby asked its mother.

❡ She answered, half-crying, half-laughing, and clasping the baby to her breast: " You were hidden in my heart as its desire, my darling.

" You were in the dolls of my childhood's games; and when with clay I made the image of my god every morning, I made and unmade you then.

" You were enshrined with our household deity; in his worship I worshiped you.

" In all my hopes and my loves, in my life, in the life of my mother, you have lived

" In the lap of the deathless Spirit who rules our home you have been nursed for ages."—Rabindranath Tagore.

⁂

HEN, and indeed for many years after, it seemed as though there was no end to the money needed to carry on and develop the business. As our successes began to come, I seldom put my head upon the pillow at night without speaking a few words to myself in this wise:

" Now a little success, soon you will fall down, soon you will be overthrown. Because you have got a start, you think you are quite a merchant; look out, or you will lose your head—go steady." These intimate conversations with myself, I am sure had a great influence on my life.—John D. Rockefeller.

⁂

HE old idea of romance: The country boy goes to the city, marries his employer's daughter, enslaves some hundreds of his fellow humans, gets rich, and leaves a public library to his home town.

❡ The new idea of romance: To undo some of the mischief done by the old idea of romance.—Seymour Deming.

⁂

THINK the first virtue is to restrain the tongue; he approaches nearest to the gods who knows how to be silent, even though he is in the right.—Cato.

OVE is the only bow on life's dark cloud. It is the Morning and the Evening Star. It shines upon the cradle of the babe, and sheds its radiance upon the quiet tomb. It is the mother of Art, inspirer of poet, patriot and philosopher. It is the air and light of every heart, builder of every home, kindler of every fire on every hearth. It was the first to dream of immortality. It fills the world with melody, for Music is the voice of Love. Love is the magician, the enchanter, that changes worthless things to joy, and makes right royal kings and queens of common clay. It is the perfume of the wondrous flower—the heart—and without that sacred passion, that divine swoon, we are less than beasts; but with it, earth is heaven and we are gods.—Robert G. Ingersoll.

THOUSANDS of channels there are through which the beauty of our soul may sail even unto our thoughts. Above all is there the wonderful, central channel of love. For is it not in love that are found the purest elements of beauty that we can offer to the soul? Some there are who do thus in beauty love each other. And to love thus means that, little by little, the sense of ugliness is lost; that one's eyes are closed to all the littlenesses of life, to all but the freshness and virginity of the very humblest of souls. Loving thus, we can no longer have anything to conceal, for that the ever-present soul transforms all things into beauty. It is to behold evil in so far only as it purifies indulgence, and teaches us no longer to confound the sinner with the sin Loving thus do we raise on high within ourselves all those about us who have attained an eminence where failure has become impossible: heights whence a paltry action has so far to fall that, touching earth, it is compelled to yield up its diamond soul. It is to transform, though all unconsciously, the feeblest intention that hovers about us into illimitable movement. It is to summon all that is beautiful in earth, heaven or soul, to the banquet of love. It means that the least gesture will call forth the presence of the soul with all its treasure. It means that the beauty that turns into love is undistinguishable from the love that turns into beauty. It means to be able no longer to tell where the ray of a star leaves off and the kiss of an ordinary thought begins. It means that each day will reveal to us a new beauty in that mysterious angel, and that we shall walk together in a goodness that shall ever become more and more living, loftier and loftier.—Maeterlinck.

CHERISH the spirit of our people and keep alive their attention. Do not be too severe upon their errors, but reclaim them by enlightening them. If once they become inattentive to public affairs, you and I, and Congress and Assemblies, judges and governors, shall all become wolves. It seems to be the law of our general nature, in spite of individual exceptions; and experience declares that man is the only animal which devours his own kind; for I can apply no milder term to the governments of Europe, and to the general prey of the rich on the poor.—Thomas Jefferson.

I DO not despise genius—indeed, I wish I had a basketful of it instead of a brain, but yet, after a great deal of experience and observation, I have become convinced that industry is a better horse to ride than genius. It may never carry any one man as far as genius has carried individuals, but industry—patient, steady intelligent industry—will carry thousands into comfort and even into celebrity, and this it does with absolute certainty; whereas genius often refuses to be tamed and managed, and often goes with wretched morals. If you are to wish for either, wish for industry.
—Julian Ralph.

The more a man is educated, the more is it necessary, for the welfare of the State, to instruct him how to make a proper use of his talents. Education is like a double-edged sword. It may be turned to dangerous usages if it is not properly handled.—Wu Ting-Fang.

EQUALITY is the life of conversation; and he is as much out who assumes to himself any part above another, as he who considers himself below the rest of society. Familiarity in inferiors is sauciness: in superiors it is condescension; neither of which are to have being among companions, the very word implying that they are to be equal. When, therefore, we have extracted the company from all considerations of their equality or fortune, it will immediately appear that, to make it happy and polite, there must nothing be started which shall discover that our thoughts run upon any such distinctions ᴞ Hence it will arise that benevolence must become the rule of society, and he that is most obliging must be most diverting.

—Richard Steele.

NE has achieved success who has lived well, laughed often and loved much; who has gained the respect of intelligent men and the love of little children; who has filled his niche and accomplished his task; who has left the world better than he found it, whether by an improved poppy, a perfect poem or a rescued soul; who has never lacked appreciation of earth's beauty or failed to express it; who has looked for the best in others and given the best he had; whose life was an inspiration; whose memory is a benediction.

Mrs. A. J. Stanley.

IT is said that in love we idolize the object, and, placing him apart and selecting him from his fellows, look on him as superior in nature to all others. We do so; but even as we idolize the object of our affections, do we idolize ourselves: if we separate him from his fellow-mortals, so do we separate ourselves, and glorying in belonging to him alone feel lifted above all other sensations, all other joys and griefs, to one hallowed circle from which all but his idea is banished: we walk as if a mist, or some more potent charm, divided us from all but him; a sanctified victim, which none but the priest set apart for that office could touch and not pollute, enshrined in a cloud of glory, made glorious through beauties not our own.

—Mrs. M. W. Shelley.

BEAUTY is an all-pervading presence. It unfolds to the numberless flowers of the Spring; it waves in the branches of the trees and in the green blades of grass; it haunts the depths of the earth and the sea, and gleams out in the hues of the shell and the precious stone. And not only these minute objects, but the ocean, the mountains, the clouds, the heavens, the stars, the rising and the setting sun, all overflow with beauty. The universe is its temple; and those men who are alive to it can not lift their eyes without feeling themselves encompassed with it on every side. Now, this beauty is so precious, the enjoyment it gives so refined and pure, so congenial without tenderest and noblest feelings, and so akin to worship, that it is painful to think of the multitude of men as living in the midst of it, and living almost as blind to it as if, instead of this fair earth and glorious sky, they were tenants of a dungeon. An infinite joy is lost to the world by the want of culture of this spiritual endowment. The greatest truths are wronged if not linked with beauty, and they win their way most surely and deeply into the soul when arrayed in this their natural and fit attire.—W. E. Channing.

WHAT a place to be in is an old library! It seems as if all the souls of all the writers that had bequeathed their labors to these Bodleians were reposing here as in some dormitory, or middle state. I do not want to handle, to profane the leaves, their winding-sheets. I could as soon dislodge a shade. I seem to inhale learning, walking amid their foliage; and the odor of their old moth-scented coverings is fragrant as the first bloom of these sciential apples which grew amid the happy orchard.—Charles Lamb.

Doubt whom you will, but never yourself.—Bovee.

LIFE appears to me to be too short to be spent in nursing animosity or in registering wrongs. We are, and must be, one and all, burdened with faults in this world; but the time will come when, I trust, we shall put them off in putting off our corruptible bodies: when debasement and sin will fall from us and only the spark will remain, the impalpable principle of life and thought, pure as when it left the Creator to inspire the creature: whence it came, it will return, perhaps to pass through gradations of glory. ❡ It is a creed in which I delight, to which I cling. It makes Eternity a rest, a mighty home; not a terror and an abyss. Besides, with this creed revenge never worries my heart, degradation never too deeply disgusts me, injustice never crushes me too low: I live in calm looking to the end.—Charlotte Brontë.

IS it a fact, or have I dreamt it, that by means of electricity the world of matter has become a great nerve, vibrating thousands of miles in a breathless point of time? Rather, the round globe is a vast head, a brain, instinct with intelligence: or shall we say it is itself a thought, and no longer the substance which we dreamed it.—Nathaniel Hawthorne.

Sentiment is the poetry of the imagination.—Lamartine.

These I have loved:
White plates and cups, clean-gleaming,
Ringed with blue lines; and feathery,
*   faery dust;*
Wet roofs, beneath the lamplight; the
*   strong crust*
Of friendly bread; and many-tasting food;
Rainbows; and the blue bitter smoke of
*   wood;*
And radiant raindrops couching in cool
*   flowers;*
And flowers themselves, that sway
*   through sunny hours,*
Dreaming of moths that drink them
*   under the moon;*
Then, the cool kindliness of sheets, that
*   soon*
Smooth away trouble; and the rough
*   male kiss*
Of blankets; grainy hair; live hair; that is
Shining and free; blue-massing clouds;
*   the keen*
Unpassioned beauty of a great machine;
The benison of hot water; furs to touch;
The good smell of old clothes; and
*   others such—*
The comfortable smell of friendly fingers,
Hair's fragrance, and the musty reek
*   that lingers*
About dead leaves and last year's ferns.
    " The Great Lover," *by Rupert Brooke*

FIRST of all, we must observe that in all these matters of human action the too little and the too much are alike ruinous, as we can see (to illustrate the spiritual by the natural) in matters of strength and health. Too much and too little exercise alike impair the strength, and too much meat and drink and too little both alike destroy the health, but the fitting amount produces and preserves them. So, too, the man who takes his fill ot every pleasure and abstains from none becomes a profligate; while he who shuns all becomes stolid and insusceptible.

—Aristotle.

TAKE life too seriously, and what is it worth? ❡ If the morning wake us to no new joys, if the evening bring us not the hope of new pleasures, is it worth while to dress and undress? Does the sun shine on me today that I may reflect on yesterday? That I may endeavor to foresee and to control what can neither be foreseen nor controlled—the destiny of tomorrow?—Goethe.

EVEN the cleverest and most perfect circumstantial evidence is likely to be at fault after all, and therefore ought to be received with great caution. Take the case of any pencil sharpened by any woman; if you have witnesses, you will find she did it with a knife, but if you take simply the aspect of the pencil, you will say she did it with her teeth.—Twain.

AM the printing press, born of the mother earth. My heart is of steel, my limbs are of iron, and my fingers are of brass.

I sing the songs of the world, the oratorios of history, the symphonies of all time.

I am the voice of today, the herald of tomorrow. I weave into the warp of the past the woof of the future. I tell the stories of peace and war alike. I make the human heart beat with passion or tenderness. I stir the pulse of nations, and make brave men do braver deeds, and soldiers die.

I inspire the midnight toiler, weary at his loom, to lift his head again and gaze, with fearlessness, into the vast beyond, seeking the consolation of a hope eternal.

¶ When I speak, a myriad people listen to my voice. The Saxon, the Latin, the Celt, the Hun, the Slav, the Hindu, all comprehend me.

I am the tireless clarion of the news. I cry your joys and sorrows every hour. I fill the dullard's mind with thoughts uplifting. I am light, knowledge, power. I epitomize the conquests of mind over matter.

I am the record of all things mankind has achieved. My offspring comes to you in the candle's glow, amid the dim lamps of poverty, the splendor of riches; at sunrise, at high noon and in the waning evening.

I am the laughter and tears of the world, and I shall never die until all things return to the immutable dust. ¶ I am the printing-press.

—Robert H. Davis.

⸙ ⸙

DO your work—not just your work and no more, but a little more for the lavishing's sake; that little more which is worth all the rest. And if you suffer as you must, and if you doubt as you must, do your work. Put your heart into it and the sky will clear. Then out of your very doubt and suffering will be born the supreme joy of life.—Dean Briggs.

⸙ ⸙

Corrupted freemen are the worst of slaves—Garrick.

HUMAN and mortal though we are, we are, nevertheless, not mere insulated beings, without relation to past or future. Neither the point of time nor the spot of earth in which we physically live bounds our rational and intellectual enjoyments. We live in the past by a knowledge of its history, and in the future by hope and anticipation. By ascending to an association with our ancestors; by contemplating their example, and studying their character; by partaking of their sentiments and imbibing their spirit; by accompanying them in their toils; by sympathizing in their sufferings and rejoicing in their successes and their triumphs—we mingle our own existence with theirs and seem to belong to their age. We become their contemporaries, live the lives which they lived, endure what they endured, and partake in the rewards which they enjoyed.—Daniel Webster.

⸙ ⸙

TO achieve what the world calls success a man must attend strictly to business and keep a little in advance of the times.

The man who reaches the top is the one who is not content with doing just what is required of him. He does more. ¶ Every man should make up his mind that if he expects to succeed, he must give an honest return for the other man's dollar.

Grasp an idea and work it out to a successful conclusion. That 's about all there is in life for any of us.

—Edward H. Harriman.

⸙ ⸙

INASMUCH as most good things are produced by labor, it follows that all such things ought to belong to those whose labor has produced them. But it has happened in all ages of the world that some have labored, and others, without labor, have enjoyed a large proportion of the fruits. This is wrong, and should not continue. To secure to each laborer the whole product of his labor as nearly as possible is a worthy object of any good government.

—Abraham Lincoln.

FINE as friendship is, there is nothing irrevocable about it. The bonds of friendship are not iron bonds, proof against the strongest of strains and the heaviest of assaults. A man by becoming your friend has not committed himself to all the demands which you may be pleased to make upon him. Foolish people like to test the bonds of their friendships, pulling upon them to see how much strain they will stand. When they snap, it is as if friendship itself had been proved unworthy. But the truth is that good friendships are fragile things and require as much care in handling as any other fragile and precious things. For friendship is an adventure and a romance, and in adventures it is the unexpected that happens. It is the zest of peril that makes the excitement of friendship. All that is unpleasant and unfavorable is foreign to its atmosphere; there is no place in friendship for harsh criticism or faultfinding. We will " take less " from a friend than we will from one who is indifferent to us.—Randolph S. Bourne.

FEAR is lack of faith. Lack of faith is ignorance. Fear can only be cured by vision.

Give the world eyes. It will see. Give it ears. It will hear. Give it a right arm. It will act.

Man needs time and room. Man needs soil, sunshine and rain. Needs a chance.

¶ Open all your doors and windows. Let everything pass freely in and out, out and in.

Even the evil. Let it pass out and in, in and out.

No man hates the truth. But most men are afraid of the truth.

Make the truth easier than a lie. Make the truth welcomer than its counterfeits

Then men will no longer be afraid.

Being afraid is being ignorant. Being ignorant is being without faith.

— Horace Traubel.

You may be as orthodox as the Devil, and as wicked.—John Wesley.

MY son, remember you have to work. Whether you handle pick or wheelbarrow or a set of books, digging ditches or editing a newspaper, ringing an auction bell or writing funny things, you must work. Don't be afraid of killing yourself by overworking on the sunny side of thirty. Men die sometimes, but it is because they quit at nine p. m. and don't go home until two a. m. It 's the intervals that kill, my son. The work gives you appetite for your meals; it lends solidity to your slumber; it gives you a perfect appreciation of a holiday. There are young men who do not work, but the country is not proud of them. It does not even know their names; it only speaks of them as old So-and-So's boys. Nobody likes them; the great, busy world does n't know they are here. So find out what you want to be and do. Take off your coat and make dust in the world. The busier you are, the less harm you are apt to get into, the sweeter will be your sleep, the brighter your holidays, and the better satisfied the whole world will be with you.—Bob Burdette.

WHAT can I do? I can talk out when others are silent. I can say man when others say money. I can stay up when others are asleep. I can keep on working when others have stopped to play. I can give life big meanings when others give life little meanings. I can say love when others say hate. I can say every man when others say one man. I can try events by a hard test when others try it by an easy test.

What can I do? I can give myself to life when other men refuse themselves to life.—Horace Traubel.

IT is of dangerous consequence to represent to man how near he is the level of beasts without showing him at the same time his greatness. It is likewise dangerous to let him see his greatness without his meanness. It is more dangerous yet to leave him ignorant of either; but very beneficial that he should be made sensible of both.—Pascal.

Beauty is truth, truth beauty.—Keats.

HERE is a life that is worth living now as it was worth living in the former days, and that is the honest life, the useful life, the unselfish life, cleansed by devotion to an ideal. There is a battle that is worth fighting now as it was worth fighting then, and that is the battle for justice and equality: to make our city and our State free in fact as well as in name; to break the rings that strangle real liberty and to keep them broken; to cleanse, so far as in our power lies, the fountains of our national life from political, commercial and social corruption; to teach our sons and daughters, by precept and example, the honor of serving such a country as America—that is work worthy of the finest manhood and womanhood. The wellborn are those who are born to do that work; the wellbred are those who are bred to be proud of that work; the well-educated are those who see deepest into the meaning and the necessity of that work. Nor shall their labor be for naught, nor the reward of their sacrifice fail them; for high in the firmament of human destiny are set the stars of faith in mankind, and unselfish courage and loyalty to the ideal.

—Henry Van Dyke.

Behind him lay the gray Azores,
Behind the Gates of Hercules;
Before him not the ghost of shores;
Before him only shoreless seas.
The good mate said: "Now must we pray,
For lo! the very stars are gone.
Brave Adm'r'l, speak; what shall I say?"
"Why, say: 'Sail on! and on!'"

"My men grow mutinous day by day;
My men grow ghastly wan and weak."
The stout mate thought of home; a spray
Of salt wave washed his swarthy cheek.
"What shall I say, brave Adm'r'l, say,
If we sight naught but seas at dawn?"
"Why, you shall say at break of day:
'Sail on! sail on! sail on! and on!'"

They sailed and sailed, as winds might blow,
Until at last the blanched mate said:
"Why, now not even God would know
Should I and all my men fall dead.
These very winds forget their way,
For God from these dread seas is gone.

(Concluded on next page)

ENTHUSIASM is the greatest asset in the world. It beats money and power and influence. Single-handed the enthusiast convinces and dominates where the wealth accumulated by a small army of workers would scarcely raise a tremor of interest. Enthusiasm tramples over prejudice and opposition, spurns inaction, storms the citadel of its object, and like an avalanche overwhelms and engulfs all obstacles. It is nothing more or less than faith in action Faith and initiative rightly combined remove mountainous barriers and achieve the unheard of and miraculous.

❡ Set the germ of enthusiasm afloat in your plant, in your office, or on your farm; carry it in your attitude and manner; it spreads like contagion and influences every fiber of your industry before you realize it; it means increase in production and decrease in costs; it means joy, and pleasure, and satisfaction to your workers; it means life, real, virile; it means spontaneous bedrock results—the vital things that pay dividends.—Henry Chester.

THE sole aristocracy of today is the aristocracy of wealth; the sole aristocracy of tomorrow will be the eternal divine, beneficent aristocracy of intellect and virtue—at its highest, genius; but that, like everything that descends from God, will rise among the people and labor for the people.—Mazzini.

My son Hannibal will be a great general, because of all my soldiers he best knows how to obey.—Hamilcar.

EVERY school boy and girl who has arrived at the age of reflection ought to know something about the history of the art of printing.

—Horace Mann.

AN is arrogant in proportion to his ignorance. Man's natural tendency is toward egotism. Man, in his infancy of knowledge, thinks that all creation was formed for him. For several ages he saw, in the countless worlds that sparkle through space like the bubbles of a shoreless ocean, only the petty candles, the household torches, that Providence had been pleased to light for no other purpose but to make the night more agreeable to man. Astronomy has corrected this delusion of human vanity, and man now reluctantly confesses that the stars are worlds, larger and more glorious than his own—that the earth on which he crawls is a scarcely visible speck on the vast chart of creation.

But in the small as in the vast, God is equally profuse of life. The traveller looks upon the tree, and fancies its boughs were formed for his shelter in the Summer sun, or his fuel in the Winter frosts. But in each leaf of these boughs the Creator has made a world —it swarms with innumerable races. Each drop of water in a moat is an orb more populous than a kingdom is of men. ❡ Everywhere, then, in this immense design, science brings new life to light. Life is the one pervading principle, and even the thing that seems to die and putrefy but engenders new life, and changes to fresh forms of matter.

—Bulwer Lytton.

The victory of success is half won when one gains the habit of work.

—Sarah A. Bolton.

*Now speak, brave Adm'r'l; speak and
say—"
He said: "Sail on! sail on! and on!"*

*They sailed. They sailed. Then spake the
mate:
"This mad sea shows his teeth tonight.
He curls his lip, he lies in wait,
With lifted teeth, as if to bite!
Brave Adm'r'l, say but one good word:
What shall we do when hope is gone?"
The words leapt like a leaping sword:
"Sail on! sail on! sail on! and on!"*

*Then, pale and worn, he kept his deck,
And peered through darkness. Ah, that
night
Of all dark nights! And then a speck—
A light! A light! A light! A light!
It grew, a starlit flag unfurled!
It grew to be Time's burst of dawn.
He gained a world; he gave that world
Its grandest lesson: "On! sail on!"*

" Columbus," by Joaquin Miller

GET the confidence of the public and you will have no difficulty in getting their patronage. Inspire your whole force with the right spirit of service; encourage every sign of the true spirit. So display and advertise wares that customers shall buy with understanding. Treat them as guests when they come and when they go, whether or not they buy Give them all that can be given fairly, on the principle that to him that giveth shall be given. Remember always that the recollection of quality remains long after the price is forgotten Then your business will prosper by a natural process.

—H. Gordon Selfridge.

THE man who lacks faith in other men loses his best chances to work and gradually undermines his own power and his own character. We do not realize to what extent others judge us by our beliefs. But we are in fact judged in that way; and it is right that we should be judged in that way. The man who is cynical, whether about women or business or politics, is assumed to be immoral in his relations to women or business or politics. The man who has faith in the integrity of others in the face of irresponsible accusations is assumed to have the confidence in other's goodness because he is a good man himself.

—President Hadley.

When you define liberty you limit it, and when you limit it you destroy it.

—Brand Whitlock.

BELIEVE in boys and girls, the men and women of a great tomorrow, that whatsoever the boy soweth, the man shall reap. I believe in the curse of ignorance, in the efficacy of schools, in the dignity of teaching, and the joy of serving another. I believe in wisdom as revealed in human lives as well as in the pages of a printed book; in lessons taught not so much by precept as by example: in ability to work with the hands as well as to think with the head; in everything that makes life large and lovely. I believe in beauty in the schoolroom, in the home, in the daily life and out of doors. I believe in laughing, in all ideals and distant hopes that lure us on. I believe that every hour of every day we receive a just reward for all we do. I believe in the present and its opportunities, in the future and its promises, and in the divine joy of living.—Edwin Osgood Grover.

GOOK love, my friends, is your pass to the greatest, the purest, and the most perfect pleasure that God has prepared for His creatures. It lasts when all other pleasures fade. It will support you when all other recreations are gone. It will last you until your death. It will make your hours pleasant to you as long as you live.—Anthony Trollope.

ALL Nature speaks the voice of dissolution. The highway of history and of life is strewn with the wrecks that Time, the great despoiler, has made. We listen sorrowfully to the Autumn winds as they sigh through dismantled forests, but we know their breath will be soft and vernal in the Spring, and the dead flowers and withered foliage will blossom and bloom again. And if a man die, shall he, too, not live again? Is earth the end of all, and death an eternal sleep? Not so, but beyond the grave in the distant Aiden, hope provides an Elysium of the soul where the mortal shall assume immortality, and life become an endless splendor.
—D. W. Voorhees.

DISTINGUISHED beauty, brilliant talents, and the heroic qualities that play a more or less important part in the affairs of life, sink into a comparatively minor place among the elements of married happiness. Marriage brings every faculty and gift into play, but in degrees and proportions very different from public life or casual intercourse and relations. Power to soothe, to sympathize, to counsel, and to endure, are more important than the highest qualities of the hero or the saint. It is by these alone that the married life attains its full measure of perfection.—W. E. H. Lecky.

YOU don't have to preach honesty to men with a creative purpose. Let a human being throw the energies of his soul into the making of something, and the instinct of workmanship will take care of his honesty. The writers who have nothing to say are the ones you can buy; the others have too high a price. A genuine craftsman will not adulterate his product. The reason is n't because duty says he should n't, but because passion says he could n't.
—Walter Lippmann.

IT is right and necessary that all men should have work to do which shall be worth doing, and be of itself pleasant to do: and which should be done under such conditions as would make it neither over-wearisome nor over-anxious. Turn that claim about as I may, think of it as long as I can, I can not find that it is an exorbitant claim; yet again I say if Society would or could admit it the face of the world would be changed; discontent and strife and dishonesty would be ended. To feel that we were doing work useful to others and pleasant to ourselves, and that such work and its due reward could not fail us! What serious harm could happen to us then?—William Morris.

FAR away there in the sunshine are my highest aspirations. I may not reach them, but I can look up and see their beauty, believe in them, and try to follow where they lead.—L. M. Alcott.

UMOR has been defined as the salt of life. It is a caprice of our natures, or rather that quality which gives to ideas a ludicrous or fantastic turn, the effect of it being to excite the pleasurable emotions which we exhibit in laughter or mirth. Its unfailing power to win an audience is well known, and it is to this emotion that the amateur's attention is first attracted. It may take the form of a play of wit, sarcasm, satire, irony or the like; in any case, it is certain to meet with a prompt response from the average audience. Comedy which is the term under which we class the different forms of humor, is therefore an essential element in drama. It does not deal with emotions that are heartsearching nor terrifying incidents, but trades rather in eccentricities of character and quaintness of manner; consequently, its chief dramatic use is to relieve the tension of a serious action. It is in this manner that it was used by the Elizabethan playwrights, who fully appreciated the tastes and weaknesses of their audience. However, comedy is not an absolute essential to the success of a play. Nearly all the best tragedies and certain of the most powerful dramas have not a ray of humor in them. The reason is not far to seek, for serious subjects, such as deal with the dignified and noble qualities of the human nature, admit only of a serious and earnest presentation. It has been said that the direct appeal of the drama is to make the audience think,

A murdered man, ten miles away,
Will hardly shake your peace,
Like one red stain upon your hand;
And a tortured child in a distant land
Will never check one smile today,
Or bid one fiddle cease.

The News
It came along a little wire,
Sunk in a deep sea;
It thins in the clubs to a little smoke
Between one joke and another joke,
For a city in flames is less than the fire
That comforts you and me.

The Diplomats
Each was honest after his way,
Lukewarm in faith, and old;
And blood, to them, was only a word,
And the point of a phrase their only sword,
And the cost of war, they reckoned it
In little disks of gold.

From " The Wine Press," *by Alfred Noyes*

feel or laugh, and certainly a drama which does not accomplish at least one of these results is a failure; but to combine all these qualities in the proper proportions in a single play demands the greatest ability, and few playwrights can accomplish it. Humor in the hands of an artist has an unfailing power to win an audience, and it is the best means which the playwright has at his command for relieving the stress of a serious action.
—O. R. Lamb.

OCIETY, as we have constituted it, will have no place for me, has none to offer; but Nature, whose sweet rains fall on unjust and just alike, will have clefts in the rocks where I may hide, and sweet valleys in whose silence I may weep undisturbed. She will hang the night with stars so that I may walk abroad in the darkness without stumbling, and send the wind over my footprints so that none may track me to my hurt; she will cleanse me in great waters, and with bitter herbs make me whole.—Oscar Wilde.

CLIMB the mountains and get their good tidings. Nature's peace will flow into you as sunshine flows into trees. The winds will blow their own freshness into you, and the storms their energy, while cares will drop away from you like the leaves of Autumn.—John Muir.

I love to be alone. I never found the companion that was so companionable as solitude.—Thoreau.

THANK Heaven, every Summer's day of my life, that my lot was humbly cast within the hearing of romping brooks, and beneath the shadow of oaks. And from all the tramp and bustle of the world, into which fortune has led me in these latter years of my life, I delight to steal away for days and for weeks together, and bathe my spirit in the freedom of the old woods, and to grow young again, lying upon the brookside and counting the white clouds that sail along the sky, softly and tranquilly, even as holy memories go stealing over the vault of life. I like to steep my soul in a sea of quiet, with nothing floating past me, as I lie moored to my thought, but the perfume of flowers, and soaring birds, and shadows of clouds. ❧ Two days ago, I was sweltering in the heat of the city, jostled by the thousand eager workers, and panting under the shadow of the walls. But I have stolen away, and for two hours of healthful regrowth into the darkling past, I have been this blessed Summer's morning lying upon the grassy bank of a stream that babbled me to sleep in boyhood. Dear, old stream, unchanging, unfaltering—never growing old—smiling in your silver rustle, and calming yourself in the broad, placid pools—I love you, as I love a friend!—Donald G. Mitchell.

THERE is first the literature of knowledge, and secondly the literature of power. The function of the first is—to teach; the function of the second is—to move; the first is a rudder, the second an oar or a sail. The first speaks to the mere discursive understanding; the second speaks ultimately, it may happen to the higher understanding or reason, but always through affections of pleasure and sympathy.
—Thomas De Quincey.

HE who helps a child helps humanity with an immediateness which no other help given to human creature in any other stage of human life can possibly give again.—Phillips Brooks.

TRUE love of country is not mere blind partisanship. It is regard for the people of one's country and all of them; it is a feeling of fellowship and brotherhood for all of them; it is a desire for the prosperity and happiness of all of them; it is kindly and considerate judgment toward all of them. The first duty of popular self-government is individual self-control. The essential condition of true progress is that it shall be based upon grounds of reason, and not of prejudice. Lincoln's noble sentiment of charity for all and malice toward none was not a specific for the Civil War, but is a living principle of action.
—Elihu Root.

EACH day it becomes more and more apparent that all questions in this country must be settled at the bar of public opinion. If our laws regulating large business concerns provide for proper and complete publicity—so that the labor of a concern will know what it is doing, so that the stockholders will know what is being done, and the public will have as much information as either—many of our present difficulties will disappear. In place of publicity being an element of weakness to a business concern, it will be an element of strength.
—George W. Perkins.

TO act in obedience to the hidden precepts of Nature—that is rest; and in this special case, since man is meant to be an intelligent creature, the more intelligent his acts are, the more he finds repose in them. When a child acts only in a disorderly, disconnected manner, his nervous force is under a great strain; while, on the other hand, his nervous energy is positively increased and multiplied by intelligent actions.
—Maria Montessori.

HE who freely magnifies what hath been nobly done, and fears not to declare as freely what might be done better, gives ye the best covenant of his fidelity.—John Milton.

DO not think that I exaggerate the importance or the charms of pedestrianism, or our need as a people to cultivate the art. I think it would tend to soften the national manners, to teach us the meaning of leisure, to acquaint us with the charms of the open air, to strengthen and foster the tie between the race and the land. No one else looks out upon the world so kindly and charitably as does the pedestrian; no one gives and takes so much from the country he passes through. Next to the laborer in the fields, the walker holds the closest relation to the soil; and he holds a closer and more vital relation to Nature because he is freer and his mind more at leisure.

Man takes root at his feet, and at best he is no more than a potted plant in his house or carriage till he has established communication with the soil by the loving and magnetic touch of his soles to it. Then the tie of association is born; then those invisible fibers and rootlets through which character comes to smack of the soil, and which makes a man kindred to the spot of earth he inhabits. ❡ The roads and paths you have walked along in Summer and Winter weather, the meadows and hills which you have looked upon in lightness and gladness of heart, where fresh thought have come into your mind, or some noble prospect has opened before you, and especially the quiet ways, where you have walked in sweet converse with your friend—pausing under the trees, drinking at the spring—henceforth they are not the same; a new charm is added; those thoughts spring there perennial, your friend walks there forever.—John Burroughs.

The fountains mingle with the river,
  And the rivers with the ocean,
The winds of heaven mix forever
  With a sweet emotion;
Nothing in the world is single;
  All things by a law divine
In one another's being mingle;—
  Why not I with thine?

See the mountains kiss high heaven,
  And the waves clasp one another;
No sister flower would be forgiven
  If it disdained its brother;
And the sunlight clasps the earth,
  And the moonbeams kiss the sea;
What are all these kissings worth,
  If thou kiss not me?

" Love's Philosophy,"
  by Percy Bysshe Shelley

EVERY time that we allow ourselves to be penetrated by Nature, our soul is opened to the most touching impressions. Whether Nature smiles and adorns herself on her most beautiful days, or whether she becomes pale, gray, cold and rainy, in Autumn and in Winter, there is something in her which moves not only the surface of the soul, but even its inmost depths, and awakens a thousand memories which to all appearances have no connection whatever with the outward scene, but which, nevertheless, undoubtedly hold communion with the soul of Nature through sympathies that may be entirely unknown to us, because her methods seem to be beyond the touch of our thought—Maurice de Guerin.

MY garden, with its silence and the pulses of fragrance that come and go on the airy undulations, affects me like sweet music. Care stops at the gates, and gazes at me wistfully through the bars. Among my flowers and trees, Nature takes me into her own hands, and I breathe freely as the first man.
—Alexander Smith.

A LAKE is the landscape's most beautiful and expressive feature. It is earth's eye; looking into which the beholder measures the depth of his own nature. The fluviatile trees next the shore are the slender eyelashes which fringe it, and the wooded hills and cliffs around are its overhanging brows.—Thoreau.

NO man lives without jostling and being jostled; in all ways he has to elbow himself through the world, giving and receiving offense.—Carlyle.

E follow the stream of amber and bronze brawling along its bed with its frequent cascades and snow-white foam. Through the canyon we fly —mountains not only each side, but seemingly, till we get near, right in front of us—every road a new view flashing, and each flash defying description—on the almost perpendicular sides, clinging pines, cedars, crimson sumach bushes, spruces, spots of wild grass—but dominating all, those towering rocks, rocks, rocks, bathed in delicate vari-colors, with the clear sky of Autumn overhead. New scenes, new joys, seem developed. Talk as you like, a typical Rocky Mountain canyon, or a limitless sea-like stretch of the great Kansas or Colorado plains, under favoring circumstances, tallies, perhaps expresses, certainly awakes, those grandest and subtlest element-emotions in the human soul, that all marble temples and sculptures from Phidias to Thorwaldsen—all paintings, poems, reminiscences or even music— probably never can.—Walt Whitman.

BY thy name they shall call thee, at the place where thou belongest they shall see thee, what is thine they shall give to thee, no man touches that which is destined for his neighbor.—Rabbi Ben Azai.

THE thing needed is not plans, but men. A well-thought-out plan without a man to execute it is a waste of money; and as a rule, the more comparatively the details have been thought out by a man who is not going to execute them himself, the larger will be the amount of money wasted. Get a man with a plan, and the more money he has the greater is his chance of doing a larger work; but a plan without a man is as bad as a man without a plan—the more he has the more he wastes.—Arthur T. Hadley.

THOSE who love Nature can never be dull. They may have other temptations; but at least they will run no risk of being beguiled, by ennui, idleness or want of occupation, " to buy the merry madness of an hour with the long peni-

tence of after-time." The love of Nature, again, helps us greatly to keep ourselves free from those mean and petty cares which interfere so much with calm and peace of mind. It turns " every ordinary walk into a morning or evening sacrifice," and brightens life until it becomes almost like a fairy-tale.—John Lubbock.

BE glad of life because it gives you the chance to love and to work and to play and to look up at the stars.
—Henry Van Dyke.

THAT life should appear commonplace to any man is evidence that he has invested it with the coarse habit of his thinking. Life is beautiful to whomsoever will think beautiful thoughts. There are no common people but they who think commonly and without imagination or beauty. Such are dull enough.
—Stanton Davis Kirkham.

THERE is nothing holier in this life of ours than the first consciousness of love—the first fluttering of its silken wings—the first rising sound and breath of that wind which is so soon to sweep through the soul, to purify or to destroy.
—Longfellow.

I WOULD compromise war. I would compromise glory. I would compromise everything at that point where hate comes in, where misery comes in, where love ceases to be love, and life begins its descent into the valley of the shadow of death. But I would not compromise Truth. I would not compromise the right.—Henry Watterson.

WHAT then do you call your soul? What idea have you of it? You can not of yourselves, without revelation, admit the existence within you of anything but a power unknown to you of feeling and thinking.—Voltaire.

The longer I live the more my mind dwells upon the beauty and the wonder of the world. I hardly know which feeling leads, wonderment or admiration.
- John Burroughs.

HOUGH not often consciously recognized, perhaps this is the great pleasure of Summer: to watch the earth, the dead particles, resolving themselves into the living case of life, to see the seed-leaf push aside the clod and become by degrees the perfumed flower. From the tiny, mottled egg come the wings that by and by shall pass the immense sea. It is in this marvelous transformation of clods and cold matter into living things that the joy and the hope of Summer reside. Every blade of grass, each leaf, each separate floret and petal is an inscription speaking of hope. Consider the grasses and the oaks, the swallows, the sweet, blue butterfly—they are one and all a sign and token showing before our eyes earth made into life. So that my hope becomes as broad as the horizon afar, reiterated by each leaf, sung on every bough, reflected in the gleam of every flower. There is so much for us yet to come, so much to be gathered and enjoyed. Not for you or me, now, but for our race, who will ultimately use this magical secret for their happiness. Earth holds secrets enough to give them the life of the fabled Immortals. My heart is fixed firm and stable in the belief that ultimately the sunshine and the Summer, the flowers and the azure sky, shall become, as it were, interwoven into man's existence. He shall take from all their beauty and enjoy their glory.—Richard Jefferies.

※ ※

GREAT deal of talent is lost in the world for want of a little courage. Every day sends to their graves obscure men whom timidity prevented from making a first effort; who, if they could have been induced to begin, would in all probability have gone great lengths in the career of fame. The fact is, that to do anything in the world worth doing, we must not stand back shivering and thinking of the cold and danger, but jump in and scramble through as well as we can. It will not do to be perpetually calculating risks and adjusting nice chances; it did very well before the Flood, when a man would consult his friends upon an intended publication for a hundred and fifty years, and live to see his success afterwards; but at present, a man waits, and doubts, and consults his brother, and his particular friends, till one day he finds he is sixty years old and that he has lost so much time in consulting cousins and friends that he has no more time to follow their advice.—Sydney Smith.

※ ※

E are told of the Chinese sage Mengtsen, that when he was a child, his mother's home was near a slaughter-house, and that she instantly left her home when she saw the child watching with indifference the pain inflicted upon animals. Her second home was near a graveyard, and again she left when she saw the boy imitating at his play the rites of superstition.

—Dean Farrar.

※ ※

UR great thoughts, our great affections, the truths of our life, never leave us. Surely they can not separate from our consciousness, shall follow it whithersoever that shall go, and are of their nature divine and immortal.

—Thackeray.

※ ※

AN has not yet reached his best. He never will reach his best until he walks the upward way side by side with woman. Plato was right in his fancy that man and woman are merely halves of humanity, each requiring the qualities of the other in order to attain the highest character. Shakespeare understood it when he made his noblest women strong as men, and his best men tender as women. The hands and breasts that nursed all men to life are scorned as the forgetful brute proclaims his superior strength and plumes himself so he can subjugate the one who made him what he is.—Eugene V. Debs.

※ ※

Life is a fragment, a moment between two eternities, influenced by all that has preceded, and to influence all that follows. The only way to illumine it is by extent of view.

—William Ellery Channing.

NEVER-CEASING flood of discharged convicts pours back into our penitentiaries, not because they have found life there a paradise, but because the thumbscrew of present want exercises a pressure far more potent than does the fear of future, but uncertain, punishment, however severe. Here is the true answer to the question why deterrence, pushed to the very limits of human endurance, does not deter ✷ We know well that the prison is but part of the great social question— that, as a general rule, poverty is the parent and the slum the kindergarten of vice. But we also know that, while these prepare the soil, it is the administration of our criminal law that plants the seed and supplies the tropical conditions that bring it to the instant maturity of crime.
—Griffith J. Griffith.

✷ ✷

I think that I shall never see
A poem lovely as a tree.

A tree whose hungry mouth is prest
Against the earth's sweet flowing breast;

A tree that looks at God all day
And lifts her leafy arms to pray;

A tree that may in summer wear
A nest of robins in her hair.

Upon whose bosom snow has lain;
Who intimately lives with rain.

Poems are made by fools like me,
But only God can make a tree.
" Trees," *by Joyce Kilmer*

AS I grow older, I simplify both my science and my religion. Books mean less to me; prayers mean less; potions, pills and drugs mean less; but peace, friendship, love and a life of usefulness mean more, infinitely more.
—Silas Hubbard, M. D.

✷ ✷

GIVE us, O give us the man who sings at his work! Be his occupation what it may, he is equal to any of those who follow the same pursuit in silent sullenness. He will do more in the same time— he will do it better—he will persevere longer. One is scarcely sensible to fatigue while he marches to music. The very stars are said to make harmony as they revolve in their spheres.—Carlyle.

✷ ✷

Shadow owes its birth to light.—Gray.

I THINK we may assert that in a hundred men there are more than ninety who are what they are, good or bad, useful or pernicious to society, from the instruction they have received. It is on education that depend the great differences observable among them. The least and most imperceptible impressions received in our infancy have consequences of long duration. It is with these first impressions as with a river, whose waters we can easily turn, by different canals, in opposite courses; so that from the insensible direction the stream receives at its source, it takes different directions, and at last arrives at places far different from each other; and with the same facility we may; I think, turn the minds of children to what direction we choose.—Locke.

✷ ✷

HOW much easier our work would be if we put forth as much effort trying to improve the quality of it as most of us do trying to find excuses for not properly attending to it.
—George W. Ballinger.

✷ ✷

LIFE is a tender thing and is easily molested. There is always something that goes amiss. Vain vexations—vain sometimes, but always vexatious. The smallest and slightest impediments are the most piercing; and as little letters most tire the eyes, so do little affairs most disturb us.—Montaigne.

✷ ✷

THE joys and sorrows of others are ours as much as theirs, and in proper time as we feel this and learn to live so that the whole world shares the life that flows through us, do our minds learn the Secret of Peace.—Annie Besant.

HE man who, by some sudden revolution of fortune, is lifted up all at once into a condition of life greatly above what he had formerly lived in, may be assured that the congratulations of his best friends are not all of them perfectly sincere. An upstart, though of the greatest merit, is generally disagreeable, and a sentiment of envy commonly prevents us from heartily sympathizing with his joy. If he has any judgment, he is sensible of this, and, instead of appearing to be elated with his good fortune, he endeavors, as much as he can, to smother his joy, and keep down that elevation of mind with which his new circumstances naturally inspire him. He affects the same plainness of dress, and the same modesty of behavior, which became him in his former station. He redoubles his attention to his old friends, and endeavors more than ever to be humble, assiduous and complaisant. And this is the behavior which in his situation we most approve of; because we expect, it seems, that he should have more sympathy with our envy and aversion to his happiness, than we have with his happiness. It is seldom that with all this he succeeds. We suspect the sincerity of his humility, and he grows weary of this constraint. —Adam Smith.

THE man who starts out with the idea of getting rich won't succeed; you must have a larger ambition. There is no mystery in business success. If you do each day's task successfully, stay faithfully within the natural operations of commercial law, and keep your head clear, you will come out all right.—Rockefeller.

Trusty, dusky, vivid, true,
With eyes of gold and bramble-dew,
Steel true and blade straight
The great Artificer made my mate.

Honor, anger, valor, fire,
A love that life could never tire,
Death quench, or evil stir,
The mighty Master gave to her.

Teacher, tender comrade, wife,
A fellow-farer true through life,
Heart-whole and soul-free,
The August Father gave to me.

" Trusty, Dusky, Vivid, True,"
by Robert Louis Stevenson

BESIDES theology, music is the only art capable of affording peace and joy of the heart like that induced by the study of the science of divinity. The proof of this is that the Devil, the originator of sorrowful anxieties and restless troubles, flees before the sound of music almost as much as he does before the Word of God. This is why the prophets preferred music before all the other arts, proclaiming the Word in psalms and hymns My heart, which is full to overflowing, has often been solaced and refreshed by music when sick and weary.

—Martin Luther.

SCIENCE seems to me to teach in the highest and strongest manner the great truth which is embodied in the Christian conception of entire surrender to the will of God. Sit down before the fact as a little child, be prepared to give up every preconceived notion, follow humbly wherever and to whatever abysses Nature leads, or you shall learn nothing. I have only begun to learn content and peace of mind since I have resolved at all risks to do this.—Huxley.

WITHOUT distinction, without calculation, without procrastination, love. Lavish it upon the poor, where it is very easy; especially upon the rich, who often need it most; most of all upon our equals, where it is very difficult, and for whom perhaps we each do least of all.

—Henry Drummond.

Live and think.—Samuel Lover.

Let us endeavor so to live that when we come to die even the undertaker will be sorry.—Mark Twain.

HERE is no more valuable subordinate than the man to whom you can give a piece of work and then forget it, in the confident expectation that the next time it is brought to your attention it will come in the form of a report that the thing has been done. When this self-reliant quality is joined to executive power, loyalty and common sense, the result is a man whom you can trust.

On the other hand, there is no greater nuisance to a man heavily burdened with the direction of affairs than the weak-backed assistant who is continually trying to get his chief to do his work for him on the feeble plea that he thought the chief would like to decide this or that himself. The man to whom an executive is most grateful, the man whom he will work hardest and value most, is the man who accepts responsibility willingly.—Gifford Pinchot.

WHILE the railroads of the United States may have mistakes to answer for, they have created the most effective, useful, and by far the cheapest system of land transportation in the world. This has been accomplished with very little legislation and against an immense volume of opposition and interference growing out of ignorance and misunderstanding. It is not an exaggeration to say that in the past history of this country the railway, next after the Christian religion and the public school, has been the largest single contributing factor to the welfare and happiness of the people.—James J. Hill.

THERE is music in the beauty, and the silent note that Cupid strikes, far sweeter than the sound of an instrument; for there is music wherever there is harmony, order or proportion; and thus far we may maintain the music of the spheres.

—Sir Thomas Browne.

Happiness grows at our own firesides, and is not to be picked in stranger's gardens.

—Douglas Jerrold.

YOU want a better position than you now have in business, a better and fuller place in life. All right; think of that better place and you in it as already existing. Form the mental image. Keep on thinking of that higher position, keep the image constantly before you, and —no, you will not suddenly be transported into the higher job, but you will find that you are preparing yourself to occupy the better position in life—your body, your energy, your understanding, your heart will all grow up to the job—and when you are ready, after hard work, after perhaps years of preparation, you will get the job and the higher place in life.—Joseph H. Appel.

I KNOW the beds of Eastern princes, and the luxurious couches of Occidental plutocrats, but under the rafters of a farmhouse, where the mud-wasp's nest answers for a Rembrandt and the cobweb takes the place of a Murillo, there is a feather-bed into which one softly sinks until his every inch is soothed and fitted, and settling down and farther down falls into sweet unconsciousness, while the screech-owl is calling from the moonlit oak and frost is falling upon the asters. Stocks may fluctuate and panic seize the town, but there is one man who is in peace.

—Robert T. Morris.

BANISH the future; live only for the hour and its allotted work. Think not of the amount to be accomplished, the difficulties to be overcome, but set earnestly at the little task at your elbow, letting that be sufficient for the day; for surely our plain duty is " not to see what lies dimly at a distance, but to do what lies clearly at hand."—Osler.

THE best way for a young man who is without friends or influence to begin is: first, to get a position; second, to keep his mouth shut; third, observe; fourth, be faithful; fifth, make his employer think he would be lost in a fog without him; sixth, be polite.

—Russell Sage.

HAT is music? This question occupied my mind for hours last night before I fell asleep. The very existence of music is wonderful, I might even say miraculous. Its domain is between thought and phenomena. Like a twilight mediator, it hovers between spirit and matter, related to both, yet differing from each. It is spirit, but it is spirit subject to the measurement of time. It is matter, but it is matter that can dispense with space.—Heinrich Heine.

TO renounce your individuality, to see with another's eyes, to hear with another's ears, to be two and yet but one, to so melt and mingle that you no longer know you are you or another, to constantly absorb and constantly radiate, to reduce earth, sea and sky and all that in them is to a single being, to give yourself to that being so wholly that nothing whatever is withheld, to be prepared at any moment for sacrifice, to double your personality in bestowing it—that is love.—Gautier

MELODY has by Beethoven been freed from the influence of Fashion and changing Taste, and raised to an ever-valid, purely human type. Beethoven's music will be understood to all time, while that of his predecessors will, for the most part, only remain intelligible to us through the medium of reflection on the history of art.—Richard Wagner.

NATURE, like a loving mother, is ever trying to keep land and sea, mountain and valley, each in its place, to hush the angry winds and waves, balance the extremes of heat and cold, of rain and drought, that peace, harmony and beauty may reign supreme.
—Elizabeth Cady Stanton.

WHY should we call ourselves men, unless it be to succeed in everything, everywhere? Say of nothing, " This is beneath me," nor feel that anything is beyond our powers. Nothing is impossible to the man who can will.
—Mirabeau.

IF we do our best; if we do not magnify trifling troubles; if we look resolutely, I will not say at the bright side of things, but at things as they really are; if we avail ourselves of the manifold blessings which surround us, we can not but feel that life is indeed a glorious inheritance.—John Lubbock.

THE passions are the only orators that always persuade; they are, as it were, a natural art, the rules of which are infallible; and the simplest man with passion is more persuasive than the most eloquent without it.
—La Rochefoucauld.

ALL those who love Nature she loves in turn, and will richly reward, not perhaps with the good things, as they are commonly called, but with the best things, of this world—not with money and titles, horses and carriages, but with bright and happy thoughts, contentment and peace of mind.
—John Lubbock.

IT is indisputably evident that a great part of every man's life must be employed in collecting materials for the exercise of genius. Invention, strictly speaking, is little more than a new combination of those images which have been previously gathered and deposited in the memory: nothing can come of nothing: he who has laid up no materials can produce no combinations. The more extensive, therefore, your acquaintance is with the works of those who have excelled, the more extensive will be your powers of invention, and, what may appear still more like a paradox, the more original will be your conceptions.
—Sir Joshua Reynolds.

WE are never better understood than when we speak of a " Roman virtue"—a " Roman outline." There is somewhat indefinite, somewhat yet unfulfilled, in the thought of Greece, of Spain, of modern Italy; but Rome, it stands by itself a clear word. The power of Will, the dignity of a fixed purpose, is what it utters.—Margaret Fuller.

CONFESS I am not at all charmed with the ideal of life held out by those who think that the normal state of human beings is that of struggling to get on; that the trampling, crushing, elbowing, and treading on each other's heels, which form the existing type of human life, are the most desirable lot of humankind, or anything but the disagreeable symptoms of one of the phases of industrial progress.—J. S. Mill.

WITHOUT free speech no search for truth is possible; without free speech no discovery of truth is useful; without free speech progress is checked and the nations no longer march forward toward the nobler life which the future holds for man. Better a thousandfold abuse of free speech than denial of free speech. The abuse dies in a day, but the denial slays the life of the people, and entombs the hope of the race.
—Charles Bradlaugh.

THE longer I live, the more deeply I am convinced that that which makes the difference between one man and another—between the weak and the powerful, the great and the insignificant —is energy, invincible determination, a purpose once formed and then death or victory.—Powell Buxton.

EVERY year I live I am more convinced that the waste of life lies in the love we have not given, the powers we have not used, the selfish prudence that will risk nothing, and which, shirking pain, misses happiness as well. No one ever yet was the poorer in the long run for having once in a lifetime " let out all the length of all the reins."
—Mary Cholmondeley.

I HAVE ever gained the most profit, and the most pleasure also, from the books which have made me think the most; and, when the difficulties have once been overcome, these are the books which have struck the deepest root, not only in my memory and understanding, but likewise in my affections.—A. W. Hare.

THANK God every morning when you get up that you have something to do which must be done, whether you like it or not. Being forced to work, and forced to do your best, will breed in you temperance, self-control, diligence, strength of will, content, and a hundred other virtues which the idle never know.
—Charles Kingsley.

THE study of art possesses this great and peculiar charm, that it is absolutely unconnected with the struggles and contests of ordinary life. By private interests and by political questions, men are deeply divided and set at variance; but beyond and above all such party strifes, they are attracted and united by a taste for the beautiful in art. It is a taste at once engrossing and unselfish, which may be indulged without effort and yet has the power of exciting the deepest emotions—a taste able to exercise and to gratify both the nobler and the softer parts of our nature—the imagination and the judgment, love of emotion and power of reflection, the enthusiasm and the critical faculty, the senses and the reason.—Guizot.

THERE is no short-cut, no patent tram-road, to wisdom. After all the centuries of invention, the soul's path lies through the thorny wilderness which must still be trodden in solitude, with bleeding feet, with sobs for help, as it was trodden by them of old time.
—George Eliot.

I HONOR any man who in the conscious discharge of his duty dares to stand alone; the world, with ignorant, intolerant judgment, may condemn; the countenances of relatives may be averted, and the hearts of friends grow cold; but the sense of duty done shall be sweeter than the applause of the world, the countenances of relatives, or the hearts of friends.—Charles Sumner.

Abraham Lincoln was as just and generous to the rich and well-born as to the poor and humble—a thing rare among politicians.—John Hay.

MANY a woman committing herself to a course that disregards the edicts of society knows with her mind that she is doing a foolish thing, while with her heart she rejoices in her folly and lauds herself for her high indifference to convention. Then when she finds herself suspected, assailed or ridiculed, she is amazed and deeply wounded, though with her intellect she has clearly understood the inevitableness of her reward ‰ This propensity to divorce impulse from good judgment, to do a rash thing for affection's sake, and then to writhe when the condemnation ‰ comes—is there any more truly feminine bit of sophistry in the strange round of woman's reason? The ostrich with her head in the sand is not more pathetic or absurd than a woman thus hoodwinking herself.

—Margaret Ashmun.

THIS earth with its infinitude of life and beauty and mystery, and the universe in the midst of which we are placed, with its overwhelming immensities of suns and nebulae, of light and motion, are as they are, firstly, for the development of life culminating in man; secondly, as a vast schoolhouse for the higher education of the human race in preparation for the enduring spiritual life to which it is destined.

—Alfred Russel Wallace.

Wonder is involuntary praise.—Young.

Does the road wind up-hill all the way?
  Yes, to the very end.
Will the day's journey take the whole
  long day?
  From morn till night, my friend.

But is there for the night a resting-place?
  *A roof for when the slow dark hours
  begin.*
May not the darkness hide it from
  my face?
  You can not miss that inn.

Shall I meet other wayfarers at night?
  Those who have gone before.
Then must I knock, or call when just
  in sight?
  *They will not keep you standing at
  that door.*

Shall I find comfort, travel-sore and weak?
  Of labor you shall find the sum.
Will there be beds for me and all who
  seek?
  Yea, beds for all who come.
    " Up-Hill," by Christina G. Rossetti

THE sun is just rising on the morning of another day, the first day of a new year. What can I wish that this day, this year, may bring to me? Nothing that shall make the world or others poorer, nothing at the expense of other men; but just those few things which in their coming do not stop with me, but touch me rather, as they pass and gather strength:

❡ A few friends who understand me, and yet remain my friends.

❡ A work to do which has real value without which the world would feel the poorer.

A return for such work small enough not to tax unduly any one who pays.

❡ A mind unafraid to travel, even though the trail be not blazed.

An understanding heart ‰ ‰

A sight of the eternal hills and unresting sea, and of something beautiful the hand of man has made.

A sense of humor and the power to laugh. ❡ A little leisure with nothing to do. ❡ A few moments of quiet, silent meditation. The sense of the presence of God ‰ ‰

And the patience to wait for the coming of these things, with the wisdom to know them when they come.—"A Morning Wish," by W. R. Hunt.

THERE is quite as much education and true learning in the analysis of an ear of corn as in the analysis of a complex sentence; ability to analyze clover and alfalfa roots savors of quite as much culture as does the study of the Latin and Greek roots.

O. H. Benson.

O lead a people in revolution wisely and successfully, without ambition and without crime, demands indeed lofty genius and unbending virtue. But to build their State amid the angry conflict of passion and prejudice, to peacefully inaugurate a complete and satisfactory government—this is the very greatest service that a man can render to mankind. But this also is the glory of Washington

With the sure sagacity of a leader of men, he selected at once for the three highest stations the three chief Americans. Hamilton was the head, Jefferson was the heart, and John Jay the conscience of his administration. Washington's just and serene ascendency was the lambent flame in which these beneficent powers were fused; and nothing else than that ascendency could have ridden the whirlwind and directed the storm that burst around him. Party spirit blazed into fury. John Jay was hung in effigy; Hamilton was stoned; insurrection raised its head in the West; Washington himself was denounced. But the great soul was undismayed. Without a beacon, without a chart, but with unwavering eye and steady hand, he guided his country safe through darkness and through storm. He held his steadfast way, like the sun across the firmament, giving life and health and strength to the new nation; and upon a searching survey of his administration, there is no great act which his country would annul; no word spoken, no line written, no deed done by him, which justice would reverse or wisdom deplore.—George William Curtis.

I WAS born an American; I live an American; I shall die an American; and I intend to perform the duties incumbent upon me in that character to the end of my career. I mean to do this with absolute disregard of personal consequences. What are the personal consequences? What is the individual man, with all the good or evil that may betide him, in comparison with the good or evil which may befall a great country, and in the midst of great transactions which concern that country's fate? Let the consequences be what they will, I am careless. No man can suffer too much, and no man can fall too soon, if he suffer, or if he fall, in the defense of the liberties and constitution of his country.
—Daniel Webster.

NO man today can lay claim to a liberal education unless he knows something of the reach and sweep of those peaks of poesy and learning raised by the spirit of man in the civilizations of Greece and Rome.—Edwin Markham.

WORK is the mission of mankind on this earth. A day is ever struggling forward, a day will arrive, in some approximate degree, when he who has no work to do, by whatever name he may be called, will not find it good to show himself in our quarter of the solar system but may go and look out elsewhere if there be any idle planet discoverable. Let all honest workers rejoice that such law, the first of Nature, has been recognized by them.
—George Bernard Shaw.

THE sheet-anchor of the Ship of State is the common school. Teach, first and last, Americanism. Let no youth leave the school without being thoroughly grounded in the history, the principles, and the incalculable blessings of American liberty. Let the boys be the trained soldiers of constitutional freedom, the girls the intelligent lovers of freemen.—Chauncey M. Depew.

HE is not to be called a true lover of wisdom who loves it for the sake of gain. And it may be said that the true philosopher loves every part of wisdom, and wisdom every part of the philosopher, inasmuch as she draws all to herself, and allows no one of his thoughts to wander to other things.—Dante.

The church says the earth is flat, but I know that it is round, for I have seen the shadow on the moon, and I have more faith in a shadow than in the church.—Magellan.

OTHING is more essential than that permanent, inveterate antipathies against particular nations and passionate attachments for others should be excluded, and that, in place of them, just and amicable feelings toward all should be cultivated. The nation which indulges toward another a habitual hatred or a habitual fondness is in some degree a slave. It is a slave to its animosity or to its affection, either of which is sufficient to lead it astray from its duty and its interest. Antipathy in one nation against another disposes each more readily to offer insult and injury, to lay hold of slight causes of umbrage, and to be haughty and intractable when accidental or trifling occasions of dispute occur. Hence, frequent collisions; obstinate, envenomed and bloody contests. Against the insidious wiles of foreign influence (I conjure you to believe me, fellow citizens), the jealousy of a free people ought to be constantly awake, since history and experience prove that foreign influence is one of the most baneful foes of republican government. But that jealousy, to be useful, must be impartial.—George Washington.

I THINK it rather fine, this necessity for the tense bracing of the will before anything worth doing can be done. I rather like it myself. I feel it is to be the chief thing that differentiates me from the cat by the fire.
—Arnold Bennett.

MODERN civilization rests upon physical science, for it is physical science that makes intelligence and moral energy stronger than brute force. The whole of modern thought is steeped in science. It has made its way into the works of our best poets, and even the mere man of letters, who affects to ignore and despise science, is unconsciously impregnated with her spirit and indebted for his best products to her methods. She is teaching the world that the ultimate court of appeal is observation and experience, not authority. She is creating a firm and living faith in the existence of immutable moral and physical laws, perfect obedience to which is the highest possible aim of an intelligent being.
—Huxley.

ONE fact stands out in bold relief in the history of men's attempts for betterment. That is that when compulsion is used, only resentment is aroused, and the end is not gained. Only through moral suasion and appeal to men's reason can a movement succeed.
—Samuel Gompers.

WE have grown literally afraid to be poor. We despise any one who elects to be poor in order to simplify and save his inner life. We have lost the power of even imagining what the ancient idealization of poverty could have meant; the liberation from material attachments, the unbribed soul, the manlier indifference, the paying our way by what we are or do, and not by what we have, the right to fling away our life at any moment irresponsibly—the more athletic trim; in short, the moral fighting shape. It is certain that the prevalent fear of poverty among the educated classes is the worst moral disease from which our civilization suffers.—William James.

THE manner in which one single ray of light, one single precious hint, will clarify and energize the whole mental life of him who receives it, is among the most wonderful and heavenly of intellectual phenomena.
—Arnold Bennett.

Friendship is the highest degree of perfection in society.—Montaigne.

Brutality to an animal is cruelty to mankind—it is only the difference in the victim.—Lamartine.

Blessed are they who have the gift of making friends, for it is one of God's best gifts. It involves many things, but above all, the power of going out of one's self, and appreciating whatever is noble and loving in another.
—Thomas Hughes.

E are spinning our own fates, good or evil, never to be undone. Every smallest stroke of virtue or vice leaves its never-so-little scar. The drunken Rip Van Winkle, in Jefferson's play, excuses himself for every fresh dereliction by saying, " I won't count this time! " Well, he may not count it, and a kind Heaven may not count it; but it is being counted none the less. Down among his nerve-cells and fibers the molecules are counting it, registering and storing it up to be used against him when the next temptation comes. Nothing we ever do is, in strict scientific literalness, wiped out. Of course, this has its good side as well as its bad one. As we become permanent drunkards by so many separate drinks, so we become saints in the moral, and authorities and experts in the practical and scientific spheres, by so many separate acts and hours of work. Let no youth have any anxiety about the upshot of his education, whatever the line of it may be. If he keep faithfully busy each hour of the working day, he may safely leave the final result to itself. He can with perfect certainty count on waking up some fine morning to find himself one of the competent ones of his generation in whatever pursuit he may have singled out. Silently, between all the details of his business, the *power of judging* in all that class of matter will have built itself up within him as a possession that will never pass away. Young people should know this truth in advance. The ignorance of it has probably engendered more discouragement and faint-heartedness in youths embarking on arduous careers than all other causes put together.—William James.

HE early sunlight filtered through the filmy draperies to where a wondering baby stretched his dimpled hands to catch the rays that lit his face and flesh like dawn lights up a rose. His startled gaze caught and held the dawn of day in rapturous looks that spoke the dawn of Self, for with the morning gleam out came the greater wonder. It was the mystery of Life. Across a cradle where, sunk in satin pillows, lay a still, pale form as droops a rose from some fierce heat, the evening shadows fell aslant, and spoke of peace. The twilight calm enclosed the world in silence deep as Truth, and on the little face the wondering look had given place to one of sweet repose. It was the mystery of Death. At head and foot the tapers burned, a golden light that clove the night as Hope the encircling gloom. Across the cot where lay the fair, frail form, his hand reached out to hers and met and clasped in tender burning touch. Into the eyes of each there came the look! That is the light of life; that spoke of self to each, yet told they two were one. It was the mystery to which the mysteries of Life and Death bow down—the mystery of Love.—James Hunt Cook.

She walks—the lady of my delight—
A shepherdess of sheep.
Her flocks are thoughts. She keeps them white;
She guards them from the steep.
She feeds them on the fragrant height.
And folds them in for sleep.

She roams maternal hills and bright,
Dark valleys safe and deep.
Into that tender breast at night
The chastest stars may peep.
She walks—the lady of my delight—
A shepherdess of sheep.

She holds her little thoughts in sight,
Though gay they run and leap,
She is so circumspect and right;
She has her soul to keep.
She walks—the lady of my delight—
A shepherdess of sheep.
" The Shepherdess," *by Alice Meynell*

Genius is mainly an affair of energy, and poetry is mainly an affair of genius; therefore a nation characterized by energy may well be eminent in poetry.
—Matthew Arnold.

HE world-story after all is nothing more than the story of human sentiment. The causes that have been lost and won, the victories and defeats, the Reformation and the Renaissance, all the great things that have been done, have been first achieved in the emotional life, in the human spirit. The immense material resources of Asia hurl themselves against Greek sentiment and are shattered. The Roman empire, robbed of Roman spirit, falls apart; China, the unalterable, the anesthetic, is dying ✺ Napoleon's cynical remark that Heaven espoused the cause of the larger army was nowhere better disproved than in his own history. A handful of colonial farmers is worth a regiment of Hessians. To one man comes a supreme passion—the unity of Italy, it may be, the reality of the Fatherland, the liberation of Greece; and behold, it is an accomplished fact.

It is impossible to exaggerate the omnipotence of human feeling, of human emotion, of human desire.

The miller looks to his millrace; the engineer replenishes his coalbin; the sailor regards the quarter of the wind; so must we people who have more important concerns on hand look for the carrying out of them to the strength and purity of the feelings. As men we must see to it that the heart beats high; as educators we must see to it that the tide of childish feeling is at the flood; as sociologists we must see to it that the people care. As we do this, we are strong; as we fail to do it, we are weak. Pagan defeat and superseding came when the human heart grew faint. It is the same world, this in which we live; the source of its power is still in the round tower of the heart.—C. Hanford Henderson.

✺ ✺

IN the democracy of the dead all men at last are equal. There is neither rank nor station nor prerogative in the republic of the grave. At this fatal threshold the philosopher ceases to be wise, and the song of the poet is silent. Dives relinquishes his millions and Lazarus his rags. The poor man is as rich as the richest, and the rich man is as poor as the pauper. The creditor loses his usury, and the debtor is acquitted of his obligation. There the proud man surrenders his dignities, the politician his honors, the worldling his pleasures; the invalid needs no physician, and the laborer rests from unrequited toil.

Here at last is Nature's final decree in equity. The wrongs of time are redressed. Injustice is expiated, the irony of Fate is refuted; the unequal distribution of wealth, honor, capacity, pleasure and opportunity, which makes life such a cruel and inexplicable tragedy, ceases in the realm of death. The strongest there has no supremacy, and the weakest needs no defence. The mightiest captain succumbs to that invincible adversary, who disarms alike the victor and the vanquished.—John J. Ingalls.

✺ ✺

The world is blessed most by men who do things, and not by those who merely talk about them.—James Oliver.

When you are old and gray and full of sleep,
And nodding by the fire, take down this book,
And slowly read and dream of the soft look
Your eyes had once, and of their shadows deep;

How many loved your moments of glad grace,
And loved your beauty with love false or true;
But one man loved the pilgrim soul in you,
And loved the sorrows of your changing face.

And bending down beside the glowing bars
Murmur, a little sadly, how love fled
And paced upon the mountains overhead
And hid his face amid a crowd of stars.
" When You Are Old," *by William Butler Yeats*

THE world has become one city. We begin to see that only a sophomoric and stupendous conceit can justify the claims of any race of people to be wholly superior to any other. No one race can be made perfect without the virtues of every other, or without the universal fellowship of all the children of men.

Darkness will cover the earth, until we learn the lesson of universal brotherhood. Away with national and racial prejudice! By our practice and our testimony, let us stand fearlessly and lovingly for the unity of mankind.
—Benjamin Fay Mills.

I BELIEVE in the spirit of peace, and in sole and absolute reliance on truth and the application of it to the hearts and consciences of the people. I do not believe that the weapons of liberty ever have been, or can be, the weapons of despotism. I know that those of despotism are the sword, the revolver, the cannon, the bombshell; and therefore, the weapons to which tyrants cling and upon which they depend are not the weapons for me, as a friend of liberty.—W. L. Garrison.

TWELVE Things to Remember—1. The value of time. 2. The success of perseverance. 3. The pleasure of working. 4. The dignity of simplicity. 5. The worth of character. 6. The power of kindness. 7. The influence of example. 8. The obligation of duty. 9. The wisdom of economy. 10. The virtue of patience. 11. The improvement of talent. 12. The joy of originating.—Marshall Field.

THERE are two kinds of discontent in this world: the discontent that works, and the discontent that wrings its hands. The first gets what it wants, and the second loses what it has. There's no cure for the first but success; and there's no cure at all for the second.
—Gordon Graham.

Life is made up of sobs, sniffles and smiles with sniffles predominating.—O. Henry.

THE toxin of fatigue has been demonstrated; but the poisons generated by evil temper and emotional excess over non-essentials have not yet been determined, although without a doubt they exist. Explosions of temper, emotional cyclones, and needless fear and panic over disease or misfortune that seldom materialize, are simply bad habits. By proper ventilation and illumination of the mind it is possible to cultivate tolerance, poise, and real courage without being a bromide-taker.
—Metchnikoff.

HE who proclaims the existence of the Infinite—and none can avoid it —accumulates in that affirmation more of the supernatural than is to be found in all the miracles of all the religions; for the notion of the Infinite presents that double character that it forces itself upon us and yet is incomprehensible. When this notion seizes upon our understanding, we can but kneel. . . . I see everywhere the inevitable expression of the Infinite in the world; through it, the supernatural is at the bottom of every heart. The idea of God is a form of the idea of the Infinite. As long as the mystery of the Infinite weighs on human thought, temples will be erected for the worship of the Infinite, whether God is called Brahma, Allah, Jehovah or Jesus; and on the pavement of those temples men will be seen kneeling, prostrated, annihilated in the thought of the Infinite.—Louis Pasteur.

THERE are three kinds of silence. Silence from words is good, because inordinate speaking tends to evil. Silence or rest from desires or passions is still better, because it prompts quickness of spirit. But the best of all is silence from unnecessary and wandering thoughts, because that is essential to internal recollection, and because it lays a foundation for a proper regulation and silence in other respects.
—Madame Guyon.

Co-operation, and not Competition, is the life of trade.—William C. Fitch.

ND numerous indeed are the hearts to which Christmas brings a brief season of happiness and enjoyment. How many families whose members have been dispersed and scattered far and wide, in the restless struggle of life, are then reunited, and meet once again in that happy state of companionship and mutual good-will, which is a source of such pure and unalloyed delight, and one so incompatible with the cares and sorrows of the world, that the religious belief of the most civilized nations, and the rude traditions of the roughest savages, alike number it among the first days of a future state of existence, provided for the blest and happy! How many old recollections, and how many dormant sympathies, Christmas-time awakens! ⌷ We write these words now, many miles distant from the spot at which, year after year, we met on that day, a merry and joyous circle. Many of the hearts that throbbed so gaily then, have ceased to beat; many of the looks that shone so brightly then, have ceased to glow; the hands we grasped, have grown cold; the eyes we sought, have hid their luster in the grave; and yet the old house, the room, the merry voices and smiling faces, the jest, the laugh, the most minute and trivial circumstance connected with those happy meetings, crowd upon our mind at each recurrence of the season, as if the last assemblage had been but yesterday. Happy, happy Christmas, that can win us back to the delusions of our childish days, recall to the old man the pleasures of his youth, and transport the traveler back to his own fireside and quiet home!
—Charles Dickens.

THE bread of bitterness is the food on which men grow to their fullest stature; the waters of bitterness are the debatable ford through which they reach the shores of wisdom; the ashes boldly grasped and eaten without faltering are the price that must be paid for the golden fruit of knowledge.—Ouida.

THE great duty of life is not to give pain; and the most acute reasoner can not find an excuse for one who voluntarily wounds the heart of a fellow-creature. Even for their own sakes, people should show kindness and regard for their dependents. They are often better served in trifles, in proportion as they are rather feared than loved; but how small is this gain compared with the loss sustained in all the weightier affairs of life! Then the faithful servant shows himself at once a friend, while the one who serves from fear shows himself an enemy.—Frederica Bremer.

IF thou workest at that which is before thee, following right reason seriously, vigorously, calmly, without allowing anything else to distract thee, but keeping thy divine part sure, if thou shouldst be bound to give it back immediately; if thou holdest to this, expecting nothing, fearing nothing, but satisfied with thy present activity according to Nature, and with heroic truth in every word and sound which thou utterest, thou wilt live happy. And there is no man who is able to prevent this.
—Marcus Aurelius.

I DO not remember that in my whole life I ever wilfully misrepresented anything to anybody at any time. I have never knowingly had connection with a fraudulent scheme. I have tried to do good in this world, not harm, as my enemies would have the world believe. I have helped men and have attempted in my humble way to be of some service to my country.
—J. Pierpont Morgan.

FLOWERS have an expression of countenance as much as men or animals. Some seem to smile; some have a sad expression; some are pensive and diffident; others again are plain, honest and upright, like the broadfaced sunflower and the hollyhock.
—Henry Ward Beecher.

When love and skill work together expect a masterpiece.—John Ruskin.

NO one understands the nature of love; it is like a bird of heaven that sings a strange language. It lights down among us, coming from whence we know not, going we know not how or when, striking out wild notes of music that make even fatigued and heavy hearts to throb and give back a tone of courage. . . . .

Shall we say that the creature without love is like the lamp unlit? There it is and no one needs it. But touch it with flame, and it trembles and glows and becomes the center of the room where it stands. Everything that falls under its rays is new-gilt. So does the lover see all natural things quite new.

Or take the image of the withering plant that is dying of drought. The sun's rays have parched it; the roots have searched and searched for moisture in a soil that grows every day harder and drier. The plant wilts and hangs its head; it is fainting and ready to die, when down comes the rain in a murmuring multitude of round scented drops, the purest thing alive, a distilled essence, necessary to life. Under that baptism the plant lifts itself up; it drinks and rejoices. In the night it renews its strength; in the morning the heat it has had from the sun, reinforced by the rain, bursts out into colored flowers. So I have known a man battered by hard life and the excess of his own passions: I have seen love come to such a man and take him up and cleanse him and set him on his feet; and from him has burst forth a flood of color and splendor—creative work that now lends its fiery stimulus to thousands.

¶ Another image might be of the harp that stands by itself in golden aloofness. Then comes the beautiful arms, the curving fingers that pluck at the strings, and the air is filled with melody; the harp begins to live, thrilling and rejoicing, down to its golden foot.

Or picture the unlighted house, empty at fall of night. The windows are dark; the door shut; the clean wind goes about and around it; and can not find an entrance. The dull heavy air is faint within; it longs to be reunited to the wind of the world outside. Then comes the woman with the key, and in she steps; the windows are opened, the imprisoned air rushes out, the wind enters; the lamps and the fire are lit; so that light fills windows and doors. The tables are set, there is the sound of footsteps; and more footsteps. The house glows and lives.

—Grace Rhys.

O ELOQUENT, just, and mighty Death! Whom none could advise, thou hast persuaded; what none hath dared, thou hast done; and whom all the world hath flattered, thou only hast cast out of the world and despised: thou hast drawn together all the far-stretched greatness, all the pride, cruelty and ambition of man, and covered it all over with these two narrow words—*Hic iacet !*—Raleigh.

OH, the eagerness and freshness of youth! How the boy enjoys his food, his sleep, his sports, his companions, his truant days! His life is an adventure, he is widening his outlook, he is extending his dominion, he is conquering his kingdom. How cheap are his pleasures, how ready his enthusiasms! In boyhood I have had more delight on a haymow with two companions and a big dog— delight that came nearer intoxication— than I have ever had in all the subsequent holidays of my life. When youth goes, much goes with it. When manhood comes, much comes with it. We exchange a world of delightful sensations and impressions for a world of duties and studies and meditations. The youth enjoys what the man tries to understand. Lucky is he who can get his grapes to market and keep the bloom upon them, who can carry some of the freshness and eagerness and simplicity of youth into his later years, who can have a boy's heart below a man's head.

—John Burroughs.

The lawyer who uses his knowledge to stir up strife among the industrious and impede the path of commerce, that he himself may thrive, is unworthy of our respect.—W. H. Seward.

HE difference between a precious stone and a common stone is not an essential difference—not a difference of substance, but of arrangement of the particles—the crystallization. In substance, the charcoal and the diamond are one, but in form and effect, how widely they differ! The pearl contains nothing that is not found in the coarsest oyster-shell ❧ Two men have the same thoughts; they use about the same words in expressing them; yet with one the product is real literature, with the other it is platitude.

The difference is all in presentation; a finer and more compendious process has gone on in the one case than in the other. The elements are better fused and knitted together; they are in some way heightened and intensified. Is not here a clue to what we mean by style? ❧ ❧

Style transforms common quartz into an Egyptian pebble. We are apt to think of style as something external, that can be put on, something in and of itself.

But it is not; it is in the inmost texture of the substance itself.

Polish, choice words, faultless rhetoric, are only the accidents of style.

Indeed, perfect workmanship is one thing; style, as the great writers have it, is quite another. It may, and often does, go with faulty workmanship. It is the choice of words in a fresh and vital way, so as to give us a vivid sense of a new spiritual force and personality. In the best work the style is found and hidden in the matter.

I heard a reader observe, after finishing one of Robert Louis Stevenson's books,

O, like a queen's her happy tread,
And like a queen's her golden head!
But O, at last, when all is said,
Her woman's heart for me!

We wandered where the river gleamed
'Neath oaks that mused and pines that
dreamed.
A wild thing of the woods she seemed,
So proud, and pure, and free!

All heaven drew nigh to hear her sing,
When from her lips her soul took wing;
The oaks forgot their pondering,
The pines their reverie.

And O, her happy, queenly tread,
And O, her queenly golden head!
But O, her heart, when all is said,
Her woman's heart for me!
"*Song,*" *by William Watson*

"How well it is written!" I thought it a doubtful compliment. It should have been so well written that the reader would not have been conscious of the writing at all.

If we could only get the writing, the craft, out of our stories and essays and poems, and make the reader feel he was face to face with the real thing! The complete identification of the style with the thought; the complete absorption of the man with his matter, so that the reader shall say, " How good, how real, how true! "—that is the great success. Seek ye the kingdom of truth first, and all things shall be added ❧ ❧

I think we do feel, with regard to some of Stevenson's books, like *An Inland Voyage, Travels With a Donkey,* etc., how well they are written ❧ Certainly one would not have the literary skill any less, but would have one's attention kept from it by the richness of the matter. Hence I think a British critic hits the mark when he says Stevenson lacks homeliness.

Doctor Holmes wrote fine and eloquent poems, yet I think one does not feel that he is essentially a poet. His work has not the inevitableness of Nature; it is a skilful literary feat; we admire it, but seldom return to it. His poetry is a stream in an artificial channel; his natural channel is his prose; here we get his freest and most spontaneous activity.

❡ One fault I find with our younger and more promising school of novelists is that their aim is too literary; we feel they are striving mainly for artistic effects. Do we feel this at all in Scott, Dickens, Hawthorne or Tolstoy? These men are not thinking about art, but about life—

how to produce life. ❡ In essayists like Pater, Wilde, Lang, the same thing occurs; we are constantly aware of the literary artist; they are not in love with life, reality, so much as they are with words, style, literary effects ﬌ Their seriousness is mainly an artistic seriousness. It is not so much that they have something to say, as that they are filled with a desire to say something.

Nearly all our magazine poets seem filled with the same desire; what labor, what art and technique; but what a dearth of feeling and spontaneity! I read a few lines or stanzas and then stop. I see it is only deft handicraft, and that the heart and soul are not in it.

One day my boy killed what an old hunter told him was a mock duck. It looked like a duck, it acted like a duck, but when it came upon the table—it mocked us.

These mock poems of the magazines remind me of it.

Is it not unfair to take any book, certainly any great piece of literature, and deliberately sit down to pass judgment upon it? Great books are not addressed to the critical judgment, but to the life, the soul. They need to slide into one's life earnestly, and find him with his guard down, his doors open, his attitude disinterested. The reader is to give himself to them, as they give themselves to him; there must be self-sacrifice.

We find the great books when we are young, eager, receptive. After we grow hard and critical we find few great books. A recent French critic says: " It seems to me, works of art are not made to be judged, but to be loved, to please, to dissipate the cares of real life. It is precisely by wishing to judge them that one loses sight of their true significance."

❡ " How can a man learn to know himself? " inquires Goethe. " Never by reflection, only by action." Is not this a half-truth? One can only learn his powers of action by action, and his powers of thought by thinking. He can only learn whether or not he has power to command, to lead, to be an orator or legislator, by actual trial. Has he courage, self-control, self-denial, fortitude, etc.?

In life alone can he find out. Action tests his moral virtues, reflection his intellectual. If he would define himself to himself he must think.

" We are weak in action," says Renan, " by our best qualities; we are strong in action by will and a certain one-sidedness." " The moment Byron reflects," says Goethe, " he is a child." Byron had no self-knowledge. We have all known people who were ready and sure in action, who did not know themselves at all. Your weakness or strength as a person comes out in action; your weakness or strength as an intellectual force comes out in reflection.—John Burroughs.

﬌ ﬌

AS long as nations meet on the fields of war—as long as they sustain the relations of savages to each other—as long as they put the laurel and the oak on the brows of those who kill—just so long will citizens resort to violence, and the quarrels be settled by dagger and revolver.—Robert G. Ingersoll.

﬌ ﬌

I DO not belong to the amiable group of " men of compromise." I am in the habit of giving candid and straightforward expression to the convictions which a half-century of serious and laborious study has led me to form. If I seem to you an iconoclast, I pray you to remember that the victory of pure reason over superstition will not be achieved without a tremendous struggle.

—Ernst Haeckel.

﬌ ﬌

BELIEVE me when I tell you that thrift of time will repay you in after-life, with a usury of profit beyond your most sanguine dreams; and that waste of it will make you dwindle alike in intellectual and moral stature, beyond your darkest reckoning.

—W. E. Gladstone.

﬌ ﬌

I never work better than when I am inspired by anger. When I am angry I can write, pray, and preach well; for then my whole temperament is quickened, my understanding sharpened, and all mundane vexations and temptations depart.

—Luther.

HO can describe the pleasure and delight, the peace of mind and soft tranquillity, felt in the balmy air and among the green hills and rich woods of an inland village?

Who can tell how scenes of peace and quietude sink into the minds of pain-worn dwellers in close and noisy places, and carry their own freshness deep into their jaded hearts?

Men who have lived in crowded, pent-up streets, through whole lives of toil, and never wished for change; men to whom custom has indeed been second nature, and who have come almost to love each brick and stone that formed the narrow boundaries of their daily walks—even they, with the hand of death upon them, have been known to yearn at last for one short glimpse of Nature's face, and, carried far from the scenes of their old pains and pleasures, have seemed to pass at once into a new state of being, and crawling forth from day to day to some green, sunny spot, have had such memories wakened up within them by the mere sight of sky, and hill, and plain, and glistening water, that a foretaste of heaven itself has soothed their quick decline, and they have sunk into their tombs as peacefully as the sun, whose setting they watched from their lonely chamber window but a few hours before, faded from their dim and feeble sight!

❡ The memories which peaceful country scenes call up are not of this world or of its thoughts and hopes. Their gentle influence may teach us to weave fresh garlands for the graves of those we loved, may purify our thoughts and bear down before it old enmity and hatred; but beneath all this there lingers in the least reflective mind a vague and half-formed consciousness of having held such feelings long before in some remote and distant time, which calls up solemn thoughts of distant times to come, and bends down pride and worldliness beneath it.—Charles Dickens.

The happiness of a man in this life does not consist in the absence but in the mastery of his passions.—Tennyson.

OUR friendships hurry to short and poor conclusions, because we have made them a texture of wine and dreams, instead of the tough fiber of the human heart. The laws of friendship are great, austere, and eternal, of one web with the laws of nature and of morals. But we have aimed at a swift and petty benefit, to such a sudden sweetness. We snatch at the slowest fruit in the whole garden of God, which many summers and many winters must ripen. We seek our friend not sacredly, but with an adulterate passion which would appropriate him to ourselves

I do not wish to treat friendships daintily, but with roughest courage. When they are real, they are not glass threads or frost-work, but the solidest thing we know

The end of friendship is a commerce the most strict and homely that can be joined; more strict than any of which we have experienced. It is for aid and comfort through all the relations and passages of life and death. It is fit for serene days, and graceful gifts, and country rambles, but also for rough roads and hard fare, shipwreck, poverty and persecution. It keeps company with the sallies of the wit and the trances of religion. We are to dignify to each other the daily needs and offices of man's life, and embellish it by courage, wisdom and unity. It should never fall into something usual and settled, but should be alert and inventive, and add rhyme and reason to what was drudgery.—Emerson.

I CAN not commend to a business house any artificial plan for making men producers—any scheme for driving them into business-building. You must lead them through their self-interest. It is this alone that will keep them keyed up to the full capacity of their productiveness.—Charles H. Steinway.

The cynic is one who knows the price of everything and the value of nothing.
—Oscar Wilde.

Snobbery is the pride of those who are not sure of their position.—Berton Braley.

HEN the telegram came, early one Monday morning, what was our first thought, as soon as the immediate numbness of sorrow passed and the selfish instinct began to reassert itself (as it always does) and whisper " What have *I* lost? What is the difference to *me?*" Was it not something like this—" Put away books and paper and pen. Stevenson is dead. Stevenson is dead, and now there is nobody left to write for." Our children and grandchildren shall rejoice in his books; but we of this generation possessed in the living man something that they will not know. So long as he lived, though it were far from Britain—though we had never spoken to him and he, perhaps, had barely heard our names— we always wrote our best for Stevenson. To him each writer amongst us —small or more than small—had been proud to have carried his best. That best might be poor enough. So long as it was not slipshod. Stevenson could forgive. While he lived, he moved men to put their utmost even into writings that quite certainly would never meet his eye. Surely another age will wonder over this curiosity of letters—that for five years the needle of literary endeavor in Great Britain has quivered towards a little island in the South Pacific, as to its magnetic pole.

Yet he founded no school, though most of us from time to time have poorly tried to copy him. He remained altogether inimitable, yet never seemed conscious of his greatness. It was native in him to rejoice in the successes of other men at least as much as in his own triumphs. One almost felt that, so long as good books were written, it was no great concern to him whether he or others wrote them. Born with an artist's craving for beauty of expression, he achieved that beauty with infinite pains. Confident in romance and in the beneficence of joy, he cherished the flame of joyous romance with more than Vestal fervor, and kept it ardent in a body which Nature, unkind from the beginning, seemed to delight in visiting with more unkindness— a " soul's dark cottage, battered and decayed" almost from birth. And his books leave the impression that he did this chiefly from a sense of duty: that he labored and kept the lamp alight chiefly because, for the time, other and stronger men did not ๑ ๑ Had there been another Scott, another Dumas—

The royal feast was done; the King
* Sought some new sport to banish care,*
And to his jester cried: "Sir Fool,
* Kneel now, and make for us a prayer."*

The jester doffed his cap and bells,
* And stood the mocking court before;*
They could not see the bitter smile
* Behind the painted grin he wore.*

He bowed his head, and bent his knee
* Upon the monarch's silken stool;*
His pleading voice arose: "O Lord,
* Be merciful to me, a fool!*

"No pity, Lord, could change the heart
* From red with wrong to white as wool;*
The rod must heal the sin: but Lord,
* Be merciful to me, a fool!*

" 'T is not by guilt the onward sweep
* Of truth and right, O Lord, we stay;*
'T is by our follies that so long
* We hold the earth from heaven away.*

"These clumsy feet, still in the mire,
* Go crushing blossoms without end;*

(Concluded on next page)

if I may change the image—to take up the torch of romance and run with it, I doubt if Stevenson would have offered himself. I almost think in that case he would have consigned with Nature and sat at ease, content to read of new Ivanhoes and new D'Artagnans: for—let it be said again—no man had less of the ignoble itch for merely personal success. Think, too, of what the struggle meant for him: how it drove him unquiet about the world, if somewhere he might meet with a climate to repair the constant drain upon his feeble vitality; and how at last it flung him, as by a " sudden freshet," upon Samoa—to die " far from

Argos, dear land of home." ⓠ And then consider the brave spirit that carried him—the last of a great race—along this far and difficult path; for it is the man we must consider now, not, for the moment, his writings. Fielding's voyage to Lisbon was long and tedious enough; but almost the whole of Stevenson's life has been a voyage to Lisbon, a voyage in the very penumbra of death. Yet Stevenson spoke always as gallantly as his great predecessor. Their "cheerful stoicism," which allies his books with the best British breeding, will keep them classical as long as our nation shall value breeding ﾟ ﾟ It shines to our dim eyes now, as we turn over the familiar pages of *Virginibus Puerisque*, and from page after page—in sentences and fragments of sentences —" It is not altogether ill with the invalid after all." " Who would find heart enough to begin to live, if he dallied with the consideration of death?" . . . " What sorry and pitiful quibbling all this is!" . . . " It is better to live and be done with it, than to die daily in the sick-room. By all means begin your folio; even if the doctor does not give you a year, even if he hesitates over a month, make one brave push and see what can be accomplished in a week. . . . For surely, at whatever age it overtake the man, this is to die young."

I remember now (as one remembers little things at such times) that, when first I heard of his going to Samoa, there came into my head (Heaven knows why) a trivial, almost ludicrous passage from his

These hard, well-meaning hands we thrust
Among the heart-strings of a friend.

"The ill-timed truth we might have kept—
Who knows how sharp it pierced and stung?
The word we had not sense to say—
Who knows how grandly it had rung!

"Our faults no tenderness should ask,
The chastening stripes must cleanse them all;
But for our blunders—oh, in shame
Before the eyes of heaven we fall.

"Earth bears no balsam for mistakes;
Men crown the knave, and scourge the tool
That did his will; but Thou, O Lord,
Be merciful to me, a fool!"

The room was hushed; in silence rose
The King, and sought his gardens cool,
And walked apart, and murmured low,
"Be merciful to me, a fool!"
" The Fool's Prayer," *by Edward Rowland Sill*

favorite, Sir Thomas Browne: a passage beginning " He was fruitlessly put in hope of advantage by change of Air, and imbibing the pure Aerial Nitre of those Parts; and therefore, being so far spent, he quickly found Sardinia in Tivoli, and the most healthful air of little effect, where Death had set her Broad Arrow." A statelier sentence of the same author occurs to me now: " To live indeed, is to be again ourselves, which being not only a hope, but an evidence in noble believers, it is all one to lie in St. Innocent's Churchyard, as in the sands of Egypt. Ready to be anything in the ecstasy of being ever, and as content with six foot as the *moles* of Adrianus." This one lies, we are told, on a mountain-top, overlooking the Pacific. At first it seemed so much easier to distrust a News Agency than to accept Stevenson's loss. " O captain, my captain!" One needs not be an excellent writer to feel that writing will be thankless work, now that Stevenson is gone. But the papers by this time leave no room for doubt. "A grave was dug on the summit of Mount Vaea, thirteen hundred feet above the sea. The coffin was carried up the hill by Samoans with great difficulty, a track having to be cut through the thick bush which covers the side of the hill, from the base to the peak." For the good of man, his father and grandfather planted the high sea-lights upon the Inchcape and the Tyree Coast. He, the last of their line, nursed another light and tended it. Their lamps still shine upon the Bell Rock and the

Skerryvore; and—though in alien seas, upon a rock of exile—this other light shall continue, unquenchable by age, beneficent, serene.
" The Death of Robert Louis Stevenson," by Sir A. T. Quiller-Couch.

❧ ❧

MUSIC is to me an ethereal rain, an ever-soft distillation, fragrant and liquid and wholesome to the soul, as dew to flowers; an incomprehensible delight, a joy, a voice of mystery, that seems to stand on the boundary between the sphere of the senses and the soul, and plead with pure, unrefined human nature to ascend into regions of seraphic uncontained life.
O wondrous power! Art thou not the nearest breath of God's own beauty, born to us amid the infinite, whispering gallery of His reconciliation! Type of all love and reconciliation, solvent of hard, contrary elements—blender of soul with soul, and all with the Infinite Harmony.—John S. Dwight.

❧ ❧

LAUGHTER, while it lasts, slackens and unbraces the mind, weakens the faculties, and causes a kind of remissness and dissolution in all the powers of the soul; and thus far it may be looked upon as a weakness in the composition of human nature. But if we consider the frequent reliefs we receive from it, and how often it breaks the gloom which is apt to depress the mind and damp our spirits, with transient, unexpected gleams of joy, one would take care not to grow too wise for so great a pleasure of life.—Addison.

❧ ❧

THE highest compact we can make with our fellow is, let there be truth between us two forevermore. It is sublime to feel and say of another, I need never meet, or speak, or write to him; we need not reinforce ourselves, or send tokens of remembrance; I rely on him as on myself; if he did not thus or thus, I know it was right.—Emerson.

❧ ❧

There are whole worlds of fact waiting to be discovered by inference.
—Woodrow Wilson.

NOW blessings light on him that first invented this same sleep: it covers a man all over, thoughts and all, like a cloak; it is meat for the hungry, drink for the thirsty, heat for the cold, and cold for the hot. It is the current coin that purchases all the pleasures of the world cheap; and it is the balance that sets the king and the shepherd, the fool and the wise man, even. There is only one thing, which somebody once put into my head, that I dislike in sleep: it is, that it resembles death; there is very little difference between a man in his first sleep and a man in his last sleep.
—Cervantes.

❧ ❧

THE true rule, in determining to embrace or reject anything, is not whether it have any evil in it, but whether it have more of evil than of good. There are few things wholly evil or wholly good. Almost everything, especially of government policy, is an inseparable compound of the two, so that our best judgment of the preponderance between them is continually demanded ❧
—A. Lincoln.

❧ ❧

TO pursue trifles is the lot of humanity; and whether we bustle in a pantomime, or strut at a coronation, or shout at a bonfire, or harangue in a senate-house—whatever object we follow, it will at last conduct us to futility and disappointment. The wise bustle and laugh as they walk in the pageant, but fools bustle and are important; and this probably is all the difference between them.—Oliver Goldsmith.

❧ ❧

I PAINFULLY reflect that in almost every political controversy of the last fifty years the leisured classes, the educated classes, the wealthy classes, the titled classes, have been in the wrong. The common people—the toilers, the men of uncommon sense—these have been responsible for nearly all of the social reform measures which the world accepts today.—W. E. Gladstone.

❧ ❧

Laws are not made for the good.
—Socrates.

CAN conceive of a national destiny surpassing the glories of the present and the past—a destiny which meets the responsibilities of today and measures up to the possibilities of the future

Behold a republic, resting securely upon the foundation stones quarried by revolutionary patriots from the mountain of eternal truth—a republic applying in practice and proclaiming to the world the self-evident proposition that all men are created equal; that they are endowed with inalienable rights; that governments are instituted among men to secure these rights; that governments derive their just powers from the consent of the governed.

Behold a republic in which civil and religious liberty stimulate all to earnest endeavor, and in which the law restrains every hand uplifted for a neighbor's injury—a republic in which every citizen is a sovereign, but in which no one cares to wear a crown.

Behold a republic standing erect, while empires all around are bowed beneath the weight of their own armaments—a republic whose flag is loved, while other flags are only feared.

Behold a republic increasing in population, in wealth, in strength and influence, solving the problems of civilization and hastening the coming of universal brotherhood—a republic which shakes thrones and dissolves aristocracies by its silent example, and gives light and protection to those who sit in darkness. ❡ Behold a republic gradually but surely becoming the supreme moral factor in the world's progress and the accepted arbiter of the world's disputes—a republic whose history, like the path of the just, is "as the shining light that shineth more and more unto the perfect day."—"The Ideal Republic," by William Jennings Bryan.

I wandered lonely as a cloud
That floats on high o 'er vales and hills,
When all at once I saw a crowd,
A host, of golden daffodils;
Beside the lake, beneath the trees,
Fluttering and dancing in the breeze.

Continuous as the stars that shine
And twinkle in the milky way,
They stretched in never-ending line
Along the margin of a bay:
Ten thousand saw I at a glance,
Tossing their heads in sprightly dance.

The waves beside them danced; but they
Out-did the sparkling waves in glee:
A poet could not but be gay,
In such a jocund company:
I gazed—and gazed—but little thought
What wealth the show to me had brought:

For oft, when on my couch I lie
In vacant or in pensive mood,
They flash upon that inward eye
Which is the bliss of solitude;
And then my heart with pleasure fills,
And dances with the daffodils.
" I Wandered Lonely As A Cloud,"
by William Wordsworth

YOU will succeed best when you put the restless, anxious side of affairs out of mind, and allow the restful side to live in your thoughts. —Margaret Stowe.

HE is an eloquent man who can treat humble subjects with delicacy, lofty things impressively and moderate things temperately.—Cicero.

I DO not know what I may appear to the world, but to myself I seem to have been only like a boy playing on the seashore, and diverting myself in now and then finding a prettier shell, or a smoother pebble than ordinary, whilst the great ocean of truth lay all undiscovered before me. —Newton.

AS a writer, I have only one desire—to fill you with fire, to pour into you the distilled essence of the sun itself. I want every thought, every word, every act of mine to make you feel that you are receiving into your body, into your mind, into your soul, the sacred spirit that changes clay into men and men into gods.—Thomas Dreier.

FOURSCORE and seven years ago our fathers brought forth on this continent a new nation, conceived in liberty and dedicated to the proposition that all men are created equal. Now we are engaged in a great civil war, testing whether that nation, or any nation so conceived and so dedicated, can long endure. We are met on a great battlefield of that war. We have come to dedicate a portion of that field as a final resting-place for those who here gave their lives that that nation might live. It is altogether fitting and proper that we should do this. But in a larger sense we can not dedicate, we can not consecrate, we can not hallow this ground. The brave men, living and dead, who struggled here have consecrated it far above our poor power to add or detract. The world will little note nor long remember what we say here, but it can never forget what they did here. It is for us, the living, rather to be dedicated here to the unfinished work which they who fought here have thus far so nobly advanced. It is rather for us to be here dedicated to the great task remaining before us, that from these honored dead we take increased devotion to that cause for which they gave the last full measure of devotion; that we here highly resolve that these dead shall not have died in vain; that this nation, under God, shall have a new birth of freedom, and that government of the people, by the people and for the people shall not perish from the earth.—" Address at Gettysburg," by Abraham Lincoln.

☙ ❧

GENIUS is its own reward: for a man's best qualities must necessarily benefit himself. " He who is born with a talent, for a talent, finds in it his happiest existence," says Goethe. If we look up to a great man of the past, we do not say, " How happy he is to be still admired by all of us;" but " How happy he must have been in the direct enjoyment of a mind whose traces continue to delight mankind for centuries." Not fame itself is of value, but that wherewith it is acquired; and in the begetting of immortal children lies the real enjoyment.—Schopenhauer.

☙ ❧

IF it 's near dinner-time, the foreman takes out his watch when the jury have retired and says: " Dear me, gentlemen, ten minutes to five, I declare! I dine at five, gentlemen." " So do I," says everybody else except two men who ought to have dined at three, and seem more than half-disposed to stand out in consequence. The foreman smiles and puts up his watch: " Well, gentlemen, what do we say? Plaintiff, defendant, gentlemen? I rather think, so far as I am concerned, gentlemen—I say I rather think—but don't let that influence you—I rather think the plaintiff's the man."—Charles Dickens.

☙ ❧

IMMORTALITY is a word that Hope through all the ages has been whispering to Love ☙ The miracle of thought we can not understand. The mystery of life and death we can not comprehend. This chaos called world has never been explained. The golden bridge of life from gloom emerges, and on shadow rests. Beyond this we do not know. Fate is speechless, destiny is dumb, and the secret of the future has never yet been told. We love; we wait; we hope. The more we love, the more we fear. Upon the tenderest heart the deepest shadows fall. All paths, whether filled with thorns or flowers, end here. Here success and failure are the same. The rag of wretchedness and the purple robe of power all differences and distinction lose in this democracy of death. Character survives; goodness lives; love is immortal.—Robert G. Ingersoll.

☙ ❧

THERE is an idea abroad among moral people that they should make their neighbors good. One person I have to make good: myself. But my duty to my neighbor is much more nearly expressed by saying that I have to make him happy if I may.—R. L. Stevenson.

☙ ❧

Some people are so painfully good that they would rather be right than be pleasant.—L. C. Ball.

NE man when he has done a service to another is ready to set it down to his account as a favor conferred. Another is not ready to do this, but still in his own mind he thinks of the man as his debtor, and he knows what he has done. A third in a manner does not even know what he has done, but he is like a vine which has produced grapes, and seeks for nothing more after it has once produced its proper fruit. As a horse when he has run, a dog when he has caught the game, a bee when it has made its honey, so a man when he has done a good act does not call out for others to come and see, but he goes on to another act, as a vine goes on to produce again the grapes in season. Must a man then be one of these, who in a manner acts thus without observing it? Yes. What more dost thou want when thou hast done a man a service? Art thou not content that thou hast done something comfortable to thy nature, and dost thou seek to be paid for it, just as if the eye demanded a recompense for seeing, or the feet should demand a recompense for walking?—Marcus Aurelius.

I regard ideas only in my struggles: to the persons of my opponents I am indifferent, bitterly as they have attacked and slandered my own person.

—Ernst Haeckel.

HE equal right of all men to the use of land is as clear as their equal right to breathe the air—it is a right proclaimed by the fact of their existence. For we can not suppose that some men have a right to be in this world, and others no right.—Henry George.

I went to Europe, said my friend,
  Expecting wonders rare
To open vistas without end,
  And lay the future bare.

Paris, of course, would be in style;
  And Berlin, London, Rome,
Would show me something more worth
    while
  Than anything at home.

And then to hear them cheer a crown,
  Or praise some rusty thing
That the dark ages handed down,
  Was—was astonishing.

  "Travel," by William Griffith

RT is not a sermon, and the artist is not a preacher. Art accomplishes by indirection. The beautiful refines. The perfect in art suggests the perfect in conduct. The harmony in music teaches, without intention, the lesson of proportion in life. The bird in his song has no moral purpose, and yet the influence is humanizing. The beautiful in nature acts through appreciation and sympathy. It does not browbeat, neither does it humiliate. It is beautiful without regard to you. Roses would be unbearable if in their red and perfumed hearts were mottoes to the effect that bears eat bad boys and that honesty is the best policy. Art creates an atmosphere in which the proprieties, the amenities, and the virtues unconsciously grow. The rain does not lecture the seed. The light does not make rules for the vine and flower. The heart is softened by the pathos of the perfect.—Robert G. Ingersoll.

N imperfect soul seeing what is good and great and true, but very often failing in the attempt to attain it, is apt to be very harsh in its judgments on the shortcomings of others. But a divine and sovereign soul—a soul that has more nearly attained to the measure of the perfect man—takes a calmer and gentler, because a larger-hearted view of those little weaknesses and indirectnesses which it can not but daily see.—Farrar.

USTICE is as strictly due between neighbor nations as between neighbor citizens. A highwayman is as much a robber when he plunders in a gang, as when single; and a nation that makes an unjust war is only a *great gang*.

—Franklin.

ET us ask ourselves, what is education? Above all things, what is our ideal of a thoroughly liberal education? —of that education which, if we could begin life again, we would give ourselves—of that education which, if we could mould the fates to our own will, we would give our children. Well, I know not what may be your conception upon this matter, but I will tell you mine, and I hope I shall find that our views are not very discrepant.

Suppose it were perfectly certain that the life and fortune of every one of us would, one day or other, depend upon his winning or losing a game of chess. Don't you think that we should all consider it to be a primary duty to learn at least the names and the moves of the pieces; to have a notion of a gambit, and a keen eye for all the means of giving and getting out of check? Do you not think that we should look with a disapprobation, even scorn, upon the father who allowed his son, or the state which allowed its members, to grow up without knowing a pawn from a knight? Yet it is a very plain and elementary truth, that the life, the fortune, and the happiness of every one of us, and, more or less, of those who are connected with us, do depend upon our knowing something of the rules of a game infinitely more difficult and complicated than chess. It is a game which has been played for untold ages, every man and woman of us being one of the two players in a game of his or her own. The chessboard is the world, the pieces are the phenomena of the universe, the rules of the game are what we call the laws of Nature. The player on the other side is hidden from us. We know that his play is always fair, just, and patient. But also we know, to our cost, that he never overlooks a mistake or makes the smallest allowance for ignorance. To the man who plays well, the highest stakes are paid, with that sort of overflowing generosity with which the strong shows delight in strength. And one who plays ill is checkmated—without haste, but without remorse.

My metaphor will remind some of you of the famous picture in which Retzsch has depicted Satan playing at chess with man for his soul. Substitute for the mocking fiend in that picture, a calm, strong angel who is playing for love, as we say, and would rather lose than win— and I should accept it as an image of human life.

Well, what I mean by Education is learning the rules of this mighty game. In other words, education is the instruction of the intellect in the laws of Nature, under which name I include not merely things and their forces, but men and their ways; and the fashioning of the affections and of the will into an earnest and loving desire to move in harmony with those laws ✒ For me, education means neither more nor less than this. Anything which professes to call itself education must be tried by this standard and if it fails to stand the test, I will not call it education, whatever may be the force of authority, or of numbers, upon the other side.

It is important to remember that, in strictness, there is no such thing as an uneducated man ✒ Take an extreme case. Suppose that an adult man, in the full vigor of his faculties, could be suddenly placed in the world, as Adam is said to have been, and then left to do as he best might. How long would he be left uneducated? Not five minutes. Nature would begin to teach him, through the eye, the ear, the touch, the properties of objects. Pain and pleasure would be at his elbow telling him to do this and avoid that; and by slow degrees the man would receive an education, which, if narrow, would be thorough, real, and adequate to his circumstances though there would be no extras and very few accomplishments.

And if to this solitary man entered a second Adam, or, better still, an Eve, a new and greater world, that of social and moral phenomena, would be revealed. Joys and woes, compared with which all others might seem but faint shadows, would spring from the new relations. Happiness and sorrow would take the place of the coarser monitors, pleasure and pain; but conduct would still be shaped by the observation of the natural consequences of actions; or, in other words, by the laws of the nature of man.

¶ To every one of us the world was once as fresh and new as to Adam. And then, long before we were susceptible of any other mode of instruction, Nature took us in hand, and every minute of waking life brought its educational influence, shaping our actions into rough accordance with Nature's laws, so that we might not be ended untimely by too gross disobedience. Nor should I speak of this process of education as past, for any one, be he as old as he may. For every man, the world is as fresh as it was at the first day, and as full of untold novelties for him who has the eyes to see them. And Nature is still continuing her patient education of us in that great university, the universe of which we are all members—Nature having no Test-Acts.

Those who take honors in Nature's university, who learn the laws which govern men and things and obey them, are the really great and successful men in this world. The great mass of mankind are the " Poll," who pick up just enough to get through without much discredit. Those who won't learn at all are plucked; and then you can't come up again. Nature's pluck means extermination.

¶ Thus the question of compulsory education is settled so far as Nature is concerned. Her bill on that question was framed and passed long ago. But, like all compulsory legislation, that of Nature is harsh and wasteful in its operation. Ignorance is visited as sharply as wilful disobedience—incapacity meets with the same punishment as crime. Nature's discipline is not even a word and a blow, and the blow first; but the blow without the word. It is left you to find out why your ears are boxed.

The object of what we commonly call education—that education in which man intervenes and which I shall distinguish as artificial education—is to make good these defects in Nature's methods; to prepare the child to receive Nature's education, neither incapably nor ignorantly, nor with wilful disobedience; and to understand the preliminary symptoms of her displeasure, without waiting for the box on the ear. In short, all artificial education ought to be an anticipation of natural education. And a liberal education is an artificial education which has not only prepared a man to escape the great evils of disobedience to natural laws, but has trained him to appreciate and to seize upon the rewards, which Nature scatters with as free a hand as her penalties.

That man, I think, has had a liberal education, who has been so trained in youth that his body is the ready servant of his will, and does with ease and pleasure all the work that, as a mechanism, it is capable of; whose intellect is a clear, cold, logic engine, with all its parts of equal strength, and in smooth working order; ready, like a steam engine, to be turned to any kind of work, and spin the gossamers as well as forge the anchors of the mind; whose mind is stored with a knowledge of the great and fundamental truths of Nature and of the laws of her operations; one who, no stunted ascetic, is full of life and fire, but whose passions are trained to come to heel by a vigorous will, the servant of a tender conscience; who has learned to love all beauty, whether of Nature or of art, to hate all vileness, and to respect others as himself.

Such an one, and no other, I conceive, has had a liberal education; for he is, as completely as a man can be, in harmony with Nature. He will make the best of her, and she of him. They will get on together rarely; she as his ever beneficent mother; he as her mouthpiece, her conscious self, her minister and interpreter.

—Huxley.

THERE is but one straight road to success, and that is merit. The man who is successful is the man who is useful. Capacity never lacks opportunity. It can not remain undiscovered, because it is sought by too many anxious to use it.—Bourke Cockran.

Blessed are the joymakers.—N. P. Willis.

HE boy is indeed the true apple-eater, and is not to be questioned how he came by the fruit with which his pockets are filled. It belongs to him, and he may steal it if it can not be had in any other way. His own juicy flesh craves the juicy flesh of the apple. Sap draws sap. His fruit-eating has little reference to the state of his appetite. Whether he be full of meat or empty of meat he wants the apple just the same. Before meal or after meal it never comes amiss ∾ The farm-boy munches apples all day long. He has nests of them in the hay-mow, mellowing, to which he makes frequent visits. ℭ The apple is indeed the fruit of youth. As we grow old we crave apples less. It is an ominous sign. When you are ashamed to be seen eating them on the street; when you can carry them in your pocket and your hand not constantly find its way to them; when your neighbor has apples and you have none, and you make no nocturnal visits to his orchard; when your lunch-basket is without them and you can pass a winter's night by the fireside with no thought of the fruit at your elbow, then be assured you are no longer a boy, either in heart or years.

—John Burroughs.

∾ ∾

VIL is unnatural—goodness the natural state of man. Earth has no hopeless islands or continents. We live in a redemptive world. Poverty will end; sin will die; love will triumph and hope will plant flowers on every grave.

—David Swing.

∾ ∾

T is in the nature of things that those who are incapable of happiness should have no idea of it. Happiness is not for wild animals, who can only oscillate between apathy and passion. To be happy, even to conceive happiness, you must be reasonable or (if Nietzsche prefers the word) you must be tamed. You must have taken the measure of your powers, tasted the fruits of your passions and learned your place in the world and what things in it can really serve you. To be happy you must be wise. This happiness is sometimes found instinctively, and then the rudest fanatic can hardly fail to see how lovely it is; but sometimes it comes of having learned something by experience (which empirical people never do) and involves some chastening and renunciation; but it is not less sweet for having this touch of holiness about it, and the spirit of it is healthy and beneficent.

—George Santayana.

∾ ∾

HE Bible has been the Magna Charta of the poor and of the oppressed. Down to modern times, no state has had a constitution in which the interests of the people are so largely taken into account; in which the duties, so much more than the privileges, of rulers are insisted upon, as that drawn up for Israel in Deuteronomy and Leviticus. Nowhere is the fundamental truth, that the welfare of the state, in the long run, depends upon the righteousness of the citizen, so strongly laid down. The Bible is the most democratic book in the world.—Huxley.

∾ ∾

RINTING is a good business. It is clean, honorable, respectable. It is celebrated as a trainer of men for higher stations in life. It has many inspiring traditions and legends. It combines the need for knowledge of everything under the sun: mathematics, mechanics, language, spelling, grammar, color, composition, salesmanship; there is indeed no limit to the accomplishments that are required of the printer. The printer is brought into contact with all other vocations and professions. No vocation or profession can really exist without the printing-press. From text-books to novels, from pamphlets to newspapers, from tickets to tax-bills, no man can evade the printed word.

—Henry P. Porter.

∾ ∾

The world is a looking-glass, and gives back to every man the reflection of his own face. Frown at it, and it in turn will look sourly upon you; laugh at it and with it, and it is a jolly, kind companion.

—William Makepeace Thackeray.

T is said that the Persians, in their ancient constitution, had public schools in which virtue was taught as a liberal art or science; and it is certainly of more consequence to a man, that he has learned to govern his passions in spite of temptation, to be just in his dealings, to be temperate in his pleasures, to support himself with fortitude under his misfortunes, to behave with prudence in all his affairs, and in every circumstance of life; I say, it is of much more real advantage to him, to be thus qualified, than to be a master of all the arts and sciences in the whole world beside. ❡ Virtue itself alone is sufficient to make a man great, glorious and happy. He that is acquainted with Cato, as I am, can not help thinking, as I do now, and will acknowledge he deserves the name, without being honored by it. Cato is a man whom fortune has placed in the most obscure part of the country. His circumstances are such, as only put him above necessity, without affording him many superfluities; yet who is greater than Cato? I happened but the other day to be at a house in town, where, among others, were met men of the most note in this place. Cato had business with some of them, and knocked at the door. The most trifling actions of a man, in my opinion, as well as the smallest features and lineaments of the face, give a nice observer some notion of his mind. Methought he rapped in such a peculiar manner, as seemed of itself to express there was one, who deserved as well as desired admission. He appeared in the plainest country garb; his great coat was coarse, and looked old and threadbare; his linen was homespun; his beard, perhaps of seven days' growth; his shoes thick and heavy; and every part of his dress corresponding. Why was this man received with such concurring respect from every person in the room, even from those who had never known him or seen him before? It was not an exquisite form of person, or grandeur of dress, that struck us with admiration. ❡ I believe long habits of virtue have a sensible effect on the countenance. There was something in the air of his face, that manifested the true greatness of mind, which likewise appeared in all he said, and in every part of his behaviour, obliging us to regard him with a sort of veneration. His aspect is sweetened with humanity and benevolence, and at the same time emboldened with resolution, equally free from diffident bashfulness and an unbecoming assurance. The consciousness of his own innate worth and unshaken integrity renders him calm and undaunted in the presence of the most great and powerful, and upon the most extraordinary occasions. His strict justice and known impartiality make him the arbitrator and decider of all differences, that arise for many miles around him, without putting his neighbors to the charge, perplexity and uncertainty of lawsuits. He always speaks the thing he means, which he is never afraid or ashamed to do, because he knows he always means well, and therefore is never obliged to blush, and feel the confusion of finding himself detected in the meanness of a falsehood. He never contrives ill against his neighbors, and therefore is never seen with a lowering, suspicious aspect. A mixture of innocence and wisdom makes him ever seriously cheerful. His generous hospitality to strangers, according to his ability; his goodness, his charity, his courage in the cause of the oppressed, his fidelity in friendship, his humility, his honesty and sincerity, his moderation, and his loyalty to the

God with His million cares

Went to the left or right,

Leaving our world; and the day

Grew night.

Back from a sphere He came

Over a starry lawn,

Looked at our world; and the dark

Grew dawn.

"Dawn and Dark," by Norman Gale

government; his piety, his temperance, his love to mankind, his magnanimity, his public-spiritedness, and, in fine, his consummate virtue, make him justly deserve to be esteemed the glory of his country.—Franklin.

THE power of a man increases steadily by continuance in one direction. He becomes acquainted with the resistances and with his own tools; increases his skill and strength and learns the favorable moments and favorable accidents. He is his own apprentice, and more time gives a great addition of power, just as a falling body acquires momentum with every foot of the fall.—Emerson.

Truth is such a precious article let us all economize in its use.—Mark Twain.

IT is great, and there is no other greatness—to make one nook of God's creation more fruitful, better, more worthy of God; to make some human heart a little wiser, manlier, happier—more blessed, less accursed.
—Carlyle.

IF time be of all things most precious, wasting time must be the greatest prodigality, since lost time is never found again; and what we call time enough always proves little enough. Let us then be up and doing, and doing to a purpose; so by diligence shall we do more with less perplexity.—Franklin.

ALWAYS in our dreams we hear the turn of the key that shall close the door of the last brothel; the clink of the last coin that pays for the body and soul of a woman; the falling of the last wall that encloses artificially the activity of woman and divides her from man; always we picture the love of the sexes as once a dull, slow, creeping form; then a torpid, earthly chrysalis; at last the full-winged insect, glorious in the sunshine of the future
Today, as we row hard against the stream of life, is it only blindness in our eyes, which have been too long strained, which makes us see, far up the river where it fades into distance, through all the mists that rise from the river-banks, a clear, golden light? Is it only a delusion of the eyes which makes us grasp our oars more lightly and bend our backs lower; though we know well that long before the boat reaches those stretches, other hands than ours will man the oars and guide its helm? Is it all a dream?
—Olive Schreiner.

I KNOW not if I deserve that a laurel-wreath should one day be laid on my coffin. Poetry, dearly as I have loved it, has always been to me but a divine plaything I have never attached any great value to poetical fame; and I trouble myself very little whether people praise my verses or blame them. But lay on my coffin a *sword;* for I was a brave soldier in the Liberation War of humanity.—Heinrich Heine.

I never make the mistake of arguing with people for whose opinions I have no respect.—Gibbon.

TO AWAKEN each morning with a smile brightening my face, to greet the day with reverence, for the opportunities it contains; to approach my work with a clean mind; to hold ever before me, even in the doing of little things, the Ultimate Purpose toward which I am working; to meet men and women with laughter on my lips and love in my heart; to be gentle, kind and courteous through all the hours; to approach the night with weariness that ever wooes sleep and the joy that comes from work well done—this is how I desire to waste wisely my days.
—Thomas Dreier.

WE are foolish, and without excuse foolish, in speaking of the superiority of one sex to the other, as if they could be compared in similar things! Each has what the other has not; each completes the other; they are in nothing alike; and the happiness and perfection of both depend on each asking and receiving from the other what the other only can give.—John Ruskin.

NOT many generations ago, where you now sit, encircled with all that exalts and embellishes civilized life, the rank thistle nodded in the wind, and the wild fox dug his hole unscared. Here lived and loved another race of beings. Beneath the same sun that rolls over your head; the Indian hunter pursued the panting deer; gazing on the same moon that smiles for you, the Indian lover wooed his dusky mate.

❡ Here the wigwam blaze beamed on the tender and helpless, and the councilfire glared on the wise and daring. Now, they dipped their noble limbs in yon sedgy lakes, and now, they paddled the light canoe along yon rocky shores. Here they warred; the echoing whoop, the bloody grapple, the defying death-song, all were here; and when the tiger-strife was over, here curled the smoke of peace ൟ ൟ

Here, too, they worshiped; and from many a dark bosom went up a fervent prayer to the Great Spirit. He had not written his laws for them on tables of stone, but he had traced them on the tables of their hearts. The poor child of Nature knew not the God of Revelation, but the God of the universe he acknowledged in everything around.

And all this has passed away. Across the ocean came a pilgrim bark, bearing the seeds of life and death. The former were sown for you; the latter sprang up in the path of the simple native.

Here and there, a stricken few remain; but how unlike their bold, untamable progenitors. As a race, they have withered from the land. Their arrows are broken, their springs are dried up, their cabins are in dust. Their council-fire has long since gone out on the shore, and their war cry is fast fading to the untrodden west. Slowly and sadly they climb the distant mountains, and read their doom in the setting sun.

—"The Indians," by Charles Sprague.

ൟ ൟ

A more perfect race means a more soulful race, a more soulful race a race having greater capacity for love.—Ellen Key.

IT is by affliction chiefly that the heart of man is purified, and that the thoughts are fixed on a better state. Prosperity, unalloyed and imperfect as it is, has power to intoxicate the imagination, to fix the mind upon the present scene, to produce confidence and elation, and to make him who enjoys affluence and honors forget the hand by which they were bestowed. It is seldom that we are otherwise than by affliction awakened to a sense of our imbecility, or taught to know how little all our acquisitions can conduce to safety or quiet, and how justly we may inscribe to the superintendence of a higher power those blessings which in the wantonness of success we considered as the attainments of our policy and courage.

—Samuel Johnson.

ൟ ൟ

ALL business as now conducted—particularly those lines of business which embrace the so-called industries—requires specialized training and technical education, in fact so much scientific knowledge that the distinctive line between " business" and " profession" is fast disappearing.

Any one who hopes to achieve success, even the average, must know more, or at least as much, about some one thing as any other one, and not only know, but know how to do—and how to utilize his experience and knowledge for the benefit of others.

The crying evil of the young man who enters the business world today is the lack of application, preparation, and thoroughness, with ambition but without the willingness to struggle to gain his desired end. Mental and physical strength comes only through the exercise and working of mind and body.

There is too little idea of personal responsibility; too much of " the world owes me a living," forgetting that if the world does owe you a living you yourself must be your own collector.

—Theodore N. Vail.

ൟ ൟ

It may make a difference to all eternity whether we do right or wrong today.

—James Freeman Clarke.

HAT Raphael is to color, what Mozart is in music, that Burns is in song. With his sweet words, " the mother soothes her child, the lover wooes his bride, the soldier wins his victory." ❧ His biographer says his genius was so overmastering that the news of Burns' arrival at the village inn drew farmers from their fields and at midnight wakened travelers, who left their beds to listen, delighted, until the morn ❧ ❧

One day this child of poverty and obscurity left his plow behind, and entering the drawing-rooms of Edinburgh, met Scotland's most gifted scholars, her noblest lords and ladies. Mid these scholars, statesmen and philosophers, he blazed " like a torch amidst the tapers," showing himself wiser than the scholars, wittier than the humorist, kinglier than the courtliest. And yet, in the very prime of his mid-manhood, Burns lay down to die, a broken-hearted man. He who had sinned much suffered much, and being the victim of his own folly, he was also the victim of ingratitude and misfortune. Bewildered by his debts, he seems like an untamed eagle beating against bars he can not break. The last time he lifted his pen upon the page it was not to give immortal form to some exquisite lyric he had fashioned, but to beg a friend in Edinburgh for a loan of ten pounds to save him from the terrors of a debtor's prison. By contrast with the lot of other worthies, Robert Burns seems to have been the child of good fortune. In the last analysis the blame is with the poet himself. Not want of good fortune without, but want of good guidance within, wrecked his youth. Save Saul alone, history holds no sadder tragedy that that of Burns, who sang " the short and simple annals of the poor."—Newell Dwight Hillis.

❧ ❧

NATURE gives to every time and season some beauties of its own; and from morning to night, as from the cradle to the grave, is but a succession of changes so gentle and easy that we can scarcely mark their progress.—Dickens.

HEALTH is, indeed, so necessary to all the duties as well as pleasures of life, that the crime of squandering it is equal to the folly; and he that for a short gratification brings weakness and diseases upon himself, and for the pleasure of a few years passed in the tumults of diversion and clamors of merriment, condemns the maturer and more experienced part of his life to the chamber and the couch, may be justly reproached, not only as a spendthrift of his happiness, but as a robber of the public; as a wretch that has voluntarily disqualified himself for the business of his station, and refused that part which Providence assigns him in the general task of human nature.—Samuel Johnson.

❧ ❧

Courage and perseverance have a magical talisman, before which difficulties disappear and obstacles vanish into air.—John Quincy Adams.

❧ ❧

AMERICA is God's crucible, the great Melting-Pot where all the races of Europe are melting and reforming! Here you stand, good folk, think I, when I see them at Ellis Island, here you stand in your fifty groups, with your fifty languages and histories, and your fifty blood hatreds and rivalries. But you won't be long like that, brothers, for these are the fires of God you 've come to—these are the fires of God. A fig for your feuds and vendettas! Germans and Frenchmen, Irishmen and Englishmen, Jews and Russians—into the Crucible with you all! God is making the American. The real American has not yet arrived. He is only in the crucible, I tell you—he will be the fusion of all races, the common superman.
—Israel Zangwill.

❧ ❧

IT 'S good to have money and the things that money can buy, but it 's good, too, to check up once in a while and make sure you have n't lost the things that money can't buy.
—George Horace Lorimer.

❧ ❧

He is the happiest, be he king or peasant, who finds peace in his home.—Goethe.

GREAT many people run down jealousy on the score that it is an artificial feeling, as well as practically inconvenient. This is scarcely fair; for the feeling on which it merely attends, like an ill-humored courtier, is self artificial in exactly the same sense and to the same degree. I suppose what is meant by that objection is that jealousy has not always been a character of man; formed no part of that very modest kit of sentiments with which he is supposed to have begun the world; but waited to make its appearance in better days and among richer natures. And this is equally true of love, and friendship, and love of country, and delight in what they call the beauties of nature, and most other things worth having. Love, in particular, will not endure any historical scrutiny: to all who have fallen across it, it is one of the most incontestable facts in the world; but if you begin to ask what it was in other periods and countries, in Greece for instance, the strangest doubts begin to spring up, and everything seems so vague and changing that a dream is logical in comparison. Jealousy, at any rate, is one of the consequences of love; you may like it or not, at pleasure; but there it is.

—Robert Louis Stevenson

The law of worthy life is fundamentally the law of strife. It is only through labor and painful effort, by grim energy and resolute courage, that we move on to better things.—Theodore Roosevelt.

If I should die tonight
And you should come to my cold corpse
and say,
Weeping and heartsick o'er my lifeless
clay—
If I should die tonight,
And you should come in deepest grief
and woe—
And say: " Here 's that ten dollars that
I owe,"
I might arise in my large white cravat
And say, "What 's that? "

If I should die tonight
And you should come to my cold corpse
and kneel,
Clasping my bier to show the grief you feel,
I say, if I should die tonight
And you should come to me, and there
and then
Just even hint at paying me that ten,
I might arise the while,
But I 'd drop dead again.
" If I Should Die To-Night," *by Ben King*

IN China letters are respected not merely to a degree but in a sense which must seem, I think, to you unintelligible and overstrained. But there is a reason for it. Our poets and literary men have taught their successors, for long generations, to look for good not in wealth, not in power, not in miscellaneous activity, but in a trained, a choice, an exquisite appreciation of the most simple and universal relations of life. To feel, and in order to feel to express, or at least to understand the expression of all that is lovely in Nature, all that is poignant and sensitive in man, is to us in itself a sufficient end. A rose in a moonlit garden, the shadow of trees on the turf, almond bloom, scent of pine, the wine-cup and the guitar, these and the pathos of life and death, the long embrace, the hand stretched out in vain, the moment that glides for ever away, with its freight of music and light, into the shadow and hush of the haunted past, all that we have, all that eludes us, a bird on the wing, a perfume escaped on the gale—to all these things we are trained to respond, and the response is what we call literature.—G. Lowes Dickinson.

Reason elevates our thoughts as high as the stars, and leads us through the vast space of this mighty fabric; yet it comes far short of the real extent of our corporeal being.—Samuel Johnson.

The man who trusts men will make fewer mistakes than he who distrusts them.—Cavour.

THERE are two sorts of people in the world, who, with equal degrees of health and wealth, and the other comforts of life, become, the one happy, and the other miserable. This arises very much from the different views in which they consider things, persons and events; and the effect of those different views upon their own minds.

In whatever situation men can be placed they may find conveniences and inconveniences; in whatever company they may find persons and conversation more or less pleasing; at whatever table they may meet with meats and drinks of better and worse taste, dishes better and worse dressed; in whatever climate they will find good and bad weather; under whatever government, they may find good and bad laws, and good and bad administration of those laws; in whatever poem or work of genius they may see faults and beauties; in almost every face and every person they may discover fine features and defects, good and bad qualities.

Under these circumstances the two sorts of people above mentioned fix their attention; those who are disposed to be happy, on the convenience of things, the pleasant parts of conversations, the well-dressed dishes, the goodness of the wines, the fine weather, etc., and enjoy all with cheerfulness. Those who are to be unhappy think and speak only of the contraries. Hence they are continually discontented themselves, and by their remarks, sour the pleasure of society, offend personally many people, and make themselves everywhere disagreeable. If this turn of mind was founded in nature, such unhappy persons would be the more to be pitied. But as the disposition to criticise, and to be disgusted, is perhaps taken up originally by imitation, and is unawares grown into a habit, which, though at present strong, may nevertheless be cured, when those who have it are convinced of its bad effects on their felicity. . . . If these people will not change this bad habit, and condescend to be pleased with what is pleasing, without fretting themselves and others about the contraries, it is good for others to avoid an acquaintance with them; which is always disagreeable, and sometimes very inconvenient, especially when one finds one's self entangled in their quarrels.—Franklin.

I NEED not tell you what it is to be knocking about in an open boat. I remember nights and days of calm when we pulled, we pulled, and the boat seemed to stand still, as if bewitched within the circle of the sea horizon. I remember the heat, the deluge of rain-squalls that kept us bailing for dear life (but filled our water-cask), and I remember sixteen hours on end with a mouth dry as a cinder and a steering-oar over the stern to keep my first command head on to a breaking sea. I did not know how good a man I was till then. I remember the drawn faces, the dejected figures of my two men, and I remember my youth and the feeling that will never come back any more—the feeling that I could last for ever, outlast the sea, the earth, and all men; the deceitful feeling that lures us on to joys, to perils, to love, to vain effort—to death; the triumphant conviction of strength, the heat of life in the handful of dust, the glow in the heart that with every year grows dim, grows cold, grows small, and expires—and expires, too soon—before life itself.—Joseph Conrad.

TO be strong and true; to be generous in praise and appreciation of others; to impute worthy motives even to enemies; to give without expectation of return; to practise humility, tolerance and self-restraint; to make the best use of time and opportunity; to keep the mind pure and the judgment charitable; to extend intelligent sympathy to those in distress; to cultivate quietness and non-resistance; to seek truth and righteousness; to work, love, pray and serve daily, to aspire greatly, labor cheerfully, and take God at His word—this is to travel heavenward.—Grenville Kleiser.

Manners,—the final and perfect flower of noble character.—William Winter.

MEN I find to be a sort of beings very badly constructed, as they are generally more easily provoked than reconciled, more disposed to do mischief to each other than to make reparation, much more easily deceived than undeceived, and having more pride and even pleasure in killing than in begetting one another; for without a blush they assemble in great armies at noonday to destroy, and when they have killed as many as they can, they exaggerate the number to augment the fancied glory.

In what light we are viewed by superior beings may be gathered from a piece of late West India news. A young angel of distinction being sent down to this world on some business, for the first time, had an old courier-spirit assigned him as a guide. They arrived over the seas of Martinico, in the middle of the long day of obstinate fight between the fleets of Rodney and De Grasse. When, through the clouds of smoke, he saw the fire of the guns, the decks covered with mangled limbs, and bodies dead or dying; the ships sinking, burning, or blown into the air; and the quantity of pain, misery, and destruction, the crews yet alive were thus with so much eagerness dealing round to one another, he turned angrily to his guide, and said: " You blundering blockhead, you are ignorant of your business; you undertook to conduct me to the earth, and you have brought me into hell!" " No, Sir," says the guide, " I have made no mistake; this is really the earth, and these are men. Devils never treat one another in this cruel manner; they have more sense, and more of what men (vainly) call humanity."—Franklin.

No man is the absolute lord of his life.
—Owen Meredith.

IT is now sixteen or seventeen years since I saw the Queen of France, then the Dauphiness, at Versailles; and surely never lighted on this orb, which she hardly seemed to touch, a more delightful vision. I saw her just above the horizon, decorating and cheering the elevated sphere she just began to move in; glittering like the morning star, full of life and splendor, and joy. Oh! what a revolution! and what a heart must I have to contemplate without emotion that elevation and that fall! Little did I dream when she added titles of veneration to those of enthusiastic, distant, respectful love, that she should ever be obliged to carry the sharp antidote against disgrace concealed in that bosom; little did I dream that I should have lived to see such disasters fallen upon her in a nation of gallant men, in a nation of men of honor and of cavaliers ⚬ I thought ten thousand swords must have leaped from their scabbards to avenge even a look that threatened her with insult. But the age of Chivalry is gone. That of sophisters, economists, and calculators has succeeded, and the glory of Europe is extinguished for ever. Never, never more, shall we behold that generous loyalty to rank and sex, that proud submission, that dignified obedience, that subordination of the heart, which kept alive, even in servitude itself, the spirit of an exalted freedom. The unbought grace of life, the cheap defence of nations, the nurse of manly sentiments and heroic enterprise is gone! It is gone, that sensibility of principle, that chastity of honor, which felt a stain like a wound, which inspired courage whilst it mitigated ferocity, which ennobled whatever it touched, and under which vice itself lost half its evil, by losing all its grossness.—Edmund Burke.

WE make daily great improvements in *natural*, there is one I wish to see in *moral* philosophy; the discovery of a plan, that would induce and oblige nations to settle their disputes without first cutting one another's throats ⚬ When will human reason be sufficiently improved to see the advantage of this? When will men be convinced, that even successful wars become misfortunes, who unjustly commenced them, and who triumphed blindly in their success, not seeing all its consequences.—Franklin.

THE presence that thus rose strangely beside the waters, is expressive of what in the ways of a thousand years men had come to desire. Hers is the head upon which " all the ends of the world are come," and the eyelids are a little weary. It is a beauty wrought out from within upon the flesh, the deposit, little cell by cell, of strange thoughts and fantastic reveries and exquisite passions. Set it for a moment beside one of those white Greek goddesses or beautiful women of antiquity, and how would they be troubled by this beauty, into which the soul with all its maladies has passed! All the thoughts and experience of the world have etched and moulded there, in that which they have of power to refine and make expressive the outward form, the animalism of Greece, the lust of Rome, the reverie of the middle age with its spiritual ambition and imaginative loves, the return of the Pagan world, the sins of the Borgias. She is older than the rocks among which she sits; like the vampire, she has been dead many times, and learned the secrets of the grave; and has been a diver in deep seas, and keeps their fallen day about her; and trafficked for strange webs with Eastern merchants; and, as Leda, was the mother of Helen of Troy, and, as Saint Anne, the mother of Mary; and all this has been to her but as the sound of lyres and flutes, and lives only in the delicacy with which it has moulded the changing lineaments, and tinged the eyelids and the hands.
An appreciation of da Vinci's Mona Lisa (" La Gioconda"), by Walter Pater.

Over the shoulders and slopes of the dune
I saw the white daisies go down to the sea,
A host in the sunshine, an army in June,
The people God sends us to set our heart free.

The bobolinks rallied them up from the dell,
The orioles whistled them out of the wood;
And all of their saying was, "Earth, it is well! "
And all of their dancing was, " Life, thou art good!"

" Daisies," *by Bliss Carman*

PERFECT love has this advantage in it, that it leaves the possessor of it nothing farther to desire. There is one object (at least) in which the soul finds absolute content, for which it seeks to live, or dares to die. The heart has, as it were, filled up the moulds of the imagination. The truth of passion keeps pace with and outvies the extravagance of mere language. There are no words so fine, no flattery so soft, that there is not a sentiment beyond them, that it is impossible to express, at the bottom of the heart where true love is. What idle sounds the common phrases, *adorable creature, angel, divinity,* are! What a proud reflection it is to have a feeling answering to all these, rooted in the breast, unalterable unutterable, to which all other feelings are light and vain! Perfect love reposes on the object of its choice, like the halcyon on the wave; and the air of heaven is around it.—William Hazlitt

I LAY very little stress either upon asking or giving advice. Generally speaking, they who ask advice know what they wish to do, and remain firm to their intentions. A man may allow himself to be enlightened on various points, even upon matters of expediency and duty; but, after all, he must determine his course of action for himself.
—Wilhelm von Humboldt.

Bed is a bundle of paradoxes; we go to it with reluctance, yet we quit it with regret; we make up our minds every night to leave it early, but we make up our bodies every morning to keep it late.—Colton.

UT the iniquity of oblivion blindly scattereth her poppy, and deals with the memory of men without distinction to merit of perpetuity. Who can but pity the founder of the pyramids? Herostratus lives that burnt the temple of Diana, he is almost lost that built it; Time hath spared the epitaph of Adrian's horse, confounded that of himself. In vain we compute our felicities by the advantages of our good names, since bad have equal durations; and Thersites is like to live as long as Agamemnon ◦ Who knows whether the best of men be known, or whether there be not more remarkable persons forgot, than any that stand remembered in the known account of Time? . . . ¶ Oblivion is not to be hired; the greater part must be content to be as though they had not been; to be found in the register of God, not in the record of man. . . . The number of the dead long exceedeth all that shall live. The night of time far surpasseth the day, and who knows when was the Equinox? Every hour adds unto that current arithmetic, which scarce stands one moment. And since death must be the Lucina of life, and even Pagans could doubt whether thus to live were to die; since our longest sun sets at right descensions, and makes but winter arches, and therefore it can not be long before we lie down in darkness and have our light in ashes; since the brother of Death daily haunts us with dying Mementoes, and Time that grows old itself bids us hope no long duration, diuturnity is a dream and folly of expectation.

Darkness and light divide the course of Time, and oblivion shares with memory a great part even of our living beings; we slightly remember our felicities, and the smartest strokes of affliction leave but short smart upon us.

In vain do individuals hope for immortality, or any patent from oblivion, in preservations below the Moon. . . . But man is a noble animal, splendid in ashes and pompous in the grave, solemnizing nativities and deaths with equal lustre, nor omitting ceremonies of bravery in the infamy of his nature. —Sir Thomas Browne.

◦ ◦

Sun set and evening star,
*   And one clear call for me!*
And may there be no moaning of the bar
*   When I put out to sea.*

But such a tide as moving seems asleep,
*   Too full for sound and foam,*
When that which drew from out the
*   boundless deep*
*   Turns again home.*

Twilight and evening bell,
*   And after that the dark!*
And may there be no sadness of farewell
*   When I embark.*

For tho' from out our bourne of Time
*   and place*
*   The flood may bear me far,*
I hope to see my Pilot face to face
*   When I have crost the bar.*
"Crossing the Bar," *by Alfred Lord Tennyson*

OW it appears to me that almost any Man may, like the spider, spin from his own inwards his own airy Citadel—the points of leaves and twigs on which the spider begins her work are few, and she fills the air with a beautiful circuiting. Man should be content with as few points to tip with the fine Web of his Soul, and weave a tapestry empyrean—full of symbols for his spiritual eye, of softness for his spiritual touch, of space for his wandering, of distinctness for his luxury. . . . I was led into these thoughts, my dear Reynolds, by the beauty of the morning operating on a sense of Idleness. I have not read any Books—the Morning said I was right— I had no idea but of the Morning, and the Thrush said I was right.
—John Keats.

◦ ◦

What we can do for another is the test of powers; what we can suffer for is the test of love.—Bishop Westcott.

◦ ◦

A picture is a poem without words.
—Horace.

E that hath wife and children hath given hostages to fortune; for they are impediments to great enterprises, either of virtue or mischief. Certainly the best works, and of greatest merit for the public, have proceeded from the unmarried or childless men, which both in affection and means have married and endowed the public. Yet it were great reason that those that have children should have greatest care of future times, unto which they know they must transmit their dearest pledges. Unmarried men are best friends, best masters, best servants; but not always best subjects; for they are light to run away—and almost all fugitives are of that condition. A single life doth well with churchmen, for charity will hardly water the ground where it must first fill a pool. It is indifferent for judges and magistrates; for if they be facile and corrupt, you shall have a servant five times worse than a wife. For soldiers, I find generals commonly, in their hortatives, put men in mind of their wives and their children, and I think the despising of marriage amongst the Turks maketh the vulgar soldier more base. Certainly, wife and children are a kind of discipline of humanity; and single men, though they be many times more charitable, because their means are less exhaust, yet, on the other side, they are more cruel and hardhearted (good to make severe inquisitors), because their tenderness is not so oft called upon. Wives are young men's mistresses; companions for middle age, and old men's nurses; so that a man may have a quarrel to marry when he will

But yet he was reputed one of the wise men that made answer to the question when a man should marry: " A young man, not yet; an elder man, not at all."—Francis Bacon.

Success lies, not in achieving what you aim at, but in aiming at what you ought to achieve, and pressing forward, sure of achievement here, or if not here, hereafter.—R. F. Horton.

TIBERIUS, maintaining an honorable and just cause, and possessed of eloquence sufficient to have made a less creditable action appear plausible, was no safe or easy antagonist, when, with the people crowding around the hustings, he took his place and spoke in behalf of the poor. " The savage beasts," said he, " in Italy, have their particular dens, they have their places of repose and refuge; but the men who bear arms, and expose their lives for the safety of their country, enjoy in the meantime nothing in it but the air and light; and, having no houses or settlements of their own, are constrained to wander from place to place with their wives and children." He told them that the commanders were guilty of a ridiculous error, when, at the head of their armies, they exhorted the common soldiers to fight for their sepulchers and altars; when not any amongst so many Romans is possessed of either altar or monument, neither have they any houses of their own, or hearths of their ancestors to defend. They fought indeed and were slain, but it was to maintain the luxury and the wealth of other men. They were styled the masters of the world, but had not one foot of ground they could call their own.—Plutarch.

ALL real and wholesome enjoyments possible to man have been just as possible to him since first he was made of the earth as they are now; and they are possible to him chiefly in peace. To watch the corn grow, and the blossoms set; to draw hard breath over plowshare or spade; to read, to think, to love, to hope, to pray—these are the things that make men happy. . . . Now and then a wearied king, or a tormented slave, found out where the true kingdoms of the world were, and possessed himself, in a furrow or two of garden ground, of a truly infinite dominion.

—John Ruskin.

Great minds have purposes, others have wishes. Little minds are tamed and subdued by misfortune; but great minds rise above them—Washington Irving.

KNOW not whether others share in my feelings on this point; but I have often thought that if I were compelled to forego England, and to live in China, and among Chinese manners and modes of life and scenery, I should go mad. The causes of my horror lie deep; and some of them must be common to others ଽ Southern Asia, in general, is the seat of awful images and associations. As the cradle of the human race, it would alone have a dim and reverential feeling connected with it. But there are other reasons. No man can pretend that the wild, barbarous and capricious super stitions of Africa, or of savage tribes elsewhere, affect him in the way that he is affected by the ancient, monumental, cruel and elaborate religions of Indostan, etc. The mere antiquity of Asiatic things, of their institutions, histories, modes of faith, etc., is so impressive, that to me the vast age of the race and name overpowers the sense of youth in the individual ଽ A young Chinese seems to me an antediluvian man renewed. Even Englishmen, though not bred in any knowledge of such institutions, can not but shudder at the mystic sublimity of *castes* that have flowed apart, and refused to mix, through such immemorial tracts of time; nor can any man fail to be awed by the names of the Ganges or the Euphrates. It contributes much to these feelings, that Southern Asia is, and has been for thousands of years, the part of the earth most swarming with human life: the great *officina gentium*. Man is a weed in those regions. The vast empires also, into which the enormous population of Asia has always been cast, give a further sublimity to the feelings associated with all Oriental names or images. In China,

Do you fear the force of the wind,
The slash of the rain?
Go face them and fight them,
Be savage again.
Go hungry and cold like the wolf,
Go wade like the crane:
The palms of your hands will thicken
The skin of your cheek will tan,
You 'll grow ragged and weary and swarthy,
But you 'll walk like a man!

"Do You Fear the Wind?" *by Hamlin Garland*

over and above what it has in common with the rest of Southern Asia, I am terrified by the modes of life, by the manners, and the barrier of utter abhorrence and want of sympathy placed between us by feelings deeper than I can analyze. I could sooner live with lunatics or brute animals. All this, and much more than I can say, or have time to say, the reader must enter into before he can comprehend the unimaginable horror which these dreams of Oriental imagery and mythological tortures impressed upon me. Under the connecting feeling of tropical heat and vertical sunlights, I brought together all creatures, birds, beasts, reptiles, all trees and plants, usages and appearances, that are found in all tropical regions, and assembled them together in China or Indostan. From kindred feelings, I soon brought Egypt and all her gods under the same law. I was stared at, hooted at, grinned at, chattered at, by monkeys, by parroquets, by cockatoos. I ran into pagodas; and was fixed, for centuries, at the summit or in secret rooms; I was the idol; I was the priest; I was worshiped; I was sacrificed. I fled from the wrath of Brama through all the forests of Asia; Vishnu hated me; Seeva laid wait for me. I came suddenly upon Isis and Osiris: I had done a deed, they said, which the ibis and the crocodile trembled at. I was buried, for a thousand years, in stone coffins, with mummies and sphinxes, in narrow chambers at the heart of eternal pyramids. I was kissed, with cancerous kisses, by crocodiles; and laid, confounded with all unutterable slimy things, amongst reeds and Nilotic mud ଽ ଽ

I thus give the reader some slight abstraction of my Oriental dreams, which always filled me with such amazement at the monstrous scenery, that horror seemed absorbed, for a while, in sheer astonishment. Sooner or later came a reflux of feeling that swallowed up the astonishment, and left me, not so much in terror, as in hatred and abomination of what I saw. Over every form, and threat, and punishment, and dim, sightless incarceration, brooded a sense of eternity and infinity that drove me into an oppression as of madness. Into these dreams only it was, with one or two slight exceptions, that any circumstances of physical horror entered. All before had been moral and spiritual terrors. But here the main agents were ugly birds, or snakes, or crocodiles; especially the last. The cursed crocodile became to me the object of more horror than almost all the rest. I was compelled to live with him; and (as was always the case almost in my dreams) for centuries. I escaped sometimes, and found myself in Chinese houses, with cane tables, etc. All the feet of the tables, sofas, etc., soon became instinct with life: the abominable head of the crocodile, and his leering eyes, looked out at me, multiplied into a thousand repetitions; and I stood loathing and fascinated. And so often did this hideous reptile haunt my dreams, that many times the very same dream was broken up in the very same way: I heard gentle voices speaking to me (I hear everything when I am sleeping); and instantly I awoke: it was broad noon; and my children were standing, hand in hand, at my bedside; come to show me their colored shoes, or new frocks, or to let me see them dressed for going out. I protest that so awful was the transition from the crocodile, and the other unutterable monsters and abortions of my dreams, to the sight of innocent *human* natures and of infancy, that, in the mighty and sudden revulsion of mind I wept, and could not forbear it, as I kissed their faces.—" Opium Dreams," by Thomas de Quincey.

०० ००

The tallest and the smallest among us are so alike diminutive and pitifully base, it is a meanness to calculate the difference.—Thackeray.

HERE is my creed. I believe in one God, the creator of the universe. That he governs it by his Providence. That he ought to be worshiped. That the most acceptable service we render to him is doing good to his other children. That the soul of man is immortal, and will be treated with justice in another life respecting its conduct in this. These I take to be the fundamental points in all sound religion.

As to Jesus of Nazareth, I think his system of morals and his religion as he left them to us, the best the world ever saw or is like to see; but I apprehend it has received various corrupting changes, and I have some doubts as to his divinity; though it is a question I do not dogmatize upon, having never studied it, and think it needless to busy myself with it now, when I expect soon an opportunity of knowing the truth with less trouble. I see no harm, however, in its being believed, if that belief has the good consequence, as probably it has, of making his doctrines more respected and more observed; especially as I do not perceive, that the Supreme takes it amiss, by distinguishing the unbelievers in his government of the world with any peculiar marks of his displeasure. ❡ I shall only add, respecting myself, that, having experienced the goodness of that Being in conducting me prosperously through a long life, I have no doubt of its continuance in the next, though without the smallest conceit of meriting such goodness.—Franklin.

०० ००

So to conduct one's life as to realize oneself—this seems to me the highest attainment possible to a human being. It is the task of one and all of us, but most of us bungle it.—Ibsen.

०० ००

DEBT, grinding debt, whose iron face the widow, the orphan, and the sons of genius fear and hate; debt, which consumes so much time, which so cripples and disheartens a great spirit with cares that seem so base, is a preceptor whose lessons can not be foregone, and is needed most by those who suffer from it most.
—Emerson.

POOR Relation is one of the most irrelevant things in nature—a piece of impertinent correspondency,—an odious approximation,—a haunting conscience,—a preposterous shadow, lengthening in the noon-tide of our prosperity,—an unwelcome remembrancer,—a perpetually recurring mortification,—a drain on your purse, a more intolerable dun upon your pride,—a drawback upon success,—a rebuke to your rising,—a stain in your blood,—a blot on your 'scutcheon—a rent in your garment,—a death's head at your banquet,—Agothocle's pot,—a Mordecai in your gate, a Lazarus at your door,—a lion in your path,—a frog in your chamber,—a fly in your ointment,—a mote in your eye,—a triumph to your enemy, an apology to your friends,—the one thing not needful,—the hail in harvest,—the ounce of sour in a pound of sweet. ❡ He is known by his knock. Your heart telleth you, " That is Mr.—." A rap, between familiarity and respect; that demands, and at the same time seems to despair of, entertainment. He entereth smiling and—embarrassed. He holdeth out his hand to you to shake, and—draweth it back again. He casually looketh in about dinner-time—when the table is full. He offereth to go away, seeing you have company,—but is induced to stay. He filleth a chair, and your visitor's two children are accommodated at a side-table. He never cometh upon open days, when your wife says, with some complacency, " My dear, perhaps Mr.—— will drop in today." He remembereth birthdays—and professeth he is fortunate to have stumbled upon one. He declareth against

The violet is much too shy,
The rose too little so;
I think I 'll ask the buttercup
If I may be her beau.

When winds go by, I 'll nod to her
And she will nod to me,
And I will kiss her on the cheek
As gently as may be.

And when the mower cuts us down,
Together we will pass,
I smiling at the buttercup,
She smiling at the grass.

" A Song the Grass Sings,"
by Charles G. Blanden

fish, the turbot being small,—yet suffereth himself to be importuned into a slice against his first resolution. He sticketh by the port,—yet will be prevailed upon to empty the remaining glass of claret, if a stranger press it upon him. He is a puzzle to the servants, who are fearful of being too obsequious, or not civil enough, to him. The guests think " they have seen him before." Every one speculateth upon his condition; and the most part take him to be—a tide-waiter. He calleth you by your Christian name, to imply that his other is the same with your own. He is too familiar by half, yet you wish he had less diffidence. With half the familiarity, he might pass for a casual dependant; with more boldness, he would be in no danger of being taken for what he is. He is too humble for a friend; yet taketh on him more state than befits a client. He is a worse guest than a country tenant, inasmuch as he bringeth up no rent—yet 't is odds, from his garb and demeanor, that your guests take him for one. He is asked to make one at the whist-table; refuseth on the score of poverty, and—resents being left out. When the company break up, he profereth to go for a coach—and lets the servant go. He recollects your grandfather; and will thrust in some mean and quite unimportant anecdote—of the family as " he is blest in seeing it now." He reviveth past situations, to institute what he calleth—favorable comparisons. With a reflecting sort of congratulation, he will inquire the price of your furniture; and insults you with a special commendation of your window-curtains ๑ He is of opinion that the urn is the more elegant shape, but after all, there was something more comfortable about the old tea-kettle; which you must remember. He dare say you must find a great convenience in having a carriage of your own, and appealeth to your lady if it is not so. Inquireth if you have had your arms done in vellum yet; and did not know, till lately, that such-and-such had been the crest of the family. His memory is unseasonable; his compliments perverse; his talk a trouble; his stay pertinacious; and when he goeth away, you dismiss his chair into a corner, as precipitately as possible, and feel fairly rid of two nuisances.

There is a worse evil under the sun, and that is—a female Poor Relation. You may do something with the other; you may pass him off tolerably well; but your indigent she-relation is hopeless. " He is an old humorist," you may say, " and affects to go threadbare. His circumstances are better than folks would take them to be. You are fond of having a Character at your table, and truly he is one." But in the indications of female poverty there can be no disguise. No woman dresses below herself from mere caprice *so so*

The truth must out without shuffling. " She is plainly related to the L——s; or what does she at their house? " She is, in all probability, your wife's cousin. Nine times out of ten, at least, this is the case. Her garb is something between a gentlewoman and a beggar, yet the former evidently predominates. She is most provokingly humble, and ostentatiously sensible to her inferiority. He may require to be repressed sometimes,—*aliquando sufflaminadus erat,* —but there is no raising her. You send her soup at dinner, and she begs to be helped—after the gentlemen. Mr.—— requests the honor of taking wine with her; she hesitates between Port and Madeira, and chooses the former— because he does. She calls the servant *Sir;* and insists on not troubling him to hold her plate. The housekeeper patronizes her. The children's governess takes upon her to correct her, when she has mistaken the piano for harpsichord.
—Charles Lamb.

THE poet is chiefly distinguished from other men by a greater promptness to think and feel without immediate external excitement, and a greater power in expressing such thoughts and feelings as are produced in him in that manner. ¶ But these passions and thoughts and feelings are the general passions and thoughts and feelings of men. And with what are they connected? Undoubtedly with our moral sentiments and animal sensations, and with the causes which excite these; with the operations of the elements, and the appearances of the visible universe; with storm and sunshine, with the revolutions of the seasons, with cold and heat, with loss of friends and kindred, with injuries and resentments, gratitude and hope, with fear and sorrow. These, and the like, are the sensations and objects which the Poet describes, as they are the sensations of other men and the objects which interest them.—William Wordsworth.

so so

I SEND you herewith a bill for ten louis d'ors. I do not pretend to *give* such a sum; I only *lend* it to you. When you shall return to your country with a good character, you can not fail of getting into some business, that will in time enable you to pay all your debts. In that case, when you meet with another honest man in similar distress, you must pay me by lending this sum to him; enjoining him to discharge the debt by a like operation, when he shall be able, and shall meet with such another opportunity. I hope it may thus go through many hands, before it meets with a knave that will stop its progress. This is a trick of mine for doing a deal of good with a little money. I am not rich enough to afford *much* in good works, and so am obliged to be cunning and make the most of a *little.*—Franklin.

so so

JUSTICE is the only worship. Love is the only priest. Ignorance is the only slavery. Happiness is the only good. The time to be happy is now. The place to be happy is here. The way to be happy is to make other people happy.—R. G. Ingersoll.

N the early days of the anti-slavery agitation, a meeting was called at Faneuil Hall, in Boston, which a good-natured mob of soldiers was hired to suppress. They took possession of the floor and danced breakdowns and shouted choruses and refused to hear any of the orators upon the platform. The most eloquent pleaded with them in vain. They were urged by the memories of the Cradle of Liberty, for the honor of Massachusetts, for their own honor as Boston boys, to respect liberty of speech. ℂ But they still laughed and sang and danced, and were proof against every appeal. At last a man suddenly arose from among themselves, and began to speak. Struck by his tone and quaint appearance, and with the thought that he might be one of themselves, the mob became suddenly still. " Well, fellow-citizens," he said, " I would n't be quiet if I did n't want to." The words were greeted with a roar of delight from the mob, which supposed it had found its champion, and the applause was unceasing for five minutes, during which the strange orator tranquilly awaited his chance to continue. The wish to hear more hushed the tumult, and when the hall was still he resumed: " No, I certainly would n't stop if I had n't a mind to; but then, if I were you, I would have a mind to!" ℂ The oddity of the remark and the earnestness of the tone, held the crowd silent, and the speaker continued: " Not because this is Faneuil Hall, nor for the honor of Massachusetts, nor because you are Boston boys, but because you are men, and because honorable and generous men always love fair play." ✦ The mob was conquered. Free speech and fair play were secured. Public opinion can do what it has a mind to do in this country. If it be debased and demoralized, it is the most odious of tyrants. It is Nero and Caligula multiplied by millions. Can there then be a more stringent public duty for every man —and the greater the intelligence the greater the duty— than to take care, by all the influence he can command, that the country, the majority, public opinion, shall have a mind to do only what is just and pure, and humane?—George William Curtis.

✦ ✦

I must go down to the seas again, to the lonely sea and the sky,
And all I ask is a tall ship and a star to steer her by;
And the wheel's kick and the wind's song and the white sail's shaking,
And a gray mist on the sea's face and a gray dawn breaking.

I must go down to the seas again, for the call of the running tide
Is a wild call and a clear call that may not be denied;
And all I ask is a windy day with the white clouds flying,
And the flung spray and the blown spume, and the sea-gulls crying.

I must go down to the seas again, to the vagrant gypsy life,
To the gull's way and the whale's way where the wind's like a whetted knife,
And all I ask is a merry yarn from a laughing fellow-rover,
And quiet sleep and a sweet dream when the long trick's over.

" Sea-Fever," *by John Masefield,*

T is all very fine to talk about tramps and morality. Six hours of police surveillance (such as I have had), or one brutal rejection from an inn door, change your views upon the subject like a course of lectures. As long as you keep in the upper regions, with all the world bowing to you as you go, social arrangements have a very handsome air; but once get under the wheels, and you wish Society were at the devil. I will give most respectable men a fortnight of such a life, and then I will offer them two pence for what remains of their morality.—Robert Louis Stevenson.

✦ ✦

When a firm, decisive spirit is recognized it is curious to see how the space clears around a man and leaves him room and freedom.—John Foster.

IKE all highly developed literatures, the Bible contains a great deal of sensational fiction, imagined with intense vividness, appealing to the most susceptible passions, and narrated with a force which the ordinary man is quite unable to resist. Perhaps only an expert can thoroughly appreciate the power with which a story well told, or an assertion well made, takes possession of a mind not specially trained to criticize it. Try to imagine all that is most powerful in English literature bound into one volume, and offered to a comparatively barbarous race as an instrument of civilization invested with supernatural authority! Indeed, let us leave what we call barbarous races out of the question, and suppose it offered to the English nation on the same assumptions as to its nature and authority which the children in our popular schools are led to make today concerning the Bible under the School Board compromise! ᔰ How much resistance would there be to the illusion created by the art of our great storytellers? Who would dare to affirm that the men and women created by Chaucer, Shakespeare, Bunyan, Fielding, Goldsmith, Scott and Dickens had never existed? Who could resist the force of conviction carried by the tremendous assertive power of Cobbett, the gorgeous special-pleading of Ruskin, or the cogency of Sir Thomas More, or even Matthew Arnold? Above all, who could stand up against the inspiration and moral grandeur of our prophets and poets, from Langland to Blake and Shelley? The power of Scripture has not waned with the ages. Why not teach children the realities of inspiration and revelation as they work daily through scribes and lawgivers? It would, at all events, make better journalists and parish councillors of them—George Bernard Shaw.

ᔰ ᔰ

The man who foolishly does me wrong, I will return to him the protection of my most ungrudging love; and the more evil comes from him, the more good shall go from me.—Buddha.

HERE is only one wish realizable on the earth; only one thing that can be perfectly attained: Death. And from a variety of circumstances we have no one to tell us whether it be worth attaining. ❡ A strange picture we make on our way to our chimeras, ceaselessly marching, grudging ourselves the time for rest; indefatigable, adventurous pioneers. It is true that we shall never reach the goal; it is even more than probable that there is no such place; and if we lived for centuries, and were endowed with the powers of a god, we should find ourselves not much nearer what we wanted at the end. O toiling hands of mortals! O unwearied feet, travelling ye know not whither! Soon, soon, it seems to you, you must come forth on some conspicuous hilltop, and but a little way further, against the setting sun, descry the spires of El Dorado. Little do ye know your own blessedness; for to travel hopefully is a better thing than to arrive, and the true success is to labor.
—Robert Louis Stevenson.

ᔰ ᔰ

HAT is the best solitude that comes closest in the human form—your friend, your other self, who leaves you alone, yet cheers you: who peoples your house or your field and wood with tender remembrances: who stands between your yearning heart and the great outward void that you try in vain to warm and fill; who in his own person and spirit clothes for you, and endows with tangible form, all attractions and subtle relations and meanings that draw you to the woods and fields. What the brooks and the trees and the birds said so faintly and vaguely, he speaks with warmth and directness. Indeed, your friend complements and completes your solitude and you experience its charm without desolation.—John Burroughs.

ᔰ ᔰ

AD we lived, I should have a tale to tell of the hardihood, the endurance and the courage of my companions which would have stirred the hearts of every Englishman. These rough notes and our dead bodies must tell the story.
—Captain Robert F. Scott.

RIENDS, who would have acquitted me, I would like to talk with you about this thing which has happened, before I go to the place at which I must die. Stay then awhile, for we may as well talk with one another while there is time. You are my friends, and I should like to show you the meaning of this event which has happened to me ☞ O my judges—for so I may truly call you, I should like to tell you of a wonderful circumstance: Hitherto the familiar oracle within me has constantly been in the habit of opposing me, even in trifles, if I was going to make a slip or err in any matter; and now, as you see, there has come upon me the last and worst evil. But the oracle made no sign of opposition, either as I was leaving my house and going out in the morning, or while I was speaking, at anything which I was going to say; and yet I have often been stopped in the middle of a speech; but now in nothing that I either said or did touching this matter has the oracle opposed me. What do I take to be the explanation of this! I will tell you. I regard this as a great proof that what has happened to me is a good; and that those who think that death is an evil are in error. For the customary sign would surely have opposed me had I been going to evil and not to good.

Let us reflect in another way, and we shall see that there is no great reason to hope that death is a good. For one of two things—either death is a state of nothingness; or, as men say, there is a change and migration of the soul from this world to another.

Now if you suppose that there is no consciousness, but a sleep like the sleep of him who is undisturbed even by the sight of dreams, death will be an unspeakable gain. For if a person were to select the night in which his sleep was undisturbed even by dreams, and were to compare this with the other days and nights of his life; and then were to tell us how many days and nights he had passed in the course of his life better and more pleasantly than this one, I think this man—I will not say a private man, but even the great king—will not find many such days or nights, when compared with others. Now if death is like this I say that to die is gain; for eternity is then only a single night. ❡ But if death is the journey to another place—and there, as men say, all the dead are—what good can be greater than this? If, indeed, when the pilgrim arrives in the world below, he is delivered from the professors of justice in this world, and finds the true judges who are said to give judgment there—Minos, and Rhadamanthus, and Æacus, and Triptolemus, and other sons of God who were righteous in their own life—that pilgrimage will be worth making.

Above all, I shall then be able to continue my search into true and false knowledge, as in this world, so also in that. And I shall find out who is wise, and who pretends to be wise and is not. What would not a man give to be able to examine the leader of the Trojan expedition; or Odysseus, or Sisyphus, or numberless others—men and women, too! What infinite delight would there be in conversing with them and asking questions!—in another world they do not put a man to death for asking questions; assuredly not. For besides being happier in that world than in this, they will be immortal, if what is said be true. Wherefore, be of good cheer about death, and know of a certainty that no evil can happen to a good man, either in this life or after death. He and his are not neglected by the gods, nor has my own

I strove with none; for none was worth my strife.

Nature I loved and, next to Nature, Art!

I warmed both hands before the fires of life;

It sinks, and I am ready to depart.

"I Strove With None," *by Walter Savage Landor*

approaching end happened by mere chance. But I see clearly that to die and be released was better for me; and therefore the oracle gave no sign.

For which reason, also, I am not angry with my condemners or with my accusers. They have done me no harm, although they did not mean to do me any good; and for this I may gently blame them. Still I have a favor to ask of them ⧴ When my sons grow up, I would ask you, my friends, to punish them. And I would have you trouble them, as I have troubled you, if they seem to care about riches or anything more. than about virtue. ⧉ Or if they pretend to be something when they are really nothing, then reprove them, as I have reproved you, for not caring about that for which they ought to care, and thinking that they are really something when they are really nothing. And if you do this, I and my sons will have received justice at your hands ⧴ ⧴

The hour of my departure has arrived, and we go our ways—I to die, and you to live. Which is better, God only knows. —From Socrates' Talk to His Friends before Drinking the Hemlock.

⧴ ⧴

Would ye learn the road to Laughter-
town,
O ye who have lost the way?
Would ye have young heart though your
hair be gray?
Go learn from a little child each day.
Go serve his wants and play his play,
And catch the lilt of his laughter gay,
And follow his dancing feet as they stray;
For he knows the road to Laughter-
town,
O ye who have lost the way!
—Katherine D. Blake.

A little work, a little play
To keep us going—and so, good-
day !
A little warmth, a little light
Of love's bestowing—and so, good-
night !
A little fun, to match the sorrow
Of each day's growing—and so,
good morrow!
A little trust that when we die
We reap our sowing! And so—
good-bye!

" A Little Work," *by George du Maurier*

ISSIPATIONS, vices, ... a certain class of philosophers have asserted to be a natural preparative for entering on active life; a kind of mud bath, in which the youth is, as it were, necessitated to steep, and, we suppose, cleanse himself, before the real toga of Manhood can be laid on him. We shall not dispute much with this class of philosophers; we hope they are mistaken; for Sin and Remorse so easily beset us at all stages of life, and are always such indifferent company, that it seems hard we should, at any stage, be forced and fated not only to meet but to yield to them, and even serve for a term in their leprous armada. We hope it is not so.

Clear we are, at all events, it can not be the training one receives in this Devil's service, but only our determining to desert from it, that fits us for true manly Action. We become men, not after we have been dissipated, and disappointed in the chase of false pleasure; but after we have ascertained, in any way, what impassable barriers hem us in through this life; how mad it is to hope for contentment to our infinite soul from the *gifts* of this extremely finite world; that a man must be sufficient for himself; and that for suffering and enduring there is no remedy but striving and doing. Manhood begins when we have in any way made truce with Necessity; begins even when we have surrendered to Necessity, as the most part only do; but begins joyfully and hopefully only when we have reconciled ourselves to Necessity; and thus, in reality, triumphed over it, and felt that in Necessity we are free.—Burns.

⧴ ⧴

God is the I of the Infinite.—Hugo.

REASON, murder, rape, and burning a dwelling house, were all the crimes that were liable to be punished with death by our good old common law. And such was the tenderness, such the reluctance to shed blood, that if recompense could possibly be made, life was not to be touched. Treason being against the King, the remission of the crime was in the crown. In case of murder itself, if compensation could be made, the next of kin might discharge the prosecution, which if once discharged, could not be revived. If a ravisher could make the injured woman satisfaction, the law had no power over him; she might marry the man under the gallows, if she pleased, and take him from the jaws of death to the lips of matrimony. But so fatally are we deviated from the benignity of our ancient laws, that there is now under sentence of death an unfortunate clergyman, who made satisfaction for the injury he attempted: the satisfaction was accepted, and yet the acceptance of the satisfaction and the prosecution bear the same date.

The Mosaic law ordained that for a sheep or an ox, four and five fold should be restored; and for robbing a house, double; that is one fold for reparation, the rest for example; and the forfeiture was greater, as the property was more exposed. If the thief came by night, it was lawful to kill him; but if he came by day, he was only to make restitution and if he had nothing he was to be sold for his theft. This is all that God required in felonies, nor can I find in history any sample of such laws as ours, except a code that was framed at Athens by Draco. He made every offense capital,

To suffer woes which Hope thinks infinite;
To forgive wrongs darker than death or
   night;
   To defy Power, which seems
    omnipotent;
   To love, and bear; to hope till Hope
    creates
From its own wreck the thing it contem-
   plates;
   Neither to change, nor falter, nor
    repent;
This, like thy glory, Titan, is to be
Good, great and joyous, beautiful and
   free;
This is alone Life, Joy, Empire, and
   Victory.

From " Prometheus Unbound,"
             by Percy Bysshe Shelley

upon this modern way of reasoning— " That petty crimes deserved death, and he knew nothing worse for the greatest." His laws, it is said, were written, not with ink, but with blood; but they were of short duration, being all repealed by Solon, except one, for murder . . . .

An attempt was made some years ago to repeal some of the most absurd and cruel of our capital laws. The bill passed this house, but was rejected by the Lords for this reason: "It was an innovation, they said, and subversive of law." The very reverse is truth ∞ These hanging laws are themselves innovations. No less than three and thirty of them passed the last reign. I believe I myself was the first person to check the progress of them. When the great Alfred came to the throne, he found the kingdom overrun with robbers; but the silly expedient of hanging never came into his head; he instituted a police, which was, to make every township answerable for the felonies committed in it. Thus property became the guardian of property, and all robbery was so effectually stopped that in a very short time a man might travel through the kingdom unarmed, with his purse in his hand. . . .

Even in crimes which are seldom or never pardoned, death is no prevention. Housebreakers, forgers and coiners are sure to be hanged; yet housebreaking, forgery and coining are the very crimes which are oftenest committed. Strange it is that in the case of blood, of which we ought to be most tender, we should still go on, against reason and against experience to make unavailing slaughter of our fellow-creatures. A recent event has proved that policy will do what

blood can not do—I mean the late regulation of the coinage. Thirty years together men were continually hanged for coining; still it went on: but on the new regulation of the gold coin it ceased . . . .
❡ There lies at this moment in Newgate, under sentence to be burnt alive, a girl just turned fourteen; at her master's bidding, she hid some whitewashed farthings behind her stays, on which the jury has found her guilty, as an accomplice with her master in the treason. The master was hanged last Wednesday; and the faggots all lay ready—no reprieve came till just as the cart was setting out, and the girl would have been burnt alive on the same day, had it not been for the humane but casual interference of Lord Weymouth. Sir, are we taught to execrate the incendiary fires of Smithfield, and we are lighting them now to burn a poor harmless child for hiding a whitewashed farthing! And yet this barbarous sentence, which ought to make men shudder at the thought of shedding blood for such trivial causes, is brought as a reason for more hanging and burning. —From Speech of Sir William Meredith in the House of Commons, May 13, 1777.

❧ ❧

EVERY man is said to have his peculiar ambition. Whether it be true or not, I can say, for one, that I have no other so great as that of being truly esteemed of my fellow-men, by rendering myself worthy of their esteem. How far I shall succeed in gratifying this ambition is yet to be developed. I am young and unknown to many of you. I was born, and have ever remained, in the most humble walks of life. I have no wealthy or popular relations or friends to recommend me. My case is thrown exclusively upon the independent voters of the country; and, if elected, they will have conferred a favor upon me for which I shall be unremitting in my labors to compensate ❧ ❧
But, if the good people in their wisdom shall see fit to keep me in the background, I have been too familiar with disappointments to be very much chagrined.—Lincoln, to the People of Sangamon, March 9, 1832.

 T is customary to say that age should be considered, because it comes last ❧ It seems just as much to the point, that youth comes first. And the scale fairly kicks the beam, if you go on to add that age, in a majority of cases, never comes at all. Disease and accidents make short work of even the most prosperous persons. To be suddenly snuffed out in the middle of ambitious schemes is tragical enough at the best; but when a man has been grudging himself his own life in the meanwhile, and saving up everything for the festival that was never to be, it becomes that hysterically moving sort of tragedy which lies on the confines of farce. . . To husband a favorite claret until the batch turns sour is not at all an artful stroke of policy; and how much more with a whole cellar— a whole bodily existence! People may lay down their lives with cheerfulness in the sure expectation of a blessed mortality; but that is a different affair from giving up youth with all its admirable pleasures, in the hope of a better quality of gruel in a more than problematic, nay, more than improbable old age. We should not compliment a hungry man, who should refuse a whole dinner and reserve all his appetite for the dessert, before he knew whether there was to be any dessert or not. If there be such a thing as imprudence in the world, we surely have it here. We sail in leaky bottoms and on great and perilous waters; and to take a cue from the dolorous old naval ballad, we have heard the mermaids singing, and know that we shall never see dry land any more. Old and young, we are all on our last cruise. If there is a fill of tobacco among the crew, for God's sake pass it round, and let us have a pipe before we go!—Robert Louis Stevenson.

❧ ❧

ADVERSITY is a medicine which people are rather fond of recommending indiscriminately as a panacea for their neighbors. Like other medicines, it only agrees with certain constitutions. There are nerves which it braces, and nerves which it utterly shatters.
—Justin McCarthy.

ELIUS LAMIA, born in Italy of illustrious parents, had not yet discarded the *toga prœtexta* when he set out for the schools of Athens to study philosophy ๑ Subsequently he took up his residence at Rome, and in his house on the Esquiline, amid a circle of youthful wastrels, abandoned himself to licentious courses. But being accused of engaging in criminal relations with Lepida, the wife of Sulpicius Quirinus, a man of consular rank, and being found guilty, he was exiled by Tiberius Cæsar. At that time he was just entering his twenty-fourth year ๑ ๑ During the eighteen years that his exile lasted he traversed Syria, Palestine, Cappadocia, and Armenia, and prolonged visits to Antioch, Cæsarea, and Jerusalem. When, after the death of Tiberius, Caius was raised to the purple, Lamia obtained permission to return to Rome. He even regained a portion of his possessions. Adversity had taught him wisdom. . . . With a mixture of surprise and vexation he recognized that age was stealing upon him ๑ In his sixty-second year, being afflicted with an illness which proved in no slight degree troublesome, he decided to have recourse to the waters of Baiæ. The coast at that point, once frequented by the halcyon, was at this date the resort of the wealthy Roman, greedy of pleasure. For a week Lamia lived alone, without a friend in the brilliant crowd. Then one day, after dinner, an inclination to which he yielded urged him to ascend the inclines which, covered with vines that resembled bacchantes, looked out upon

It is not raining rain for me,
It 's raining daffodils;
In every dimpled drop I see
Wild flowers on the hills.

The clouds of gray engulf the day
And overwhelm the town;
It is not raining rain to me,
It 's raining roses down.

It is not raining rain to me,
But fields of clover bloom,
Where any buccaneering bee
Can find a bed and room.

A health unto the happy,
A fig for him who frets!
It is not raining rain to me,
It 's raining violets.

"April Rain," *by Robert Loveman*

the waves. ❦ Having reached the summit he seated himself by the side of a path beneath a terebinth, and let his glances wander over the lovely landscape. . . . ❦ Lamia drew from a fold of his toga a scroll containing the *Treatise upon Nature*, extending himself upon the ground, and began to read. But the warning cries of a slave necessitated his rising to allow of the passage of a litter which was being carried along the narrow pathway through the vineyards. The litter being uncurtained, permitted Lamia to see stretched upon the cushions as it was borne nearer to him the figure of an elderly man of immense bulk, who, supporting his head on his hand, gazed out with a gloomy and disdainful expression. His nose, which was aquiline, and his chin, which was prominent, seemed desirous of meeting across his lips, and his jaws were powerful. ❦ From the first moment Lamia was convinced that the face was familiar to him. He hesitated a moment before the name came to him. Then suddenly hastening towards the litter with a display of surprise and delight—

"Pontius Pilate!" he cried. "The gods be praised who have permitted me to see you once again!"

The old man gave a signal to the slaves to stop, and cast a keen glance upon the stranger who had addressed him.

"Pontius, my dear host," resumed the latter, "have twenty years so far whitened my hair and hollowed my cheeks that you no longer recognize your friend Ælius Lamia?"

At this name Pontius Pilate dismounted

from the litter as actively as the weight of his years and the heaviness of his gait permitted him, and embraced Ælius Lamia again and again.

" Gods! what a treat it is to me to see you once more! But, alas, you call up memories of those long-vanished days when I was Procurator of Judæa, in the province of Syria. Why, it must be thirty years ago that I first met you. It was at Cæsarea, whither you came to drag out your weary term of exile. I was fortunate enough to alleviate it a little, and out of friendship, Lamia, you followed me to that depressing place Jerusalem, where the Jews filled me with bitterness and disgust. You remained for more than ten years my guest and my companion, and in converse about Rome and things Roman we both of us managed to find consolation—you for your misfortunes, and I for my burdens of State."

Lamia embraced him afresh. . . .

" You were preparing to suppress a Samaritan rising when I set out for Cappadocia, where I hoped to draw some profit from the breeding of horses and mules. I have not seen you since then. How did that expedition succeed? Pray tell me. Everything interests me that concerns you in any way."

Pontius Pilate sadly shook his head.

❡ " My natural disposition," he said, " as well as a sense of duty, impelled me to fulfil my public responsibilities, not merely with diligence, but even with ardor ✒ But I was pursued by unrelenting hatred. Intrigues and calumnies cut short my career in its prime, and the fruit it should have looked to bear has withered away. You ask me about the Samaritan insurrection. Let us sit down on this hillock. I shall be able to give you an answer in few words. These occurrences are as vividly presented to me as if they had happened yesterday.

" A man of the people, of persuasive speech—there are many such to be met with in Syria—induced the Samaritans to gather together in arms on Mount Gerizim (which in that country is looked upon as a holy place) under the promise that he would disclose to their sight the

sacred vessels which in the ancient days of Evander and our father Æneas, had been hidden away by an eponymos hero, or rather a tribal deity, named Moses. Upon this assurance the Samaritans rose in rebellion; but having been warned in time to forestall them, I dispatched detachments of infantry to occupy the mountain, and stationed cavalry to keep the approaches to it under observation ✒ ✒

" These measures of prudence were urgent. The rebels were already laying siege to the town of Tyrathaba, situated at the foot of Mount Gerizim. I easily dispersed them, and stifled the as yet scarcely organized revolt. Then, in order to give a forcible example with as few victims as possible, I handed over to execution the leaders of the rebellion. But you are aware, Lamia, in what strait dependence I was kept by the proconsul Vitellius, who governed Syria not in, but against the interests of Rome, and looked upon the provinces of the empire as territories which could be farmed out to tetrarchs. The head men among the Samaritans, in their resentment against me, came and fell at his feet lamenting. To listen to them nothing had been further from their thoughts than to disobey Cæsar. It was I who had provoked the rising, and it was purely in order to withstand my violence that they had gathered together around Tyrathaba ✒ Vitellius listened to their complaints, and handing over the affairs of Judæa to his friend Marcellus, commanded me to go and justify my proceedings before the Emperor himself. With a heart overflowing with grief and resentment I took ship. Just as I approached the shores of Italy, Tiberius, worn out with age and the cares of empire, died suddenly on the self-same Cape Misenum, whose peak we see from this very spot magnified in the mists of evening. I demanded justice of Caius, his successor, whose perception was naturally acute, and who was acquainted with Syrian affairs. But marvel with me, Lamia, at the maliciousness of fortune, resolved on my discomfiture. Caius then had in his suite at Rome the Jew Agrippa, his companion, the friend of his childhood, whom he cherished as his own eyes. Now Agrippa favored Vitellius, inasmuch as Vitellius was the enemy of Antipas, whom Agrippa pursued with his hatred. The Emperor adopted the prejudices of his beloved Asiatic, and refused even to listen to me.". . . .

"Pontius," replied Lamia, "I am persuaded that you acted towards the Samaritans according to the rectitude of your character, and solely in the interests of Rome. But were you not perchance on that occasion a trifle too much influenced by that impetuous courage which has always swayed you? You will remember that in Judæa it often happened that I who, younger than you, should naturally have been more impetuous than you, was obliged to urge you to clemency and suavity."

"Suavity towards the Jews!" cried Pontius Pilate "Although you have lived amongst them, it seems clear that you ill understand those enemies of the human race. Haughty and at the same time base, combining an invincible obstinacy with a despicably mean spirit, they weary alike your love and your hatred. My character, Lamia, was formed upon the maxims of the divine Augustus. When I was appointed Procurator of Judæa, the world was already penetrated with the majestic ideal of the *pax romana*. No longer, as in the days of our internecine strife, were we witnesses to the sack of a province for the aggrandisement of a proconsul. I knew where my duty lay. I was careful that my actions should be governed by prudence and moderation. The gods are my witnesses that I was resolved upon mildness, and upon mildness only. . . . Before the immortal gods I swear that never once during my term of office did I flout justice and the laws. But I am grown old. My enemies and detractors are dead. I shall die unavenged. Who will not retrieve my character?"

He moaned and lapsed into silence. Lamia replied:

"That man is prudent who neither hopes nor fears anything from the uncertain events of the future. Does it matter in the least what estimate men may form of us hereafter? We ourselves are, after all, our own witnesses and our own judges. You must rely, Pontius Pilate, on the testimony you yourself bear to your own rectitude. Be content with your personal respect and that of your friends.". . . . .

"We'll say no more at present," said Pontius. . . . "I must hasten on. Adieu! But now that I have rediscovered a friend, I should wish to take advantage of my good fortune. Do me the favor, Ælius Lamia, to give me your company at supper at my house tomorrow. My house stands on the seashore, at the extreme end of the town in the direction of Misenum. You will easily recognize it by the porch, which bears a painting representing Orpheus surrounded by tigers and lions, whom he is charming with the strains from his lyre.

"Till tomorrow, Lamia," he repeated, as he climbed once more into his litter. "Tomorrow we will talk about Judæa."

The following day at the supper hour Lamia presented himself at the house of Pontius Pilate. Two couches were in readiness for occupants. . . . As they proceeded with their repast, Pontius and Lamia interchanged inquiries with one another about their ailments, the symptoms of which they described at considerable length, mutually emulous of communicating the various remedies which had been recommended to them. . . After a time they turned to the subject of the great engineering feats that had been accomplished in the country, the prodigious bridge constructed by Caius between Puteoli and Baiæ, and the canals which Augustus excavated to convey the waters of the ocean to Lake Avernus and the Lucrine lake.

"I also," said Pontius, with a sigh, "I also wished to set afoot public works of great utility. When, for my sins, I was appointed Governor of Judæa, I conceived the idea of furnishing Jerusalem with an abundant supply of pure water by means of an aqueduct. . . . But far from viewing with satisfaction the construction of that conduit, which was intended to carry to their town upon its massive arches not only water but health, the inhabitants of Jerusalem gave vent to lamentable outcries ✎ They gathered tumultuously together exclaiming against the sacrilege and impiousness, and hurling themselves upon the workmen, scattered the very foundation stones. Can you picture to yourself, Lamia, a filthier set of barbarians? Nevertheless, Vitellius decided in their favor, and I received orders to put a stop to the work." ❡ " It is a knotty point," said Lamia, " how far one is justified in devising things for the commonweal against the will of the populace." ✎ ✎ Pontius Pilate continued as though he had not heard this interruption. . ❡ "I was appointed by Rome not for the destruction, but for the upholding of their customs, and over them I had the power of the rod and the axe ✎ At the outset of my term of office I endeavored to persuade them to hear reason. I attempted to snatch their miserable victims from death. But this show of mildness only irritated them the more; they demanded their prey, fighting around me like a horde of vultures with wing and beak. Their priests reported to Cæsar that I was violating their law, and their appeals, supported by Vitellius, drew down upon me a severe reprimand. How many times did I long, as the Greeks used to say, to dispatch accusers and accused in one convoy to the crows!". . . .

Lamia exerted himself to lead the conversation back to a less acrimonious note. " Pontius, " he said, " it is not difficult for me to understand both your long-standing resentment and your sinister forebodings. Truly, what you have experienced of the character of the Jews is nothing to their advantage. But I lived in Jeru-

Into the woods My Master went,
Clean forspent, forspent.
Into the woods my Master came,
Forspent with love and shame.
But the olives they were not blind to Him;
The little gray leaves were kind to Him;
The thorn-tree had a mind to Him
When into the woods He came.

Out of the woods my Master went,
And He was well content.
Out of the woods my Master came,
Content with death and shame.
When Death and Shame would woo Him
  last,
From under the trees they drew Him last:
'T was on a tree they slew Him—last
When out of the woods He came.

" A Ballad of Trees and the Master,"
by Sidney Lanier

salem as an interested onlooker, and mingled freely with the people, and I succeeded in detecting certain obscure virtues in these rude folk which were altogether hidden from you. I have met Jews who were all mildness, whose simple manners and faithfulness of heart recalled to me what our poets have related concerning the Spartan lawgiver. And you yourself, Pontius, have seen perish beneath the cudgels of your legionaries simpleminded men who have died for a cause they believed to be just without revealing their names. Such men do not deserve our contempt ✎ I am saying this because it is desirable in all things to preserve moderation and an even mind. ✎ But I own that I never experienced any lively sympathy for the Jews. ✎ The Jewess, on the contrary, I found extremely pleasing. I was young, then, and the Syrian women stirred all my senses to response. Their ruddy lips, their liquid eyes that shone in the shade, their sleepy gaze pierced me to the very marrow. Painted and stained, smelling the nard and myrrh, steeped in odors, their physical attractions are both rare and delightful."

Pontius listened impatiently to these praises ✎ ✎

" I was not the kind of man to fall into the snares of the Jewish women," he said, " and since you have opened the subject yourself, Lamia, I was never able to approve of your laxity. If I did not express with sufficient emphasis formerly how culpable I held you for having intrigued at Rome with the wife of a man of consular rank, it was because you were then enduring heavy penance for your misdoings. Marriage from the patrician point of view is a sacred tie; it is one of the institutions which are the support of Rome. As to foreign women and slaves such relations as one may enter into with them would be of little account were it not that they habituate the body to a humiliating effeminacy. Let me tell you that you have been too liberal in your offerings to the Venus of the Market-place; and what, above all, I blame in you is that you have not married in compliance with the law and given children to the Republic, as every good citizen is bound to do."

But the man who had suffered exile under Tiberius was no longer listening to the venerable magistrate ✣ Having tossed off his cup of Falernian, he was smiling at some image visible to his eye alone ✣ ✣

After a moment's silence he resumed in a very deep voice, which rose in pitch by little and little:

"With what languorous grace they dance, those Syrian women! I knew a Jewess at Jerusalem who used to dance in a poky little room, on a threadbare carpet, by the light of one smoky little lamp, waving her arms as she clanged her cymbals. Her loins arched, her head thrown back, and, as it were dragged down by the weight of her heavy red hair, her eyes swimming with voluptuousness, eager, languishing, compliant, she would have made Cleopatra herself grow pale with envy. I was in love with her barbaric dances, her voice—a little raucous and yet so sweet—her atmosphere of incense, the semi-somnolescent state in which she seemed to live. I followed her everywhere. I mixed with the vile rabble of soldiers, conjurers and extortioners with which she was surrounded. One day, however, she disappeared, and I saw her no more. Long did I seek her in disreputable alleys and taverns. It was more difficult to learn to do without her than to lose the taste for Greek wine. Some months after I lost sight of her, I learned by chance that she had attached herself to a small company of men and women who were followers of a young Galilean thaumaturgist. His name was Jesus; he came from Nazareth, and he was crucified for some crime, I don't quite know what. Pontius, do you remember anything about the man?"

Pontius Pilate contracted his brows, and his hand rose to his forehead in the attitude of one who probes the deeps of memory. Then after a silence of some seconds:

"Jesus?" he murmured, "Jesus—of Nazareth? I can not call him to mind."

—"The Procurator of Judea" (abbreviated), by Anatole France.

✣ ✣

FOR money enters in two different characters into the scheme of life. A certain amount, varying with the number and empire of our desires, is a true necessity for each one of us in the present order of society; but beyond that amount, money is a commodity to be bought or not to be bought, a luxury in which we may either indulge or stint ourselves, like any other. And there are many luxuries that we may legitimately prefer to it, such as a grateful conscience, a country life, or the woman of our inclination. Trite, flat, and obvious as this conclusion may appear, we have only to look round us in society to see how scantily it has been recognized; and perhaps even ourselves, after a little reflection, may decide to spend a trifle less for money, and indulge ourselves a trifle more in the article of freedom.

—Robert Louis Stevenson.

✣ ✣

IT strikes me dumb to look over the long series of faces, such as any full Church, Courthouse, London-Tavern Meeting, or miscellany of men will show them. Some score or two of years ago, all these were little red-colored infants; each of them capable of being kneaded, baked into any social form you chose: yet see now how they are fixed and hardened—into artisans, artists, clergy, gentry, learned sergeants, unlearned dandies, and can and shall now be nothing else henceforth.—Carlyle.

✣ ✣

Music was a thing of the soul—a rose-lipped shell that murmured of the eternal sea—a strange bird singing the songs of another shore.—J. C. Holland.

E are spirits ◦ That bodies should be lent us, while they can afford us pleasure, assist us in acquiring knowledge, or in doing good to our fellow creatures, is a kind and benevolent act of God. When they become unfit for these purposes, and afford us pain instead of pleasure, instead of an aid become an incumbrance, and answer none of the intentions for which they were given, it is equally kind and benevolent, that a way is provided by which we may get rid of them ◦ Death is that way. Our friend and we were invited abroad on a party of pleasure, which is to last forever. His chair was ready first and he has gone before us. We could not all conveniently start together; and why should you and I be grieved at this, since we are soon to follow, and know where to find him.—Franklin.

◦ ◦

IT begins now to be everywhere surmised that the real Force, which in this world all things must obey, is Insight, Spiritual Vision and Determination. The Thought is parent of the Deed, nay, is living soul of it, and last and continual, as well as first mover of it; is the foundation and beginning and essence, therefore, of man's whole existence here below. In this sense, it has been said, the Word of man (the uttered Thought of man) is still a magic formula, whereby he rules the world. Do not the winds and waters, and all tumultuous powers, inanimate and animate, obey him? A poor, quite mechanical Magician speaks; and fire-winged ships cross the Ocean at his bidding. Or mark, above all, that " raging of the nations," wholly in contention, desperation and dark chaotic fury; how the meek voice of a Hebrew Martyr and Redeemer stills it into order, and a savage |Earth becomes kind and beautiful, and the habitation of horrid cruelty a temple of peace. The true Sovereign of the world, who moulds the world like soft wax, according to his pleasure, is he who lovingly *sees* into the world; the " inspired Thinker," whom in these days we name Poet. The true Sovereign is the Wise Man.

ABOVE all, it is ever to be kept in mind, that not by material, but by moral power, are men and their actions governed. How noiseless is thought! No rolling of drums, no tramp of squadrons or immeasurable tumult of baggage-wagons, attends its movements: in what obscure and sequestered places may the head be meditating, which is one day to be crowned with more than imperial authority; for Kings and Emperors will be among its ministering servants; it will rule not over, but *in,* all heads, and with these its solitary combinations of ideas, as with magic formulas, bend the world to its will! The time may come when Napoleon himself may be better known for his laws than for his battles; and the victory of Waterloo prove less momentous than the opening of the first Mechanics' Institute.—Carlyle.

◦ ◦

IN the mind of him who is pure and good will be found neither corruption nor defilement nor any malignant taint. Unlike the actor who leaves the stage before his part is played, the life of such a man is complete whenever death may come. He is neither cowardly nor presuming; not enslaved to life nor indifferent to its duties; and in him is found nothing worthy of condemnation nor that which putteth to shame.
Test by a trial how excellent is the life of the good man—the man who rejoices at the portion given him in the universal lot and abides therein content; just in all his ways and kindly minded toward all men.
This is moral perfection: to live each day as though it were the last; to be tranquil, sincere, yet not indifferent to one's fate.—Marcus Aurelius.

◦ ◦

I THINK that to have known one good, old man—one man, who, through the chances and mischances of a long life, has carried his heart in his hand, like a palm-branch, waving all discords into peace—helps our faith in God, in ourselves, and in each other more than many sermons.—G.W.Curtis.

◦ ◦

Life is but a thought.—Coleridge.

HE is no madman, but the best bundle of nerves I ever saw; cut, bruised and battered, and chained beside, he showed himself to be a man of courage and fortitude. He is a fanatic, of course, beyond all reason, but he thinks himself a Christian, and believes honestly he is called of God to free the negroes. They say when one son was dead by his side, he held his rifle in one hand, and felt the pulse of another who was dying, all the time cautioning his men to be cool and sell their lives dearly. ❡ "While I was talking with him," continued Governor Wise, "some one called out that he was a robber and a murderer ✿ Brown replied, 'You slave-holders are the robbers.' ❡ "I said to him, 'Captain Brown, your hair is matted with blood and you are speaking hard words. Perhaps you forget I am a slave-holder; you had better be thinking on eternity. Your wounds may be fatal, and if they are not, you will have to stand trial for treason, conspiracy and murder, and how can you hope to escape, when you admit your guilt?' " The old man leaned on his elbow, and beneath the bandages on his broken face I saw the blue eyes flash and he answered me: 'Governor Wise, you call me old, but after all I have only ten or fifteen years, at most, the start of you in that journey to eternity, of which you speak. I will leave this world first, but you must follow. I will meet you across Death's border, and I tell you, Governor Wise, prepare for eternity. You admit you are a slave-holder. You have a responsibility weightier than mine ✿ Prepare to meet your God!' "—Governor Henry A. Wise's Interview with John Brown.

✿ ✿

Search thy own heart; what paineth thee in others in thyself may be.—J. G. Whittier.

✿ ✿

I who am dead a thousand years,
And wrote this sweet archaic song,
Send you my words for messengers
The way I shall not pass along.

I care not if you bridge the seas,
Or ride secure the cruel sky,
Or build consummate palaces
Of metal or of masonry.

But you have wine and music still,
And statues and a bright-eyed love,
And foolish thoughts of good and ill,
And prayers to them that sit above?

How shall we conquer? Like a wind
That falls at eve our fancies blow,
And old Mœonides the blind
Said it three thousand years ago.

O friend, unseen, unborn, unknown,
Student of our sweet English tongue,
Read out my words at night, alone:
I was a poet, I was young.

Since I can never see your face,
And never shake you by the hand,
I send my soul through time and space
To greet you. You will understand.

"To a Poet a Thousand Years Hence,"
by James Elroy Flecker

I HAVE, may it please the Court, a few words to say.

In the first place I deny everything, but what I have all along admitted: of a design on my part to free the slaves. I intended certainly to have made a clean thing of the matter, as I did last winter when I went to Missouri and there took slaves without the snapping of a gun on either side, moving them through the country, and finally leaving them in Canada. I designed to have done the same thing again on a larger scale. That was all I intended. I never did intend murder, or treason, or the destruction of property, or to excite or incite slaves to rebellion, or to make insurrection.

I have another objection, and that is that it is unjust that I should suffer such a penalty. Had I interfered in the manner in which I admit, and which I admit has been fairly proved—for I admire the truthfulness and candor of the greater portion of the witnesses who have testified in this case—had I so interfered in behalf of the rich, the powerful, the intelligent, the so-called great, or in behalf of any of their friends, either father, mother, brother, sister, wife or children, or any of that class, and suffered and sacrificed what I have in this interference, it would have been all right. Every man of this Court would have deemed it an act worthy of reward rather than punishment so so

This Court acknowledges, too, as I suppose, the validity of the law of God. I see a book kissed, which I suppose to be the Bible, or at least the New Testament, which teaches me that all things whatsoever I would that men should do to me, I should do even so to them. It teaches me further to remember them that are in bonds as bound with them. I endeavored to act up to that instruction. I say I am yet too young to understand that God is any respecter of persons.

I believe that to have interfered as I have done, as I have always freely admitted I have done, in behalf of his despised poor, I did no wrong, but right. Now if it is deemed necessary that I should forfeit my life for the furtherance of the ends of justice, and mingle my blood further with the blood of my childdren and with the blood of millions in this slave country whose rights are disregarded by wicked, cruel and unjust enactments, I say let it be done.

Let me say one word further. I feel entirely satisfied with the treatment I have received on my trial. Considering all the circumstances, it has been more generous than I expected. But I feel no consciousness of guilt. I have stated from the first what was my intention, and what was not. I never had any design against the liberty of any person, nor any disposition to commit treason or incite slaves to rebel or make any general insurrection so so

I never encouraged any man to do so, but always discouraged any idea of that kind so so

Let me say, also, in regard to the statements made by some of them that I have induced them to join me. But the contrary is true. I do not say this to injure them, but as regretting their weakness.

Not one but joined me of his own accord, and the greater part at their own expense. A number of them I never saw, and never had a word of conversation with till the day they came to me, and that was for the purpose I have stated. Now, I have done.—John Brown's Address to the Court.

so so

IF you accept art, it must be part of your daily lives, and the daily life of every man. It will be with us wherever we go, in the ancient city full of traditions of past time, in the newly cleared farm in America or the colonies, where no man has dwelt for tradition to gather around him; in the quiet country-side, as in the busy town, no place shall be without it. You will have it with you in your sorrow as in your joy, in your work-a-day as in your leisure. It shall be no respecter of persons, but be shared by gentle and simple, learned and unlearned, and be as a language that all can understand. It will not hinder any work that is necessary to the life of man at the best, but it will destroy all degrading toil, all enervating luxury, all foppish frivolity. It will be the deadly foe of ignorance, dishonesty and tyranny, and will foster good-will, fair dealing and confidence between man and man. It will teach you to respect the highest intellect with a manly reverence but not to despise any man who does not pretend to be what he is not.—William Morris.

so so

THE scholar only knows how dear these silent yet eloquent companions of pure thoughts and innocent hours become in the season of adversity. When all that is worldly turns to dross around us, these only retain their steady value. When friends grow cold, and the converse of intimates languishes into vapid civility and commonplace these only continue the unaltered countenance of happier days, and cheer us with that true friendship which never deceived hope nor deserted sorrow.

—Washington Irving.

so so

Divinity consists in use and practise, not in speculation.—Luther.

T seems to me that the truest way to understand [the art of] conversation, is to know the faults and errors to which it is subject and from thence each man to form maxims to himself whereby it may be regulated, because it requires few talents to which most men are not born, or at best may acquire, without any great genius or study. For nature hath left every man a capacity of being agreeable, though not of shining in company; and there are a hundred men sufficiently qualified for both, who, by a very few faults, that they might correct in half an hour, are not so much as tolerable ✖ ✖ For instance: nothing is more generally exploded than the folly of talking too much, yet I rarely remember to have seen five people together, when some one among them has not been predominant in that kind, to the great constraint and disgust of all the rest. But among such as deal in multitudes of words, none are comparable to the sober, deliberate talker, who proceeds with much thought and caution, makes his preface, branches out into several digressions, finds a hint that puts him in mind of another story, which he promises to tell you when this is done; comes back regularly to his subject, can not readily call to mind some person's name, holding his head, complains of his memory; the whole company all this while in suspense; at length says, it is no matter, and so goes on. And, to crown the business, it perhaps proves at last a story the company has heard fifty times before; or, at best, some insipid adventure of the relator. ❡ Another general fault in conversation is that of those who affect to talk of themselves; some, without any ceremony will run over the history of their lives; will relate the annals of their diseases, with the several symptoms and circumstances of them; will enumerate the hardships and injustice they have suffered in court, in parliament, in love, or in law. Others are more dexterous, and with great art will be on the watch to hook in their own praise; they will call a witness to remember they always foretold what would happen in such a case, but none would believe them; they advised such a man from the beginning and told him the consequences, just as they happened; but he would have his own way. Others make a vanity of telling their faults, they are the strangest men in the world; they can not dissemble; they own it is a folly; they have lost abundance of advantages by it; but if you would give them the world; they can not help it; there is something in their nature that abhors insincerity and constraint; with many other insufferable topics of the same altitude ✖ ✖ Of such mighty importance every man is to himself, and ready to think he is so to others; without once making this easy and obvious reflection, that his affairs can have no more weight with other men, than theirs have with him; and how little that is, he is sensible enough. When a company has met, I often have observed two persons discover, by some accident, that they were bred together at the same school or university; after which the rest are condemned to silence, and to listen while these two are refreshing each other's memory, with the arch tricks and passages of themselves and their comrades.

Come, I will make the continent indissoluble,
I will make the most splendid race the sun ever shone upon,
I will make divine magnetic lands,
   With the love of comrades,
    With the life-long love of comrades.

I will plant companionship thick as trees along all the rivers of America, and along the shores of the great lakes, and all over the prairies,
I will make inseparable cities with their arms about each other's necks,
   By the love of comrades,
    By the manly love of comrades.

" For You O Democracy," *by Walt Whitman*

There are some faults in conversation, which none are so subject to as men of wit, nor even so much as when they are with each other. If they have opened their mouths, without endeavoring to say a witty thing, they think it is so many words lost; it is a torment to the hearers, as much as to themselves, to see them upon the rack for invention, and in perpetual constraint, with so little success. They must do something extraordinary, in order to acquit themselves, and answer their character, else the standers-by may be disappointed, and be apt to think them only like the rest of mortals. I have known two men of wit, industriously brought together, in order to entertain the company, when they have made a very ridiculous figure, and provided all the mirth at their own expense.

℘ I know a man of wit, who is never easy but when he can be allowed to dictate and preside: he never expects to be informed or entertained, but to display his own talents. His business is to be good company, and not good conversation; and therefore he chooses to frequent those who are content to listen and profess themselves his admirers.

℘ Raillery is the finest part of conversation; but as it is our usual custom, to counterfeit and adulterate whatever is too dear to us, so we have done with this, and turned it all into what is generally called repartee, or being smart; just as when an expensive fashion comes up, those who are not able to reach it, content themselves with some paltry imitation. It now passes for raillery to run a man down in discourse, to put him out of countenance, and make him ridiculous; sometimes to expose the defects of his person or understanding; on all which occasions he is obliged not to be angry, to avoid the imputation of not being able to take a jest. It is admirable to observe one who is dexterous in this art, singling out a weak adversary, getting the laugh on his side, and then carrying all before him. The French, from whom we borrow the word, had a quite different idea of the thing, and so had we in the politer age of our fathers. Raillery was to say something that at first appeared a reproach or reflection, but by some turn of wit, unexpected and surprising, ended always in a compliment, and to the advantage of the person it was addressed to. And surely one of the best rules in conversation is, never to say a thing which any of the company can reasonably wish we had left unsaid; nor can there anything be well more contrary for the ends to which people meet together, than to part unsatisfied with each other or themselves.

There are some men excellent at telling a story, and provided with a plentiful stock of them, which they can draw upon occasion in all companies; and considering how long conversation runs now among us, it is not altogether a contemptible talent; however, it is subject to two unavoidable defects, frequent repetition, and being soon exhausted; so that, whoever values this gift in himself, has need of a good memory, and ought frequently to shift his company, that he may not discover the weakness of his fund; for those who are thus endued have seldom any other revenue, but live upon the main stock.

Great speakers in public are seldom agreeable in private conversation, whether their faculty be natural, or acquired by practice, and often venturing. Natural elocution, although it may seem a paradox, usually springs from a barrenness of invention, and of words; by which men who have only one stock of notions upon every subject, and one set of phases to express them in, they swim in the superfices, and offer themselves on every occasion; therefore, men of much learning, and who know the compass of a language, are generally the worst talkers of a sudden until much practice has inured and emboldened them; because they are confounded with plenty of matter, variety of notions, and of words, which they can not readily choose, but are perplexed and entangled by too great a choice; which is no disadvantage in private conversation; where, on the other side, the talent of haranguing is of all others, the most insupportable.

℘ Thus we see how human nature is most debased, by the abuse of that faculty which is held the great distinction between men and brutes; and how little advantage we make of that, which might be the greatest, the most lasting, and the most innocent, as well as useful, pleasure of life.—Jonathan Swift.

ॐ ॐ

It suffices not that beauty should keep solitary festival in life; it has to become a festival of every day.—Maeterlinck.

ॐ ॐ

WHEN those difficult cases occur, they are difficult, chiefly because, while we have them under consideration, all the reasons *pro* and *con* are not present to the mind at the same time; but sometimes one set present themselves, and at other times another, the first being out of sight. Hence the various purposes or inclinations that alternately prevail, and the uncertainty that perplexes us *ॐ ॐ*

To get over this, my way is, to divide half a sheet of paper by a line into two columns; writing over the one *pro* and the other *con;* then during three or four days' consideration, I put down under the different heads short hints of the different motives, that at different times occur to me, *for* or *against* the measure. When I have thus got them all together in one view, I endeavor to estimate their respective weights; and, where I find two (one on each side) that seem equal, I strike them both out. If I find a reason *pro* equal to some *two* reasons *con,* I strike out the *three.* If I judge some *two* reasons *con,* equal to some *three* reasons *pro,* I strike out the *five;* and thus proceeding I find at length where the *balance* lies; and if, after a day or two of further consideration, nothing new that is of importance occurs on either side, I come to a determination accordingly *ॐ* And, though the weight of reasons can not be taken with the precision of algebraic quantities, yet, when each is thus considered separately and comparatively, and the whole lies before me, I think I can judge better, and am less liable to make a rash step; and in fact I have found great value from this kind of equation, in what may be called *moral* or *prudential* algebra.—Franklin.

YOU may believe me, when I assure you in the most solemn manner that, so far from seeking this employment, I have used every effort in my power to avoid it, not only from my unwillingness to part with you and the family, but from a consciousness of its being a trust too great for my capacity; and I should enjoy more real happiness in one month with you at home than I have the most distant prospect of finding abroad, if my stay were to be seven times seven years. But as it has been kind of destiny that has thrown me upon this service, I shall hope that my undertaking it is designed to answer some good purpose. . . . .

I shall rely confidently on that Providence which has heretofore preserved and been bountiful to me, not doubting but that I shall return safe to you in the fall. I shall feel no pain from the toil or danger of the campaign; my unhappiness will flow from the uneasiness I know you will feel from being left alone. I therefore beg that you will summon your whole fortitude, and pass your time as agreeably as possible. Nothing will give me so much sincere satisfaction as to hear this, and to hear it from your own pen.—George Washington, Letter to His Wife, 1775.

ॐ ॐ

A GREAT factory with the machinery all working and revolving with absolute and rhythmic regularity and with the men all driven by one impulse and moving in unison as though a constituent part of the mighty machine, is one of the most inspiring examples of directed force that the world shows. I have rarely seen the face of a mechanic in the act of creation which was not fine, never one which was not earnest and impressive.—Thomas Nelson Page.

ॐ ॐ

THERE is no moment like the present. The man who will not execute his resolutions when they are fresh upon him can have no hope from them afterwards: they will be dissipated, lost, and perish in the hurry and scurry of the world, or sunk in the slough of indolence.—Maria Edgeworth.

NOW feeble words seem here! How can I hope to utter what your hearts are full of? I fear to disturb the harmony which his life breathes round this home. One and another of you, his neighbors, say, "I have known him five years," "I have known him ten years." It seems to me as if we had none of us known him. How our admiring, loving wonder has grown, day by day, as he has unfolded trait after trait of earnest, brave, tender, Christian life! We see him walking with radiant, serene face to the scaffold, and think, what an iron heart, what devoted faith! We take up his letters, beginning, "My dear wife and children, every one,"—see him stoop on the way to the scaffold and kiss that negro child—and this iron heart seems all tenderness. Marvelous old man! We hardly said it when the loved forms of his sons, in the bloom of young devotion, encircle him, and we remember he is not alone, only the majestic center of a group. Your neighbor farmer went, surrounded by his household, to tell the slaves there will still be hearts and right arms ready and nerved for the service. From this roof four, from a neighboring roof two, to make up that score of heroes. How resolutely each looked into the face of Virginia, how loyally each stood at his forlorn post, meeting death cheerfully, till that master voice said, "It is enough." And these weeping children and widow see so lifted up and consecrated by long, single-hearted devotion to his great purpose that we dare, even at this moment, to remind them how blessed they are in the privilege of thinking that in the last throbs

Be still, my soul, be still; the arms you
    bore are brittle,
  Earth and high heaven are fixt of old
    and founded strong.
I think rather,—call to thought, if now
    you grieve a little,
  The days when we had rest, O soul,
    for they were long.

Men loved unkindness then, but lightless
    in the quarry
  I slept and saw not; tears fell down,
    I did not mourn;
Sweat ran and blood sprang out and
    I was never sorry:
  Then it was well with me, in days
    ere I was born.

(Concluded on next page)

of these brave young hearts, which lie buried on the banks of the Shenandoah, thoughts of them mingled with love to God and hope for the slave.

He has abolished slavery in Virginia. You may say this is too much. Our neighbors are the last men we know. The hours that pass us are the ones that we appreciate least. Men walked Boston streets when night fell on Bunker's Hill, and pitied Warren, saying, "Foolish man! Threw away his life! Why did n't he measure his means better?" Now we see him standing colossal on that blood-stained sod, and severing that day the tie which bound Boston to Great Britain. That night George III ceased to rule in New England. History will date Virginia Emancipation from Harper's Ferry. True, the slave is still there. So, when the tempest uproots a pine on your hills, it looks green for months—a year or two. Still it is timber, not a tree. John Brown has loosened the roots of the slavery system; it only breathes—it does not live—hereafter.—"The Burial of John Brown," by Wendell Phillips.

THE house-builder at work in cities or anywhere,
The preparatory jointing, squaring, sawing, mortising,
The hoist-up of beams, the push of them in their places, laying them regular.
Setting the studs by their tenons in the mortises, according as they were prepared,
The blows of the mallets and hammers—
Pæans and praises to him!
            —Walt Whitman.

Today is yesterday's pupil.—Franklin.

HE functions of the poetical faculty are twofold; by one it creates new materials of knowledge, and power, and pleasure; by the other it engenders in the mind a desire to reproduce and arrange them according to a certain rhythm and order which may be called the beautiful and good. The cultivation of poetry is never more to be desired than at periods when, from an excess of the selfish and calculating principle, the accumulation of the materials of external life exceed the quantity of the power of assimilating them to the internal laws of human nature. The body has then become too unwieldy for that which animates it.

Poetry is indeed something divine. It is at once the center and circumference of knowledge; it is that which comprehends all science, and that to which all science must be referred. It is at the same time the root and blossom of all other systems of thought; it is that from which all spring, and that which adorns all; and that which, if blighted, denies the fruit and the seed, and withholds from the barren world the nourishment and the succession of the scions of the tree of life. It is the perfect and consummate surface and bloom of all things; it is as the odor and the color of the rose to the texture of the elements which compose it, as the form and splendor of unfaded beauty to the secrets of anatomy and curruption ✒ What were virtue, love, patriotism, friendship—what were the scenery of this beautiful universe which we inhabit—what were our consolations on this side of the **grave**—and what were our aspirations **beyond** it, if poetry did not ascend to

Now, and I muse for why and never find the reason,
I pace the earth, and drink the air, and feel the sun.
Be still, be still, my soul; it is but for a season:
Let us endure an hour and see injustice done.

Ay, look: high heaven and earth ail from the prime foundation;
All thoughts to rive the heart are here, and all are vain;
Horror and scorn and hate and fear and indignation—
Oh, why did I awake? when shall I sleep again?

" Be Still, My Soul," *by A. E. Houseman*

bring light and fire from those eternal regions where the owl-winged faculty of calculation dare not ever soar?

Poetry is not like reasoning, a power to be exerted according to the determination of the will. A man can not say it: " I will compose poetry." The greatest poet even can not say it; for the mind in creation is as a fading coal, which some invisible influence, like an inconstant wind, awakens to transitory, brightness; this power arises from within, like the color of a flower which fades and changes as it is developed, and the conscious portions of our natures are unprophetic either of its approach or its departure ✒ Could this influence be durable in its original purity and force, it is impossible to predict the greatness of the results; but when composition begins, inspiration is already on the decline, and the most glorious poetry that has ever been communicated to the world is probably a feeble shadow of the original conception of the poet.

Poetry is the record of the best and happiest moments of the happiest and best minds. We are aware of evanescent visitations of thought and feeling sometimes associated with place or person, sometimes regarding our own mind alone, and always arising unforeseen and departing unbidden, but elevating and delightful beyond all expression: so that even in the desire and the regret they leave, there can not but be pleasure, participating as it does in the nature of its object. It is as it were the interpenetration of a diviner nature through our own; but its footsteps are like those of a wind over the sea which the coming calm erases, and whose traces remain only, as on the wrinkled sand which paves it.

These and corresponding conditions of being are experienced principally by those of the most delicate sensibility and the most enlarged imagination; and the state of mind produced by them is at war with every base desire. The enthusiasm of virtue, love, patriotism, and friendship is essentially linked with such emotions; and while they last, self appears as what it is, an atom to a universe. Poets are not only subject to these experiences as spirits of the most refined organization, but they can color all that they combine with the evanescent hues of this ethereal world; a word, a trait in the representation of a scene or a passion, will touch the enchanted chord, and reanimate, in those who have ever experienced these emotions, the sleeping, the cold, the buried image of the past. Poetry thus makes immortal all that is best and most beautiful in the world; it arrests the vanishing apparitions which haunt the interlunations of life, and veiling them or in language or in form, sends them forth among mankind, bearing sweet news of kindred joy to those with whom their sisters abide—abide, because there is no portal of expression from the caverns of the spirit which they inhabit into the universe of things. Poetry redeems from decay the visitations of the divinity in man.

—Percy Bysshe Shelley

Patience is bitter, but its fruit sweet.
—Rousseau.

Every man is a volume, if you know how to read him—Channing.

Wit consists in knowing the resemblance of things which differ, and the difference of things which are alike.
—Madame De Stael.

Our whole social life is in essence but a long, slow striving for the victory of justice over force.—John Galsworthy.

There would be no perceptible influence on the morals of the race if Hell were quenched and Heaven burned.
—Charles W. Eliot.

MANY lovable people miss each other in the world, or meet under some unfavorable star. There is the nice and critical moment of declaration to be got over. From timidity or lack of opportunity a good half of possible love cases never get so far, and at least another quarter do there cease and determine. A very adroit person, to be sure, manages to prepare the way and out with his declaration in the nick of time. And then there is a fine, solid sort of man, who goes on from snub to snub; and if he has to declare forty times will continue imperturbably declaring amid the astonished consideration of men and angels, until he has a favorable answer ✆ I daresay, if one were a woman, one would like to marry a man who was capable of doing this, but not quite one who had done so. It is just a little bit abject, and somehow just a little bit gross; and marriages in which one of the parties has been thus battered into consent scarcely form agreeable subjects for meditation. Love should run out to meet love with open arms. Indeed, the ideal story is that of two people who go into love step for step, with a fluttered consciousness, like a pair of children venturing together in a dark room. From the first moment when they see each other, with a pang of curiosity, through stage after stage of growing pleasure and embarrassment, they can read the expression of their own trouble in each other's eyes. There is here no declaration properly so called; the feeling is so plainly shared, that as soon as the man knows what is in his own heart, he is sure of what is in the woman's.—Robert Louis Stevenson.

EVERY man, however obscure, however far removed from the general recognition, is one of a group of men impressible for good, and impressible for evil, and it is in the nature of things that he can not really improve himself without in some degree improving other men.—Charles Dickens.

Be not prodigal of your opinions, lest by sharing them with others you be left without.—Ambrose Bierce.

HERE is something extremely fascinating in quickness; and most men are desirous of appearing quick. The great rule for becoming so is, *by not attempting to appear quicker than you really are;* by resolving to understand yourself and others, and to know what *you* mean, and what *they* mean, before you speak or answer.

¶ Every man must submit to be slow before he is quick; and insignificant before he is important. The too early struggle against the pain of obscurity corrupts no small share of understandings ✺ Well and happily has that man conducted his understanding who has learned to derive from the exercise of it regular occupation and rational delight; who, after having overcome the first pain of application, and acquired a habit of looking inwardly upon his own mind, perceives that every day is multiplying the relations confirming the accuracy, and augmenting the number of his ideas; who feels that he is rising in the scale of intellectual beings, gathering new strength with every new difficulty which he subdues, and enjoying today as his pleasure that which yesterday he labored at as his toil.

There are many consolations in the mind of such a man which no common life can ever afford, and many enjoyments which it has not to give! It is not the mere cry of moralists, and the flourish of rhetoricians; but it is *noble* to seek truth, and it is *beautiful* to find it. It is the ancient feeling of the human heart—that knowledge is better than riches; and it is deeply and *sacredly true!* ✺ ✺

To mark the course of human passions as they have flowed on in the ages that are past; to see why nations have risen, and why they have fallen; to speak of heat, and light, and winds; to know what man has discovered in the heavens above, and in the earth beneath; to hear the chemist unfold the marvelous properties that the Creator has locked up in a speck of earth; to be told that there are worlds so distant from our sun that the quickness of light traveling from the world's creation has never yet reached us; to wander in the creations of poetry, and grow warm again, with that eloquence which swayed the democracies of the old world; to go up with great reasoners to the First Cause of all, and to perceive in the midst of all this dissolution and decay, and cruel separation, that there *is* one thing unchangeable, indestructible, and everlasting;—it is worth while in the days of our youth to strive hard for this great discipline; to pass sleepless nights for it, to give up to it laborious days; to spurn for it present pleasures; to endure for it afflicting poverty; to wade for it through darkness, and sorrow, and contempt, as the great spirits of the world have done in all ages and all times.—Sidney Smith.

✺ ✺

PLAY is pleasurable mental and physical competitive exercise where the issues involved are trivial and transient. It is a fit preparation for more important tasks. And it is the law of life that you only do those important tasks well at which you have played in childhood.—Stanley Hall.

✺ ✺

The worst sorrows in life are not in its losses and misfortunes, but its fears.
—A. C. Benson.

Who drives the horses of the sun
Shall lord it but a day;
Better the lowly deed were done,
And kept the humble way.

The rust will find the sword of fame,
The dust will hide the crown;
Ay, none shall nail so high his name
Time will not tear it down.

The happiest heart that ever beat
Was in some quiet breast
That found the common daylight sweet,
And left to Heaven the rest.

" The Happiest Heart," *by John Vance Cheney*

IR—The bearer of this, who is going to America, presses me to give him a letter of recommendation, though I know nothing of him, not even his name. This may seem extraordinary, but I assure you it is not uncommon here. Sometimes, indeed, one unknown person brings another equally unknown, to recommend him; and sometimes they recommend one another! ◊ As to this gentleman, I must refer you to himself for his character and merits, with which he is certainly better acquainted than I can possibly be. I recommend him, however, to those civilities which every stranger, of whom one knows no harm, has a right to; and I request you will do him all the favor that, on further acquaintance, you shall find him to deserve. I have the honor to be, etc.—Paris, April 2, 1777.—Franklin.

◊ ◊

When the state is most corrupt, then laws are most multiplied.—Tacitus.

◊ ◊

HUSBANDMAN who had a quarrelsome family, after having tried in vain to reconcile them by words, thought he might more readily prevail by an example. So he called his sons and bade them lay a bundle of sticks. before him. Then having tied them up into a fagot, he told the lads, one after another, to take it up and break it. They all tried, but tried in vain. Then, untying the fagot, he gave them the sticks to break one by one. This they did with the greatest ease. Then said the father: " Thus, my sons, as long as you remain united, you are a match for all your enemies; but differ and separate, and you are undone."—Æsop.

◊ ◊

The nation that has the schools has the future.—Bismarck.

◊ ◊

HEN man has come to the Turnstiles of Night, all the creeds in the world seem to him wonderfully alike and colorless.—Rudyard Kipling.

◊ ◊

Love comes unseen; we only see it go.
—Austin Dobson.

HOEVER examines, with due circumspection, into the *Annual Records of Time,* will find it remarked, that war is the child of pride, and pride the daughter of riches—the former of which assertions may be soon granted, but one can not so easily subscribe to the latter; for pride is nearly related to beggary and want, either by father or mother, and sometimes by both: and to speak naturally, it very seldom happens among men to fall out when all have enough: invasions usually travelling from north to south, that is to say, from poverty to plenty. The most ancient and natural grounds of quarrels, are lust and avarice; which, though we may allow to be brethren, or collateral branches of pride, are certainly the issues of want.—Jonathan Swift.

◊ ◊

'T is the mind that makes the body rich.
—Shakespeare.

◊ ◊

ERHAPS none of Shelley's poems is more purely and typically Shelleian than " The Cloud," and it is interesting to note how essentially it springs from the faculty of make-believe. The same thing is conspicuous, though less purely conspicuous, throughout his singing; it is the child's faculty of make-believe raised to the " nth " power. He is still at play, save only that his play is such as manhood stops to watch, and his playthings are those which the gods give their children. The universe is the box of toys. He dabbles his fingers in the day-fall. He is gold-dusty with tumbling amidst the stars. He makes bright mischief with the moon ◊ The meteors nuzzle their noses in his hand. He teases into growling the kennelled thunder, and laughs at the shaking of its fiery chain. He dances in and out of the gates of heaven; its floor is littered with his broken fancies. He runs wild over the fields of ether. He chases the rolling world. He gets between the feet of the horses of the sun. He stands in the lap of patient Nature, and twines her loosened tresses after a hundred wilful fashions, to see how she will look nicest in his song.—Francis Thompson.

EN differ from each other in quality rather than in quantity of life. It is true, some are granted more years than others; but after all that is not so important. One would rather live a year than vegetate for a century, though I grant you it would be better to live for a hundred years than for one, if we could be sure we were living all the time and not simply staying above the ground. Yet everyone interprets life in terms of its quality rather than its quantity. Looking back over the past one often finds a day or a week standing out longer in memory than years that preceded and followed it ❧ It was longer in significance, one lived more, and so the day had deeper meaning for the spirit than years of mere routine existence. We have lived, not so many days and years, but so much work and love and struggle and joy and heart-ache. Life is always measured in terms of its quality by the standards of the soul ❧ ❧

There is, morever, one most encouraging and consoling law in human development: we grow, not in an arithmetical, but in a geometrical ratio, the increment of new life being multiplied into the old and not simply added to it. A new thought achieved is not added to the sum of one's past thinking, but multiplied into it, becoming a new point of view, from which one sees in changing perspective all other facts and ideas. One step up in the mountain widens the horizon in all directions. . . .

It is the increment of new life multiplied into the old that so largely determines the whole product of life, as far as it is within our own control ❧ We can no longer change yesterday: it arches over us as fate, but we can influence decidedly the factor of today's life which is multiplied into the whole achievement of the past ❧ ❧

That is why the margin of time we have to spend as we please is so sacred; and the briefer the margin, the more precious it becomes. If you have ten hours a day to spend as you please, you may perhaps afford to waste an hour of it—perhaps; but if you have only half an hour each day at your own free disposal that half-hour becomes a sacred opportunity of life, the chance to change the quality of your existence, to multiply the capital on which you are doing business in the vocation of living. . . .

❦ No, the river of time sweeps on with regular, remorseless current. There are hours when we would give all we possess if we could but check the flow of its waters, there are other hours when we long to speed them more rapidly; but desire and effort alike are futile. Whether we work or sleep, are earnest or idle, rejoice or moan in agony, the river of time flows on with the same resistless flood; and it is only while the water of the river of time flows over the mill-wheel of today's life that we can utilize it. Once it is past, it is in the great, unreturning sea of eternity. Other opportunities will come, other waters will flow; but that which has slipped by unused is lost utterly and will return not again.

—Edward Howard Griggs.

❧ ❧

I don't think much of a man who is not wiser today than he was yesterday.

—Abraham Lincoln.

The Body
of
Benjamin Franklin, Printer
(Like the cover of an old book,
Its contents torn out,
And stripped of its lettering and gilding,)
Lies here food for worms.
Yet the work itself shall not be lost,
For it will (as he believes) appear once
more
In a new
And more beautiful Edition
Corrected and Amended
By
The Author

" Franklin's self-written epitaph "

APOLEON is the world's greatest example of the Will-to-Power, perhaps without an equal in his individual mastery over conditions and over men ✒ ✒

It has been said of him that " he leaped the Mediterranean; he dashed across the desert; threw himself against the gate of the Orient, and its hinges, rusted by five hundred years of disuse, were shattered. He smote slothful Europe, and its medieval systems crumbled to dust. He infused armies, lawyers, artists, builders, with the electric force of the revolution, and, at his command, codes were formulated, arches and bridges were built, roads were made and canals were dug. The ruler of Italy at twenty-six, the despot of Egypt at twenty-eight, the dictator of France at thirty, the master of Europe at thirty-two," and for twenty years thereafter the central figure and the most dramatic of the world's history.

His dispatches are filled with the words: Success, Riches, Glory, Fame—these were the talismanic words of Napoleon, and yet there is in all the tragic story of man no sadder failure. Even in the days of his power, he was called " The Great Unloved." Though master of the world, save only one little island lying off in the fog of the North Atlantic—" that wart on the nose of Europe," as he persisted in calling England—though master of the world, yet of him his friend could only affirm: " Napoleon, grand, gloomy and peculiar, sits upon his throne a sceptered hermit, wrapped in the solitude of his own ambition."

Made dizzy by his own power, drunken

I am tired of planning and toiling
In the crowded hives of men;
Heart-weary of building and spoiling,
And spoiling and building again.
And I long for the dear old river,
Where I dreamed my youth away;
For a dreamer lives forever.
And a toiler dies in a day.

I am sick of the showy seeming,
Of a life that is half a lie;
Of the faces lined with scheming
In the throng that hurries by,
From the sleepless thought endeavor
I would go where the children play;
For a dreamer lives forever,
And a toiler dies in a day.

(Concluded on next page)

with his own success, he attempts to stride the world like a Colossus. And in an evil hour, more by his own failure, than through the strength of his foes, he falters and fails, as power always does and always will, for it is certain, sooner or later, to encounter a greater power or perish through internal dissension and corruption. ¶ Now turn for a moment to the Man of Galilee. What is the heart of his philosophy—" so simple," as Canon Farrar used to say, " that a little child can understand it—so profound that all the wisdom of the world can not exhaust it?" ✒ Jesus taught that all men are children of one Heavenly Father, and that, therefore, the natural condition of men is one of mutual helpfulness and of universal friendship. He conceived of the race as one human family. He refused to recognize the gulf the leaders of his people had fixed between Jew and Gentile or between the righteous and the wicked. That man is great, according to the Nazarene's gospel, who has the strength to serve and the patience to suffer—one who conquers not the world but his own selfish heart and lives to bless his fellows.

Jesus was the incarnation of the spirit that allays strife, changes animosity to friendship—his was the spirit that helps and heals. Jesus was the Prince of Peace as between man and man, nation and nation, race and race. Jesus was the Prince of Compassion. He saw the multitude poor and distressed and said, with infinite tenderness, " I have compassion on the multitude." Jesus was the Prince of Forgiveness and taught the deadliness of hate to the one who hates. Jesus was the Prince of Love and, because of this, as a great Frenchman has said, the " arch-seducer of souls." His royal proclamation was, " Come unto me and I will give you rest." His last benediction was, " Peace I leave with you, my peace I give unto you."

Napoleon, on the other hand, was the Prince of War, the incarnation of its spirit, an exemplar of its cruelty—he was the Prince of Destructive Energy, of devastating force. His empire was builded upon the sorrows of his fellowmen and cemented by their blood and tears ᴥ᷄ He was the Prince of Hate and sowed the seeds of lasting hate and bitterness. And lastly, he was the Prince of Unrelieved Despair, " The Great Unloved," therefore most miserable.—William Day Simonds.

ᴥᴥ

*O*EAR Friends: I am going to do that which the dead oft promised he would do for me.

The loved and loving brother, husband, father, friend, died where manhood's morning almost touches noon, and while the shadows still were falling toward the west ᴥᴥ

He had not passed on life's highway the stone that marks the highest point; but being weary for a moment, he lay down by the wayside, and using his burden for a pillow, fell into that dreamless sleep that kisses down his eyelids still. While yet in love with life and raptured with the world, he passed to silence and pathetic dust.

Yet, after all, it may be best, just in the happiest, sunniest hour of all the voyage, while eager winds are kissing every sail, to dash against the unseen rock, and in an instant hear the billows roar above a sunken ship. For whether in midsea or 'mong the breakers of the farther shore, a wreck at last must mark the end of each and all. And every life, no matter if its every hour is rich with love and every moment jeweled with a joy, will, at its close, become a tragedy as sad and deep and dark as can be woven of the warp and woof of mystery and death. ⬤ This brave and tender man in every storm of life was oak and rock; but in the sunshine he was vine and flower. He was the friend of all heroic souls. He climbed the heights and left all superstitions far below, while on his forehead fell the golden dawning of the grander day.

He loved the beautiful, and was with color, form, and music touched to tears. He sided with the weak, the poor, and wronged, and lovingly gave alms. With loyal heart and with the purest hands he faithfully discharged all public trusts.

He was a worshiper of liberty, a friend of the oppressed. A thousand times I have heard him quote these words: " For Justice all place a temple, and all season, summer." He believed that happiness is the only good, reason the only torch, justice the only worship, humanity the only religion, and love the only priest. He added to the sum of human joy; and were every one to whom he did some loving service to bring a blossom to his grave, he would sleep tonight beneath a wilderness of flowers.

Life is a narrow vale between the cold and barren peaks of two eternities. We strive in vain to look beyond the heights. We cry aloud, and the only answer is the echo of our wailing cry. From the voiceless lips of the unreplying dead there comes no word; but in

I can feel no pride, but pity
　For the burdens the rich endure;
There is nothing sweet in the city,
　But the patient lives of the poor.
O, the little hands too skilful.
　And the child mind choked with weeds,
The daughter's heart grown wilful,
　And the father's heart that bleeds.

No, no, from the street's rude bustle,
　From trophies of mart and stage,
I would fly to the wood's low rustle
　And the meadow's kindly page.
Let me dream as of old by the river.
　And be loved for the dream alway;
For a dreamer lives forever,
　And a toiler dies in a day.

" The Dreamer," *by John Boyle O'Reilly*

the night of death hope sees a star and listening love can hear the rustle of a wing ๑๑ ๑๑

He who sleeps here, when dying, mistaking the approach of death for the return of health, whispered with his latest breath, " I am better now." Let us believe, in spite of doubts and dogmas, of fears and tears, that these dear words are true of all the countless dead. ℂ The record of a generous life runs like a vine around the memory of our dead, and every sweet, unselfish act is now a perfumed flower.

And now, to you, who have been chosen, from among the many men he loved, to do the last sad office for the dead, we give his sacred dust.

Speech can not contain our love. There was, there is, no gentler, stronger, manlier man ๑๑ ๑๑

—Robert G. Ingersoll. (Tribute to His Brother, Ebon C. Ingersoll.)

๑๑ ๑๑

The greater the obstacle the more glory in overcoming it.—Molière.

๑๑ ๑๑

WHEN I left camp that morning I had not expected so soon the result that was then taking place, and consequently was in rough garb. I was without a sword—as I usually was when on horseback on the field—and wore a soldier's blouse for a coat, with the shoulder-straps of my rank to indicate to the army who I was. When I went into the house I found General Lee. We greeted each other, and after shaking hands, took our seats. I had my staff with me, a good portion of whom were in the room during the whole of the interview. . . . . General Lee was dressed in a full uniform, which was entirely new, and was wearing a sword of considerable value—very likely the sword which had been presented by the State of Virginia; at all events, it was an entirely different sword from the one which would ordinarily be worn in the field. In my rough traveling suit—the uniform of a private, with the straps of a lieutenant-general—I must have contrasted very strangely with a man so handsomely dressed, six feet high, and of faultless form. But this was

not a matter that I thought of until afterward. ℂ We soon fell into a conversation about old army times. He remarked that he remembered me very well in the old army; and I told him that as a matter of course I remembered him perfectly; but from the difference between our ranks and years (there being about sixteen years' difference between our ages), I had thought it very likely that I had not attracted his attention sufficiently to be remembered by him after such a long interval. Our conversation grew so pleasant that I almost forgot the object of our meeting.

After the conversation had run on in this way for some time, General Lee called my attention to the object of our meeting, and said that he had asked for this interview for the purpose of getting from me the terms I proposed to give his army. I said that I merely meant that his army should lay down their arms, not to take them up again during the war unless duly and properly exchanged. He said that he had so understood my letter. Then we gradually fell off into conversation about matters foreign to the subject which had brought us together. This continued for some time, when General Lee again interrupted the course of the conversation by suggesting that the terms I proposed to give his army ought to be written out. I called to General Parker, secretary on my staff, for writing materials, and commenced writing out the terms . . . . . When I put my pen to the paper I did not know the first word that I should make use of in writing the terms. I only knew what was in my mind, and I wished to express it clearly, so that there could be no mistaking it. As I wrote on, the thought occurred to me that the officers had their own private horses and effects, which were important to them, but of no value to us; also that it would be an unnecessary humiliation to call upon them to deliver their side-arms. ℂ No conversation—not one word— passed between General Lee and myself either about private property, side-arms or kindred subjects. When he read over that part of the terms about side-arms, horses, and private property of the officers, he remarked, with some feeling, I thought, that this would have a happy effect upon his army . . . . The much-talked-of surrendering of Lee's sword and my handing it back—this and much more that has been said about it is the purest romance. The word sword or side-arms was not mentioned by either of us until I wrote it in the terms. There was no premeditation, and it did not occur to me until the moment I wrote it down. If I had happened to omit it, and General Lee had called my attention to it, I should have put it in the terms, precisely as I acceded to the provision about the soldiers retaining their horses. . . . Lee and I separated as cordially as we had met, he returning to his own line; and all went into bivouac for the night at Appomattox.

—General U. S. Grant. (Meeting with General Robert E. Lee at Appomattox.)

๑ ๑

When I don't know whether to fight or not, I always fight.—Nelson.

๑ ๑

"THE cost of a thing," says Thoreau, " is the amount of what I will call life which is required to be exchanged for it, immediately or in the long run." I have been accustomed to put it to myself, perhaps more clearly, that the price we have to pay for money is paid in liberty. Between these two ways of it, at least, the reader will probably not fail to find a third definition of his own, and it follows, on one or other, that a man may pay too dearly for his livelihood by giving in Thoreau's terms, his whole life for it, or, in mine, bartering for it the whole of his available liberty, and becoming a slave till death. There are two questions to be considered—the quality of what we buy, and the price we have to pay for it. Do you want a thousand a year, a two thousand a year or a ten thousand a year, livelihood? and can you afford the one you want? It is a matter of taste; it is not in the least degree a question of duty, though commonly supposed so. But there is no authority for that view anywhere. It is nowhere in the Bible. It is true that we might do a vast amount of good if we were wealthy, but

it is also highly improbable; not many do; and the art of growing rich is not only quite distinct from that of doing good, but the practice of the one does not at all train a man for practising the other. " Money might be of great service to me," writes Thoreau, " but the difficulty now is that I do not improve my opportunities, and therefore I am not prepared to have my opportunities increased." It is a mere illusion that, above a certain income, the personal desires will be satisfied and leave a wider margin for the generous impulse. It is as difficult to be generous, or anything else, except perhaps a member of Parliament, on thirty thousand as on two thousand a year.

—Robert Louis Stevenson.

๑ ๑

I owe all my success in life to having been always a quarter of an hour beforehand.—Lord Nelson.

๑ ๑

"DEAR MADAM: I have been shown in the files of the War Department a statement of the Adjutant-General of Massachusetts that you are the mother of five sons who have died gloriously on the field of battle. I feel how weak and fruitless must be any words of mine which should attempt to beguile you from the grief of a loss so overwhelming. But I can not refrain from tendering to you the consolation that may be found in the thanks of the Republic they died to save. I pray that our heavenly Father may assuage the anguish of your bereavement, and leave you only the cherished memory of the loved and lost, and the solemn pride that must be yours to have laid so costly a sacrifice upon the altar of freedom.—Abraham Lincoln. (Letter to Mrs. Bixby. Washington, November 21, 1864.)

๑ ๑

LUCK means the hardships and privations which you have not hesitated to endure; the long nights you have devoted to work. Luck means the appointments you have never failed to keep; the trains you have never failed to catch.—Max O'Rell.

EVER, perhaps, did any man suffer death with more justice, or deserve it less. The first step he took, after his capture, was to write a letter to General Washington, conceived in terms of dignity without insolence, and apology without meanness. The scope of it, was to vindicate himself from the imputation of having assumed a mean character for treacherous or interested purposes; asserting that he had been involuntarily an impostor; that contrary to his intention which was to meet a person for intelligence on neutral ground, he had been betrayed within our posts, and forced into the vile condition of an enemy in disguise: soliciting only that, to whatever rigor policy might devote him, a decency of treatment might be observed, due to a person, who, though unfortunate, had been guilty of nothing dishonorable. His request was granted in its full extent; for, in the whole progress of the affair, he was treated with the most scrupulous delicacy. When brought before the Board of Officers, he met with every mark of indulgence, and was required to answer no interrogatory which could even embarrass his feelings. On his part, while he carefully concealed everything that might involve others, he frankly confessed all the facts relating to himself; and, upon his confession, without the trouble of examining a witness, the board made their report. The members of it were not more impressed with the candor and firmness, mixed with a becoming sensibility, which he displayed, than he was penetrated with their liberality and politeness. He acknowledged the gener-

O Captain! my Captain! our fearful trip
*　　is done,*
The ship has weathered every rack, the
*　　prize we sought is won.*
The port is near, the bells I hear, the
*　　people all exulting,*
While follow eyes the steady keel, the
*　　vessel grim and daring;*
*　But O heart! heart! heart!*
*　　O the bleeding drops of red,*
*　Where on the deck my Captain lies,*
*　　Fallen cold and dead.*

O Captain! my Captain! rise up and hear
*　　the bells;*
Rise up—for you the flag is flung—for
*　　you the bugle trills,*
For you bouquets and ribboned wreaths
*　　—for you the shores a-crowding,*

(Concluded on next page)

osity of the behavior toward him in every respect, but particularly in this, in the strongest terms of manly gratitude. In a conversation with a gentleman who visited him after his trial, he said he flattered himself he had never been illiberal; but if there were any remains of prejudice in his mind, his present experience must obliterate them. ❡ In one of the visits I made to him, (and I saw him several times during his confinement,) he begged me to be the bearer of a request to the general, for permission to send an open letter to Sir Henry Clinton. " I foresee my fate," said he, ''and though I pretend not to play the hero, or to be indifferent about life, yet I am reconciled to whatever may happen, conscious that misfortune, not guilt, has brought it upon me. There is only one thing that disturbs my tranquillity. Sir Henry Clinton has been too good to me; he has been lavish of his kindness. I am bound to him by too many obligations, and love him too well, to bear the thought that he should reproach himself, or that others should reproach him, on the supposition of my having conceived myself obliged, by his instructions, to run the risk I did. I would not, for the world, leave a sting in his mind that should embitter his future days." He could scarce finish the sentence, bursting into tears in spite of his efforts to suppress them; and with difficulty collected himself enough afterward to add: " I wish to be permitted to assure him, I did not act under this impression, but submitted to a necessity imposed upon me, as contrary to my own inclination as to his orders." His request was readily complied with; and he wrote the letter, annexed, with which I dare say you will be as much pleased as I am, both for the diction and sentiment.

¶ When his sentence was announced to him, he remarked, that since it was his lot to die, there was still a choice in the mode, which would make a material difference in his feelings; and he would be happy, if possible, to be indulged with a professional death. He made a second application, by letter, in concise but persuasive terms. It was thought this indulgence, being incompatible with the customs of war, could not be granted; and it was therefore determined, in both cases, to evade an answer, to spare him the sensations which a certain knowledge of the intended mode would inflict.

In going to the place of execution, he bowed familiarly, as he went along, to all those with whom he had been acquainted in his confinement ঌ A smile of complacency expressed the serene fortitude of his mind. Arrived at the fatal spot, he asked, with some emotion, " Must I then die in this manner?" He was told it had been unavoidable. " I am reconciled to my fate," said he, " but not to the mode." Soon, however, recollecting himself, he added: " It will be but a momentary pang;" and, springing upon the cart, performed the last offices to himself, with a composure that excited the admiration and melted the hearts of the beholders ঌ Upon being told the final moment was at hand, and asked if he had anything to say, he answered, " Nothing, but to request you will witness to the world, that I die like a brave man." Among the extraordinary circumstances that attended him, in the midst of his enemies, he died universally esteemed and universally regretted.

I am aware that a man of real merit is never seen in so favorable a light as through the medium of adversity: the clouds that surround him are shades that set off his good qualities. Misfortune cuts down the little vanities that, in prosperous times, serve as so many spots in his virtues; and gives a tone of humility that makes his worth more amiable. His spectators, who enjoy a happier lot, are less prone to detract from it, through envy, and are more disposed, by compassion, to give him the credit he deserves, and perhaps even to magnify it.

I speak not of André's conduct in this affair as a philosopher, but as a man of the world. The authorized maxims and practices of war are the satires of human nature. They countenance almost every species of seduction as well as violence; and the general who can make most traitors in the army of his adversary, is frequently most applauded. On this scale we acquit André; while we could not but condemn him, if we were to examine his conduct by the sober rules of philosophy and moral rectitude.—Alexander Hamilton. (The Fate of André).

ঌ ঌ

HALF the joy of life is in little things taken on the run. Let us run if we must—even the sands do that—but let us keep our hearts young and our eyes open that nothing worth our while shall escape us. And everything is worth its while if we only grasp it and its significance.—Victor Cherbuliez.

ঌ ঌ

Equality causes no war.—Solon.

For you they call, the swaying mass,
their eager faces turning;
Here Captain! dear father!
This arm beneath your head!
It is some dream that on the deck
You 've fallen cold and dead.

My Captain does not answer, his lips are
pale and still,
My father does not feel my arm, he has
no pulse nor will,
The ship is anchored safe and sound, its
voyage closed and done,
From fearful trip the victor ship comes in
with object won;
Exult O shores, and ring O bells!
But I with mournful tread,
Walk the deck my Captain lies,
Fallen cold and dead.

"O Captain! My Captain!" by Walt Whitman

IFE is indeed a strange gift, and its privileges are most mysterious. No wonder when it is first granted to us that our gratitude, our admiration and our delight should prevent us from reflecting on our own nothingness, or from thinking it will ever be recalled. Our first and strongest impressions are borrowed from the mighty scene that is opened to us, and we unconsciously transfer its durability, as well as its splendor, to ourselves. So newly found we can not think of parting with it yet, or at least put off that consideration *sine die*. Like a rustic at a fair, we are full of amazement and rapture, and have no thought of going home, or that it will soon be night. We know our existence only by ourselves, and confound our knowledge with the objects of it. We and nature are therefore one. Otherwise the illusion, the " feast of reason and the flow of soul," to which we are invited, is a mockery and a cruel insult. We do not go from a play till the last act is ended, and the lights are about to be extinguished. But the fairy face of nature still shines on: shall we be called away before the curtain falls, or ere we have scarce had a glimpse of what is going on? Like children, our step-mother nature holds us up to see the raree-show of the universe, and then, as if we were a burden to her to support, let us fall down again. Yet what brave sublunary things does not this pageant present, like a ball or *fete* of the universe!

To see the golden sun, the azure sky, the outstretched ocean; to walk upon the green earth, and to be lord of a thousand creatures; to look down yawning precipices or over distant sunny vales; to see the world spread out under one's feet as a map; to bring the stars near; to view the smallest insects through a microscope; to read history and consider the revolutions of empire and the successions of generations; to hear of the glory of Tyre, of Sidon, of Babylon, and of Susa, and to say all these were before me and are now nothing; to say I exist in such a point of time, and in such a point of space; to be a spectator and a part of its ever-moving scene; to witness the change of season, of spring and autumn, of winter and summer; to feel hot and cold, pleasure and pain, beauty and deformity, right and wrong; to be sensible to the accidents of nature; to consider the mighty world of eye and ear; to listen to the stock-dove's notes amid the forest deep; to journey over moor and mountain; to hear the midnight sainted choir; to visit lighted halls, or the cathedral's gloom, or sit in crowded theaters and see life itself mocked; to study the works of art, and refine the sense of beauty to agony; to worship fame and to dream of immortality; to look upon the Vatican and to read Shakespeare; to gather up the wisdom of the ancients and to pry into the future; to listen to the trump of war, the shout of victory; to question history as to the movements of the human heart; to seek for truth; to plead the cause of humanity; to overlook the world as if time and nature poured their treasures at our feet—to be and to do all this, and then in a moment to be nothing—to have it all snatched from us by a juggler's trick, or a phantasmagoria! There is something in this transition from all to nothing that shocks us and damps the enthusiasm of youth new flushed with hope and pleasure, and we cast the comfortless thought as far from us as we can . . . . The world is a witch that puts us off with false shows and appearances.

—William Hazlitt.

VERY young man should have this sentiment planted and nourished in him, that he is to regard himself as one of Nature's failures, but as also a proof of her great and wonderful intention; she succeeded ill, he must say to himself, but I will honor her intention by serving towards her better future success.

—Schopenhauer.

Our hope for eternal life in the hereafter does not spring from a longing for a spiritual existence, but grows out of our love for life upon this earth, which we have tried and found good.

—Robert J. Shores.

AKE not anxious thought as to the results of your work nor of our work. If you are doing all that you can, the results, immediate or eventual, are not your affair at all. Such seed of truth as we plant can but grow. If we do not see the fruits here, we know nevertheless that here or somewhere they do spring up.

It would be great if we could succeed now; it will be greater if we patiently wait for success, even though we never see it ourselves. For it will come. Do not be fretted by abuse. Those who abuse you do not know what they are doing. We also were at one time deluded and cruel, therefore forgive.

Do not be worried by bigotry. We can not help it, we are not responsible for it —we are responsible to ourselves and for ourselves and for no one else. Do not be angry at opposition either; no one can really oppose the order of Nature or the decrees of God, which are one and the same. Our plans may be upset—there are greater plans than ours.

They may not be completed in the time we would wish, but our works and the work of those who follow us, they will be carried out.

Do not grieve over your own troubles: you would not have them if you did not need them. Do not grieve over the troubles of "others;" there are no others ∞ ∞

Therefore let us keep God in our hearts and quiet in our minds, for though in the flesh we may never stand upon our edifice, we are building that which shall never be pulled down.—Bolton Hall.

∞ ∞

Don't part with your illusions. When they are gone you may still exist, but you have ceased to live.—Mark Twain.

∞ ∞

A LITTLE while ago, I stood by the grave of the old Napoleon—a magnificent tomb of gilt and gold, fit almost for a dead deity—and gazed upon the sarcophagus of rare and nameless marble, where rest at last the ashes of that restless man. I leaned over the balustrade and thought about the career of the greatest soldier of the modern world. ❡ I saw him walking upon the banks of the Seine, contemplating suicide. I saw him at Toulon—I saw him putting down the mob in the streets of Paris—I saw him at the head of the army of Italy—I saw him crossing the bridge of Lodi with the tricolor in his hand—I saw him in Egypt in the shadows of the pyramids— I saw him conquer the Alps and mingle the eagles of France with the eagles of the crags. I saw him at Marengo—at Ulm and Austerlitz. I saw him in Russia, where the infantry of the snow and the cavalry of the wild blast scattered his legions like winter's withered leaves. I saw him at Leipsic in defeat and disaster—driven by a million bayonets back upon Paris—clutched like a wild beast— banished to Elba. I saw him escape and retake an empire by the force of his genius. I saw him upon the frightful field of Waterloo, where Chance and Fate combined to wreck the fortunes of their former king. And I saw him at St. Helena, with his hands crossed behind him, gazing out upon the sad and solemn sea ∞ ∞

I thought of the orphans and widows he had made—of the tears that had been shed for his glory, and of the only woman who ever loved him, pushed from his heart by the cold hand of ambition. And I said I would rather have been a French peasant and worn wooden shoes. I would rather have lived in a hut with a vine growing over the door, and the grapes growing purple in the kisses of the autumn sun. I would rather have been that poor peasant with my loving wife by my side, knitting as the day died out of the sky—with my children upon my knees and their arms about me—I would rather have been that man and gone down to the tongueless silence of the dreamless dust, than to have been that imperial impersonation of force and murder, known as "Napoleon the Great."
—Robert G. Ingersoll.

∞ ∞

No man is worth his salt who is not ready at all times to risk his body, to risk his well-being, to risk his life, in a great cause.—Theodore Roosevelt.

HE pretty fable by which the Duchess of Orleans illustrates the character of her son, the regent, might, with little change, be applied to Byron. All the fairies, save one, had been bidden to his cradle. All the gossips had been profuse of their gifts. One had bestowed nobility, another genius, a third beauty. The malignant elf who had been uninvited came last, and, unable to reverse what her sisters had done for their favorite, had mixed up a curse with every blessing. He was sprung of a house, ancient indeed and noble, but degraded and impoverished by a series of crimes and follies, which had attained a scandalous publicity. The kinsman whom he succeeded had died poor, and, but for merciful judges, would have died upon the gallows ∾ The young peer had great intellectual powers; yet there was an unsound part in his mind. He had naturally a generous and tender heart; but his temper was irritable and wayward. He had a head which statuaries loved to copy, and a foot the deformity of which the beggars in the street mimicked. Distinguished at once by the strength and by the weakness of his intellect, affectionate yet perverse, a poor lord, and a handsome cripple, he required, if ever man required, the firmest and the most judicious training. But, capriciously as nature had dealt with him, the relative to whom the office of forming his character was entrusted was more capri-

cious still. She passed from paroxysms of rage to paroxysms of fondness. At one time she stifled him with her caresses, at another time she insulted his deformity. ℂ He came into the world, and the world treated him as his mother treated him—sometimes with kindness, sometimes with severity, never with justice. It indulged him without discrimination, and punished him without discrimination. He was truly a spoilt child; not merely the spoilt child of his parents, but the spoilt child of nature, the spoilt child of fortune, the spoilt child of fame, the spoilt child of society. His first poems were received with a contempt which feeble as they were, they did not absolutely deserve. The poem which he published on his return from his travels was, on the other hand, extolled far above its merits. At twenty-four he found himself on the highest pinnacle of literary fame, with Scott, Wordsworth, Southey, and a crowd of other distinguished writers, beneath his feet. There is scarcely an instance in history of so sudden a rise to so dizzy an eminence. ℂ Everything that could stimulate, and everything that could gratify the strongest propensities of our nature—the gaze of a hundred drawing-rooms, the acclamations of the whole nation, the applause of applauded men, the love of the loveliest women—all this world, and the glory of it, were at once offered to a young man, to whom nature had given violent passions, and whom education

My new-cut ashlar takes the light
Where crimson-blank the windows flare.
By my own work before the night,
Great Overseer, I make my prayer.

If there be good in that I wrought,
Thy Hand compelled it, Master, Thine—
Where I have failed to meet Thy Thought
I know, through Thee, the blame was mine.

The depth and dream of my desire,
The bitter paths wherein I stray—
Thou knowest Who hast made the Fire,
Thou Knowest Who hast made the Clay.

Who, lest all thought of Eden fade,
Bring'st Eden to the craftsman's brain—
Godlike to muse o'er his own trade,
And manlike stand with God again!

One stone the more swings into place
In that dread Temple of Thy worth.
It is enough that, through Thy Grace,
I saw naught common on Thy Earth.

Take not that vision from my ken—
Oh whatsoe'er may spoil or speed.
Help me to need no aid from men
That I may help such men as need!
    "A Dedication," *by Rudyard Kipling*

had never taught to control them. He lived as many men live who have no similar excuses to plead for his faults. But his countrymen and his countrywomen would love him and admire him. They were resolved to see in his excesses only the flash and outbreak of the same fiery mind which glowed in his poetry. He attacked religion; yet in religious circles his name was mentioned with fondness, and in many religious publications his works were censured with singular tenderness. He lampooned the Prince Regent; yet he could not alienate the Tories. Everything, it seems, was to be forgiven to youth, rank and genius ✒ Then came the reaction. Society, capricious in its indignation as it had been capricious in its fondness, flew into a rage with its froward and petted darling. He had been worshiped with an irrational idolatry ✒ He was persecuted with an irrational fury. Much has been written about those unhappy domestic occurrences, which decided the fate of his life. Yet nothing ever was positively known to the public but this—that he quarreled with his lady, and that she refused to live with him. There have been hints in abundance and shrugs and shakings of the head, and " Well, well, we know," and " We could if we would," and " If we list to speak," and " There be that might an they list." But we are not aware that there is before the world, substantiated by credible, or even by tangible evidence,

Tiger, tiger, burning bright
In the forests of the night,
What immortal hand or eye
Could frame thy fearful symmetry?

In what distant deeps or skies
Burnt the fires of thine eyes?
On what wings dare he aspire?
What the hand dare seize the fire?

And what shoulder, and what art,
Could twist the sinews of thy heart?
And when thy heart began to beat,
What dread hand? and what dread feet?

What the hammer? what the chain?
In what furnace was thy brain?
What the anvil? what dread grasp
Dare its deadly terrors clasp?

When the stars threw down their spears,
And water'd heaven with their tears,
Did he smile his work to see?
Did he who made the lamb make thee?

Tiger, tiger, burning bright
In the forests of the night,
What immortal hand or eye
Dare frame thy fearful symmetry?

" The Tiger," *by William Blake*

a single fact indicating that Lord Byron was more to blame than any other man who is on bad terms with his wife. The professional men whom Lady Byron consulted were undoubtedly of the opinion that she ought not to live with her husband. But it is to be remembered that they formed that opinion without hearing both sides. We do not say, we do not mean to insinuate, that Lady Byron was in any respect to blame. We think that those who condemn her on the evidence which is now before the public are as rash as those who condemn her husband. ⁌ We will not pronounce any judgment; we can not, even in our own minds, form any judgment on a transaction which is so imperfectly known to us ✒ It would have been well if, at the time of the separation, all those who knew as little about the matter then as we know about it now, had shown that forbearance, which, under such circumstances, is but common justice.

We know no spectacle so ridiculous as the British public in one of its periodical lifts of morality. In general, elopements, divorces, and family quarrels pass with little notice. We read the scandal, talk about it for a day, and forget it. But once in six or seven years, our virtue becomes outrageous. We can not suffer the laws of religion and decency to be violated. We must make a stand against vice. We must teach libertines that the English people appreciate the importance of domestic ties. Accordingly, some unfortunate man, in no respect more depraved than hundreds whose offenses have been treated with lenity, is singled out as an expiatory sacrifice. If he has children, they are to be taken from him. If he has a profession, he is to be driven from it. He is cut by the higher orders, and hissed by the lower. He is, in truth, a sort of whipping-boy, by whose vicarious agonies all the other transgressors of the same class are, it is supposed, sufficiently chastised ❧ We reflect very complacently on our own severity, and compare with great pride the high standard of morals established in England, with the Parisian laxity. At length our anger is satiated. Our victim is ruined and heartbroken. And our virtue goes quietly to sleep for seven years more. ❡ It is clear that those vices which destroy domestic happiness ought to be as much as possible repressed. It is equally clear that they can not be repressed by penal legislation ❧ It is therefore right and desirable that public opinion should be directed against them. But it should be directed against them uniformly, steadily, and temperately, not by sudden fits and starts. There should be one weight and one measure. Declamation is always an objectionable mode of punishment. It is the resource of judges too indolent and hasty to investigate facts, and to discriminate nicely between shades of guilt. It is an irrational practice, even when adopted by military tribunals. When adopted by the tribunal of public opinion, it is infinitely more irrational. It is good that a certain portion of disgrace should constantly attend on certain bad actions. But it is not good that the offenders merely have to stand the risks of a lottery of infamy that ninety-

So, we'll go no more a-roving
  So late into the night,
Though the heart be still as loving
  And the moon be still as bright.

For the sword outwears its sheath,
  And the soul wears out the breast,
And the heart must pause to breathe,
  And love itself have rest.

Though the night was made for loving
  And the day returns too soon,
Yet we'll go no more a-roving
  By the light of the moon.

"We'll Go No More A-Roving," *by Lord Byron*

nine out of every hundred should escape; and that the hundredth, perhaps the most innocent of the hundred, should pay for all. . . .

We can not even now retrace those events without feeling something of what was felt by the nation when it was first known that the grave had closed over so much sorrow and so much glory—something of what was felt by those who saw the hearse, with its long train of coaches turn slowly northward, leaving behind it that cemetery, which had been consecrated by the dust of so many great poets, but of which the doors were closed against all that remained of Byron. We well remember that, on that day, rigid moralists could not refrain from weeping for one so young, so illustrious, so unhappy, gifted with such rare gifts and tried by such strong temptations. It is unnecessary to make any reflections. The history carries its moral with it. Our age has indeed been fruitful of warnings to the eminent and of consolation to the obscure ❧ Two men have died within our recollection, who at a time of life at which few people have completed their education, had raised themselves, each in his own department, to the height of glory. One of them died at the height of glory. One of them (Napoleon) died at Longwood, the other (Byron) at Missolonghi.—Lord Macaulay.

❧ ❧

If those who are the enemies of innocent amusements had the direction of the world, they would take away the spring, and youth; the former from the year, the latter from human life.

—Balzac.

❧ ❧

To believe with certainty we must begin by doubting.—Stanislaus.

F Turner's correspondence very little is in existence, and little can have been worth preserving. He could write a simple note, especially to an intimate friend; and though his spelling was always uncertain, he sometimes, by happy accident, could get through a few sentences without a blunder ◦ Like most uneducated men, he disliked letter writing, and he carried this dislike to a degree involving positive discourtesy to others.

He received a good many dinner invitations and though not what was called a diner-out, was on the other hand frequently disposed to profit by that rule of society which allows a bachelor to receive hospitality without returning it; so that although nobody could be sure he would accept an invitation, nobody, on the other hand, could be certain that he would invariably prefer his bachelor's fireside ◦ ◦

His dislike to the trouble of letter writing made him treat invitations in a very peculiar manner, and in a manner which only very kind and indulgent friends would have put up with. Sometimes he answered them, but he did n't by any means consider it an obligation to do so; and he would go to dine, and determine at the last minute not to go, just as we go to the theater, without writing anything to the provider of the entertainment. Whenever he went beyond a simple note his letters were ill-spelled and ungrammatical ◦ ◦

The reader may find it a relief to see a specimen of Turner's prose—a philo-sophical piece about morality and art. Let him study it as long as he thinks it worth his attention and he will find it utterly impossible to understand one single sentence in the paragraph: " They wrong virtue, enduring difficulties or worth in the bare imitation of nature, all the force received in some brain; but where these demands arise above mediocrity it assuredly would not be a little sacrifice to those who perceive the value of the success to foster it by terms as cordial that can not look so easy away as those spoken of convey doubts to the accepting individual. If as the line that unites the above to grace, and those forces forming a new style, not that soul can guess as ethics. Teach them both, but many serve as the body and soul, and but presume more as the beacon headland which would be a warning to the danger of mannerism and disgustful."

❡ This criticism of Turner as a writer may here come to an end. Enough has been said to prove the truth of the assertion made at the beginning of this biography, to the effect that he did not know the English language. His unsuccessful attempt to learn Latin with Mr. Trimmer is a proof that he did not know Latin. His outrageous spelling of French names is equally good evidence that he never mastered French, and there is not a trace of proof that he ever knew any other tongue. The plain truth is, that he never possessed any language whatever. Hundreds of foreigners can write better English than he could. There are English letters on my table from Dutchmen at Amsterdam, at the Hague,

_Hark you such sound as quivers? Kings
    will hear,
  As kings have heard, and tremble on
    their thrones;
The old will feel the weight of mossy
    stones;
The young alone will laugh and scoff
    at fear.
It is the tread of armies marching near,
  From scarlet lands to lands forever
    pale;
  It is a bugle dying down the gale;
Is the sudden gushing of a tear.
And it is hands that grope at ghostly
    doors;
  And romp of spirit-children on the
    pave;
  It is the tender sighing of the brave
Who fell, ah! long ago, in futile wars;
  It is such sound as death; and, after all,
  'Tis but the forest letting dead leaves
    fall._

" November," _by Mahlon Leonard Fisher_

at Leyden, which are far superior in grammar, spelling and construction to anything that Turner could compose after living in London for fifty years, with access to the best society in England ❧ ❧

Is there any use, it may be asked, in dwelling upon these weak points of a great genius. Would it not be at once more agreeable and more becoming to veil them gently in forgetfulness? Perhaps it might, but assuredly the agreeable and the becoming are not the only purposes of this biography. When we study the life of a man who is famous for what he has done, it is good for us to have no illusions about the range of his powers, and the degree of his cultivation. The quotations which have been made will quite certainly prevent any reader from forming in his own mind the image of an ideal Turner and worshiping it. Beyond this benefit, which is not to be despised, we have the other advantage of noting how completely, in Turner, the man was sacrificed to the artist, as gardeners sacrifice certain fruit trees to their fruit. The pruning was not done intentionally in his case ❧ One dominant faculty absorbed all the sap of his intelligence, and left him as inferior to the mass of educated men in common things as he was superior to them in the perception of natural beauty. It may be a consolation to mediocrities, to reflect that if they can not paint, they would infinitely outshine Turner at a grammar school examination; but without desiring to soothe the jealousies of artists who spell better than they paint, we may assuredly affirm that it remains, and must ever remain, an open question, whether when you compare Turner with what we call an educated gentleman, the sum of superiorities will not be on the side of the gentleman.

The case of Turner is just one of those cases which conform to the prejudice against artists, as craftsmen who have developed a special skill at the cost of more necessary knowledge and accomplishments. It throws, too, a very strong light upon the question whether artistic genius is a special faculty, or an exceptionally high condition of all the faculties. I think that the case of Turner proves artistic genius to be a special faculty only. If all his mental powers had been of a high order he would have written his native language easily and correctly as a matter of course, and even composed good poetry, since he had feeling and imagination. On the other hand, his career proves conclusively that literary talent and the sort of education which fosters it, are now, as so many believe, absolutely essential to the attainment of distinction and success in life. The lesson which such men leave to us, when we understand both their excellence and their deficiency, is not to humiliate ourselves, not to lose our self-respect in their presence, and on the other hand not to attach too much importance to our own superiorities over them, since they have done so easily without our accomplishments ❧ It is probable that every reader of these pages is greatly superior to Turner in what is held to be an education of the general order. At the same time, it is impossible to forget that this unpolished and illiterate being had the rarest gifts of nature of a special kind, all of which is clear proof that the knowledge of language is not necessary to the exercise of high faculties.—Philip G. Hamerton. (Life of J. M. W. Turner.)

❧ ❧

War does not of choice destroy bad men, but good ever.—Sophocles.

❧ ❧

There is only one way to get ready for immortality, and that is to love this life and live it as bravely and faithfully, and cheerfully as we can.
—Henry van Dyke.

❧ ❧

The darkest hour in any man's life is when he sits down to plan how to get money without earning it.
—Horace Greeley.

❧ ❧

A handful of pine-seed will cover mountains with the green majesty of forest. I too will set my face to the wind and throw my handful of seed on high.
—Fiona Macleod.

EAR SIR:—I have read your manuscript with some attention. By the argument it contains against a particular Providence, though you allow a general Providence, you strike at the foundations of all religion. For, without the belief of a Providence that takes cognizance of, guards, and guides, and may favor particular persons, there is no motive to worship a Deity, to fear his displeasure or to pray for his protection. I will not enter into any discussion of your principles, though you seem to desire it *so* At present I shall only give you my opinion that, though your reasons are subtile, and may prevail with some readers, you will not succeed so as to change the general sentiments of mankind on that subject, and the consequence of printing this piece will be, a great deal of odium drawn upon yourself, mischief to you, and no benefit to others. He that spits against the wind spits in his own face.

But were you to suceed, do you imagine any good would be done by it? You yourself may find it easy to live a virtuous life, without the assistance afforded by religion; you having a clear perception of the advantages of virtue, and the disadvantage of vice, and possessing a strength of resolution sufficient to enable you to resist common temptations. But think how great a portion of mankind consists of weak and ignorant men and women, and of inexperienced, inconsiderate youth of both sexes, who have need of the motives of religion to restrain them from vice, to support their virtue, and retain them in the practice of it till it becomes habitual, which is the great point for its security. And perhaps you are indebted to her originally, that is, to your religious education, for the habits of virtue upon which you now justly value yourself. You might easily display your excellent talents of reasoning upon a less hazardous subject, and thereby obtain a rank with our most distinguished authors *so* For among us it is not necessary, as among the Hottentots, that a youth, to be raised into the company of men, should prove his manhood by beating his mother. ❡ I would advise you, therefore, not to attempt unchaining the tiger, but to burn this piece before it is seen by any other person; whereby you will save yourself a great deal of mortification by the enemies it may raise against you, and perhaps a good deal of regret and repentance. If men are so wicked with religion, what would they be if without it. I intend this letter itself as a proof of my friendship, and therefore add no professions to it; but subscribe simply yours,

B. Franklin.

When I consider Life and its few years—
A wisp of fog betwixt us and the sun;
A call to battle, and the battle done
Ere the last echo dies within our ears;
A rose choked in the grass; an hour of
fears;
The gusts that past a darkening shore do
beat;
The burst of music down an unlistening
street—
I wonder at the idleness of tears.
Ye old, old dead, and ye of yesternight,
Chieftains, and bards, and keepers of the
sheep,
By every cup of sorrow that you had,
Loose me from tears, and make me see
aright
How each hath back what once he stayed
to weep;
Homer his sight, David his little lad!

"Tears," by Lizette Woodworth Reese

so so

O man will ever be a big executive who feels that he must, either openly or under cover, follow up every order he gives and see that it is done—nor will he ever develop a capable assistant.

—John Lee Mahin.

so so

Behavior is the theory of manners practically applied.—Mme. Necker.

so so

Whatever strengthens and purifies the affections, enlarges the imagination, and adds spirit to sense, is useful.—Shelley.

HERE are few things of more common occurrence than shaking hands; and yet I do not recollect that much has been speculated upon the subject. I confess, when I consider to what unimportant and futile concerns the attention of writers and readers has been directed, I am surprised that no one has been found to *handle* so important a matter as this, and attempt to give the public a rational view of the doctrine and discipline of shaking hands.

I have been unable to find in the ancient writers any distinct mention of shaking hands. They followed the heartier practice of hugging or embracing, which has not wholly disappeared among grown persons in Europe, and children in our own country, and has unquestionably the advantage on the score of cordiality. When the ancients trusted the business of salutation to the hands alone, they joined but did not shake them; and although I find frequently such phrases as *jungere dextras hospitio,* I do not recollect to have met with that of *agitare dextras.* I am inclined to think that the practice grew up in the ages of chivalry, when the cumbrous iron mail, in which the knights were cased, prevented their embracing; and when, with fingers clothed in steel, the simple touch or joining of the hands would have been but cold welcome; so that a prolonged junction was a natural resort, to express cordiality; and as it would have been awkward to keep the hands unemployed in this position, a gentle agitation or shaking might have been naturally introduced. How long the practice may have remained in this incipient stage it is impossible, in the silence of history, to say; nor is there anything in the chronicles, in Philip de Comines or the Byzantine historians, which enables us to trace the progress of the art into the forms in which it now exists among us.—Edward Everett.

➳ ➳

There are two worlds; the world that we can measure with line and rule, and the world that we feel with our hearts and imagination.—Leigh Hunt.

WHEN Turner became an Academician, he took his old father away from his business of barber, and gave him a home in his own house. It is said that he was kind and respectful to the old man, invariably; which we may easily believe, though there have been stories to the contrary, originating in the simple habits of both father and son. It seemed to both of them perfectly natural that the elder man, having now so much time on his hands, should occupy himself in little tasks which would save a shilling here and there; but that the painter readily consented to this, was it not the most delicate conduct possible under the circumstances? Old William Turner had been industrious and economical all his life, and like all old men who have been accustomed to work for a living, he felt the need of useful occupation ➳ ➳

It is said that he acted as porter at his son's gallery, would stretch canvases for him, and do other little things, in all of which there is certainly no real humiliation, but simply the gratification of an old man's wish to be useful. The relation between father and son is indeed quite the prettiest part of the life-story we have to tell. The artist was never hindered by his father, but aided by him in all possible ways with tender parental care and sagacious foresight. The son, on his part, was dutiful and filial to the last, taking the old man to his home and drawing closer the bonds of affection as the social distance between them became wider. Thus it is precisely when the painter wins the full honors of the Academy, honors which got the recognized and envied position in London society, that he takes his father home. A meaner nature would have tried to keep the old man at a safe distance.
—Philip G. Hamerton. (Life of J. M. W. Turner).

➳ ➳

Poverty is uncomfortable, as I can testify; but nine times out of ten the best thing that can happen to a young man is to be tossed overboard and compelled to sink or swim for himself.
—James A. Garfield.

JUST now the whole effort of our country is bent toward securing an adequate food-supply ❧ If our dietitians could only learn the truth, how easy it would be to get a supply of this kind! We eat brands when we ought to be eating bran. Our wheat has all its vitality taken out of it to make white flour. We care more for the dairy cow than we do for the American citizen ❧ She gets the real cream of wheat and we get what she is supposed to have—the husks ❧ ❧

Simple, wholesome wheat-bread and porridge, an abundance of fruits in season, succulent vegetables, particularly the potato, spinach and asparagus, with a generous supply of pure, fresh, clean, tuberculin-tested milk, will give the citizen a diet wholesome, nutritious and full of vitamins. To this may be added a moderate supply of good meat and eggs.

❧ In so far as food is concerned, the common idea that beer, whisky and wine have food value is largely an illusion. It is true that a moderate amount of alcohol is burned in the tissues of the body, furnishing heat and energy. The effort of the body to get rid of the ingested poison, however, takes out all of this heat and energy, so that little or none of it is available for the other business of life.

Let me prescribe the diet of the country: I do not care who makes its laws.

—Dr. Harvey W. Wiley.

❧ ❧

Originality is simply a pair of fresh eyes.

—T. W. Higginson.

❧ ❧

GBERNARD SHAW will never be a character universally loved. I think if Bernard Shaw felt himself universally loved he would be the most chagrined individual that Nature has ever produced. George Bernard Shaw loves nothing so much as being hated, if the hatred is sincere; he loves nothing so much as being criticized, if the criticism is honest; he loves nothing so much as being intellectually knocked down, if the individual that attempts it has the capacity to achieve the effort. George Bernard Shaw is a fighter through and through, an intellectual warrior, a man who I might say is pre-eminently one of us; he belongs to this age.

Every one of his intellectual efforts is but a reflection and reproduction of the intellectualism of this present age. Shaw is made by the age, is part of the age, is the articulation of the age, and is pre-eminently so because he articulates no one phase of it: he reflects no one facet of the universal crystal; he exhibits no one characteristic that marks the peculiarities of our time; but in a sort of cosmopolitan universalism Bernard Shaw seems to reflect the refined potentialities of the age in which we live.

—Dr. Henry Frank.

❧ ❧

Manhood, not scholarship, is the first aim of education.

—Ernest Thompson Seton.

❧ ❧

THE leader for the time being, whoever he may be, is but an instrument, to be used until broken and then to be cast aside; and if he is worth his salt he will care no more when he is broken than a soldier cares when he is sent where his life is forfeit in order that the victory may be won. In the long fight for righteousness the watchword for all of us, is spend and be spent. It is a little matter whether any one man fails or succeeds; but the cause shall not fail, for it is the cause of mankind. We, here in America, hold in our hands the hope of the world, the fate of the coming years; and shame and disgrace will be ours if in our eyes the light of high resolve is dimmed, if we trail in the dust the golden hopes of men. If on this new continent we merely build another country of great but unjustly divided material prosperity, we shall have done nothing; and we shall do as little if we merely set the greed of envy against the greed of arrogance, and thereby destroy the material well-being of all of us.—Theodore Roosevelt.

❧ ❧

I envy the beasts two things—their ignorance of evil to come, and their ignorance of what is said about them.

—Voltaire.

HERE was Lamb himself, the most delightful, the most provoking, the most witty and sensible of men. He always made the best pun, and the best remark in the course of the evening

His serious conversation, like his serious writing, is his best. No one ever stammered out such fine, piquant, deep, eloquent things in a half a dozen half-sentences as he does His jests scald like tears; and he probes a question with a play upon words. What a keen, laughing, hare-brained vein of home-felt truth! What choice venom! How often did we cut into the haunch of letters, while we discussed the haunch of mutton on the table! How we skimmed the cream of criticism! How we got into the heart of controversy! How we picked out the marrow of authors! " And, in our flowing cups, many a good name and true was freshly remembered."

❡ Recollect (most sage and critical reader) that in all this I was but a guest!

❡ Need I go over the names? They were but the old everlasting set—Milton and Shakespeare, Pope and Dryden, Steele and Addison, Swift and Gay, Fielding, Smollett, Sterne, Richardson, Hogarth's prints, Claude's landscapes, the Cartoons at Hampton Court, and all those things that, having once been, must ever be. The Scotch Novels had not then been heard of: so we said nothing about them. In general, we were hard upon the moderns. The author of the *Rambler* was only tolerated in Boswell's *Life* of him; and it was as much as any one could do to edge in a word for *Junius*.

❡ Lamb could not bear *Gil Blas*. This

If the red slayer think he slays,
Or if the slain think he is slain,
They know not well the subtle ways
I keep, and pass, and turn again.

Far or forgot to me is near;
Shadow and sunlight are the same;
The vanished gods to me appear;
And one to me are shame and fame.

They reckon ill who leave me out;
When me they fly, I am the wings;
I am the doubter and the doubt,
And I the hymn the Brahmin sings.

The strong gods pine for my abode.
And pine in vain the sacred Seven;
But thou, meek lover of the good!
Find me, and turn thy back on heaven.
" Brahma," *by Ralph Waldo Emerson*

was a fault I remember the greatest triumph I ever had was in persuading him, after some years' difficulty, that Fielding was better than Smollett.

On one occasion, he was for making out a list of persons famous in history that one would wish to see again—at the head of which were Pontius Pilate, Sir Thomas Browne, and Dr. Faustus—but we blackballed most of his list!

❡ But with what a gusto would he describe his favorite authors, Donne, or Sir Philip Sidney, and find their most crabbed passages *delicious!* He tried them on his palate as epicures taste olives, and his observations had a smack in them, like a roughness, on the tongue. With what discrimination he hinted a defect in what he admired most—as in saying that the display of the sumptuous banquet in *Paradise Regained* was not in true keeping, as the simplest fare was all that was necessary to tempt the extremity of hunger—and stating that Adam and Eve in *Paradise Lost* were too much like married people.

—" Charles Lamb," by W. Hazlitt.

THE truth is, progress and reaction are but words to mystify the millions. They mean nothing, they are nothing, they are phases and not facts. In the structure, the decay, and the development of the various families of man, the vicissitudes of history find their main solution—all is race.—Disraeli.

We must not blame God for the fly, for man made him. He is the resurrection, the reincarnation of our own dirt and carelessness.

—Woods Hutchinson, M. D.

THE supreme consolation which I find is in the view that life is a grand tragedy. There are islands of joy, havens of pure bliss; there is the laughter of children, the effulgence of love in young, hyacinthian days, and there is the steady glow of love in after years. I take account of all this; yet I say that around this glow and brightness, enveloping it, tragedy is always present or imminent—if no other tragedy, then the tragedy of death, which all must face. But the tragic view is not a funereal, gloomy and melancholy view. The effect of a great tragedy is elevating, not depressing. After witnessing a tragedy on the stage, when the curtain is rung down on the fifth act, the spectator finds himself in an uplifted mood, despite all the strain that has been put upon his feelings. He is not prostrated to the ground, he is uplifted. Great music rolls through his soul. He seems to float as in some high ether, and far beneath him lie the gulfs of pity and of terror through which he has passed ѕ The effect of tragedy—the tragedy on the stage, which is a mirror of life—is blended of defeat and victory. Both enter in. Ruin there is, but a glory shines above the ruin. The effect of tragedy on the stage is produced by great qualities in the hero, which we admire, but which are prevented from successful manifestation by some flaw in his nature. Or the hero strives after some high ideal, carries in his breast some noble purpose. The fault is not in him, but in his surroundings. The time is not ripe for him, the people with whom he must deal are below his standard; and he fails, but in failing he sets forth in high relief the grandeur to which he has aspired, the greatness at which he aimed.
¶ Transfer the idea of tragedy from the stage to life itself. There are high powers at work, a great and noble strain is trying to express itself in things and in men; but conditions are not fit or adequate, and the greatness is constantly breaking down, the nobility failing, not because it ought to fail, but because conditions are insufficient, because the finite can not embody the infinite ѕ Yet the failures only serve to set off the infiniteness in the tendency ѕ ѕ Work helps; sympathy helps; in all the ordinary circumstances of life, not to be sorry for one's self but to be sorry for others is the best help. But the thought that life is a grand tragedy, that over the ruins a glory shines, is to me the supreme help.—*Felix Adler.*

Break, break, break,
On thy cold gray stones, O Sea!
And I would that my tongue could utter
The thoughts that arise in me.

O, well for the fisherman's boy,
That he shouts with his sister at play!
O, well for the sailor lad,
That he sings in his boat on the bay!

And the stately ships go on,
To their haven under the hill;
But O for the touch of a vanished hand,
And the sound of a voice that is still!

Break, break, break,
At the foot of thy crags, O Sea!
But the tender grace of a day that is dead
Will never come back to me.
" Break, Break, Break,"*by Alfred, Lord Tennyson*

ѕ ѕ

THIS London City, with all its houses, palaces, steam-engines, cathedrals, and huge immeasurable traffic and tumult, what is it but a Thought, but millions of Thoughts made into One— a huge immeasurable Spirit of a Thought, embodied in brick, in iron, smoke, dust, Palaces, Parliaments, Hackney Coaches, Katherine Docks, and the rest of it! Not a brick was made but some man had to *think* of the making of that brick.
—*Carlyle.*

ѕ ѕ

The consciousness of being loved softens the keenest pang, even at the moment of parting; yea, even the eternal farewell is robbed of half its bitterness when uttered in accents that breathe love to the last sigh.—*Addison.*

ѕ ѕ

God gives all things to industry—*Franklin*

HE day is done. Soft darkness fills all space ❧ The turmoil has ceased. The clatter of hoofs and the whir of motors have died away. One late straggler shuffles past. All is quiet. The shadows hide from the white-faced moon.

I am tired of the toil of the day—weary of this fretful little earth, so full of things. My feet are hot with tramping the stolid street. My throat is choked with the dust of trivial traffic. The things of my labor have become irksome to me—mere toys that I have played with all day. I will lay them aside. What matter if I can not find them again? *Valedico,* peevish little earth, I am going out into the Universe to stroll on the Milky Way and bathe in the Ocean of Night.

O, great, good, beautiful Night, you are so calm, so pure. I gaze through the ripples of the night-wind down into your dark depths where the stars lie strewn about ❧ Are they the jewel-offerings some ill-fated lover cast in ruthless despair upon your bosom? Or are they the pebbles that sparkle in your depths? I wander down the Milky Way. I gather the Pleiades and make a necklace for my Love. I string them on a golden strand from the tresses of Andromeda. What matter if the sea-nymphs do rage? Perseus is near and he has slain the Draco. I scatter the star-gems before my feet on the path. Wait! Triumphant Orion is passing and his gaudy girdle flashes a challenge at mad Taurus.

Here are some of the flowers of Nokomis. I will gather a few and weave them into the necklace. What is that I hear? Why—it 's the chimes of Saint Francis striking the twelfth hour. Have I been dreaming? I can retire, now, and rest on my pillow. Ah, there are the things, too— the toys. Perhaps I shall play with them again tomorrow.—Hugh Robert Orr.

❧ ❧

ENCHANTED child, born into a world unchildlike; spoiled darling of nature, playmate of her elemental daughters; " pard-like spirit, beautiful and swift," laired amidst the burning fastnesses of his own fervid mind; bold foot along the verges of precipitous dream, light leaper from crag to crag of inaccessible fancies; towering Genius, whose soul, rose like a ladder between heaven and earth with the angels of song ascending and descending it—he is shrunken into the little vessel of death, and sealed with the unshatterable seal of doom, and cast down deep below the rolling tides of Time. Mighty meat for little guests, when the heart of Shelley was laid in the cemetery of Caius Cestius! Beauty, music, sweetness, tears, the mouth of the worm has fed of them all. Into that sacred bridal-gloom of death where he holds his nuptials with eternity let not our rash speculations follow him; let us hope, rather, that as, amidst material nature, where our dull eyes see only ruin, the finer art of science has discovered life in putridity and vigor in decay, seeing dissolution even and disintegration, which in the mouth of man symbolize disorder, to be in the works of God undeviating order, and the manner of our corruption to be no less wonderful than the manner of our health—so amidst the supernatural universe some tender undreamed surprise of life in doom awaited that wild nature, which, worn by warfare with itself, its Maker, and all the world, now

Sleeps, and never palates more the dug,
The beggar's nurse and Cæsar's.

—" The Death of Shelley," by **Francis Thompson** ❧ ❧

❧ ❧

IT is related by a peasant that he had persuaded himself that beyond his fields there were no others, and when he happened to lose a cow and was compelled to go in search of her, he was astonished at the great number of fields beyond his own few acres. This must also be the case of many theorists who have persuaded themselves that beyond this field or little globe of earth there lie no other worlds—simply because he has not seen them.—Spinoza.

❧ ❧

Let the farmer forevermore be honored in his calling; for they who labor in the earth are the chosen people of God.

—**Thomas Jefferson.**

NE raw morning in Spring— it will be eighty years the nineteenth day of this month —Hancock and Adams, the Moses and Aaron of that Great Deliverance, were both at Lexington; they also had " obstructed an officer" with brave words. British soldiers, a thousand strong, came to seize them and carry them over sea for trial, and so nip the bud of Freedom auspiciously opening in that early Spring. The town militia came together before daylight, " for training." A great, tall man, with a large head and a high, wide brow, their captain—one who had " seen service "—marshaled them into line, numbering but seventy, and bade " every man load his piece with powder and ball. I will order the first man shot that runs away," said . he, when some faltered. " Don't fire unless fired upon, but if they want to have a war, let it begin here." *se se*

Gentlemen, you know what followed; those farmers and mechanics " fired the shot heard around the world." A little monument covers the bones of such as before had pledged their fortune and their sacred honor to the Freedom ot America, and that day gave it also their lives. I was born in that little town, and bred up amid the memories of that day. When a boy I read the first monumental line I ever saw—" Sacred to Liberty and the Rights of Mankind." Since then I have studied the memorial marbles of Greece and Rome, in many an ancient town; nay, on Egyptian obelisks have read what was written before the Eternal roused up Moses to lead Israel out of Egypt; but no chiseled stone has ever stirred me to such emotions as those rustic names of men who fell " In the Sacred Cause of God and their Country."—Theodore Parker.

se se

It is · no time to swap horses when you are crossing the stream.

—Abraham Lincoln.

se se

It is conceivable that religion may be morally useful without being intellectually sustainable.—J. S. Mill.

HE Venice that you see in the sunlight of a summer's day—the Venice that bewilders with her glory when you land at her watergate; that delights with her color when you idle along the Riva; that intoxicates with her music as you lie in your gondola adrift on the bosom of some breathless lagoon—the Venice of mold-stained palace, quaint cafe and arching bridge; of fragrant incense, cool, dim-lighted church, and noiseless priest; of strong men and graceful women— the Venice of light and life, of sea and sky, and melody—no pen can tell this story. The pencil and palette must lend their touch when one would picture the wide sweep of her piazzas, the abandon of her gardens, the charm of her canal and street life, the happy indolence of her people, the faded sumptuousness of her homes.

If I have given to Venice a prominent place among the cities of the earth, it is because in this selfish, materialistic, money-getting age it is a joy to live, if only for a day, where a song is more prized than a soldo; where the poorest pauper laughingly shares his scanty crust; where to be kind to a child is a habit, to be neglectful of old age a shame; a city the relics of whose past are the lessons of our future; whose every canvas, stone, and bronze bear witness to a grandeur, luxury, a taste that took a thousand years of energy to perfect, and will take a thousand years of neglect to destroy *se se*

To every one of my art-loving countrymen this city should be a Mecca; to know her thoroughly is to know all the beauty and romance of five centuries.

—F. Hopkinson Smith.

se se

Flower in the crannied wall,
I pluck you out of the crannies,
I hold you here, root and all, in my hand,
Little flower—but *if* I could understand
What you are, root and all, and all in all,
I should know what God and man is.

—Tennyson.

se se

To believe in immortality is one thing, but it is first needful to believe in life.

—Robert Louis Stevenson.

Y Dear Sammy—I hope that you retain the impressions of your education, nor have forgot that the vows of God are upon you. You know that the first fruits are Heaven's by an unalienable right, and that, as your parents devoted you to the service of the altar, so you yourself made it your choice when your father was offered another way of life for you. But have you duly considered what such ѕ⊕ a choice and such a dedication imports? Consider well what separation from the world, what purity, what devotion, what exemplary virtue, are required in those who are to guide others to glory! I say *exemplary;* for low, common degrees of piety are not sufficient for those of the sacred function. You must not think to live like the rest of the world; your light must so shine before men that they may see your good works, and thereby be led to glorify your Father which is in Heaven. For my part, I can not see with what face clergymen can reprove sinners, or exhort men to lead a good life, when they themselves indulge their own corrupt inclinations, and by their practice contradict their doctrine. If the Holy Jesus be indeed their Master, and they are really His ambassadors, surely it becomes them to live like His disciples; and if they do not, what a sad account they give of their stewardship.

I would advise you, as much as possible in your present circumstances, to throw your business into a certain method, by which means you will learn to improve every precious moment, and find an unspeakable facility in the performance of your respective duties. Begin and end the day with Him who is the Alpha and Omega, and if you really experience what it is to love God, you will redeem all the time you can for His more immediate service. I will tell you what rule I used to observe when I was in my father's house, and had as little, if not less liberty than you have now. I used to allow myself as much time for recreation as I spent in private devotion; not that I always spent so much, but I gave myself leave to go so far but no farther. So in all things else, appoint so much time for sleep, eating, company, etc., but above all things, my dear Sammy, I command you, I beg, I beseech you, to be very strict in observing the Lord's Day. In all things endeavor to act on principle, and do not live like the rest of mankind, who pass through the world like straws upon a river, which are carried which way the stream or wind drives them. Often put this question to yourself: Why do I do this or that? Why do I pray, read, study, or use devotion, etc.? By which means you will come to such a steadiness and consistency in your words and actions as becomes a reasonable creature and a good Christian.

Your affectionate mother,

Sus. Wesley.

(Letter to Her Eldest Son, dated Epworth, October, 1709.)

ѕ⊕ ѕ⊕

There by the window in the old house

Perched on the bluff, overlooking miles of valley.

My days of labor closed, sitting out life's decline,

Day by day I look in my memory,

As one who gazes in an enchantress' crystal globe,

And I saw the figures of the past,

As if in a pageant glassed by a shining dream,

Move through the incredible sphere of time.

And I saw a man arise from the soil like a fabled giant

And throw himself over a deathless destiny,

Master of great armies, head of the republic,

(Concluded on next page)

Self-confidence is the first requisite to great undertakings.—Samuel Johnson.

THE Battle of Waterloo is an enigma as obscure for those who gained it as for him who lost it. To Napoleon it is a panic; Blucher sees nothing in it but fire; Wellington does not understand it at all. Look at the reports: the bulletins are confused; the commentaries are entangled; the latter stammer, the former stutter. Jomini divides the battle of Waterloo into four moments; Muffling cuts it into three acts; Charras, altho we do not entirely agree with him in all his appreciations, has alone caught with his haughty eye the characteristic lineaments of this catastrophe of human genius contending with divine chance. All the other historians suffer from a certain bedazzlement in which they grope about. It was a flashing day, in truth the overthrow of the military monarchy which, to the great stupor of the kings, has dragged down all kingdoms, the downfall of strength and the rout of war.

In this event, which bears the stamp of superhuman necessity, men play but a small part; but if we take Waterloo from Wellington and Blucher, does that deprive England and Germany of anything? No. Neither illustrious England nor august Germany is in question in the problem of Waterloo, for, thank heaven! nations are great without the mournful achievements of the sword. Neither Germany, nor England, nor France is held in a scabbard; at this day when Waterloo is only a clash of sabers, Germany has Goethe above Blucher, and England Byron above Wellington. A mighty dawn of ideas is peculiar to our age; and in this dawn England and Germany have their own magnificent flash. They are majestic because they think; the high level they bring to civilization is intrinsic to them; it comes from themselves, and not from an accident. Any aggrandizement the nineteenth century may have can not boast of Waterloo as its fountainhead for only barbarous nations grow suddenly after a victory—it is the transient vanity of torrents swollen by a storm. Civilized nations, especially at the present day, are not elevated or debased by the good or evil fortune of a captain, and their specific weight in the human family results from something more than a battle. Their honor, dignity, enlightenment, and genius are not numbers which those gamblers, heroes, and conquerors can stake in the lottery of battles. Very often a battle lost is progress gained, and less of glory, more of liberty. The drummer is silent and reason speaks; it is the game of who loses wins. Let us, then, speak of Waterloo coldly from both sides, and render to chance the things that belong to chance, and to God what is God's. What is Waterloo—a victory? No; a quine in the lottery, won by Europe, and paid by France; it was hardly worth while erecting a lion for it.

❡ Waterloo, by the way, is the strangest encounter recorded in history; Napoleon and Wellington are not enemies, but contraries. Never did God, who delights in antitheses, produce a more striking contrast or a more extraordinary con-

---

Bringing together into a dithyramb of recreative song
The epic hopes of a people:
At the some time Vulcan of sovereign fires,
Where imperishable shields and swords were beaten out
From spirits tempered in heaven.
Look in the crystal! See how he hastens on
To the place where his path comes up to the path
Of a child of Plutarch and Shakespeare.
O Lincoln, actor indeed, playing well your part,
And Booth, who strode in a mimic play within the play,
Often and often I saw you,
As the cawing crows winged their way to the wood
Over my house-top at solemn sunsets,
There by my window,
Alone.

" William H. Herndon," *by Edgar Lee Masters*

frontation. On one side precision, foresight, geometry, prudence, a retreat assured, reserves prepared, an obstinate coolness, an imperturbable method, strategy profiting by the ground, tactics balancing battalions, carnage measured by a plumb-line, war regulated, watch in hand, nothing left voluntarily to accident, old classic courage and absolute correctness. On the other side we have intuition, divination, military strangeness, superhuman instinct, a flashing glance; something that gazes like the eagle and strikes like lightning, all the mysteries of a profound mind, association with destiny; the river, the plain, the forest, and the hill summoned, and, to some extent, compelled to obey, the despot going so far as even to tyrannize over the battlefield; faith in a star, blended with strategic science, heightening, but troubling it. Wellington was the Bareme of war, Napoleon was its Michelangelo, and this true genius was conquered by calculation. On both sides somebody was expected; and it was the exact calculator who succeeded. Napoleon waited for Grouchy, who did not come; Wellington waited for Blucher, and he came.

Wellington is the classical war taking its revenge; Bonaparte, in his dawn, had met it in Italy, and superbly defeated it —the old owl fled before the young vulture. The old tactics had been not only overthrown, but scandalized. Who was this Corsican of six-and-twenty years of age? What meant this splendid ignoramus, who, having everything against him, nothing for him, without provisions, ammunition, guns, shoes, almost without an army, with a handful of men against masses, dashed at allied Europe, and absurdly gained impossible victories? Who was this new comet of war who possessed the effrontery of a planet? The academic military school excommunicated him, while bolting, and hence arose an implacable rancor of the old Cæsarism against the new, of the old saber against the flashing sword, and of the chessboard against genius. On June 18th, 1815, this rancor got the best; and beneath Lodi, Montebello, Montenotte, Mantua, Marengo, and Arcola, it wrote—

Waterloo. It was a triumph of mediocrity, sweet to majorities, and destiny consented to this irony. In his decline, Napoleon found a young Suvarov before him—in fact, it is only necessary to blanch Wellington's hair in order to have a Suvarov. Waterloo is a battle of the first class, gained by a captain of the second ∾ ∾

What must be admired in the battle of Waterloo is England, the English firmness, the English resolution, the English blood, and what England had really superb in it, is (without offense) herself; it is not her captain, but her army. Wellington, strangely ungrateful, declares in his dispatch to Lord Bathurst that his army, the one which fought on June 18th, 1815, was a " detestable army." What does the gloomy pile of bones buried in the trenches of Waterloo think of this? England has been too modest to herself in her treatment of Wellington, for making him so great is making herself small. Wellington is merely a hero, like any other man. The Scotch Grays, the Life Guards, Maitland and Mitchell's regiments, Pack and Kempt's infantry, Ponsonby and Somerset's cavalry, the Highlanders playing the bagpipes under the shower of canister. Ryland's battalions, the fresh recruits who could hardly manage a musket, and yet held their ground against the old bands of Essling and Rivoli—all this is grand. Wellington was tenacious; that was his merit, and we do not deny it to him, but the lowest of his privates and his troopers was quite as solid as he, and the iron soldier is as good as the iron duke. For our part, all our glorification is offered to the English soldier; the English army, the English nation; and if there must be a trophy, it is to England that this trophy is owing. The Waterloo column would be more just, if, instead of the figure of a man, it raised to the clouds the statue of a people.

But this great England will be irritated by what we are writing here; for she still has feudal illusions, after her 1688 and the French 1789. This people believes in inheritance and hierarchy, and while no other excels it in power and glory, it esteems itself as a nation and not as a people. As a people, it readily subordinates itself, and takes a lord as its head; the workman lets himself be despised; the soldier puts up with flogging. It will be remembered that, at the battle of Inkerman, a sergeant who, as it appears, saved the British army, could not be mentioned by Lord Raglan, because the military hierarchy does not allow any hero below the rank of officer to be mentioned in dispatches. What we admire before all, in an encounter like Waterloo, is the prodigious skill of chance. The night raid, the wall of Hougomont, the hollow of Ohain, Grouchy deaf to the cannon, Napoleon's guide deceiving him, Bulow's guide enlightening him—all this cataclysm is marvelously managed. ❡ Altogether, we will assert, there is more of a massacre than of a battle in Waterloo. Waterloo, of all pitched battles, is the one which had the smallest front for such a number of combatants. Napoleon's three-quarters of a league. Wellington's half a league, and seventy-two thousand combatants on either side. From this density came the carnage. The following calculation has been made and proportion established: loss of men, at Austerlitz, French, fourteen per cent; Russian, thirty per cent; Austrian, forty-four per cent. At Wagram, French, thirteen per cent; Austrian, fourteen per cent. At Moscow, French, thirty-seven per cent; Russian, forty-four per cent. At Bautzen, French, thirteen per cent; Russian and Prussian, fourteen per cent. At Waterloo, French, fifty-six per cent; Allies, thirty-one per cent—total for Waterloo, forty-one per cent, or out of one hundred and forty-four thousand fighting men, sixty thousand killed.

The field of Waterloo has at the present day that calmness which belongs to the earth, and resembles all plains; but at night, a sort of visionary mist rises from it, and if any traveler walk about it, and listen and dream, like Virgil on the mournful plain of Philippi, the hallucination of the catastrophe seizes upon him. The frightful June 18th lives again, the false monumental hill is leveled, the wondrous lion is dissipated, the battle-field resumes its reality, lines of infantry undulate on the plain; furious galloping crosses the horizon; the startled dreamer sees the flash of sabers, the sparkle of bayonets, the red light of shells, the monstrous collision of thunderbolts; he hears, like a death groan from the tomb, the vague clamor of the phantom battle. These shadows are grenadiers; these flashes are cuirassiers; this skeleton is Napoleon; this skeleton is Wellington; all this is non-existent, and yet still combats, and the ravines are stained purple, and the trees rustle, and there is fury even in the clouds and in the darkness, while all the stern heights, Mont St. Jean, Hougomont, Frischemont, Papelotte, and Plancenoit, seem confusedly crowned by hosts of specters exterminating one another.—Victor Hugo.

so so

I PLACE Rembrandt at the head of the moderns, and far above them all. Correggio alone approaches him at certain moments. Rembrandt did not seek after plastic beauty like the Italians, but he discovered souls, he understood them and transfigured them in his marvelous light. Titian's—or rather, the Duke of Genoa's—mistress is more beautiful than Rembrandt's Saskia, but how infinitely I prefer the latter! As a colorist, I place Rembrandt above Titian, above Veronese, above every one! Rembrandt never lets our attention wander, as the others sometimes do. He commands it, concentrates it; we can not escape him. We feel that Rembrandt was full of kindliness. He loved the poor, he painted them as they were, in all their wretchedness. There is something penetrating, kindly, acute, sensual, in his own radiantly living face, which wins the spectator's heart as he gazes.

—Meissonier.

so so

God be thanked for books. They are the voices of the distant and the dead, and make us heirs of the spiritual life of past ages.—William E. Channing.

so so

Art is more godlike than science. Science discovers; art creates.—John Opie.

HEN in my journeys among the Indian tribes of Canada, I left European dwellings, and found myself, for the first time, alone in the midst of an ocean of forests, having, so to speak, all nature prostrate at my feet, a strange change took place within me, I followed no road; I went from tree to tree, now to the right, now to the left, saying to myself, " Here there are no more roads to follow, no more towns, no more ᴣ narrow houses, no more presidents, republics, or kings —a b o v e a l l, no more laws, and no more men." Men! Yes, some good savages, who cared nothing for me, nor I for them; who, like me, wandered freely wherever their fancy led them, eating when they felt inclined, sleeping when and where they pleased. And, in order to see if I were really established in my original rights, I gave myself up to a thousand acts of eccentricity, which enraged the tall Dutchman who was my guide, and who, in his heart, thought I was mad.

Escaped from the tyrannous yoke of society, I understood then the charms of that independence of nature which far surpasses all the pleasures of which civilized man can form any idea. I understood why not one savage has become a European, and why many Europeans have become savages; why the sublime *Discourse on the Inequality of Rank* is so little understood by the most part of our philosophers. It is incredible how small and diminished the nations and their most boasted institutions appeared in my eyes; it seemed to me as if I saw the kingdoms of the earth through an inverted spy-glass, or rather that, being

A fire-mist and a planet,—
   A crystal and a cell,—
A jellyfish and a saurian,
   And caves where the cave-men dwell;
Then a sense of law and beauty,
   And a face turned from the clod,—
Some call it Evolution,
   And others call it God.

A haze on the far horizon,
   The infinite, tender sky,
The ripe, rich tint of the cornfields,
   And the wild geese sailing high,—
And all over upland and lowland
   The charm of the goldenrod,—
Some of us call it Autumn,
   And others call it God.

(Concluded on next page)

myself grown and elevated, I looked down on the rest of my degenerate race with the eye of a giant.

You who wish to write about men, go into the deserts, become for a moment the child of nature, and then—and then only—take up the pen.

Among the innumerable enjoyments of this journey one especially made a vivid impression on my mind ᴣ ᴣ

I was going then to see the famous cataract of Niagara, and I had taken my way through the Indian tribes who inhabit the deserts to the west of the American plantations. My guides were— the sun, a pocket-compass, and the Dutchman of whom I have spoken: the latter understood perfectly five dialects of the Huron language. Our train consisted of two horses, which we let loose in the forests at night, after fastening a bell to their necks. I was at first a little afraid of losing them, but my guide reassured me by pointing out that, by a wonderful instinct, these good animals never wandered out of sight of our fire.

❡ One evening, when, as we calculated that we were only about eight or nine leagues from the cataract, we were preparing to dismount before sunset, in order to build our hut and light our watch-fire after the Indian fashion, we perceived in the wood the fires of some savages who were encamped a little lower down on the shores of the same stream as we were. We went to them. The Dutchman having by my orders asked their permission for us to pass the night with them, which was granted immediately, we set to work with our hosts. After having cut down some branches, planted some stakes, torn off some bark to cover our palace, and performed some other public offices, each of us attended to his own affairs. I brought my saddle, which served me well for a pillow all through my travels; the guide rubbed down the horses; and as to his night accomodation, since he was not so particular as I am, he generally made use of the dry trunk of a tree. Work being done, we seated ourselves in a circle, with our legs crossed like tailors, around the immense fire, to roast our heads of maize, and to prepare supper. I had still a flask of brandy, which served to enliven our savages not a little. They found out that they had some bear hams, and we began a royal feast.

The family consisted of two women, with infants at their breasts, and three warriors; two of them might be from forty to forty-five years of age, although they appeared much older, and the third was a young man.

The conversation soon became general; that is to say, on my side it consisted of broken words and many gestures—an expressive language, which these nations understand remarkably well, and that I had learned among them. The young man alone preserved an obstinate silence; he kept his eyes constantly fixed on me. In spite of the black, red and blue stripes, cut ears, and the pearl hanging from his nose, with which he was disfigured, it was easy to see the nobility and sensibility which animated his countenance. How well I knew he was inclined not to love me! It seemed to me as if he were reading in his heart the history of all the wrongs which Europeans have inflicted on his native country. The two children, quite naked, were asleep at our feet

Like tides on a crescent sea-beach,
When the moon is new and thin,
Into our hearts high yearnings
Come welling and surging in,—
Come from the mystic ocean,
Whose rim no foot has trod,—
Some of us call it Longing,
And others call it God.

A picket frozen on duty—
A mother starved for her brood—
Socrates drinking the hemlock,
And Jesus on the rood;
And millions who, humble and nameless,
The straight, hard pathway plod,—
Some call it Consecration,
And others call it God.

" Each In His Own Tongue,"
by William Herbert Carruth

before the fire; the women took them quietly into their arms and put them to bed among the skins, with a mother's tenderness so delightful to witness in these so-called savages: the conversation died away by degrees, and each fell asleep in the place where he was.

I alone could not close my eyes, hearing on all sides the deep breathing of my hosts. I raised my head, and, supporting myself on my elbow, watched by the red light of the expiring fire the Indians stretched around me and plunged in sleep. I confess that I could hardly refrain from tears. Brave youth, how your peaceful sleep affects me! You, who seemed so sensible of the woes of your native land, you were too great, too high-minded to mistrust the foreigner! Europeans, what a lesson for you! These same savages whom we have pursued with fire and sword, to whom our avarice would not leave a spadeful of earth to cover their corpses in all this world, formerly their vast patrimony—these same savages receiving their enemy into their hospitable hut, sharing with him their miserable meal, and, their couch undisturbed by remorse, sleeping close to him the calm sleep of the innocent. These virtues are as much above the virtues of conventional life as the soul of the man in his natural state is above that of the man in society.

—Chateaubriand.

so so

The bed had become a place of luxury to me! I would not exchange it for all the thrones in the world.—Napoleon I.

so so

The less people speak of their greatness the more we think of it.—Bacon.

THE greatest prerogative that man has, is his freedom to work. Few words have such individual, and yet such diverse, meanings to different people as the word " work," and no form of action has more diversity in its conception, because of differing viewpoints, than work.

A little child when asked his idea of work said, "Anything I *have* to do is work, and anything I *want* to do is play"—which answer showed that the child recognized his relation to that form of activity known as work; also it demonstrated that work had been presented to his mind as drudgery.

Drudgery is work which we make difficult; which is done because we must do it, and which we regard with aversion; it is the hard, sordid form of work, seemingly without hope and apart from any of the joy of accomplishment.

Work should be a joy; it should be the motive of our lives; and it would be if we regarded it in the light of its being a labor of love; but we have come to think of what we call labor with almost a sense of pain. Most of us resolve our work into labor and, while it results in accomplishment, it becomes unpleasant and strenuous in the method of its execution ✺ ✺

The secret of the true love of work is the hope of success in that work; not for the money reward, for the time spent, or for the skill exercised, but for the successful result in the accomplishment of the work itself.

—Sidney A. Weltmer.

✺ ✺

Every man's life is a fairy-tale written by God's fingers.

—Hans Christian Andersen.

✺ ✺

I TOO, read Gautier in Paris, and pages of his *Mlle. de Maupin* still stick in my memory; like Moore, I could boast that " the stream which poured from the side of the Crucified One and made a red girdle round the world, never bathed me in its flood." I, too, loved gold and marble and purple and bands of nude youths and maidens swaying on horses without bridle or saddle against a background of deep blue as on the frieze of the Parthenon. But afterwards I learned something of what the theory of evolution implies; realized that all great men are moments in the life of mankind, and that the lesson of every great life in the past must be learned before we can hope to push further into the Unknown than our predecessors. Gradually I came to understand that Jerusalem and not Athens is the sacred city and that one has to love Jesus and his gospel of love and pity or one will never come to full stature. Born rebels even have to realize that Love is the Way, the Truth and the Life; no one cometh to wisdom but by Love. The more I studied Jesus the greater he became to me till little by little he changed my whole outlook on life. I have been convinced now for years that the modern world in turning its back on Jesus and ignoring his teaching has gone helplessly astray.

There is new hope for us in the legend of Jesus and in his stupendous success; hope and perhaps even some foundation for faith. That a man should live in an obscure corner of Judea nineteen centuries ago, speak an insignificant dialect, and yet by dint of wisdom and goodness and in spite of having suffered a shameful death, reign as God for these two thousand years and be adored by hundreds of millions of the conquering races, goes far to prove that goodness and wisdom are fed by some hidden source and are certain therefore to increase among men.

We, too, can believe as Jesus believed, that goodness perpetuates itself, increasing from age to age, while the evil is diminishing, dying, and is only relative so to speak, or growth arrested. And our high task is to help this shaping spirit to self-realization and fulfilment in our own souls, knowing all the while that roses of life grow best about the Cross.

—Frank Harris.

✺ ✺

All truth is an achievement. If you would have truth at its full value, go win it.—Munger.

S the plow is the typical instrument of industry, so the fetter is the typical instrument of the restraint or subjection necessary in a nation—either literally, for its evildoers, or figuratively, in accepted laws, for its wise and good men. You have to choose between this figurative and literal use; for depend upon it, the more laws you accept, the fewer penalties you will have to endure, and the fewer punishments to enforce. For wise laws and just restraints are to a noble nation not chains, but chain mail—strength and defense, though something also of an encumbrance. And this necessity of restraint, remember, is just as honorable to man as the necessity of labor. You hear every day greater numbers of foolish people speaking about liberty, as if it were such an honorable thing: so far from being that, it is, on the whole, and in the broadest sense, dishonorable, and an attribute of the lower creatures. No human being, however great or powerful, was ever so free as a fish. There is always something that he must or must not do; while the fish may do whatever he likes. All the kingdoms of the world put together are not half so large as the sea, and all the railroads and wheels that ever were, or will be invented are not so easy as fins. You will find, on fairly thinking of it, that it is his restraint which is honorable to man, not his liberty; and, what is more, it is restraint which is honorable even in the lower animals. A butterfly is much more free than a bee; but you honor the bee more, just because it is subject to certain laws which fit it for orderly function in bee society. And throughout the world, of the two abstract things, liberty and restraint, restraint is always the more honorable. It is true, indeed, that in these and all other matters you never can reason finally from the abstraction, for both liberty and restraint are good when they are nobly chosen, and both are bad when they are badly chosen; but of the two, I repeat, it is restraint which characterizes the higher creature and betters the lower creatures and, from the ministering of the arch-

angel to the labor of the insect—from the poising of the planets to the gravitation of a grain of dust—the power and glory of all creatures, and all matter, consist in their obedience, not in their freedom. The sun has no liberty—a dead leaf has much. The dust of which you are formed has no liberty. Its liberty will come—with its corruption. And, therefore I say that as the first power of a nation consists in knowing how to guide a plow, its second power consists in knowing how to wear the fetter.

—John Ruskin.

ISSES, groans, catcalls, drumming with the feet, loud conversation and imitations of animals went on throughout (the maiden speech of Benjamin Disraeli in the House of Commons). . . . . But. . . . it does not follow that the maiden speech of the member for Maidstone was a failure. It was indeed in one sense a very hopeful business inasmuch as the reports prove he was quite capable of holding his own amidst extraordinary interruptions
Mr. Disraeli wound up in these words, " Now, Mr. Speaker, we see the philosophical prejudices of Man. (Laughter and cheers.) I respect cheers, even when they come from the mouth of a political opponent. (Renewed laughter.) I think, sir, (Hear! Hear! and repeated cries of Question!) I am not at all surprised, sir, at the reception I have met with, (continued laughter). I have begun several things many times (laughter, and I have always succeeded at last. (Question) Ay, sir, and though I sit down now, the time will come when you will hear me."

—Disraeli.

Beauty does not lie in the face. It lies in the harmony between man and his industry. Beauty is expression. When I paint a mother I try to render her beautiful by the mere look she gives her child.—Jean Francois Millet.

Must endure
Their going hence, even as their coming hither:
Ripeness is all.—Shakespeare.

ENERAL BONAPARTE made himself as conspicuous by his character and his intellect as by his victories, and the imagination of the French began to be touched by him [1797]. His proclamations to the Cisalpine and Ligurian republics were talked of. . . . A tone of moderation and of dignity pervaded his style, which contrasted with the revolutionary harshness of the civil rulers of France. The warrior spoke in those days like a lawgiver, while the lawgivers expressed themselves with soldier-like violence. General Bonaparte had not executed in his army the decrees against the émigrés. It was said that he loved his wife, whose character is full of sweetness; it was asserted that he felt the beauties of Ossian; it was a pleasure to attribute to him all the generous qualities that form a noble background for extraordinary abilities. ❡ Such at least was my own mood when I saw him for the first time in Paris. I could find no words with which to reply to him when he came to me to tell me that he had tried to visit my father at Coppet, and that he was sorry to have passed through Switzerland without seeing him. But when I had somewhat recovered from the agitation of admiration, it was followed by a feeling of very marked fear. Bonaparte then had no power; he was thought even to be more or less in danger from the vague suspiciousness of the Directory; so that

the fear he inspired was caused only by the singular effect of his personality upon almost every one who had intercourse with him. I had seen men worthy of high respect; I had also seen ferocious men: there was nothing in the impression Bonaparte produced upon me which could remind me of men of either type. I soon perceived, on the different occasions when I met him during his stay in Paris, that his character could not be defined by the words we are accustomed to make use of: he was neither kindly nor violent, neither gentle nor cruel, after the fashion of other men. Such a being, so unlike others, could neither excite nor feel sympathy: he was more or less than man. His bearing, his mind, his language have the marks of a foreigner's nature —an advantage the more in subjugating Frenchmen . . . ❡ Far from being reassured by seeing Bonaparte often, he always intimidated me more and more. I felt vaguely that no emotional feeling could influence him. He regards a human creature as a fact or a thing, but not as an existence like his own. He feels no more hate than love. For him there is no one but himself: all other creatures are mere ciphers. The force of his will consists in the imperturbable calculations of his egotism: he is an able chess-player whose opponent is all humankind, whom he intends to checkmate. His success is due as much to the qualities he lacks as to the talents he possesses. Neither pity, nor sympathy, nor religion, nor attach-

O my luve's like a red, red rose,
*   That's newly sprung in June;*
O my luve's like the melodie
*   That's sweetly played in tune.*

As fair thou art, my bonnie lass,
*   So deep in luve am I;*
And I will luve thee still, my dear,
*   Till a' the seas gang dry.*

Till a' the seas gang dry, my dear,
*   And the rocks melt, wi' the sun;*
I will luve thee still, my dear,
*   While the sands o' life shall run.*

And fare-thee weel, my only luve!
*   And fare-thee well, a while!*
And I will come again, my luve,
*   Though it were ten thousand mile.*

" A Red, Red Rose," *by Robert Burns*

ment to any idea whatsoever would have power to turn him from his path. He has the same devotion to his own interests that a good man has to virtue: if the object were noble, his persistency would be admirable.

Every time that I heard him talk I was struck by his superiority; it was of a kind, however, that had no relation to that of men instructed and cultivated by study, or by society, such as England and France possess examples of. But his conversation indicated that quick perception of circumstances the hunter has in pursuing his prey. Sometimes he related the political and military events of his life in a very interesting manner; he had even, in narratives that admitted gaiety, a touch of Italian imagination. Nothing however, could conquer my invincible alienation from what I perceived in him. I saw in his soul a cold and cutting sword, which froze while wounding; I saw in his mind a profound irony, from which nothing fine or noble could escape, not even his own glory: for he despised the nation whose suffrages he desired; and no spark of enthusiasm mingled with his craving to astonish the human race. . . .

His face, thin and pale at that time, was very agreeable: since then he has gained flesh—which does not become him; for one needs to believe such a man to be tormented by his own character, at all to tolerate the sufferings this character causes others. As his stature is short, and yet his waist very long, he appeared

*When Earth's last picture is painted,
   and the tubes are twisted and dried,
When the oldest colors have faded, and
   the youngest critic has died,
We shall rest, and, faith, we shall need
   it—lie down for an eon or two,
Till the Master of All Good Workmen
   shall set us to work anew!*

*And those that were good shall be happy:
   they shall sit in a golden chair;
They shall splash at a ten-league canvas
   with brushes of comet's hair;
They shall find real saints to draw from—
   Magdalene, Peter, and Paul;
They shall work for an age at a sitting
   and never be tired at all!*

*And only the Master shall praise us, and
   only the Master shall blame;
And no one shall work for money, and
   and no one shall work for fame;
But each for the joy of the working, and
   each, in his separate star
Shall draw the Thing as he sees It for
   the God of Things as They Are!*
    "L'Envoi," by Rudyard Kipling

to much greater advantage on horseback than on foot; in all ways it is war, and war only, he is fitted for. His manner in society is constrained without being timid; it is disdainful when he is on his guard, and vulgar when he is at ease; his air of disdain suits him best, and so he is not sparing in the use of it. He took pleasure already in the part of embarrassing people by saying disagreeable things: an art which he has since made a system of, as of all other methods of subjugating men by degrading them.
—Madame de Stael

LIFE would be a perpetual flea hunt if a man were obliged to run down all the innuendoes, inveracities, insinuations and misrepresentations which are uttered against him.
—Henry Ward Beecher.

THE most joyful thing I know is the peace, the silence, that one enjoys in the woods or on the tilled lands. One sees a poor, heavily laden creature with a bundle of fagots advancing from a narrow path in the fields. The manner in which this figure comes suddenly before one is a momentary reminder of the fundamental condition of human life, toil. On the tilled land around, one watches figures hoeing and digging. One sees how this or that one rises and wipes away the sweat with the back of his hand. " In the sweat of thy face shalt thou eat bread." Is that merry, enlivening work? And yet it is here that I find the true humanity, the great poetry.
—Jean Francois Millet.

ND now, having seen a great military march through a friendly country, the pomps and festivities of more than one German court, the severe struggle of a hotly contested battle, and the triumph of victory, Mr. Esmond beheld another part of military duty; our troops entering the enemy's territory and putting all around them to fire and sword; burning farms, wasted fields, shrieking women, slaughtered sons and fathers, and drunken soldiery, cursing and carousing in the midst of tears, terror, and murder. Why does the stately Muse of History, that delights in describing the valor of heroes and the grandeur of conquest, leave out these scenes, so brutal, and degrading, that yet form by far the greater part of the drama of war? You gentlemen of England, who live at home at ease and compliment yourselves in the songs of triumph with which our chieftains are bepraised; you pretty maidens that come tumbling down the stairs when the fife and drum call you, and huzza for the British Grenadiers—do you take account that these items go to make up the amount of triumph you admire, and form part of the duties of the heroes you fondle?

Our chief (the Duke of Marlborough), whom England and all Europe, saving only the Frenchmen, worshiped almost, had this of the god-like in him: that he was impassible before victory, before danger, before defeat. Before the greatest obstacle or the most trivial ceremony; before a hundred thousand men drawn in battalia, or a peasant slaughtered at the door of his burning hovel; before a carouse of drunken German lords, or a monarch's court, or a cottage table where his plans were laid, of an enemy's battery, vomiting flame and death and strewing corpses round about him—he was always cold, calm, resolute, like fate. He performed a treason or a court bow, he told a falsehood as black as Styx, as easily as he paid a compliment or spoke about the weather. He took a mistress and left her, he betrayed his benefactor and supported him, or would have murdered him, with the same calmness always and having no more remorse than Clotho when she weaves the thread, or Lachesis when she cuts it. In the hour of battle I have heard the Prince of Savoy's officers say the prince became possessed with a sort of warlike fury: his eyes lighted up; he rushed hither and thither, raging; shrieked curses and encouragement, yelling and harking his bloody war-dogs on, and himself always at the first of the hunt. Our duke was as calm at the mouth of a cannon as at the door of a drawing-room. Perhaps he could not have been the great man he was had he had a heart either for love or hatred, or pity or fear, or regret or remorse. He achieved the highest deed of daring, or deepest calculation of thought, as he performed the very meanest action of which a man is capable; told a lie or cheated a fond woman or robbed a poor beggar of a halfpenny, with a like awful serenity, and equal capacity of the highest and lowest acts of our nature.

His qualities were pretty well-known in the army, where there were parties of all politics, and of plenty of shrewdness and wit; but there existed such a perfect confidence in him, as the first captain of the world, and such a faith and admiration in his prodigious genius and fortune, that the very men whom he notoriously cheated of their pay, the chiefs whom he used and injured—for he used all men, great and small, that came near him, as his instruments, alike, and took something of theirs, either some quality or some property: the blood of a soldier, it might be, or a jeweled hat or a hundred thousand crowns from the king, or a portion out of a starving sentinel's three farthings; or when he was young, a kiss from a woman, and the gold chain off her neck, taking all he could from woman or man, and having, as I said, this of the godlike in him, that he could see a hero perish or a sparrow fall with the same amount of sympathy for either.

Not that he had no tears, he could always order up this reserve at the proper moment to battle; he could draw upon tears or smiles alike, and whenever need was for using this cheap coin. He would cringe to a shoeblack, and he would flatter a minister or a monarch; be haughty, be humble, threaten, repent, weep, grasp your hand, or stab you whenever he saw occasion—but yet those of the army who knew him best and had suffered most from him, admired him most of all; and as he rode along the lines to battle, or galloped up in the nick of time to a battalion reeling from the enemy's charge or shot, the fainting men and officers got new courage as they saw the splendid calm of his face, and felt that his will made them irresistible.

After the great victory of Blenheim, the enthusiasm of the army for the duke, even of his bitterest personal enemies in it, amounted to a sort of rage: nay, the very officers who cursed him in their hearts were among the most frantic to cheer him. Who could refuse his meed of admiration to such a victory and such a victor? Not he who writes: a man may profess to be ever so much a philosopher, but he who fought on that day must feel a thrill of pride as he recalls it.

—William M. Thackeray.

Soft is the music that would charm forever.—William Wordsworth.

THERE is, finally, a philosophic piety which has the universe for its object. This feeling, common to ancient and modern Stoics, has an obvious justification in man's dependence upon the natural world and in its service to many sides of the mind. Such justification of cosmic piety is rather obscured than supported by the euphemisms and ambiguities in which these philosophers usually indulge in their attempt to preserve the customary religious unction ॐ For the more they personify the universe and give it the name of God the more they turn it into a devil. The universe, so far as we can observe it, is a wonderful and immense engine; its extent, its order, its beauty, its cruelty, makes it alike impressive. If we dramatize its life and conceive its spirit, we are filled with wonder, terror, and amusement, so magnificent is that spirit, so prolific, inexorable, grammatical, and dull. Like all animals and plants, the cosmos has its own way of doing things, not wholly rational nor ideally best, but patient, fatal, and fruitful. Great is this organism of mud and fire, terrible this vast, painful, glorious experiment. Why should we not look on the universe with piety? Is it not our substance? Are we made of other clay? All our possibilities lie from eternity hidden in its bosom. It is the dispenser of all our joys. We may address it without superstitious terrors; it is not wicked. It follows its own habits abstractedly; it can be trusted to be true to its word. Society is not impossible between it and us, and since it is the source of all our energies, the home of all our happiness, shall we not cling to it and praise it, seeing that it vegetates so grandly and so sadly, and that it is not for us to blame it for what, doubtless, it never knew that it did?—George Santayana.

Industry, economy, honesty and kindness form a quartette of virtues that will never be improved upon.—James Oliver.

THE main thing about a book is not in what it says, but in what it asks and suggests. The interrogation-point is the accusing finger of orthodoxy, which would rather be denounced than questioned.—Horace Traubel.

MY philosophy makes life—the system of feelings and desires—supreme; and leaves knowledge merely the post of observer. This system of feelings is a fact in our minds about which there can be no dispute, a fact of which we have intuitive knowledge, a knowledge not inferred by arguments, nor generated by reasonings which can be received or neglected as we choose. Only such face-to-face knowledge has reality. It alone can get life in motion, since it springs from life.—Fichte.

THE sublime and the ridiculous are often so nearly related that it is difficult to class them separately. One step above the sublime makes the ridiculous, and one step above the ridiculous makes the sublime again.

—Thomas Paine.

IT had been part of Nelson's prayer, that the British fleet might be distinguished by humanity in the victory which he expected. Setting an example himself, he twice gave orders to cease firing on the *Redoubtable,* supposing that she had struck, because her guns were silent; for, as she carried no flag there was no means of instantly ascertaining the fact ᔰ From this ship, which he had thus twice spared, he received his death. A ball fired from her mizzentop, which, in the then situation of the two vessels, was not more than fifteen yards from that part of the deck where he was standing, struck the epaulet on his left shoulder, about a quarter after one, just in the heat of action. He fell upon his face, on the spot which was covered with his poor secretary's blood. Hardy, who was a few steps from him, turning round, saw three men raising him up ᔰ "They have done for me at last, Hardy," said he. "I hope not," cried Hardy. "Yes," he replied; "my backbone is shot through." Yet even now, not for a moment losing his presence of mind, he observed, as they were carrying him down the ladder, that the tiller ropes, which had been shot away, were not yet replaced, and ordered that new ones should be rove immediately: then, that he might not be seen by the crew, he took out his handkerchief, and covered his face and his stars. Had he but concealed these badges of honor from the enemy, England perhaps would not have had cause to receive with sorrow the news of the battle of Trafalgar. The cockpit was crowded with wounded and dying men; over whose bodies he was with some difficulty conveyed, and laid upon a pallet in the midshipmen's berth ᔰ

ℂ It was soon perceived, upon examination, that the wound was mortal. This, however, was concealed from all except Captain Hardy, the chaplain, and the medical attendants. He himself being certain, from the sensation in his back, and the gush of blood he felt momentarily within his breast, that no human care could avail him, insisted that the surgeon should leave him, and attend to those to whom he might be useful; "for," said he, "you can do nothing for me." All that could be done was to fan him with paper, and frequently to give him lemonade to alleviate his intense thirst. He was in great pain, and expressed much anxiety for the event of the action, which now began to declare itself. As often as a ship struck, the crew of the *Victory* hurrahed; and at every hurrah a visible expression of joy gleamed in the eyes and marked the countenance of the dying hero. But he became impatient to see Hardy; and as that officer

What is this, the sound and rumor?
What is this that all men hear,
Like the wind in hollow valleys when
the storm is drawing near,
Like the rolling on of the ocean in the
eventide of fear?
'T is the people marching on.
Whither go they, and whence come they?
What are these of whom ye tell?
In what country are they dwelling 'twixt
the gates of heaven and hell?
Are they mine or thine for money? Will
they serve a master well?

   Still the rumor 's marching on.
Hark the rolling of the thunder?
Lo, the sun! and lo, thereunder
Riseth wrath and hope and wonder,
And the host comes marching on.

Forth they come from grief and torment;
on they wend towards health and
mirth,
All the wide world is their dwelling,
every corner of the earth,
Buy them, sell them for thy service!
Try the bargain what 't is worth,
   For the days are marching on.
These are they who build thy houses,
weave thy raiment, win thy wheat,
Smooth the rugged, fill the barren, turn
the bitter into sweet,
All for thee this day—and ever. What
reward for them is meet
   Till the host comes marching on?

(Concluded on next page)

though often sent for, could not leave the deck, Nelson feared that some fatal cause prevented him, and repeatedly cried: " Will no one bring Hardy to me? he must be killed; he is surely dead!"

¶ An hour and ten minutes elapsed from the time when Nelson received his wound before Hardy could come to him. They shook hands in silence; Hardy in vain struggling to suppress the feelings of that most painful and yet sublimest moment. ¶ " Well, Hardy," said Nelson, " how goes the day with us? " " Very well," replied Hardy; " ten ships have struck, but five of the van have tacked, and show an intention to bear down upon the *Victory*. I have called two or three of our fresh ships round, and have no doubt of giving them a drubbing." ¶ " I hope," said Nelson, "that none of our ships have struck!" Hardy answered, " There was no fear of that." Then, and not till then, Nelson spoke of himself; " I am going fast: it will be all over with me soon. Come nearer to me. Let my dear Lady Hamilton have my hair, and all other things belonging to me." Hardy observed that he hoped Mr. Beatty could yet hold out some prospect of life. " O no," he replied; " it is impossible. My back is shot through. Beatty will tell you so." Hardy then, once more, shook hands with him, and

*Many a hundred years passed over have
   they labored deaf and blind;
Never tidings reached their sorrow, never
   hope their toil might find.
Now at last they 've heard and hear it,
   and the cry comes down the wind,
      And their feet are marching on.
O ye rich men, hear and tremble, for with
   words the sound is rife:
"Once for you and death we labored:
   changed henceforward is the strife,
We are men, and we shall battle for the
   world of men and life;
      And our host is marching on."*

*"Is it war, then? Will ye perish as the dry
   wood in the fire?
Is it peace? then be ye of us, let your hope
   be our desire.
Come and live! for life awaketh, and the
   world shall never tire:
      And the hope is marching on."
"On we march then, we the workers,
   and the rumor that ye hear
Is the blended sound of battle and deliv-
   'rance drawing near;
For the hope of every creature is the
   banner that we bear,
      And the world is marching on."
Hark the rolling of the thunder!
Lo, the sun! and lo, thereunder
Riseth wrath and hope and wonder
   And the host comes marching on.*

"The March of the Workers," *by William Morris*

with a heart almost bursting, hastened up on deck. ¶ By this time all feeling below the breast was gone; and Nelson, having made the surgeon ascertain this, said to him: " You know I am gone. I know it. I feel something rising in my breast," putting his hand on his left side, " which tells me so." And upon Beatty's inquiring whether his pain was very great, he replied, " So great that he wished he was dead ✺ Yet," said he, in a lower voice, " one would like to live a little longer too! " And after a few minutes in the same undertone, he added: " What would become of poor Lady Hamilton, if she knew my situation!" Next to his country she occupied his thoughts. ¶ Captain Hardy, some fifty minutes after he had left the cockpit, returned; and, again taking the hand of his dying friend and commander, congratulated him on having gained a complete victory. How many of the enemy were taken he did not know, as it was impossible to perceive them distinctly; but fourteen or fifteen at least. " That's well," cried Nelson, " but I bargained for twenty." And then, in a stronger voice, he said: "Anchor, Hardy; anchor." Hardy, upon this, hinted that Admiral Collingwood would take upon himself the direction of affairs. " Not while I live, Hardy," said the dying Nelson, ineffectually endeavoring to raise himself from the bed: " do you anchor." His previous orders for preparing to anchor had shown clearly he foresaw the necessity of this. Presently, calling Hardy back, he said to him, in a low voice; "Don't throw me overboard;" and he desired that he might be buried by his parents, unless it should please the King to order otherwise. Then reverting to private feelings: " Take care of my dear Lady Hamilton, Hardy: take care of poor Lady Hamilton. Kiss me, Hardy," said he. Hardy knelt down and kissed his cheek; and Nelson said, " Now I am satisfied. Thank God, I have done my duty!" Hardy stood over him in silence for a moment or two, then knelt again and kissed his forehead. "Who is that?" said Nelson; and being informed, he replied, " God bless you, Hardy," And Hardy then left him—forever. Nelson now desired to be turned upon his right side, and said, " I wish I had not left the deck; for I shall soon be gone." Death was, indeed, rapidly approaching. He said to the chaplain, " Doctor, I have *not* been a *great* sinner;" and after a short pause, " Remember that I leave Lady Hamilton and my daughter Horatia as a legacy to my country." His articulation now became difficult; but he was distinctly heard to say, " Thank God, I have done my duty!" These words he repeatedly pronounced; and they were the last words which he uttered. He expired at thirty minutes after four—three hours and a quarter after he had received his wound.

—Robert Southey.

People do not lack strength; they lack will.—Victor Hugo.

A SOUL stood on the bank of the River of Life, and it had to cross it. And first it found a reed, and it tried to cross with it. But the reed ran into its hand at the top in fine splinters and bent when it leaned on it. Then the soul found a staff and it tried to cross with it: and the sharp end ran into the ground, and the soul tried to draw it, but it could not; and it stood in the water by its staff. ❡ Then it got out and found a broad thick log, and it said, " With this I will cross." And it went down into the water. But the log was too buoyant, it floated, and almost drew the soul from its feet. ❡ And the soul stood on the bank and cried: " Oh, River of Life! How am I to cross; I have tried all roads and they have failed me?" And the River answered, " Cross me alone." And the soul went down into the water, and it crossed.—" The River of Life," by Olive Schreiner.

Joy is not in things; it is in us.—Wagner.

WHEN thou seest the great prelates with splendid mitres of gold and precious stones on their heads, and silver croziers in hand; there they stand at the altar, decked with fine copes and stoles of brocade, chanting those beautiful vespers and masses, very slowly, and with so many grand ceremonies, so many organs and choristers, that thou art struck with amazement . . . . Men feed upon the vanities and rejoice in these pomps, and say that the Church of Christ was never so flourishing, nor divine worship so well conducted as at present . . . . likewise that the first prelates were inferior to these of our own times. The former, it is true, had fewer gold mitres and fewer chalices, for indeed what few they possessed were broken up to relieve the needs of the poor; whereas our prelates, for the sake of obtaining chalices, will rob the poor of their sole means of support. But dost thou know what I would tell thee? In the primitive church the chalices were of wood, the prelates of gold; in these days the Church hath chalices of gold and prelates of wood.—Savonarola.

Quiet minds can not be perplexed or frightened, but go on in fortune or misfortune at their own private pace, like a clock during a thunderstorm.

—Robert Louis Stevenson.

Consider how few things are worthy of anger, and thou wilt wonder that any fools should be wroth.—Robert Dodsley.

T takes," says Thoreau, in the noblest and most useful passage I remember to have read in any modern author, " two to speak truth—one to speak and another to hear." He must be very little experienced, or have no great zeal for truth, who does not recognize the fact. A grain of anger or a grain of suspicion produces strange acoustical effects, and makes the ear greedy to remark offence. Hence we find those who have once quarreled carry themselves distantly, and are ever ready to break the truce. To speak truth there must be moral equality or else no respect; and hence between parent and child intercourse is apt to degenerate into a verbal fencing bout, and misapprehensions to become ingrained. And there is another side to this, for the parent begins with an imperfect notion of the child's character, formed in early years or during the equinoctial gales of youth; to this he adheres, noting only the facts which suit with his preconception; and wherever a person fancies himself unjustly judged, he at once and finally gives up the effort to speak truth ∾ With our chosen friends, on the other hand, and still more between lovers (for mutual understanding is love's essence), the truth is easily indicated by the one and aptly comprehended by the other. A hint taken, a look understood, conveys the gist of long and delicate explanations; and where the life is known, even *yea* and *nay* become luminous. In the closest of all relations—that of a love well-founded and equally shared—speech is half discarded, like a roundabout infantile process or a ceremony of formal etiquette; and the two communicate directly by their presences, and with few looks and fewer words contrive to share their good and evil and uphold each other's hearts in joy. For love rests upon a physical basis; it is a familiarity of nature's making and apart from voluntary choice. Understanding has in some sort outrun knowledge, for the affection perhaps began with the acquaintance; and as it was not made like other relations, so it is not, like them, to be perturbed or clouded. Each knows more than can be uttered; each lives by faith, and believes by a natural compulsion; and between man and wife the language of the body is largely developed and grown strangely eloquent ∾ The thought that prompted and was conveyed in a caress would only lose to be set down in words—ay, although Shakespeare himself should be the scribe.

—Robert Louis Stevenson.

∾ ∾

Co-operation is not a sentiment—it is an economic necessity.—Charles Steinmetz.

∾ ∾

YOUTH has a certain melancholy and sadness, while Age is valiantly cheerful . . . . A chief lesson of youth should be to learn to enjoy solitude—a source of peace and happiness. . In my years of youth I was delighted when the doorbell rang, for I thought, now *it* (the great romantic adventure) had come. But in later years my feeling on the same occasion had something rather akin to terror—I thought, there it comes!

—Schopenhauer.

∾ ∾

To write well is to think well, to feel well, and to render well; it is to possess at once intellect, soul, and taste.—Buffon.

∾ ∾

SPIRITUAL forces when manifested in man exhibit a sequence, a succession of steps. It follows, therefore, that when a man at one period of his life has omitted to put forth his strength in a work which he knows to be in harmony with the divine order of things, there comes a time, sooner or later, when a void will be perceived; when the fruits of his omitted action ought to have appeared, and do not; they are the missing links in the chain of consequences. The measure of that void is the measure of his past inaction, and that man will never quite reach the same level of attainment that he might have touched, had he divinely energized his lost moments.

—Friedrich Froebel.

∾ ∾

Whoever serves his country well has no need of ancestors.—Voltaire.

IN sober verity I will confess a truth to thee, reader. I love a *Fool*—as naturally as if I were of kith and kin to him. When a child, with childlike apprehensions, that dived not below the surface of the matter, I read those *Parables*—not guessing at the involved wisdom—I had more yearnings towards that simple architect, that built his house upon the sand, than I entertained for his more cautious neighbor; I grudged at the hard censure pronounced upon the quiet soul that kept his talent; and—prizing their simplicity beyond the more provident and, to my apprehension, somewhat *unfeminine* wariness of their competitors—I felt a kindness, that almost amounted to a *tendre,* for those five thoughtless virgins. I have never made an acquaintance since that lasted, or a friend·ship that answered, with any that had not some tincture of the absurd in their characters ✦ I venerate an honest obliquity of understanding. The more laughable blunders a man shall commit in your company, the more tests he giveth you that he will not betray or overreach you. I love the safety which a palpable hallucination warrants, the security which a word out of season ratifies. And take my word for this, reader, and say a fool told it you, if you please, that he who hath not a dram of folly in his mixture hath points of much worse matter in his composition. It is observed that "the foolisher the fowl, or fish, woodcocks, dotterels, cod's head, etc.,—the finer the flesh thereof;" and what are commonly the world's received fools but such whereof the world is not worthy? And what have been some of the kindliest patterns of our species, but so many darlings of absurdity, minions of the goddess, and her white boys? Reader, if you wrest my words beyond their fair construction, it is you, and not I, that are the April Fool.

—Charles Lamb.

✦ ✦

SCHOPENHAUER'S character was made up of that combination of seeming contradictions which is the peculiarity of all great men. He had the audacity of childhood, and the timidity of genius ✦ He was suspicious of every one, and ineffably kindhearted. With stupidity in every form he was blunt, even to violence; yet his manner and courtesy were such as is attributed to gentlemen of the old school. If he was an egotist, he was also charitable to excess; and who shall say that charity is not the egotism of great natures? He was honesty itself, and yet thought every one wished to cheat him. To mislead a possible thief he labeled his valuables Arcana Medica, put his bank notes in dictionaries and his gold pieces in ink bottles. He slept on the ground floor, that he might escape easily in case of fire. If he heard a noise at night he snatched at a pistol, which he kept loaded at his bedside .... Kant's biography is full of similar vagaries, and one has but to turn to the history of any of the thinkers whose

It hain't no use to grumble and complane;
    It's jest as cheap and easy to rejoice.—
When God sorts out the weather and sends rain,
    W'y rain's my choice.

Men ginerly, to all intents—
    Although they're apt to grumble some—
Puts most theyr trust in Providence,
    And takes things as they come—
      That is, the commonality
      Of men that's lived as long as me
      Has watched the world enugh to learn
      They're not the boss of this concern.

With some, of course, it's different—
    I've saw young men that knowed it all,
And did n't like the way things went
    On this terrestchul ball;—
      But all the same, the rain, some way,
      Rained jest as hard on picnic day;
      Er, when they railly wanted it,
      It mayby would n't rain a bit!

In this existence, dry and wet
    Will overtake the best of men—
Some little skift o' clouds 'll shet
The sun off now and then.—

(Concluded on next page)

names are landmarks in literature, to find that eccentricities no less striking have also been recorded of them.

—Edgar Saltus.

IT is dangerous for a man too suddenly or too easily to believe himself. Wherefore let us examine, watch, observe, and inspect our own hearts, for we ourselves are our greatest flatterers. We should every night call ourselves to an account. What infirmity have I mastered today? What passion opposed? What temptation resisted? What virtue acquired? Our vices will abate of themselves if they be brought every day to the shrift. Oh the blessed sleep that follows such a diary! Oh the tranquillity, liberty, and greatness of that mind which is a spy upon itself, and a private censor upon its own manners! It is my custom every night, so soon as the candle is out, to run over the words and actions of the past day; and I let nothing escape me, for why should I fear the sight of my errors when I can admonish and forgive myself? I was a little too hot in such a dispute; my opinion might well have been withheld, for it gave offence and did no good. The thing was true; but all truths are not to be spoken at all times. I would I had held my tongue, for there is no contending, either with fools or with our superiors. I have done ill, but it shall be so no more. If every man would but then look into himself, it would be the better for us all. What can be more reasonable than this daily review of a life that we can not warrant for a moment? Our fate is set, and the first breath we draw is only our first motion toward our last. There is a great variety in our lives, but all tends to the same issue.

We are born to lose and to perish, to hope and to fear, to vex ourslves and others, and there is no antidote against a common calamity but virtue; for the foundation of true joy is in the conscience

—Seneca.

And mayby, whilse you're wundern who
You've fool-like lent your umbrell' to,
And want it—out'll pop the sun,
And you'll be glad you hain't got none!
It aggervates the farmers, too—
They's too much wet, er too much sun,
Er work, er waitin' round to do
Before the plowin' 's done:
And mayby, like as not, the wheat,
Jest as it's lookin' hard to beat,
Will ketch the storm—and jest about
The time the corn's a-jintin' out.
These-here cy-clones a-foolin' round—
And back'ard crops!—and wind and
rain!—
And yit the corn that's wallerd down
May elbow up again!—
They hain't no sense, as I can see,
Fer mortuls, sich as us, to be
A-faultin' Natchur's wise intents,
And lockin' horns with Providence!
It hain't no use to grumble and complane;
It's jest as cheap and easy to rejoice.
When God sorts out the weather and
sends rain,
W'y, rain's my choice.

"Wet-Weather Talk," *by James Whitcomb Riley*

IN every man's life pilgrimage, however unblest, there are holy places where he is made to feel his kinship with the Divine; where the heavens bend low over his head and angels come and minister unto him. These are the places of sacrifice, the meeting-ground of mortal and immortal, the tents of trial wherein are waged the great spiritual combats of man's life. Here are the tears and agonies and the bloody sweat of Gethsemane. Happy the man who, looking back, can say of himself: "Here, too, was the victory!"

—Michael Monahan.

Habit is a cable; we weave a thread of it every day, and at last we can not break it.—Horace Mann.

The highest and most lofty trees have the most reason to dread the thunder.

—Charles Rollin.

ECONDLY, I enjoin and require that *no ecclesiastic, missionary, or minister of any sect whatsoever, shall ever hold or exercise any station or duty whatsoever in the said College; nor shall any such person ever be admitted for any purpose, or as a visitor, within the premises appropriated to the purposes of the said College:* In making this restriction, I do not mean to cast any reflection upon any sect or person whatsoever; but as there is such a multitude of sects, and such a diversity of opinion amongst them, I desire to keep the tender minds of the orphans, who are to derive advantage from this bequest, free from the excitement which clashing doctrines and sectarian controversy are so apt to produce; my desire is, that all the instructors and teachers in the college, shall take pains to instill into the minds of the scholars, *the purest principles of morality,* so that, on their entrance into active life, they may, *from inclination and habit,* evince *benevolence toward their fellow creatures,* and *a love of truth, sobriety and industry,* adopting at the same time, such religious tenets as their *matured reason* may enable them to prefer.—From the Will of Stephen Girard.

Hubbard's Note:—The heirs tried to break this will with Daniel Webster's assistance. Their contention was founded largely upon this paragraph. Nevertheless the will prevailed before the Supreme Court of the United States.

··◁▥▷··

Go not abroad; retire into thyself, for truth dwells in the inner man.
—Saint Augustine.

··◁▥▷··

SHOULD the wide world roll away,
  Leaving black terror,
Limitless night,
Nor God, nor man, nor place to stand
Would be to me essential,
If thou and thy white arms were there
And the fall to doom a long way.
—Stephen Crane.

··◁▥▷··

You believe that easily which you hope for earnestly.—Terence.

FRIENDS: I know how vain it is to gild a grief with words, and yet I wish to take from every grave its fear. Here in this world, where life and death are equal kings, all should be brave enough to meet with all the dead have met. The future has been filled with fear, stained and polluted by the heartless past. From the wondrous tree of life the buds and blossoms fall with ripened fruit, and in the common bed of earth, the patriarchs and babes sleep side by side. Why should we fear that which will come to all that is?

We can not tell, we do not know, which is the greater blessing—life or death. We do not know whether the grave is the end of this life, or the door of another, or whether the night here is not somewhere else a dawn. Neither can we tell which is the more fortunate—the child dying in its mother's arms, before its lips have learned to form a word, or he who journeys all the length of life's uneven road, painfully taking the last slow steps with staff and crutch.

Every cradle asks us, " Whence? " and every coffin, " Whither? " ◡ The poor barbarian, weeping above his dead, can answer these questions as intelligently as the robed priest of the most authentic creed. The tearful ignorance of the one is just as consoling as the learned and unmeaning words of the other. No man, standing where the horizon of a life has touched a grave, has any right to prophesy a future filled with pain and tears. It may be that death gives all there is of worth to life. If those we press and strain against our hearts could never die, perhaps that love would wither from the earth. Maybe this common fate treads from out the paths between our hearts the weeds of selfishness and hate, and I had rather live and love where death is king, than have eternal life where love is not. Another life is naught, unless we know and love again the ones who love us here.

They who stand with aching hearts around this little grave need have no fear. The larger and the nobler faith in all that is and is to be, tells us that death, even at its worst, is only perfect rest. We know that through the common wants of life—the needs and duties of each hour—their griefs will lessen day by day, until at last this grave will be to them a place of rest and peace—almost of joy. There is for them this consolation. The dead do not suffer. And if they live again, their lives will surely be as good as ours. We have no fear. We are all children of the same mother, and the same fate awaits us all.

We, too, have our religion, and it is this: Help for the living— Hope for the dead. —Robert G. Ingersoll.

Out of the dusk a shadow,
Then a spark;
Out of the cloud a silence,
Then, a lark;
Out of the heart a rapture,
Then, a pain,
Out of the dead, cold ashes,
Life again.

"Evolution," *by John Banister Tabb*

IT is a mistake to suppose that in planting colonies in the New World the nations of Europe were moved mainly by a philanthropic impulse to extend the area of liberty and civilization. Colonies were planted for the purpose of raising up customers for home trade. It was a matter of business and speculation, carried on by joint stock companies for the benefit of corporations. ¶ While our Revolution was in progress Adam Smith, when discussing and condemning the colonial system, declared that " England had founded an empire in the New World for the sole purpose of raising customers for her trade." When the colonies had increased in numbers and wealth, the purpose of the mother country was disclosed in the legislation and regulations by which the colonies were governed. Whatever did not enhance the trade and commerce of England was deemed unfit to be a part of the colonial policy. Worse even than its effects on the industry of the colonies was the influence of this policy on political and commercial morality. The innumerable arbitrary laws enacted to enforce it created a thousand new crimes. Transactions which the colonists thought necessary to the welfare, and in no way repugnant to the moral sense of good men, were forbidden under heavy penalties. ¶ They became a nation of law-breakers. Nine-tenths of the colonial merchants were smugglers. Nearly half of the signers of the Declaration of Independence were bred to commerce, to the command of ships and to contraband trade. John Hancock was the prince of contraband traders; and with John Adams as his counsel, was on trial before the admiralty court in Boston, at the exact hour of the shedding of the first blood at Lexington, to answer for a $500,000 penalty alleged to have been incurred as a smuggler. ¶ Half the tonnage of the world was engaged in smuggling or piracy. The war of independence was a war against commercial despotism; against an industrial policy which oppressed and tortured the industry of our fathers, and would have reduced them to perpetual vassalage for the gain of England.—James A. Garfield.

HE who every morning plans the transactions of the day, and follows out that plan, carries a thread that will guide him through the labyrinth of the most busy life. The orderly arrangement of his time is like a ray of light which darts itself through all his occupations. But where no plan is laid, where the disposal of time is surrendered merely to the chance of incidents, all things lie huddled together in one chaos, which admits of neither distribution nor review.—Hugo.

Amid my list of blessings infinite,
Stands this the foremost,
" That my heart has bled."
                        —Edward Young.

It is not he that enters upon any career, or starts in any race, but he that runs well and perseveringly that gains the plaudits of others, or the approval of his own conscience.—Alexander Campbell.

HE life of a people is a tissue of crimes, miseries, and follies. That is no less true of Penguinia than of other nations ☙ ☙

Gratian, the sage, toured Penguinia in the time of the last of the Draconide dynasty. Travelling one day through a lovely valley where cow bells tinkled in the pure air, he sat down on a bench at the foot of an oak tree, near a thatched cottage. On the doorstep a woman was suckling an infant; a youngster was playing with a big dog; a blind old man, seated in the sun, was drinking in the light of day through half-opened lips.

❧ The master of the house, a robust young man, offered Gratian bread and milk and, the Marsouin philosopher after partaking of this repast, exclaimed, " Kindly inhabitants of a gentle land, I thank you. Everything here breathes joy, concord and peace."

Even as he spoke, however, a shepherd passed, playing a martial air upon his bagpipes ☙ ☙

" What is that lively tune? " demanded Gratian ☙ ☙

" That 's our war hymn against the Marsouins," replied the peasant. " Everybody here sings it. Little children know it before they can talk. We are all good Penguin patriots."

" You don't like the Marsouins? "

" We hate them."

" For what reason do you hate them? "

" How can you ask? They are our neighbors, are n't they? "

" Undoubtedly."

" Well, that 's the reason the Penguins hate the Marsouins."

" Is that a reason? "

" Certainly. Who says ' neighbors ' says ' enemies ' ☙ Look at the field which touches mine. It belongs to the man I hate most in the world. After him my worst enemies are the people of the village on the other slope of the valley at the foot of that birch wood. In this narrow valley, closed in on all sides, there is only that village and my village. Of course they are enemies. Every time our chaps meet theirs, they exchange insults and blows. And you don't see why the Penguins should be the enemies of the Marsouins! Don't you know what patriotism means? For me there are only two possible battlecries: ' Long live the Penguins! Death to the Marsouins! ' "

—Anatole France.

☙ ☙

THIS Mahomet, son of Abdallah, was a sublime charlatan. He says in his tenth chapter, " Who but God can have composed the Koran? Do you think Mahomet has forged this book? Well, try and write one chapter resembling it, and call to your aid whomsoever you please." In the seventeenth chapter, he exclaims, " Praise be to him who in a single night transported his servant from the sacred temple of Mecca to that of Jerusalem! "

This was a fine journey, but nothing compared to the one he took that same night from planet to planet. He pretended that it was five hundred years' journey from one to the other, and that he had cleft the moon in twain. His disciples who, after his death, collected in a solemn manner the verses of his Koran, suppressed this celestial journey, for they dreaded raillery and rationalization.

After all, they had more delicacy than was needed. They might have trusted to the commentators, who would have found no difficulty in explaining the itinerary ☙ Mahomet's friends should have known by experience that the marvelous is the reason of the multitude. The wise contradict in a silence, which the multitude prevents their breaking. But while the itinerary of the planets was suppressed, a few words were retained about the adventure of the moon; one can not forever be on one's guard ☙ ☙

The Koran is a rhapsody, without connection, without order, and without art. . . . It is a poem or a sort of rhymed prose, consisting of about three thousand verses ☙ No poem ever advanced the fortunes of its author so much as the Koran ☙ ☙

He has the humility to confess that he himself will not enter Paradise because of his own merits, but purely by the *will* of God. Through this same *pure Divine* will, he orders that a fifth part of the spoil shall always be reserved for the Prophet ॐ ॐ

It is not true that he excludes women from Paradise. It is hardly likely that so able a man should have chosen to embroil himself with that half of the human race by which the other half is led ॐ

Abulfeda relates that an old woman one day importuned him to tell her what she must do to get into Paradise. "My good lady," said he, "Paradise is not for old women." The good woman began to weep; but the Prophet consoled her by saying, "There will be no old women, because they will become young again." This consolatory doctrine is confirmed in the fifty-fourth chapter of the Koran. He forbade wine, because some of his followers once went intoxicated to prayers. He allowed a plurality of wives, conforming in this point to the immemorial usage of the Orientals ॐ In short, his civil laws are good; his doctrine is admirable for all it has in common with ours, but his means are shocking—charlatanry and murder ॐ ॐ

He is excused by some on the first of these charges, because, say they, the Arabs had a hundred and twenty-four thousand prophets before him, and there could be no great harm in the appearance of one more. Men, it is added, require to be deceived. But how are we to justify a man who says, "Either believe that I have conversed with the Angel Gabriel, or pay me tribute?"

How superior is Confucius—the first of mortals who did not claim to have been favored with divine revelations! He employs neither falsehood nor the sword, but only reason. As viceroy of a great province he causes the laws to be ob-

April, April,
Laugh thy girlish laughter;
Then, the moment after,
Weep thy girlish tears!
April, that mine ears
Like a lover greetest,
If I tell thee, sweetest,
All my hopes and fears,
April, April,
Laugh thy golden laughter,
But, the moment after,
Weep thy golden tears!

"Song," *by William Watson*

served and morality to flourish. Later, disgraced and poor, he teaches them ॐ He practices them, alike in greatness and in humility. He renders virtue amiable, and has for his disciples the most ancient and wisest people upon the earth ॐ ॐ

Mahomet is admired for having raised himself from being a camel driver, to be a pontiff, a legislator, and a monarch, for having subdued Arabia, which had never before been subjugated; for having given the first shock to the Roman Empire in the East, and to that of the Persians ॐ But *I* admire him still more for having kept peace in his house amongst his wives.

He changed the face of part of Europe, one half of Asia, and nearly all of Africa. Nor was his religion unlikely at one time, to subjugate the whole earth. ¶ On how trivial a circumstance will revolutions sometimes depend! A blow from a stone, a little harder than that which he received in his first battle, might have changed the destinies of the world.—Voltaire.

ॐ ॐ

He who loveth a book will never want a faithful friend, a wholesome counsellor, a cheerful companion, or an effectual comforter.—Isaac Barrow.

ॐ ॐ

EVERY man will have his own criterion in forming his judgment of others. I depend very much on the effect of affliction. I consider how a man comes out of the furnace; gold will lie for a month in the furnace without losing a grain.—Richard Cecil.

ॐ ॐ

If wrinkles must be written upon our brows, let them not be written upon the heart. The spirit should not grow old.
—James A. Garfield.

THERE is nothing to make one indignant in the mere fact that life is hard, that men should toil and suffer pain. The planetary conditions once for all are such, and we can stand it. But that so many men, by mere accidents of birth and opportunity, should have a life of *nothing else* but toil and pain and hardness and inferiority imposed upon them, should have *no* vacation, while others natively no more deserving never get any taste of this campaigning life at all—*this* is capable of arousing indignation in reflective minds. It may end by seeming shameful to all of us that some of us have nothing but campaigning, and others nothing but unmanly ease.

If now—and this is my idea—there were, instead of military conscription, a conscription of the whole youthful population to form for a certain number of years a part of the army enlisted against *Nature,* the injustice would tend to be evened out, and numerous other goods to the commonwealth would follow. The military ideals of hardihood and discipline would be wrought into the growing fiber of the people; no one would remain blind, as the luxurious classes now are blind, to man's real relations to the globe he lives on, and to the permanently sour and hard foundations of his higher life. To coal and iron mines, to freight trains, to fishing fleets in December, to dish-washing, clothes-washing, and window-washing, to road-building and tunnel-making, to foundries and stoke-holes, and to the frames of skyscrapers, would our gilded youths be drafted off, according to their choice to get the childishness knocked out of them, and to come back into society with healthier sympathies and soberer ideas ֍ They would have paid their blood-tax, done their own part in the immemorial human warfare against nature, they should tread the earth more proudly, the women would value them more highly, they would be better fathers and teachers of the following generation. ❧ Such a conscription, with the state of public opinion that would have required

it, and the many moral fruits it would bear, would preserve in the midst of a pacific civilization the manly virtues which the military party is so afraid ot seeing disappear in peace. We should get toughness without callousness, authority with as little criminal cruelty as possible, and painful work done cheerily because the duty is temporary, and threatens not as now, to degrade the whole remainder of one's life.—William James.

֍ ֍

LORD, let me never tag a moral to a tale, nor tell a story without a meaning. Make me respect my material so much that I dare not slight my work. ❧ Help me to deal very honestly with words and with people, for they are both alive. Show me that as in a river, so in a writing, clearness is the best quality, and a little that is pure is worth more than much that is mixed.
Teach me to see the local color without being blind to the inner light.
Give me an ideal that will stand the strain of weaving into human stuff on the loom of the real.
Keep me from caring more for books than for folks, for art than for life.
Steady me to do the full stint of work as well as I can; and when that is done, stop me; pay what wages Thou wilt, and help me to say, from a quiet heart, a grateful Amen.—Henry van Dyke.

֍ ֍

THE new church will be founded on moral science. Poets, artists, musicians, philosophers, will be its prophet-teachers. The noblest literature of the world will be its Bible—love and labor its holy sacraments—and instead of worshiping one savior, we will gladly build an altar in the heart for every one who has suffered for humanity.—Emerson.

֍ ֍

You can not believe in honor until you have achieved it. Better keep yourself clean and bright; you are the window through which you must see the world.
—George Bernard Shaw.

֍ ֍

Men, even when alone, lighten their labor by song, however rude it may be.
—Quintilian.

THOUGHT all the time of my mother and grandmother deprived of the help of my youth and strong arm. It gave me a pang to think of tnem left weak and failing at home, when I might have been the staff of their old age; but their hearts were too full of motherly love for them to allow me to give up my profession for their sakes. And then youth has not all the sensitiveness of riper years, and a demon within seemed to push me towards Paris ✏ I was ambitious to see and learn all that a painter ought to know. My Cherbourg masters had not spoilt me in this respect during my apprenticeship. Paris seemed to me the center of knowledge, and a museum of all great works.

I started with my heart very full, and all that I saw on the road and in Paris itself made me still sadder. The wide straight roads, the long lines of trees, the flat plains, the rich grass-pastures filled with cattle, seemed to me more like stage decorations than actual nature. And then Paris—black, muddy, smoky Paris—made the most painful and discouraging impression upon me.

It was on a snowy Saturday evening in January that I arrived there. The light of the street lamps was almost extinguished by the fog. The immense crowd of horses and carriages crossing and pushing each other, the narrow streets, the air and smell of Paris seemed to choke my head and heart, and almost stifled me. I was seized with an uncontrollable fit of sobbing. I tried to get the better of my feelings, but they were too strong for me, and I could only stop my tears by bathing my face with water at a fountain in the street.

The sensation of freshness revived my courage. I stopped before a print-seller's window and looked at his pictures, while I munched my last Gruchy apple. The plates which I saw did not please me: there were groups of half-naked grisettes, women bathing and dressing, such as Devéria and Maurin then drew, and, in my eyes, seemed only fit for milliners' and perfumer's advertisements.

Paris appeared to me dismal and insipid.

I went to an *hotel garni,* where I spent my first night in one continual nightmare. I saw again my native village, and our house, looking very sad and lonely. I saw my grandmother, mother and sister, sitting there spinning, weeping, and thinking of me, and praying that I might escape from the perdition of Paris. Then the old demon appeared again, and showed me a vision of magnificent pictures so beautiful and dazzling that they seemed to glow with heavenly splendor, and finally melt away in a celestial cloud.

But my awakening was more earthly. My room was a dark and suffocating hole. I got up and rushed out into the air. The light had come back and with it my calmness and force of will.

—Millet's First Visit to Paris.

✏ ✏

A LIFE without love in it is like a heap of ashes upon a deserted hearth —with the fire dead, the laughter stilled, and the light extinguished. It is like a winter landscape—with the sun hidden, the flowers frozen, and the wind whispering through the withered leaves ✏ God knows we need all the unselfish love that can come to us. For love is seldom unselfish. There is usually the motive and the price. Do you remember William Morris, and how his life was lived, his fortune spent, his hands busied—in the service of others? He was the father of the settlement movement, of co-operative homes for working people, and of the arts and crafts revival, in our day. He was a " soldier of the common good." After he was gone—his life began to grow in radiance and power, like a beacon set high upon a dangerous shore. In the twilight of his days he wrote what I like to think was his creed—and mine: " I 'm going your way, so let us go hand in hand. You help me and I 'll help you. We shall not be here very long, for soon death, the kind old nurse, will come back and rock us all to sleep. Let us help one another while we may."—Frank P. Tebbetts.

✏ ✏

The men who try to do something and fail are infinitely better than those who try to do nothing and succeed.—Lloyd Jones.

URING the first days after my arrival in Paris my fixed idea was to find out the gallery of Old Masters ᔒ I started early one morning with this intention, but as I did not dare ask my way, for fear of being laughed at, I wandered at random through the streets, hoping, I suppose, that the Musée would come to meet me! I lost myself several days running in this fruitless search. During my wanderings one day I came across Notre Dame for the first time. It seemed to me less fine than the Cathedral of Coutances. I thought that the Luxembourg was a fine palace, but too regularly beautiful —the work, as it were, of a coquettish and mediocre builder ᔒ ᔒ
At length, I hardly know how, I found myself on the Pont Neuf, where a magnificent pile, which from the descriptions which had been given me, I supposed must be the Louvre. Without delay I turned my steps there and climbed the great staircase with a beating heart and the hurried steps of a man who feels that the one great wish of his life is about to be fulfilled ᔒ ᔒ
My hopes were not disappointed. I seemed to find myself in a world of friends, in the midst of my own kinsfolk. My dreams were at length realized. For the next month the Old Masters were my only occupation in the daytime. I de-

voured them all: I studied them, analyzed them, and came back to them continually. The Primitives attracted me by their admirable expression of sweetness, holiness, and fervor ᔒ The great Italians fascinated me by their mastery and charm of composition. There were moments when the arrows of St. Sebastian seemed to pierce me, as I looked at the martyr of Mantegna. ¶ The masters of that age have an incomparable power. They make you feel in turn the joys and the pains which thrill their souls. But when I saw that drawing of Michelangelo's representing a man in a swoon, I felt that was a different thing. The expression of the relaxed muscles, the planes and the modeling of that form exhausted by physical suffering gave me a whole series of impressions. I felt as if tormented by the same pains. I had compassion upon him. I suffered in his body with his limbs ᔒ I saw that the man who had done this was able, in a single figure, to represent all the good and evil of humanity. It was Michelangelo! That explains all. I had already seen some bad engravings of his work at Cherbourg; but here I touched the heart and heard the voice of him who has haunted me with such power during my whole life.
—Millet's First Visit to the Louvre.

ᔒ ᔒ

Adversity has no friends.—Tacitus.

Bowed by the weight of centuries he leans
Upon his hoe and gazes upon the ground,
The emptiness of ages in his face,
And on his back the burden of the world.
Who made him dead to rapture and despair,
A thing that grieves not and that never hopes,
Stolid and stunned, a brother to the ox?
Who loosened and let down this brutal jaw?
Whose was the hand that slanted back
    this brow?
Whose breath blew out the light within
    this brain?

Is this the thing the Lord God made and gave
To have dominion over sea and land;
To trace the stars and search the heavens
    for power;
To feel the passion of Eternity?
Is this the dream He dreamed who
    shaped the suns
And marked their ways upon the ancient
    deep?
Down all the stretch of Hell to its last gulf
There is no shape more terrible than this—
More tongued with censure of the world's
    blind greed—
More filled with signs and portents for
    the soul—
More fraught with menace to the universe.

What gulfs between him and the seraphim
Slave of the wheel of labor, what to him
Are Plato and the swing of Pleiades?

(Concluded on next page)

ILLET at that time wore a curious garb. A brown overcoat, in color like a stone wall, a thick beard and long locks, covered with a woolen cape like that of a coachman, gave him a singular appearance ✷ The first time that I saw him he reminded me of the painters of the Middle Ages. His reception was cordial, but almost silent ✷ He took me for a philosopher, a philanthropist, or a politician—none of whom he cared much to see. But I talked of art to him, and seeing his Daphnis and Chloe hanging on the wall, I told him what I thought of it ✷ ✷

He looked hard at me, but still with a kind of shyness, and only said a few words in a reply. ❡ Then I caught sight of a sketch of a sower.

"That would be a fine thing," I remarked, "if you had had a country model." ✷ ✷

"Then do you not belong to Paris?" he asked.

"Yes," I replied, "but I was brought up in the country." ❡ "Ah! that is a different story," he said in his Norman patois; "we must have a little talk."

Troyon left us alone, and Millet, looking at me some moments in silence, said: "You will not care for my pictures."

"You are wrong there," I replied warmly; "it is because I like them that I have come to see you."

From that moment Millet conversed freely with me, and his remarks on art were as manly as they were generous and large-hearted ✷ ✷

"Every subject is good," he said. "All we have to do is to render it with force and clearness. In art we should have one leading thought, and see that we express it in eloquent language, also that we keep it alive in ourselves, and impart it to others as clearly as we stamp a medal ✷ Art is not a pleasure-trip; it is a battle, a mill that grinds ✷ I am no philosopher. I do not pretend to do away with pain, or to find a formula which will make me a Stoic, and indifferent to evil. Suffering is, perhaps, the one thing that gives an artist power to express himself clearly."

He spoke in this manner for some time and then stopped, as if afraid of his own words ✷ But we parted, feeling that we understood each other, and had laid the foundations of a lasting friendship."—"Millet Meets His Future Biographer."—Alfred Sensier.

What the long reaches of the peaks of song,
The rift of dawn, the reddening of the rose?
Through this dread shape the suffering ages look;
Time's tragedy is in that aching stoop;
Through this dread shape humanity betrayed,
Plundered, profaned and disinherited,
Cries protest to the Judges of the World,
A protest that is also prophecy.

O masters, lords and rulers in all lands,
Is this the handiwork you give to God,
This monstrous thing distorted and soul-quenched?
How will you ever straighten up this shape;
Touch it again with immortality;
Give back the upward looking and the light;
Rebuild in it the music and the dream;
Make right the immemorial infamies,
Perfidious wrongs, immedicable woes?

O masters, lords and rulers in all lands,
How will the Future reckon with this Man?
How answer his brute question in that hour
When whirlwinds of rebellion shake the world?
How will it be with kingdoms and with kings—
With those who shaped him to the thing he is—
When this dumb Terror shall reply to God,
After the silence of the centuries?

"The Man With the Hoe," by *Edwin Markham*

✷ ✷

APITAL is condensed labor. It is nothing until labor takes hold of it. The living laborer sets free the condensed labor and makes it assume some form of utility or beauty. Capital and labor are one, and they will draw nearer to each other as the world advances in intellect and goodness.—David Swing.

JOSEPHINE was dead. The fall of the Emperor, her hero, her Cid, had bewildered and unnerved her Frightened at the din of war that shook the whole realm, she had lived in terror at Malmaison. The allied kings paid her every attention, and in showing the King of Prussia over her lovely grounds when she was ill, broken out with an eruption, she had, it is said, brought on a fatal relapse. Murmuring the words "Elba"—"Bonaparte"—she died, while her hero was yet in exile.

It is a revelation of his true character that before setting out on his last campaign he should claim one day out of the few fate gave him, and devote it to memories, to regrets, to recollections of the frail, but tender-hearted woman who had warmed to him when all the world was growing cold. He went to Malmaison, almost alone, and, with Hortense, walked over the grounds, seeing the old familiar places, and thinking of the "old familiar faces." He lingered in the garden he himself had made, and in which he used to love to work when he was First Consul, surrounded by trees and flowers, and inhaling the breath of nature. He used to say that he could work better there than anywhere else. He wandered through the park, looking out on the trees he had planted in those brilliant days long ago. Every spot had its silent reminder ot glories that were gone, of friends he would see no more.

He asked to be told everything about Josephine—her last days, her sickness, her dying hours; no details were too trivial to escape him. And as they told the story he would break in with exclamations of interest, of fondness, of sorrow. On this visit to the chateau he wanted to see everything that could remind him of her, and of their old life together —the death-chamber at the last. Here he would have no companion "My daughter, let me go in here alone!" and he put Hortense back, entered, and closed the door. He remained a long while, and when he came out his eyes showed that he had been weeping.

—Thomas E. Watson.

SOCIETIES exist under three forms sufficiently distinguishable. 1. Without government, as among our Indians. 2. Under governments wherein the will of every one has a just influence, as is the case in England in a slight degree, and in our states, in a great one. 3. Under governments of force: as is the case in all other monarchies and in most of the other republics. To have an idea of the curse of existence under these last, they must be seen. It is a government of wolves over sheep. It is a problem, not clear in my mind, that the first condition is not the best. But I believe it to be inconsistent with any great degree of population. The second state has a great deal of good in it. The mass of mankind under that enjoys a precious degree of liberty and happiness. It has its evils too: the principal of which is the turbulence to which it is subject. But weigh this against the oppressions of monarchy, and it becomes nothing. I prefer dangerous liberty rather than quiet servitude. Even this evil is productive of good It prevents the degeneracy of government, and nourishes a general attention to the public affairs. I hold it that a little rebellion now and then is a good thing, and as necessary in the political world as storms in the physical. Unsuccessful rebellions indeed generally establish the encroachments on the rights of the people which have produced them. An observation of this truth should render honest republican governors so mild in their punishment of rebellions, as not to discourage them too much. It is a medicine necessary for the sound health of government.

—Thomas Jefferson.

Economizing for the purpose of being independent is one of the soundest indications of manly character.

—Samuel Smiles.

The true work of art is but a shadow of the divine perfection.—Michelangelo.

ENERAL:—I have placed you at the head of the Army of the Potomac. Of course, I have done this upon what appear to me to be sufficient reasons, and yet I think it best for you to know that there are some things in regard to which I am not quite satisfied with you. I believe you to be a brave and skilful soldier, which of course I like. I also believe you do not mix politics with your profession, in which you are right. You have confidence in yourself, which is a valuable if not an indispensable quality. You are ambitious, which, within reasonable bounds, does good rather than harm; but I think that during General Burnside's command of the army you have taken counsel of your ambition and thwarted him as much as you could, in which you did a great wrong to the country and to a most meritorious and honorable brother officer ✒ ✒

I have heard, in such a way as to believe it, of your recently saying that both the army and the government needed a dictator.

Of course it was not for this, but in spite of it, that I have given you the command. Only those generals who gain successes can set up dictators.

What I now ask of you is military success, and I will risk the dictatorship ✒

❡ The government will support you to the utmost of its ability, which is neither more nor less than it has done and will do for all commanders.

I much fear that the spirit which you have aided to infuse into the army, of criticizing their commander and withholding confidence from him, will now turn upon you. I shall assist you as far as I can to put it down.

Neither you nor Napoleon, if he were alive again, could get any good out of an army while such a spirit prevails in it; and now beware of rashness.

Beware of rashness, but with energy and sleepless vigilance go forward and give us victories. Yours very truly, Abraham Lincoln.—(Letter to General J. Hooker, January 26, 1863.)

I SERVED with General Washington in the Legislature of Virginia, before the Revolution, and, during it, with Doctor Franklin in Congress ✒ I never heard either of them speak ten minutes at a time, nor to any but the main point, which was to decide the question ✒ ✒

They laid their shoulders to the great points, knowing that the little ones would follow of themselves. If the present Congress errs in too much talking, how can it be otherwise, in a body to which the people send one hundred and fifty lawyers, whose trade it is to question everything, yield nothing, and talk by the hour? ✒ That one hundred and fifty lawyers should do business together ought not to be expected.

—Thomas Jefferson.

✒ ✒

KEEP your minds so filled with Truth and Love that sin, disease, and death can not enter them. It is plain that nothing can be added to the mind already full. There is no door through which evil can enter, and no space for evil to fill in a mind filled with goodness. Good thoughts are an impervious armor; clad therewith you are completely shielded from the attacks of error of every sort.

❡ And not only yourselves are safe, but all whom your thoughts rest upon are thereby benefited.

The self-seeking pride of the evil thinker injures him when he would harm others. Goodness involuntarily resists evil. The evil thinker is the proud talker and doer. The right thinker abides under the shadow of the Almighty. His thoughts can only reflect peace, good will towards men, health, and holiness.

—Mary Baker Eddy.

✒ ✒

CHILDREN are much nearer the inner truth of things than we are, for when their instincts are not perverted by the superfine wisdom of their elders, they give themselves up to a full, vigorous activity ✒ Theirs is the kingdom of heaven.—Friedrich Froebel.

✒ ✒

It is the cause, and not the death, that makes the martyr.—Napoleon.

I THINK I knew General Washington intimately and thoroughly: and were I called on to delineate his character, it should be in terms like these: His mind was great and powerful without being of the very first order; his penetration strong, though not so acute as that of a Newton, Bacon or Locke; and, as far as he saw, no judgment was ever sounder. It was slow in operation, being little aided by imagination or invention, but sure in conclusion ✍ Hence the common remark of his officers, of the advantage he derived from councils of war, where, hearing all suggestions, he selected whatever was best; and certainly, no general planned his battles more judiciously ✍ But if deranged during the course of the action, if any member of his plan was dislocated by sudden circumstances, he was slow in a readjustment. The consequence was that he often failed in the field, and rarely against an enemy in station, as at Boston and York. He was incapable of fear, meeting personal danger with the calmest unconcern.

Perhaps the strongest feature in his character was prudence, never acting until every circumstance, every consideration, was maturely weighed; refraining if he saw a doubt, but, when once decided, going through with his purpose, whether obstacles opposed. His integrity was most pure, his justice the most inflexible I have ever known, no motives of interest or consanguinity, of friendship or hatred, being able to bias his decision. He was, indeed, in every sense of the words, a wise, a good and a great man ✍ His temper was naturally irritable and high-toned; but reflection and resolution had obtained a firm and habitual ascendency over it ✍ If ever, however, it broke its bonds, he was most tremendous in his wrath. In his expenses he was honorable, but exact; liberal in contribution to whatever promised utility; but frowning and unyielding on all visionary projects, and all the unworthy calls on his charity. His heart was not warm in its affections; but he exactly calculated every man's value, and gave him a solid esteem proportioned to it ✍ His person, you know, was fine; his stature exactly what one would wish; his deportment easy, erect and noble; the best horseman of his age, and the most graceful figure that could be seen on horseback ✍ Although in the circle of his friends, where he might be unreserved with safety, he took a free share in conversation, his colloquial talents were not above mediocrity, possessing neither copiousness of ideas nor fluency of words. In public, when called on for a sudden opinion, he was unready, short and embarrassed ✍ Yet he wrote readily, rather diffusely, in an easy and correct style. This he had acquired by conversation with the world, for his education was merely reading, writing and common arithmetic, to which he added surveying at a later day. His time was employed in action chiefly, reading little, and that only in agriculture and English history. His correspondence became necessarily extensive, and, with journalizing his agricultural proceedings, occupied most of his leisure hours within doors.

On the whole, his character was, in its mass, perfect; in nothing bad, in few

---

Do not weep, maiden, for war is kind.
Because your lover threw wild hands
    toward the sky
And the affrighted steed ran on alone,
Do not weep.
War is kind.

Hoarse, booming drums of the regiment,
Little souls who thirst for fight,
These men were born to drill and die.
The unexplained glory flies above them,
Great is the battle-god, and his kingdom—
A field where a thousand corpses lie.

    . . . .

Mother, whose heart hung humble as a
    button
On the bright, splendid shroud of your son,
Do not weep.
War is kind.

    " If War Be Kind," *by Stephen Crane*

points indifferent; and it may truly be said that never did Nature and fortune combine more perfectly to make a man great, and to place him in the same constellation with whatever worthies have merited from man an everlasting remembrance. For his was the singular destiny and merit of leading the armies of his country successfully through an arduous war, for the establishment of its independence; of conducting its councils through the birth of a Government new in its forms and principles, until it had settled down into a quiet and orderly train; and of scrupulously obeying the laws through the whole of his career, civil and military, of which the history of the world furnishes no other example. . . . He has often declared to me that he considered our new constitution as an experiment on the practicability of republican government, and with what dose of liberty man could be trusted for his own good; that he was determined the experiment should have a fair trial, and would lose the last drop of his blood in support of it. I do believe that General Washington had a firm confidence in the durability of our Government. I felt on his death, with my countrymen, that, " Verily a very great man hath fallen this day in Israel."—Thomas Jefferson.

సం *సం*

The only hope of preserving what is best lies in the practice of an immense charity, a wide tolerance, a sincere respect for opinions that are not ours.
—P. G. Hamerton.

సం *సం*

Books are the ever-burning lamps of accumulated wisdom.—G. W. Curtis.

There is no tongue to speak his eulogy;
Too brightly burned his splendor for our
eyes;
Far easier to condemn his injurers,
Than for the tongue to reach his smallest
worth.
He to the realms of sinfulness came down,
To teach mankind; ascending then to God,
Heaven unbarred to him her lofty gates,
To whom his country hers refused to ope.
Ungrateful land! to its own injury,
Nurse of his fate! Well, too, does this
instruct
That greatest ills fall to the perfectest.
And, midst a thousand proofs, let this
suffice—
That, as his exile had no parallel,
So never was there man more great than
he.

" On Dante," *by Michelangelo*

WE believe the government of the United States to be at this moment the best in the world; but then the Americans are the best people; and we have a theory that the government of every State is always—excepting during the periods of actual change—that which is best adapted to the circumstances and wants of its inhabitants. But they who argue in favor of a republic, in lieu of a mixed monarchy, for Great Britain, are, we suspect, ignorant of the genius of their countrymen *సం* Democracy forms no element in the materials of English character. An Englishman is, from his mother's womb, an aristocrat. Whatever rank or birth, whatever fortune, trade, or profession may be his fate, he is, or wishes or hopes to be, an aristocrat. The insatiable love of caste that in England, as in Hindustan, devours all hearts, is confined to no walks of society, but pervades every degree, from the highest to the lowest. Of what conceivable use, then, would it be to strike down the lofty patricians that have descended to us from the days of the Normans and Plantagenets, if we of the middle class— who are more enslaved than any other to this passion—are prepared to lift up, from amongst ourselves, an aristocracy of mere wealth—not less austere, not less selfish—only less noble than that we had deposed. No! whatever changes in the course of time education may and will effect, we do not believe that England, at this moment, contains even the germs of genuine republicanism *సం* We do not, then, advocate the adoption of democratic institutions for such a people. But the examples held forth to

us by the Americans, of strict economy, of peaceful non-interference, of universal education, and of other public improvements, may, and, indeed, must be emulated by the Government of this country, if the people are to be allowed even the chance of surviving a competition with that republican community.
—Richard Cobden.

Freedom is the one purport, wisely aimed at, or unwisely, of all man's struggles, toilings and sufferings, in this earth.—Carlyle.

AS to the position that " the people always mean well," that they always mean to say and do what they believe to be right and just—it may be popular, but it can not be true. The word *people* applies to all the individual inhabitants of a country. . . . That portion of them who individually mean well never was, nor until the millennium will be, considerable. Pure democracy, like pure rum, easily produces intoxication and with it a thousand pranks and fooleries

I do not expect mankind will, before the millennium, be what they ought to be; and therefore, in my opinion, every political theory which does not regard them *as being what they are,* will prove abortive

Yet I wish to see all unjust and unnecessary discriminations everywhere abolished, and that the time may come when all our inhabitants of every color and discrimination shall be free and equal partakers of our political liberties.
—John Jay.

LET it never be forgotten that it is not by means of war that states are rendered fit for the enjoyment of constitutional freedom; on the contrary, whilst terror and bloodshed reign in the land, involving men's minds in the extremities of hopes and fears, there can be no process of thought, no education going on, by which alone can a people be prepared for the enjoyment of rational liberty.
—Richard Cobden.

SIR COUNT, I have made several designs in accordance with the ideas which you suggested, and if I believe my flatterers, I have satisfied them all. Yet I have not satisfied my own judgment, since I fear that I shall not have pleased yours. I send the designs and beg that you will make a selection, if you think any of them worthy of acceptance

Our Lord the Pope has done me great honor by throwing a considerable burden on my shoulders—that of attending to the building of St. Peter's. I hope I shall not sink under it; the more so as the model which I have made is approved by His Holiness, and praised by many intelligent persons. But I soar in thought to higher spheres—I should like to discover the beautiful forms of ancient edifices, and know not whether my flight may not be the flight of Icarus. I gather much light from Vetruvius, but not as much as I require.

With regard to " Galatea," I should consider myself a great master if it realized one half of the many things of which you write; but I gather from your words the love you bear me, and I should tell you that to paint a beauty one should see many, the sole condition being that you should be with me to make choice of the best. Good judgment being as scarce as handsome women, I make use of a certain idea which comes to my mind. But whether this, in itself, has any excellence of art, I know not; I shall do what I can to attain it.—Letter from Raphael to Count Castiglione.

WE know that a statement proved to be good must be correct New thoughts are constantly obtaining the floor. These two theories—that all is matter, or that all is Mind—will dispute the ground, until one is acknowledged to be the victor. Discussing his campaign, General Grant said: " I propose to fight it out on this line, if it takes all summer." Science says: All is Mind and Mind's idea. You must fight it out on this line. Matter can afford you no aid.
—Mary Baker Eddy.

HESE are the times that try men's souls. The summer soldier and the sunshine patriot will, in this crisis, shrink from the service of his country; but he that stands it now, deserves the love and thanks of man and woman. Tyranny, like hell, is not easily conquered; yet we have this consolation with us, that the harder the conflict, the more glorious the triumph. What we may obtain too cheap, we esteem too lightly: 't is dearness only that gives everything its value. Heaven knows how to put a proper price upon its goods ๑๑ ๑๑ It would be strange indeed if so celestial an article as freedom should not be highly rated. Britain, with an army to enforce her tyranny, has declared that she has a right (not only to tax) but " to bind us in all cases whatsoever," and if being bound in that manner, is not slavery, then is there not such a thing as slavery upon earth. Even the expression is impious, for so unlimited a power can belong only to God.

* * * * * *

I have as little superstition in me as any man living, but my secret opinion has ever been, and still is, that God Almighty will not give up a people to military destruction, or leave them unsupportedly to perish, who have so earnestly and so repeatedly sought to avoid the calamities of war, by every decent method which wisdom could invent. ⟪ Neither have I so much of the infidel in me, as to suppose that He has relinquished the government of the world, and given us up to the care of devils. —Thomas Paine (From *The Crisis*)

๑๑ ๑๑

Men and nations can only be reformed in their youth; they become incorrigible as they grow old.—Rousseau.

Where weary folk toil, black with smoke,
And hear but whistles scream,
I went, all fresh from dawn and dew,
To carry them a dream.

I went to bitter lanes and dark,
Who once had known the sky,
To carry them a dream—and found
They had more dreams than I.

"The Dream-Bearer," *by Mary Carolyn Davies*

I HARDLY know whether you would like my writing to you; yet I feel strongly disposed so far to presume on the old relation which existed between us as to express my earnest hope that you will not attach too much importance to your disappointment, whatever it may have been, at the recent examination. I believe that I attach quite as much value as is reasonable to university distinctions; but it would be a grievous evil if the good of a man's reading for three years were all to depend on the result of a single examination, affected as that result must ever in some degree be by causes independent of a man's intellectual excellence. I am saying nothing but what you know quite well already; still a momentary feeling of disappointment may tempt a man to do himself great injustice, and to think that his efforts have been attended by no proportionate fruit. I can only say, for one, that as far as the real honor of Rugby is concerned, it is the effort, a hundred times more than the issue of the effort, that is in my judgment a credit to the school: inasmuch as it shows that the men who go from here to the University do their duty there; and that is the real point which alone to my mind reflects honor either on individuals or on societies; and if such a fruit is in any way traceable to the influence of Rugby, then I am proud and thankful to have had such a man as my pupil.—Thomas Arnold. (Letter to a Student.)

๑๑ ๑๑

Do not keep the alabaster boxes of your love and tenderness sealed up until your friends are dead. Fill their lives with sweetness. Speak approving, cheering words while their ears can hear them and while their hearts can be thrilled by them.—Henry Ward Beecher.

IT is well to bear in mind that whatever other sins the South may be called to bear, when it comes to business, pure and simple, it is in the South that the Negro is given a man's chance in the commercial world.

* * * * * *

Our greatest danger is that in the great leap from slavery to freedom we may overlook the fact that the masses of us are to live by the productions of our hands, and fail to keep in mind that we shall prosper in proportion as we learn to dignify and glorify common labor and put brains and skill into the common occupations of life; shall prosper in proportion as we learn to draw the line between the superficial and the substantial, the ornamental gewgaws of life and the useful. No race can prosper till it learns that there is as much dignity in tilling a field as in writing a poem. It is at the bottom of life we must begin, and not at the top.

* * * * * *

In all things that are purely social we can be as separate as the fingers, yet one as the hand in all things essential to mutual progress.

* * * * * *

There is no defence or security for any of us except in the highest intelligence and developments of all • If anywhere there are efforts tending to curtail the fullest growth of the Negro, let these efforts be turned into stimulating, encouraging, and making him the most useful and intelligent citizen.

* * * * * *

Nearly sixteen millions of hands will aid you in pulling the load upward, or they will pull against you the load downward. We shall constitute one-third and more of the ignorance and crime of the South, or one-third its intelligence and progress; we shall contribute one-third to the business and industrial prosperity of the South, or we shall prove a veritable body of death, stagnating, depressing, retarding every effort to advance the body politic.

* * * * * *

The wisest among my race understand that the agitation of questions of social equality is the extremest folly, and that progress in the enjoyment of all the privileges that will come to us must be the result of severe and constant struggle rather than of artificial forcing. No race that has anything to contribute to the markets of the world is long in any degree ostracized.

—Booker T. Washington.

• •

IF our course of life be pure, and our actions good and right, there is no need for a reward in another world even though in this one everything to which the mere worldling attaches a value should be wanting. It indicates a trivial knowledge of the true nature, and a trivial respect for the true worth and dignity of man, if the stimulus of a reward in another world must be held out in order to rouse him to action worthy of his nature and high calling.

The feeling, the consciousness of having lived and worked in unswerving faithfulness to his true nature and dignity ought, without the need or demand of any other external satisfaction, to be at all times his highest reward • We weaken and degrade the human nature we should strengthen and raise, when we dangle before it a bait to good action, even though this bait be hung out from another world • In using an external stimulus, however seemingly spiritual, to call forth a better life, we leave undeveloped that active and independent inward force which is implanted within every man for the manifestation of ideal humanity.—Friedrich Froebel.

• •

HARMONY is produced by its Principle, is controlled by it and abides with it. Divine Principle is the Life of man. Man's happiness is not, therefore, at the disposal of physical sense. Truth is not contaminated by error. Harmony in man is as beautiful as in music, and discord is unnatural, unreal.

—Mary Baker Eddy.

• •

The ladder of life is full of splinters, but they always prick the hardest when we 're sliding down.—William L. Brownell.

EMERSON'S was an Asiatic mind, drawing its sustenance partly from the hard soil of our New England, partly, too, from the air that has known Himalaya and the Ganges. So impressed with this character of his mind was Mr. Burlingame, as I saw him, after his return from his mission, that he said to me, in a freshet of hyperbole, which was the overflow of a channel with a thread of truth running in it, "There are twenty thousand Ralph Waldo Emersons in China." ❡ What could we do with this unexpected, unprovided for, unclassified, half-unwelcome newcomer, who had been for a while potted, as it were, in our Unitarian cold green-house, but had taken to growing so fast that he was lifting off its glass roof and letting in the hailstorms? Here was a protest that outflanked the extreme left of liberalism, yet so calm and serene that its radicalism had the accents of the gospel of peace. Here was an iconoclast without a hammer, who took down our idols from their pedestals so tenderly that it seemed like an act of worship.

The scribes and pharisees made light of his oracular sayings. The lawyers could not find the witnesses to subpœna and the documents to refer to when his case came before them, and turned him over to their wives and daughters ✒ The ministers denounced his heresies, and handled his writings as if they were packages of dynamite, and the grandmothers were as much afraid of his new teachings as old Mrs. Piozzi was of geology. We had had revolutionary orators, reformers, martyrs; it was but a few years since Abner Kneeland had been sent to jail for expressing an opinion about the great First Cause; but we had had nothing like this man, with his seraphic voice and countenance, his choice vocabulary, his refined utterance, his gentle courage, which, with a different manner, might have been called audacity, his temperate statement of opinions which threatened to shake the existing order of thought like an earthquake ✒ ✒ His peculiarities of style and of thinking became fertile parents of mannerisms, which were fair game for ridicule as they appeared in his imitators. For one who talks like Emerson or like Carlyle soon finds himself surrounded by a crowd of walking phonographs, who mechanically reproduce his mental and vocal accents. Emerson was before long talking in the midst of a babbling Simonetta of echoes, and not unnaturally was now and then himself a mark for the small-shot of criticism. He had soon reached that height in the "cold thin atmosphere" of thought where "Vainly the fowler's eye might mark his distant

*Tears, idle tears, I know not what they
    mean,
Tears from the depth of some divine
    despair
Rise in the heart, and gather to the eyes,
In looking on the happy autumn fields,
And thinking of the days that are no more.*

*Fresh as the first beam glittering on a
    sail,
That brings our friends up from the under-
    world,
Sad as the last which reddens over one
That sinks with all we love below the
    verge;
So sad, so fresh, the days that are no more.*

*Ah, sad and strange as in dark summer
    dawns
The earliest pipe of half-awaken'd birds
To dying ears, when unto dying eyes
The casement slowly grows a glimmering
    square;
So sad, so strange, the days that are no
    more.*

*Dear as remember'd kisses after death,
And sweet as those by hopeless fancy
    feign'd
On lips that are for others: deep as love,
Deep as first love, and wild with all regret;
Oh, death in life! the days that are no
    more.*

"Tears, Idle Tears," *by Alfred Tennyson*

flight to do him wrong." . . . ❡ I have known something of Emerson as a talker, not nearly so much as many others who can speak and write of him. It is unsafe to tell how a great thinker talks, for perhaps, like a city dealer with a village customer, he has not shown his best goods to the innocent reporter of his sayings. However that may be in this case, let me contrast in a single glance the momentary effect in conversation of the two neighbors, Hawthorne and Emerson. Speech seemed like a kind of travail to Hawthorne. One must harpoon him like a cetacean with questions to make him talk at all ❧ Then the words came from him at last, with bashful manifestations, like those of a young girl, almost—words that gasped themselves forth, seeming to leave a great deal more behind them than they told, and died out discontented with themselves, like the monologue of thunder in the sky, which always goes off mumbling and grumbling as if it had not said half it wanted to, and ought to say. . . .

To sum up briefly what would, as it seems to me, be the text to be unfolded in his biography, he was a man of excellent common sense, with a genius so uncommon that he seemed like an exotic transplanted from some angelic nursery. His character was so blameless, so beautiful, that it was rather a standard to judge others by than to find a place for on the scale of comparison. Looking at life with the profoundest sense of its infinite significance, he was yet a cheerful optimist, almost too hopeful, peeping into every cradle to see if it did not hold a babe with the halo of a new Messiah about it. He enriched the treasure-house of literature, but, what was far more, he enlarged the boundaries of thought for the few that followed him, and the many who never knew, and do not know today, what hand it was which took down their prison walls. He was a preacher who taught that the religion of humanity included both those of Palestine, nor those alone, and taught it with such consecrated lips that the narrowest bigot was ashamed to pray for him as from a footstool nearer to the throne. "Hitch your wagon to a star:" this was his version of the divine lesson taught by that holy George Herbert whose words he loved. Give him whatever place belongs to him in the literature of our language, of the world, but remember this: the end and aim of his being was to make truth lovely and manhood valorous, and to bring our daily life nearer and nearer to the eternal, immortal, invisible.

—Oliver Wendell Holmes.

What delightful hosts are they—
  Life and Love!
Lingeringly I turn away,
  This late hour, yet glad enough
They have not withheld from me
  Their high hospitality.
So, with face lit with delight
  And all gratitude, I stay
  Yet to press their hands and say,
" Thanks.—So fine a time! Good
    night."

" A Parting Guest," *by James Whitcomb Riley*

❧ ❧

WHEN I was born, New York contained 27,000 inhabitants. The upper limits of the city were at Chambers Street. Not a single free school, either by day or night, existed. General Washington had just entered upon his first term as President of the United States, the whole annual expenditures of which did not exceed $2,500,000, being about sixty cents per head of the population. Not a single steam engine had yet been built or erected on the American continent; and the people were clad in homespun and were characterized by the simple virtues and habits which are usually associated with that primitive garb. ❡ I need not tell you what the country now is, and what the habits and the garments of its people now are, or that the expenditure, per capita, of the general government has increased fifteen-fold. But I have witnessed and taken a deep interest in every step of the marvelous development and progress which have characterized this century beyond all the centuries which have gone before. ❡ Measured by the achievements of the years I have seen, I am one of the oldest men who have ever lived; but I do not feel old, and I propose to give you the recipe by which I have preserved my youth. I have always given a friendly welcome to new ideas, and I have endeavored not to feel too old to learn, and thus, though I stand here with the snows of so many winters upon my head, my faith in human nature, my belief in the progress of man to a better social condition, and especially my trust in the ability of men to establish and maintain self-government, are as fresh and as young as when I began to travel the path of life ∾ ∾

While I have always recognized that the object of business is to make money in an honorable manner, I have endeavored to remember that the object of life is to do good. Hence I have been ready to engage in all new enterprises, and, without incurring debt, to risk in their promotion the means which I had acquired, provided they seemed to me calculated to advance the general good.

This will account for my early attempt to perfect the steam engine, for my attempt to construct the first American locomotive, for my connection with the telegraph in a course of efforts to unite our country with the European world, and for my recent efforts to solve the problem of economical steam navigation on the canals ∾ It happens to but few men to change the current of human progress, as it did to Watt, to Fulton, to Stephenson, and to Morse; but most men

may be ready to welcome laborers to a new field of usefulness, and to clear the road for their progress.

This I have tried to do, as well in the perfecting and execution of their ideas as in making such provision as my means have permitted for the proper education of the young mechanics and citizens of my native city, in order to fit them for the reception of new ideas, social, mechanical and scientific—hoping thus to economize and expand the intellectual as well as the physical forces, and provide a larger fund for distribution among the various classes which necessarily make up the total of society ∾ ∾

If our lives shall be such that we shall receive the glad welcome of "Well done, good and faithful servant," we shall then know that we have not lived in vain.—Peter Cooper (From an Address, 1874.)

Out of me unworthy and unknown
The vibrations of deathless music:
"With malice toward none, with chairty
* for all."*
Out of me the forgiveness of millions
* towards millions,*
And the beneficent face of a nation
Shining with justice and truth.
I am Anne Rutledge who sleep beneath
* these weeds,*
Beloved in life of Abraham Lincoln,
Wedded to him, not through union,
But through separation.
Bloom forever, O Republic,
From the dust of my bosom!

" Anne Rutledge," *by Edgar Lee Masters*

∾ ∾

THE less there is said of physical structure and laws, and the more there is thought and said about moral and spiritual law, the higher the standard of mortals will be, and the farther they will be removed from imbecility of mind and body.

We should master fear, instead of cultivating it. It was the ignorance of our forefathers, in the departments of knowledge broadcast in the earth, which made them more hardy than our trained physiologists, more honest than our sleek politicians.—Mary Baker Eddy.

∾ ∾

There 's a divinity that shapes our ends, Rough-hew them how we will.
                              —Shakespeare.

∾ ∾

Where law ends tyranny begins.
                              —William Pitt.

Samuel Johnson Meets His Future Biographer

R. THOMAS DAVIES the actor, who then kept a bookseller's shop in Russell street, Covent Garden, told me that Johnson was very much his friend, and came frequently to his house, where he more than once invited me to meet him; but by some unlucky accident or other he was prevented from coming to us.

Mr. Thomas Davies was a man of good understanding and talents, with the advantage of a liberal education. Though somewhat pompous, he was an entertaining companion; and his literary performances have no inconsiderable share of merit. He was a friendly and very hospitable man. Both he and his wife (who has been celebrated for her beauty), though upon the stage for many years, maintained a uniform decency of character; and Johnson esteemed them, and lived in as easy an intimacy with them as with any family which he used to visit. Mr. Davies recollected several of Johnson's remarkable sayings, and was one of the best of the many imitators of his voice and manner, while relating them. He increased my impatience more and more to see the extraordinary man whose works I highly valued, and whose conversation was reported to be so peculiarly excellent.

At last, on Monday the 16th of May, when I was sitting in Mr. Davies' back parlor, after having drunk tea with him and Mrs. Davies, Johnson unexpectedly came in the shop; and Mr. Davies having perceived him through the glass door in the room in which we were sitting, advancing toward us, he announced his awful approach to me somewhat in the manner of an actor in the part of Horatio, when he addresses Hamlet on the appearance of his father's ghost—" Look, my lord, it comes." I found that I had a perfect idea of Johnson's figure from the portrait of him painted by Sir Joshua Reynolds soon after he had published his *Dictionary,* in the attitude of sitting in his easy chair in deep meditation; which was the first picture his friend did for him, which Sir Joshua very kindly presented to me, and from which an engraving has been made for this work. Mr. Davies mentioned my name, and respectfully introduced me to him. I was much agitated, and recollecting his prejudice against the Scotch, of which I had heard much, I said to Davies, " Don't tell where I came from," " From Scotland," cried Davies, roguishly ๑๑ " Mr. Johnson," (said I) " I do indeed come from Scotland, but I can not help it." I am willing to flatter myself that I meant this as light pleasantry to soothe and conciliate him, and not as an humiliating abasement at the expense of my country. But however that might be, this speech was somewhat unlucky; for with that quickness of wit for which he was so remarkable, he seized the expression, " come from Scotland," which I used in the sense of being of that country: and as if I had said that I had come away from it, or left it, retorted, " That, sir, I find, is what a very great many of your countrymen can not help." This stroke stunned me a good deal; and when he had sat down, I felt myself not a little embarrassed, and apprehensive of what might come next. He then addressed himself to Davies: " What do you think of Garrick? He has refused me an order for the play of Miss Williams, because he knows the house will be full, and that an order would be worth three shillings." Eager to take any opening to get into conversation with him, I ventured to say, " Oh, sir, I can not think Mr. Garrick would grudge such a trifle to you."

" Sir," (said he, with a stern look) " I have known David Garrick longer than you have done; and I know no right you have to talk to me on the subject." Perhaps I deserved this check; for it was rather presumptuous in me, an entire stranger, to express any doubt of the justice of his animadversion upon his old acquaintance and pupil. I now felt myself much mortified, and began to think that the hope which I had long indulged of obtaining his acquaintance was blasted. And in truth, had not my ardor been uncommonly strong, and my resolution uncommonly persevering, so rough a reception might have deterred me forever from making any further attempts . . . . ❡ I was highly pleased with the extraordinary vigor of his conversation, and regretted that I was drawn away from it by an engagement at another place. I had for a part of the evening been left alone with him, and had ventured to make an observation now and then, which he received very civilly; so that I was satisfied that though there was a roughness in his manner, there was no ill-nature in his disposition. Davies followed me to the door, and when I complained to him a little of the hard blows which the great man had given me, he kindly took upon him to console me by saying, " Don't be uneasy. I can see he likes you very well."

A few days afterward I called on Davies, and asked him if he thought I might take the liberty of waiting on Mr. Johnson at his chambers in the Temple. He said I certainly might, and that Mr. Johnson would take it as a compliment. So on Tuesday the 24th of May, after having been enlivened by the witty sallies of Messieurs Thornton, Wilkes, Churchill, and Lloyd, with whom I had passed the morning, I boldly repaired to Johnson. His chambers were on the first floor of No. 1, Inner Temple Lane, and I entered them with an impression given me by the Rev. Dr. Blair, of Edinburgh, who had been introduced to him not long before, and described his having " found the giant in his den;" an expression which, when I came to be pretty well acquainted with Johnson, I repeated to him, and he was diverted at this picturesque account of himself. . . . .

He received me very courteously; but it must be confessed that his apartment and furniture and morning dress were sufficiently uncouth. His brown suit of clothes looked very rusty; he had on a little shriveled unpowdered wig, which was too small for his head; his shirt-neck and the knees of his breeches were loose; his black worsted stockings ill drawn up; and he had a pair of unbuckled shoes by way of slippers. But all these slovenly particularities were forgotten the moment that he began to talk. Some gentlemen, whom I do not recollect, were sitting with him; and when they went away, I also rose; but he said to me, " Nay, don't go." " Sir," (said I), " I am afraid that I intrude upon you. It is benevolent to allow me to sit and hear you." He seemed pleased with this compliment, which I sincerely paid him, and answered, " Sir, I am obliged to any man who visits me."—James Boswell.

❧

RUTH! Where is truth but in the soul itself? Facts, objects, are but phantoms, matter-woven ghosts of this earthly night, at which the soul, sleeping here in the mire and clay of matter, shudders and names its own vague tremors, sense and perception ❧ Yet, even as our nightly dreams stir in us the suspicion of mysterious and immaterial presences, unfettered by the bonds of time and space, so do these waking dreams which we call sight and sound. They are divine messengers, whom Zeus, pitying his children, even when he pent them in this prison-house of flesh, appointed to arouse in them dim recollections of that real world of souls whence they came. Awakened once to them; seeing, through the veil of sense and fact, the spiritual truth of which they are but the accidental garment, concealing the very thing which they made palpable, the philosopher may neglect the fact for the doctrine, the shell for the kernel, the body for the soul, of which it is but the symbol and the vehicle.—Hypatia.

❧

ENGLAND and America are bound up together in peaceful fetters by the strongest of all the ligatures that can bind two nations to each other, namely, commercial interests; and which, every succeeding year, renders more impossible, if the term may be used, a rupture between the two Governments.
—Richard Cobden.

❧

If you wish to appear agreeable in society, you must consent to be taught many things which you know already.
—Lavater.

O my dearest Cousin, Simone di Battesta di Carlo in Urbino ✐ ✐

Dearest, in place of a father I have received one of yours; most dear to me because it assures me that you are not angry; which indeed would be wrong considering how tiresome it is to write when one has nothing of consequence to say. But now, being of consequence, I reply to tell you as much as I am able to communicate ✐ And first, in reference to taking a wife I reply that I am quite content in respect of her whom you first wished to give me, and I thank God constantly that I took neither her nor another, and in this I was wiser than you who wished me to take her. I am sure that you too are aware that I would not have the position I now hold, since I find myself at this moment in possession of things in Rome worth three thousand ducats of gold, and receipts of fifty scudi of gold, because His Holiness has given me a salary of three hundred gold ducats for attending to the building of St. Peter's which [the salary] I shall never fail to enjoy so long as my life lasts; and I am certain of getting others, and am also paid for what I do to whatever amount I please, and I have begun to paint another room for His Holiness which will amount to one thousand two hundred ducats of gold.

So that, dearest Cousin, I do honor to you and all relatives and to my country. Yet, for all that, I hold you dear in the center of my heart, and when I hear your name, I feel as if I heard that of a father; and do not complain of me because I do not write, because I have to com-

Eternal spirit of the chainless mind!
Brightest in dungeons, Liberty! thou art:
For there thy habitation is the heart—
The heart which love of thee alone can
*   bind:*
And when thy sons to fetters are con-
*   signed—*
To fetters, and the damp vault's dayless
*   gloom*
Their country conquers with their martyr-
*   dom,*
And Freedom's fame finds wings on every
*   wind.*
Chillon! thy prison is a holy place,
And thy sad floor an altar—for 't was trod,
Until his very steps have left a trace
Worn, as if thy cold pavement were a sod,
By Bonnivard—May none those marks
*   efface!*
For they appeal from tyranny to God.
   " Sonnet on Chillon," *by Lord Byron*

plain of you that you sit pen in hand all day and let six months go by between one letter and the other. Still with all that, you will not make me angry with you, as you do wrongly with me.

I have come fairly out in the matter of a wife, but, to return to that, I answer, that you may know, that Cardinal Bibieni wants me to have one of his relatives, and with the assent of you and the cousin priest I promised to do what his reverend lordship wanted, and I can not break my word. We are now more than ever on the point of settling and presently I shall advise you of everything ✐ Have patience, as the matter is in such a good way, and then should it not come off, I will do as you may wish, and know that if Francesco Buffo has offers for me, I have some of my own also, and I can find a handsome wife of excellent repute in Rome as I have heard. She and her relatives are ready to give me three thousand gold scudi as a dowry, and I live in a house at Rome, and one hundred ducats are worth more here than two hundred there (Urbino?); of this be assured ✐ ✐

As to my stay in Rome, I can not live anywhere else for any time if only because of the building of St. Peter's, as I am in the Palace of Bramante; but what place in the world is more worthy than Rome, what enterprise more worthy than St. Peter's, which is the first temple of the world and the largest building that has ever been seen, the cost of which will exceed a million in gold? And know that the Pope has ordered the expenditure on building of sixty thousand ducats a year, and he never gives a thought to anything else ✐ He has given me a companion, a most learned old friar of more than eighty years of age 🙟 The Pope sees that he can not live long; he has resolved to give him to me as a companion, for he is a man of high reputation, and of the greatest requirements, in order that I may learn from him, and if he has any secret in architecture that I may become perfect in that art 🙟 His name is Fra Giocondo; and the Pope sends for him every day and chats a little with us about the building. ❡ I beg you will be good enough to go to the Duke and Duchess and tell them this, as I know they will be pleased to hear that one of their servants does them honor, and recommend me to them as I continually stand recommended to you. Salute all friends and relatives for me and particularly Ridolfo, who has so much love for me. The first of July, 1514, Your Raffael, painter in Rome.

Hubbard's Note:—Raphael's love for Cardinal Bibieni's niece ended in tragedy. The wedding was postponed at the request of the Pope, and she died before it occurred. Raphael's death followed soon after, at the age of 37, and his body was placed beside hers in the Pantheon.

🙟 🙟

He's truly valiant that can wisely suffer
The worst that man can breathe, and make his wrongs
His outside, to wear them like his raiment, carelessly,
And ne'er prefer his injuries to his heart,
To bring it into danger.—Shakespeare.

🙟 🙟

Make yourself an honest man, and then you may be sure that there is one rascal less in the world.—Carlyle.

The world is too much with us; late and
*   soon,*
Getting and spending, we lay waste our
*   powers:*
Little we see in Nature that is ours;
We have given our hearts away, a sordid
*   boon!*
This sea that bares her bosom to the moon,
The winds that will be howling at all hours,
And are up-gathered now like sleeping
*   flowers;*
For this, for everything, we are out of
*   tune;*
It moves us not.—Great God! I'd rather
*   be*
A pagan suckled in a creed outworn;
So might I, standing on this pleasant lea,
Have glimpses that would make me less
*   forlorn;*
Have sight of Proteus rising from the sea;
Or hear old Triton blow his wreathed
*   horn.*
*   —William Wordsworth*

I SEEM to know Cellini first of all as a man possessed by intense, absorbing egotism; violent, arrogant, self-assertive, passionate; conscious of great gifts for art, physical courage, and personal address. . . . To be self-reliant in all circumstances; to scheme and to strike, if need be, in support of his opinion or his right to take the law into his own hands for the redress of injury or insult! this appeared to him the simple duty of an honorable man. But he had nothing of the philosopher's calm, the diplomatist's prudence, the general's strategy, or the courtier's self-restraint. On the contrary, he possessed the temperament of a born artist, blent in almost equal proportions with that of a born bravo 🙟

❡ Throughout the whole of his tumultuous career these two strains contended in his nature for mastery. Upon the verge of fifty-six, when a man's blood has generally cooled, we find that he was released from prison on bail, and bound over to keep the peace for a year with some enemy whose life was probably in danger; and when I come to speak of his homicides, it will be obvious that he enjoyed killing live men quite as much as casting bronze statues. . . .
Sensitive, impulsive, rash of speech, hasty in action, with the artist's susceptibility and the bravo's heat of blood, he injured no one more than himself by his eccentricities of temper. Yet there is no trace in any of his writings that he ever laid his misadventures to their proper cause 🙟 He consistently poses as an injured man, whom malevolent scoun-

drels conspired to persecute. Nor does he do this with any bad faith. His belief in himself remained as firm as adamant, and he candidly conceived that he was under the special providence of a merciful and loving God who appreciated his high and virtuous qualities.

* * * * * *

. . . . He tells us how Pope Paul III was willing to pardon him for an outrageous murder committed in the streets of Rome. One of the Pope's gentlemen submitted that this was showing unseasonable clemency. " You do not understand the matter as well as I do," replied His Holiness. " I must inform you that men like Benvenuto, unique in their profession, are not bound by the laws." That sentence precisely paints Cellini's own conception of himself. . . .

—John Addington Symonds.

IT was in Rome that I had to do Lord Byron's statue. When my noble sitter arrived at my studio, he took his place before me and immediately put on a strange air, entirely different from his natural physiognomy.

" My lord," said I, " have the goodness to sit still, and may I beg you not to assume such an expression of misery."

" That," replied Byron, " is the expression which characterizes my countenance."

" Really," said I; and then, without troubling myself about this affectation, I worked on according to my own ideas. When the bust was finished, every one thought it strikingly like Lord Byron, but the noble poet was by no means satisfied with it.

" That face is not mine," said he; " I look much more unhappy than that." For he was determined to look unhappy.

—Thorwaldsen.

He drew a circle that shut me out—
Heretic, rebel, a thing to flout.
But love and I had the wit to win:
We drew a circle that took him in.

—Edwin Markham.

A thought is an idea in transit.

—Pythagoras.

FULL of anxieties and apprehending daily that we should hear distressing news from Boston, I walked with Mr. Samuel Adams in the State House yard [Philadelphia], for a little exercise and fresh air, before the hour of [the Continental] Congress, and there represented to him the various dangers that surrounded us.

He agreed to them all, but said, " What shall we do? " I answered him I was determined to take a step which should compel all the members of Congress to declare themselves for or against *something*. I am determined this morning to make a direct motion that Congress should adopt [as its own] the army before Boston, and appoint Colonel Washington commander of it.

Mr. Adams seemed to think very seriously of it, but said nothing.

Accordingly, when Congress had assembled, I rose in my place . . . . Mr. Washington, who happened to sit near the door, as soon as he heard me allude to him, from his usual modesty, darted into the library-room.

Mr. Hancock heard me with visible pleasure, but when I came to describe Washington for the commander, I never remarked a more sudden and striking change of countenance. Mortification and resentment were expressed as forcibly as his face could exhibit them.

Mr. Samuel Adams seconded the motion, and that did not soften the president's [Hancock's] physiognomy at all.

—John Adams.

IT is but a little time—a few days longer in this prison-house of our degradation, and each thing shall return to its own fountain; the blood-drop to the abysmal heart, and the water to the river, and the river to the shining sea; and the dewdrop which fell from heaven shall rise to heaven again, shaking off the dust grains which weighed it down, thawed from the earth frost which chained it here to herb and sward, upward and upward ever through stars and suns, through gods, and through the parents of the gods purer and purer through successive lives, until it enters The Nothing, which is the All, and finds its home at last.—Hypatia.

AT my first ball at Tortonia's, not knowing any lady, I was standing about, looking at everybody, but not dancing. All at once some one tapped me on the shoulder, and said, "You also are admiring the beautiful Englishwoman there?" What was my surprise, when on turning around, I found myself face to face with Chevalier Thorwaldsen, who was standing by the door and intently observing the beautiful creature. He had hardly asked the question when some one spoke loudly just behind me. "Where is she then? Where is the little Englishwoman? My wife has sent me to look at her, *per Bacco!*" The speaker was a slight little Frenchman, with stiff upstanding gray hair, and the Legion of Honor at his button-hole. I immediately recognized Horace Vernet. He and Thorwaldsen began a serious and learned conversation about the beauty, and what especially delighted me was to see the admiration of these two old artists for the young girl; they were never tired of looking at her, while she went on dancing with the most delicious unconsciousness. Thorwaldsen and Vernet had themselves introduced to the parents of the young English lady, and took no further trouble about me, so that I had no chance of speaking to them again. But, some days later, I was invited to the house of English friends from Venice, who wished, they said, to introduce me to some particular friends of theirs. I was delighted to discover that their friends were Thorwaldsen and Vernet. . . . In my capacity as a pianist I have enjoyed a special pleasure here. You know how Thorwaldsen loves music. He has a very good instrument in his studio, and I go to him sometimes in the mornings and play to him while he works. When I see the old artist handling his brown clay, giving the last touches, with his firm and delicate hand, to a drapery or a limb, when I see him creating those imperishable works which will win the admiration of posterity, I feel happy in that I can give him pleasure.
—Mendelssohn.

Of Heaven or Hell I have no power to sing,
I can not ease the burden of your fears,
Or make quick-coming death a little thing,
Or bring again the pleasure of past years,
Nor for my words shall ye forget your tears.
Or hope again for aught that I can say,
The idle singer of an empty day.

But, rather when aweary of your mirth,
From full hearts still unsatisfied ye sigh,
And, feeling kindly unto all the earth,
Grudge every minute as it passes by,
Made the more mindful that the sweet
    days die—
Remember me a little then I pray,
The idle singer of an empty day.

The heavy trouble, the bewildering care
That weighs us down who live and earn
    our bread
These idle verses have no power to bear:
So let me sing of names remembered,
Because they living not, can ne'er be dead,
Or long time take their memory quite away
From us poor singers of an empty day.

Dreamer of dreams, born out of my due time,
Why should I strive to set the crooked
    straight?
Let it suffice me that my murmuring rhyme
Beats with light wing against the ivory gate.
Telling a tale not too importunate
To those who in the sleepy region stay,
Lulled by the singer of an empty day.

    " The Idle Singer," by William Morris

THIS little globe which is but a mere speck, travels through space with its fellows, lost in immensity. Man, a creature about five feet tall, is certainly a tiny thing, as compared with the universe. Yet one of these imperceptible beings declares to his neighbors; "Hearken unto me. The God of all these worlds speaks with my voice. There are nine billions of us wee ants upon earth, but only my ant-hole is precious in God's sight. All the others are eternally damned by Him. Mine alone is blessed."—Voltaire.

Adversity is the path of truth.—Byron.

Y DEAREST BETSY, yesterday I received Letters from some of our Friends at the Camp informing me of the Engagement [Bunker Hill] between American troops and the Rebel Army in Charlestown. I can not but be greatly rejoyced at the tryed Valor of your Countrymen, who, by all Accounts behaved with an intrepidity becoming those who fought for their Liberties against the mercenary Soldiers of a Tyrant.

It is painful to me to reflect on the terror I must suppose you were under on hearing the Noise of War so near. Favor me, my dear, with an Account of your Apprehensions at that time, under your own hand. . . . . .

Mr. Pitts and Dr. Church inform me that my dear Son has at length escaped from the Prison at Boston . . . . Remember me to my dear Hannah and sister Polly and to all Friends.

Let me know where good old Swory is. Gage [the British General] has made me respectable by naming me first among those who are to receive no favor [of pardon] from him. I thoroughly despise him and his [amnesty] Proclamation . . . . The Clock is now striking twelve. I therefore wish you a good Night. Yours most affectionately,

S. Adams.

(Letter to his Wife, June 28th, 1775)

E [Patrick Henry] rose to reply with apparent embarrassment and some awkwardness, and began a faltering exordium. The people hung their heads at the unpromising commencement, and the clergy were observed to exchange sly looks with each other, while his father sank back in his chair in evident confusion

All this was of short duration, however. As he proceeded and warmed up to his subject, a wondrous change came over him. His attitude became erect and lofty, his face lighted up with genius, and his eyes seemed to flash fire, his gestures became graceful and impressive, his voice and his emphasis peculiarly charming. His appeals to the passions were overpowering. In the language of those who heard him, " he made the blood to run cold, and their hair to rise on end." In a word, to the astonishment of all, he suddenly burst upon them as an orator of the highest order. The surprise of the people was only equaled by their delight, and so overcome was his father that tears flowed profusely down his cheeks.

He contended that . . . . in the case now before them . . . . [the parsons] deserved to be punished with signal severity

" We have heard a great deal about the benevolence and holy zeal of our reverend clergy, but how is this manifested? Do they manifest their zeal in the cause of religion and humanity by practising the mild and benevolent precepts of the Gospel of Jesus? Do they feed the hungry and clothe the naked? Oh, no, gentlemen! Instead of feeding the hungry and clothing the naked, these rapacious harpies would, were their powers equal to their will, snatch from the hearth of their honest parishioner his last hoe-cake, from the widow and her orphan children their last milch cow! the last bed, nay, the last blanket from the lying-in woman!"

These words, uttered with all the power of the orator, aroused in the audience an intense feeling against the clergy, which became so apparent as to cause the reverend gentlemen to leave their seats on the bench, and to quit the courthouse in dismay.—William Wirt Henry, (*Life, Correspondence, and Speeches of Patrick Henry.*)

" The Parsons' Cause " (1763) Patrick Henry's First Important Case.

A SOPHISTICAL rhetorician (is Gladstone) inebriated with the exuberance of his own verbosity, and gifted with an egotistical imagination that can at all times command an interminable and inconsistent series of arguments to malign an opponent and to glorify himself.—Disraeli.

The tree of liberty must be refreshed from time to time with the blood of patriots and tyrants.—Thomas Jefferson.

HEN Zarathustra arrived at the nearest town which adjoineth the forest, he found many people assembled in the market-place; for it had been announced that a rope-dancer would give a performance ✒ And Zarathustra spake thus unto the people:

I teach you the Superman. Man is something that is to be surpassed. What have ye done to surpass man?

All beings hitherto have created something beyond themselves: and ye want to be the ebb of that great tide, and would rather go back to the beast than surpass man? ✒ ✒

What is the ape to man? A laughing-stock, a thing of shame ✒ And just the same shall man be to the Superman: a laughing-stock, a thing of shame.

Ye have made your way from the worm to man, and much within you is still worm. Once were ye apes, and even yet man is more of an ape than any of the apes ✒ ✒

Even the wisest among you is only a disharmony and hybrid of plant and phantom. But do I bid you become phantoms or plants?

Lo, I teach you the Superman!

The Superman is the meaning of the earth. Let your will say: The Superman shall be the meaning of the earth!

* * * * * *

But ye, also, my brethren, tell me: What doth your body say about your soul? Is your soul not poverty and pollution and wretched self-complacency?

Verily, a polluted stream is man. One must be a sea, to receive a polluted stream without becoming impure.

Lo, I teach you the Superman: he is that sea; in him can your great contempt be submerged ✒ ✒

What is the greatest thing ye can experience? It is the hour of great contempt. The hour in which even your happiness becometh loathsome unto you, and so also your reason and virtue.

The hour when ye say: " What good is my happiness! It is poverty and pollution and wretched self-complacency. But my happiness should justify existence itself!"

The hour when ye say: " What good is my reason! Doth it long for knowledge as the lion for his food? ✒ It is poverty and pollution and wretched self-complacency!" ✒ ✒

The hour when ye say: " What good is my virtue! As yet it hath not made me passionate. How weary I am of my good and my bad! It is all poverty and pollution and wretched self-complacency!"

❧ The hour when ye say: " What good is my justice! I do not see that I am fervor and fuel. The just, however, are fervor and fuel!"

The hour when we say: " What good is my pity! Is not pity the cross on which he is nailed who loveth man? But my pity is not a crucifixion."

Have ye ever spoken thus? Have ye ever cried thus? Ah! would that I had heard you crying thus!

It is not your sin—it is your self-satisfaction that crieth unto heaven; your very sparingness in sin crieth unto heaven! ✒ ✒

Where is the lightning to lick you with its tongue? Where is the frenzy with which ye should be inoculated?

Lo, I teach you the Superman: he is that lightning, he is that frenzy!—

When Zarathustra had thus spoken, one of the people called out: " We have heard enough of the rope-dancer; it is time now for us to see him!" And all the people laughed at Zarathustra. But the rope-dancer, who thought the words applied to him, began his performance.

—Friedrich Nietzsche.

✒ ✒

I VIEW a return to the domination of Britain with horror, and would risk all for independence; but that point ceded, I would give them advantageous commercial terms. The destruction of Old England would hurt me; I wish it well, it afforded my ancestors an asylum from persecution.—John Jay.

✒ ✒

The damps of autumn sink into the leaves and prepare them for the necessity of their fall; and thus insensibly are we, as years close around us, detached from our tenacity of life by the gentle pressure of recorded sorrow.—W. S. Landor.

HIS century, which some have called an age of iron, has been also an age of ideas, an era of seeking and finding the like of which was never known before. It is an epoch the grandeur of which dwarfs all others that can be named since the beginning of the historic period, if not since. Man first became distinctively human. In their mental habits, in their methods of inquiry, and in the data at their command, " the men of the present day who have fully kept pace with the scientific movement are separated from the men whose education ended in 1830, by an immeasurably wider gulf than has ever before divided one progressive generation of men from their predecessors."

The intellectual development of the human race has been suddenly, almost abruptly, raised to a higher plane than that upon which it had proceeded from the days of the primitive troglodyte to the days of our great-grandfathers. It is characteristic of this higher plane of development that the progress which until lately was so slow must henceforth be rapid. Men's minds are becoming more flexible, the resistance to innovation is weakening, and our intellectual demands are multiplying while the means of satisfying them are increasing. Vast as are the achievements

In Xanadu did Kubla Khan
A stately pleasure-dome decree:
Where Alph, the sacred river, ran
Through caverns measureless to man
Down to a sunless sea.

So twice five miles of fertile ground
With walls and towers were girdled round:
And there were gardens bright with
sinuous rills,
Where blossomed many an incense-
bearing tree;
And here were forests ancient as the hills,
Enfolding sunny spots of greenery.
But O! that deep romantic chasm which
slanted
Down the green hill athwart a cedarn
cover!
A savage place! as holy and enchanted
As e'er beneath a waning moon was
haunted
By woman wailing for her demon-lover!
And from this chasm, with ceaseless
turmoil seething,
As if this Earth in fast thick pants were
breathing,
A mighty fountain momently was forced,
Amid whose swift half-intermitted burst
Huge fragments vaulted like rebounding
hail,
Or chaffy grain beneath the thresher's
flail:
And 'mid these dancing rocks at once and
ever
It flung up momently the sacred river.

(Concluded on next page)

we have just passed in review, the gaps in our knowledge are immense, and every problem that is solved but opens a dozen new problems that await solution.

Under such circumstances there is no likelihood that the last word will soon be said on any subject. In the eyes of the twenty-first century the science of the nineteenth will doubtless seem very fragmentary and crude. But the men of that day, and of all future time, will no doubt point back to the age just passing away as the opening of a new dispensation, the dawning of an era in which the intellectual development of mankind was raised to a higher plane than that upon which it had hitherto proceeded

As an inevitable result of the thronging discoveries just enumerated, we find ourselves in the midst of a mighty revolution in human thought. Time-honored creeds are losing their hold upon men; ancient symbols are shorn of their value; everything is called in question. The controversies of the day are not like those of former times. It is no longer . . . a struggle between abstruse dogmas of rival churches. Religion itself is called upon to show why it should any longer claim our allegiance.

There are those who deny the existence of God ❧ There are those who would explain away the human soul as a mere group of fleeting phenomena attendant upon the collocation of sundry particles of matter. And there are many others who, without committing themselves to these positions of the atheist and the materialist, have nevertheless come to regard religion as practically ruled out from human affairs.

❧ No religious creed that man has ever devised can be made to harmonize in all its features with modern knowledge ❧ All such creeds were constructed with reference to theories of the universe which are now utterly and hopelessly discredited ❧

❧ How, then, it is asked, amid the general wreck of old beliefs, can we hope that the religious attitude in which from time immemorial we have been wont to contemplate the universe can any longer be maintained? Is not the belief in God perhaps a dream of the childhood of our race, like the belief in elves and bogarts which once was no less universal? and is not modern science fast destroying the one as it has already destroyed the other?

❧ Such are the questions which we daily hear asked, sometimes with flippant eagerness, but oftener with anxious dread. . . . . If we find in that idea, as conceived by untaught thinkers in the twilight of antiquity, an element that still survives the widest and deepest generalizations of modern times, we have the strongest possible reason for believing that the idea is permanent and answers to an Eternal Reality. It was to be expected that conceptions of Deity handed down from primitive men should undergo serious modification. If it can be shown that the essential element in these conceptions must survive the enormous additions to our knowledge which have distinguished the present age above all others since man became man, then we may believe that it will endure so long as man endures; for it is not likely that it can ever be called upon to pass a severer ordeal.

— John Fiske.

❧ ❧

I am not a good orator in my own cause.—John Knox.

❧ ❧

NOTHING is true forever ❧ A man and a fact will become equally decrepit and will tumble in the same ditch, for truth is as mortal as man, and both are outlived by the tortoise and the crow.

❧ To say that two is company and three is a crowd is to make a very temporary statement. After a short time satiety or use and wont has crept sunderingly between the two, and, if they are any company at all, they are bad company, who pray discreetly but passionately for the crowd that is censured by the proverb.

—James Stephens.

❧ ❧

Our whole life is like a play.—Ben Jonson.

*Five miles meandering with a mazy
     motion
Through wood and dale the sacred river
     ran,
Then reached the caverns measureless to
     man,
And sank in tumult to a lifeless ocean:
And 'mid this tumult Kubla heard from far
Ancestral voices prophesying war!*

*The shadow of the dome of pleasure
Floated midway on the waves;
Where was heard the mingled measure
From the fountain and the caves.
It was a miracle of rare device,
A sunny pleasure-dome with caves of ice!*

*A damsel with a dulcimer
In a vision once I saw:
It was an Abyssinian maid,
And on her dulcimer she played,
Singing of Mount Abora,
Could I revive within me
Her symphony and song,
To such a deep delight 't would win me
That with music loud and long,
I would build that dome in air,
That sunny dome! those caves of ice!
And all who heard should see them there,
And all should cry, Beware! Beware!
His flashing eyes, his floating hair!
Weave a circle round him thrice,
And close your eyes with holy dread,
For he on honey-dew hath fed,
And drunk the milk of Paradise.*

" Kubla Khan," *by Samuel Taylor Coleridge*

FTER having applied my mind with more than ordinary attention to my studies, it is my usual custom to relax and unbend it in the conversation of such as are rather easy than shining companions. This I find particularly necessary for me before I retire to rest, in order to draw my slumbers upon me by degrees and fall asleep insensibly. This is the particular use I make of a set of heavy honest men with whom I have passed many hours with much indolence though not with great pleasure ᴥ Their conversation is a kind of preparative for sleep; it takes the mind from its abstractions, leads it into the familiar traces of thought, and lulls it into that state of tranquillity which is the condition of a thinking man when he is but half-awake. . . . .

I must own it makes me very melancholy in company when I hear a young man begin a story, and have often observed that one of a quarter of an hour long, in a man of five-and-twenty, gathers circumstances every time he tells it, until it grows into a long Canterbury tale of two hours by the time he is three score.

The only way of avoiding such a trifling and frivolous old age is to lay up in our way to it such stores of knowledge and observation as may make us useful and agreeable in our declining years. The mind of man in a long life will become a magazine of wisdom or folly, and will consequently discharge itself in something impertinent or improving ᴥ For which reason, as there is nothing more ridiculous than an old trifling story-teller, so there is nothing more venerable than one who has turned his experience to the entertainment and advantage of mankind ᴥ ᴥ

In short, we who are in the last stage of life, and are apt to indulge ourselves in talk, ought to consider if what we speak be worth being heard, and endeavor to make our discourse like that of Nestor, which Homer compares to "the flowing of honey for its sweetness."—Sir Richard Steele.

ᴥ ᴥ

Point thy tongue on the anvil of truth.
—Pindar.

*T*HAT a man in his sixties should be able to write a series of works so robust, so fresh, so real, as those which Defoe, at that age, gave to the world is certainly a fact unequaled in the history of our literature. Among those works are *Robinson Crusoe,* the immortal; *Colonel Jack,* equally immortal; *Moll Flanders; Roxana;* and the *Journal of the Plague Year* ᴥ ᴥ

Here are five works, every one of which is enough by itself to make the reputation of an author; five works, one of which is read by every boy of all those who speak our English tongue, while the rest, for the student of literature, are as immortal as Robinson Crusoe himself ᴥ It is as if the writer laughed at time, or as if he would crowd into the last ten years of his life—he died at seventy—all the work which most men are contented to spread over their whole working time; or as if he would prove that even in old age he could recover the spring and flower of youth, could feel again the force of love, and be moved once more with the ambitions, the passions, the heats, the agitations—in a word, with all the emotion of youth.

Old age, for the most part, regards not the things of youth; it is the saddest thing to see the old man turning unmoved from the things which mean so much, so very much, to his grandsons. There is a senile callousness which is lamentable to witness; there is a sorrowful loosening of the hold with which the world has hitherto gripped the soul. With Defoe there is nothing of all this, absolutely nothing; he writes, save for his balanced style, as a young man of five-and-twenty.—Walter Besant.

ᴥ ᴥ

*D*EMAGOGUES and agitators are very unpleasant, and leagues and registers may be very unpleasant, but they are incidents to a free and constitutional country, and you must put up with these inconveniences or do without many important advantages.
—Disraeli

ᴥ ᴥ

Forty is the old age of youth; fifty is the youth of old age.—Victor Hugo.

OTHING is more unjust than to cast especial blame for resistance to science upon the Roman Church. The Protestant Church, though rarely able to be so severe, has been more blameworthy. The persecution of Galileo and his compeers by the older church was mainly at the beginning of the seventeenth century; the persecution of Robertson Smith, and Winchell, and Woodrow, and Toy, and the young professors at Beyrout, by various Protestant authorities, was near the end of the nineteenth century. Those earlier persecutions by Catholicism were strictly in accordance with principles held at that time by all religionists, Catholic and Protestant, throughout the world; these later persecutions by Protestants were in defiance of principles which all Protestants today hold or pretend to hold, and none make louder claim to hold them than the very sects which persecuted these eminent Christian men of our day, whose crime was that they were intelligent enough to accept the science of their time, and honest enough to acknowledge it.

Most unjustly, then, would Protestantism taunt Catholicism for excluding knowledge of astronomical truths from European Catholic universities in the seventeenth and eighteenth centuries, while real knowledge of geological and biological and anthropological truth is denied or pitifully diluted in so many American Protestant colleges and universities in the nineteenth century.

Nor has Protestantism the right to point with scorn to the Catholic *Index* and to lay stress on the fact that nearly every really important book in the last three centuries has been forbidden by it, so long as young men in so many American Protestant universities and colleges are nursed with " ecclesiastical pap " rather than with real thought, and directed to the works of " solemnly constituted impostors," or to sundry " approved courses of reading," while they are studiously kept aloof from such leaders in modern thought as Darwin, Spencer, Huxley, Draper and Lecky . . .

As to the older errors, the whole civilized world was at fault. Protestant as well as Catholic. It was not the fault of religion; it was the fault of that shortsighted linking of theological dogmas to scriptural texts which, in utter defiance of the words and works of the Blessed Founder of Christianity, narrow-minded, loud-voiced men are ever prone to substitute for religion. Justly it is said by one of the most eminent among contemporary Anglican divines that " it is because they have mistaken the dawn for a conflagration that theologians have so often been foes of light."—Andrew D. White.

LEARNED men in all ages have had their judgments free, and most commonly disagreeing from the common judgment of the world; such also have they published both with pen and tongue; notwithstanding, they themselves have lived in the common society with others, and have borne patiently with errors and imperfections which they could not amend. Plato, the philosopher, wrote his book on the commonwealth, in which he condemned many things that then were maintained in the world, and required many things to have been reformed; and yet, notwithstanding, he lived under such policies as then were universally received, without further troubling of any state. Even so, madam, am I content to do, in uprightness of heart, and with a testimony of a good conscience.

—John Knox to Mary, Queen of Scots.

WHEN it shall be said in any country in the world, " My poor are happy; neither ignorance nor distress is to be found among them; my jails are empty of prisoners, my streets of beggars; the aged are not in want, the taxes are not oppressive; the rational world is my friend, because I am a friend of its happiness "—when these things can be said, then may that country boast of its constitution and its government.

—Thomas Paine.

Ignorance is the night of the mind, but a night without moon or star.—Confucius.

T is only a poor sort of happiness that could ever come by caring very much about our own narrow pleasures. We can only have the highest happiness, such as goes along with being a great man, by having wide thoughts, and much feeling for the rest of the world as well as ourselves; and this sort of happiness often brings so much pain with it, that we can only tell it from pain by its being what we would choose before everything else, because our souls see it is good ✍ There are so many things wrong and difficult in the world that no man can be great—he can hardly keep himself from wickedness—unless he gives up thinking much about his pleasure or his rewards, and gets strength to endure what is hard and painful. My father had the greatness that belongs to integrity; he chose poverty and obscurity rather than falsehood. And there was Fra Girolamo (Savonarola); he had the greatness which belongs to a life spent in struggling against powerful wrong, and in trying to raise men to the highest deeds they are capable of. And so, my Lillo, if you mean to act nobly and seek to know the best things God has put within reach of men, you must learn to fix your mind on that end, and not on what will happen to you because of it. ❡ And remember, if you were to choose something lower, and make it the rule of your life to seek your own pleasure and escape from what is disagreeable, calamity might come just the same; and it would be calamity falling on a base mind, which is the one form of sorrow that has no balm in it, and that may well make a man say—' It would have been better for me if I had never been born.' I will tell you something, Lillo."
Romola paused for a moment. She had

Time, you old gipsy man,
Will you not stay,
Put up your caravan
Just for one day?

All things I 'll give you
Will you be my guest,
Bells for your jennet
Of silver the best,
Goldsmiths shall beat you
A great golden ring,
Peacocks shall bow to you,
Little boys sing,
Oh, and sweet girls will
Festoon you with May.
Time, you old gipsy,
Why hasten away?

(Concluded on next page)

taken Lillo's cheeks between her hands, and his young eyes were meeting hers.
❡ " There was a man to whom I was very near, so that I could see a great deal of his life, who made almost every one fond of him, for he was young, and clever, and beautiful, and his manners to all were gentle and kind. I believe, when I first knew him, he never thought of anything cruel or base. But because he tried to slip away from everything that was unpleasant, and cared for nothing else as much as his own safety, he came at last to commit some of the basest deeds—such as make men infamous. He denied his father, and left him to misery; he betrayed every trust that was reposed in him, that he might keep himself safe and get rich and prosperous. Yet calamity overtook him."
Again Romola paused. Her voice was unsteady, and Lillo was looking at her with awed wonder.
❡ " Another time, my Lillo—I will tell you—another time."—From the Epilogue to *Romola* by George Eliot.

✍ ✍

Books are the true levelers. They give to all who faithfully use them the society, the spiritual presence, of the best and greatest of our race.—W. E. Channing.

✍ ✍

Some people have a perfect genius for doing nothing, and doing it assiduously.
　　　　—Thomas C. Haliburton.

✍ ✍

THE delusive idea that men merely toil and work for the sake of preserving their bodies, and procuring for themselves bread, houses, and clothes, is degrading and not to be encouraged ✍ The true origin of man's activity and creativeness lies in his unceasing impulse to embody outside himself the divine and spiritual element within him.—Froebel.

THUS after four months of anxious toil, through the whole of a scorching Philadelphia summer, after earnest but sometimes bitter discussion, in which more than once the meeting had seemed on the point of breaking up, a colossal work had at last been accomplished, the results of which were powerfully to affect the whole future career of the human race.

¶ In spite of the high-wrought intensity of feeling which had been now and then displayed, grave decorum had ruled the proceedings; and now, though few were really satisfied, the approach to acquiescent unanimity was very remarkable. When all was over, it is said that many of the members seemed awe-struck. Washington sat with head bowed in solemn meditation. The scene was ended by a characteristic bit of homely pleasantry from Franklin ∞ ∞

Thirty-three years ago, in the days of George II, before the first mutterings of the Revolution had been heard, and when the French dominion in America was still untouched, before the banishment of the Acadians or the rout of Braddock, while Washington was still surveying lands in the wilderness, while Madison was playing in the nursery and Hamilton was not yet born, Franklin had endeavored to bring together the thirteen colonies in a federal union. Of the famous Albany plan of 1754, the first complete outline of a federal constitution for America that ever was made, he was the principal if not the sole author ∞ When he signed his name to the Declaration of Independence in this very room, his years had rounded the full period of threescore and ten. Eleven years more had passed, and he had been spared to see the noble aim of his life accomplished.

Last week in Babylon,
Last night in Rome,
Morning, and in the crush
Under Paul's dome;
Under Paul's dial
You tighten your rein—
Only a moment,
And off once again;
Off to some city
Now blind in the womb,
Off to another
Ere that's in the tomb.

Time, you old gipsy man,
Will you not stay,
Put up your caravan
Just for one day?
"Time, You Old Gipsy Man,"
by Ralph Hodgson

There was still, no doubt, a chance of failure, but hope now reigned in the old man's breast. On the back of the President's quaint black armchair there was emblazoned a half-sun, brilliant with its gilded rays. As the meeting was about to break up and Washington arose, Franklin pointed to the chair, and made it the text for prophecy ∞ "As I have been sitting here all these weeks," said he, "I have often wondered whether yonder sun is rising or setting. But now I know that it is a rising sun!"
—John Fiske.

∞ ∞

MAN is a land-animal. A land-animal can not live without land. All that man produces comes from the land; all productive labor, in the final analysis, consists in working up land, or materials drawn from land, into such forms as fit them for the satisfaction of human wants and desires. Man's very body is drawn from the land ∞ Children of the soil, we come from the land, and to the land we must return. Take away from man all that belongs to the land, and what have you but a disembodied spirit? Therefore, he who holds the land on which and from which another man must live is that man's master; and the man is his slave. The man who holds the land on which I must live, can command me to life or to death just as absolutely as though I were his chattel.

Talk about abolishing slavery! We have not abolished slavery; we have only abolished one rude form of it—chattel slavery. There is a deeper and more insidious form, a more cursed form yet before us to abolish, in this industrial slavery that makes a man a virtual slave, while taunting him and mocking him in the name of freedom.
—Henry George.

THAT to which the great sacred books of the world conform, and our own most of all, is the evolution of the highest conceptions, beliefs and aspirations of our race from its childhood through the great turning-points in its history. Herein lies the truth of all bibles, and especially of our own. Of vast value they indeed often are as a record of historical outward fact; recent researches in the East are constantly increasing this value; but it is not for this that we prize them most: they are eminently precious, not as a record of outward fact, but as a mirror of the evolving heart, soul and mind of man. They are true because they have been developed in accordance with the laws governing the evolution of truth in human history, and because in poem, chronicle, code, legend, myth, apologue or parable they reflect this development of what is best in the onward march of humanity. To say that they are not true is as if one should say that a flower or a tree or a planet is not true; to scoff at them is to scoff at the law of the universe. In welding together into noble form, whether in the book of Genesis, or in the Psalms, or in the book of Job, or elsewhere, the great conceptions of men acting under earlier inspiration, whether in Egypt, or Chaldea, or India, or Persia, the compilers of our sacred books have given to humanity a possession ever becoming more and more precious; and modern science, in substituting a new heaven and a new earth for the old —the reign of law for the reign of caprice, and the idea of evolution for that of creation—has added and is steadily adding a new revelation divinely inspired ✤ ✤
In the light of these two evolutions, then—one of the visible universe, the other of a sacred creation-legend— science and theology, if the master minds in both are wise, may at last be reconciled.—Andrew D. White.

✤ ✤

Do I contradict myself? Very well, then, I contradict myself; (I am large. I contain multitudes).—Walt Whitman.

IT is Criticism, as Arnold points out, that creates the intellectual atmosphere of the age. It is Criticism . . . that makes the mind a fine instrument . .
❡ It is Criticism, again, that, by concentration, makes culture possible ✤ It takes the cumbersome mass of creative work, and distils it into a finer essence. . . .
❡ The thread that is to guide us across the wearisome labyrinth is in the hands of Criticism. Nay more, where there is no record, and history is either lost or was never written, Criticism can re-create the past for us from the very smallest fragment of language or art, just as surely as the man of science can from some tiny bone, or the mere impress of a foot upon a rock, re-create for us the winged dragon or the Titan lizard that once made the earth shake beneath its tread, can call Behemoth out of his cave, and make Leviathan swim once more across the startled sea. Prehistoric history belongs to the philological and archæological critic ✤ It is to him that the origins of things are revealed.
The self-conscious deposits of an age are nearly always misleading . . . It is Criticism that makes us cosmopolitan . . . It is only by the cultivation of the habit of intellectual criticism that we shall be able to rise superior to race prejudices . . . Criticism will annihilate race prejudices, by insisting upon the unity of the human mind in the variety of its forms . . .
It is Criticism that, recognizing no position as final, and refusing to bind itself by the shallow shibboleths of any sect or school, creates that serene philosophic temper which loves truth for its own sake, and loves it not the less because it knows it to be unattainable.
—Oscar Wilde.

✤ ✤

The stomach is a slave that must accept everything that is given to it, but which avenges wrongs as slyly as does the slave.
—Emile Souvestre.

✤ ✤

Man is so essentially, so necessarily, a moral being that, when he denies the existence of all morality, that very denial already becomes the foundation of a new morality.—Maeterlinck.

HE changes which break up at short intervals the prosperity of men are advertisements of a nature whose law is growth. Evermore it is the order of nature to grow, and every soul is by this intrinsic necessity quitting its whole system of things, its friends, and home, and laws, and faith, as the shell-fish crawls out of its beautiful but stony case, because it no longer admits of its growth, and slowly forms a new house. ❡ In proportion to the vigor of the individual these revolutions are frequent, until in some happier mind they are incessant, and all worldly relations hang very loosely about him, becoming as it were a transparent fluid membrane through which the form is always seen and not as in most men an indurated heterogeneous fabric of many dates and of no settled character, in which the man is imprisoned. Then there can be enlargement and the man of to-day scarcely recognizes the man of yesterday. And such should be the outward biography of man in time, a putting off of dead circumstances day by day, as he renews his raiment day by day. But to us, in our lapsed state, resting not advancing, resisting not co-operating with the divine expansion, this growth comes by shocks.

We can not part with our friends. We can not let our angels go. We do not see that they only go out that archangels may come in ✺ We are idolaters of the old. We do not believe in the riches of the soul, in its proper eternity and omnipresence. We do not believe there is any force in today to rival or re-create that beautiful yesterday ✺ We linger in the ruins of the old tent, where once we had bread and shelter and organs, nor believe that the spirit can feed, cover, and nerve us again. We can not again find aught so dear, so sweet, so graceful. But we sit and weep in vain. The voice of the Almighty saith, "Up and onward for evermore!"

We can not stay amid the ruins. Neither will we rely on the new; and so we walk ever with reverted eyes, like those monsters who look backwards ✺ ✺

And yet the compensations of calamity are made apparent to the understanding also after long intervals of time. A fever, a mutilation, a cruel disappointment, a loss of wealth, the loss of friends, seems at the moment unpaid loss, and unpayable ✺ But the sure years reveal the deep remedial force that underlies all facts. The death of a dear friend, wife, brother, lover, which seemed nothing but privation, somewhat later assumes the aspect of a guide or genius; for it commonly operates revolutions in our way of life, terminates an epoch of infancy or of youth which was waiting to be closed, breaks up a wonted occupation, or a household, or style of living, and allows the formation of new ones more friendly

I went to the dances at Chandlerville,
And played snap-out at Winchester.
One time we changed partners,
Driving home in the moonlight of middle
*   June,*
And then I found Davis.
We were married and lived together for
*   seventy years,*
Enjoying, working, raising the twelve
*   children,*
Eight of whom we lost
Ere I reached the age of sixty.
I spun, I wove, I kept the house, I nursed
*   the sick,*
I made the garden, and for holiday
Rambled over the fields where sang the
*   larks,*
And by Spoon River gathering many a
*   shell,*
And many a flower and medicinal weed—
Shouting to the wooded hills, singing to
*   the green valleys.*
At ninety-six I had lived enough, that is all,
And passed to a sweet repose.
What is this I hear of sorrow and
*   weariness,*
Anger, discontent and drooping hopes?
Degenerate sons and daughters,
Life is too strong for you—
It takes life to love Life.

"Lucinda Matlock," *by Edgar Lee Masters*

to the growth of character. It permits or constrains the formation of new acquaintances, and the reception of new influences that prove of the first importance to the next years; and the man or woman who would have remained a sunny garden flower, with no room for its roots and too much sunshine for its head, by the falling of walls and the neglect of its gardener, is made the banyan of the forest, yielding shade and fruit to wide neighborhoods of men.—Emerson.

I FIND letters from God dropped in the street, and every one is signed by God's name,
And I leave them where they are, for I know that wheresoe'er I go,
Others will punctually come for ever and ever.

—Walt Whitman.

THE idea of having navies for the protection of commerce is delusive. It is putting the means of destruction for the means of protection ❧ Commerce needs no other protection than the reciprocal interest which every nation feels in supporting it—it is common stock—it exists by a balance of advantages to all; and the only interruption it meets is from the present uncivilized state of governments, and which it is its common interest to reform. . . .
There can be no such thing as a nation flourishing alone in commerce; she can only participate; and the destruction of it in any part must necessarily affect all. When, therefore, governments are at war, the attack is made upon the common stock of commerce, and the consequence is the same as if each had attacked his own.
The prosperity of any commercial nation is regulated by the prosperity of the rest. If they are poor, she can not be rich; and her condition, be it what it may, is an index of the height of the commercial tide in other nations.

—Thomas Paine.

A politician thinks of the next election; a statesman, of the next generation.

—James Freeman Clarke.

ITH respect to what are called denominations of religion, if every one is left judge of his own religion, there is no such thing as a religion that is wrong; but if they are to judge of each other's religion, there is no such thing as a religion that is right; and therefore, all the world is right, or all the world is wrong.
But with respect to religion itself, without regard to names, and as directing itself from the universal family of mankind to the divine object of all adoration, it is man bringing to his Maker the fruits of his heart; and though these fruits may differ from each other like the fruits of the earth, the grateful tribute of every one is accepted.

＊ ＊ ＊ ＊ ＊ ＊

If we suppose a large family of children who on any particular day, or particular occasion, make it a custom to present to their parents some token of their affection and gratitude, each of them would make a different offering, and most probably in a different manner.
Some would pay their congratulations in themes of verse and prose, by some little devices, as their genius dictated, or according to what they thought would please; and, perhaps, the least of all, not able to do any one of those things, would ramble into the garden, or the field, and gather what it thought the prettiest flower it could find, though, perhaps, it might be but a simple weed. The parents would be more gratified by such a variety than if the whole of them had acted on a concerted plan, and each had made exactly the same offering ❧ ❧
This would have the cold appearance of contrivance, or the harsh one of control.
⊄ But of all unwelcome things, nothing would more afflict the parents than to know that the whole of them had afterwards got together by the ears, boys and girls, fighting, reviling and abusing each other about which was the best or the worst present.—Thomas Paine.

No man but a blockhead ever wrote except for money.—Samuel Johnson.

NLY in broken gleams and partial light has the sun of Liberty yet beamed among men, yet all progress hath she called forth.

Liberty came to a race crouching under Egyptian whips, and led them forth from the House of Bondage ✒ She hardened them in the desert and made of them a race of conquerors.

❡ The free spirit of the Mosaic law took their thinkers up to heights where they beheld the unity of God, and inspired their poets with strains that yet phrase the highest exaltations of thought.

Liberty dawned on the Phœnician coast and ships passed the Pillars of Hercules to plow the unknown sea ✒ She broke in partial light on Greece, and marble grew to shapes of ideal beauty, words became the instruments of subtlest thought, and against the scanty militia of all free cities the countless hosts of the Great King broke like surges against a rock. She cast her beams on the four-acre farms of Italian husbandmen, and born of her strength a power came forth that conquered the world! She glinted from shields of German warriors, and Augustus wept his legions. Out of the night that followed her eclipse, her slanting rays fell again on free cities, and a lost learning revived, modern civilization began, a new world was unveiled; and as Liberty grew so grew art, wealth, power, knowledge and refinement ✒ ✒

In the history of every nation we may read the same truth. It was the strength born of Magna Charta that won Crecy and Agincourt. It was the revival of Liberty from the despotism of the Tudors that glorified the Elizabethan age. It was the spirit that brought a crowned tyrant to the block that planted here the seed of a mighty tree. It was the energy of ancient freedom that, the moment it had gained unity, made Spain the mightiest power of the world, only to fall to the lowest depths of weakness when tyranny succeeded liberty. ❡ See, in France, all intellectual vigor dying under the tyranny of the seventeenth century to revive in splendor as Liberty awoke in the eighteenth, and on the enfranchisement of the French peasants in the great revolution, basing the wonderful strength that has in our time laughed at disaster.

What Liberty shall do for the nation that fully accepts and loyally cherishes her, the wondrous inventions, which are the marked features of this century, give us but a hint . . . . .

❡ A hundred years have passed since the fast friend of American liberty—the great Earl Chatham—rose to make his last appeal for the preservation, on the basis of justice, of that English-speaking empire, in which he saw the grandest possibility of the future. Is it too soon to hope that the future may hold the realization of his vision in a nobler form than even he imagined, and that it may be the mission of this Republic to unite all the nations of English speech, whether they grow beneath the Northern Star or Southern Cross, in a league which by insuring justice, promoting peace, and liberating commerce, will be the forerunner of a world-wide federation that will make war the possibility of a past age, and turn to works of usefulness the enormous forces now dedicated to destruc-

*Bright Star! would I were steadfast as
    thou art—
Not in lone splendor hung aloft the night,
And watching, with eternal lids apart,
Like Nature's patient, sleepless Eremite,
The moving waters at their priest-like task
Of pure ablution round earth's human
    shores,
Or gazing on the new soft-fallen mask
Of snow upon the mountains and the
    moors—
No—yet still steadfast, still unchangeable,
Pillowed upon my fair love's ripening
    breast,
To feel for ever its soft fall and swell,
Awake for ever in a sweet unrest,
  Still, still to hear her tender-taken
    breath,
  And so live ever—or else swoon to
    death.*

" Last Sonnet," *by John Keats*

tion, ... ℂ Is this the dream of dreamers? One brought to the world the message that it might be reality. But they crucified him between two thieves. ℂ Not till it accepts that message can the world have peace. Look over the history of the past. What is it but a record of the woes inflicted by man on man, of wrong producing wrong, and crime fresh crime? It must be so till justice is acknowledged and liberty is law ✤ ✤

Who is Liberty that we should doubt her; that we should set bounds to her, and say, " Thus far shalt thou come and no farther! " Is she not peace? is she not prosperity? is she not progress? nay, is she not the goal towards which all progress strives?

Not here; but yet she cometh! Saints have seen her in their visions; seers have seen her in their trance. To heroes has she spoken, and their hearts were strong; to martyrs, and the flames were cool! ℂ She is not here, but yet she cometh. Lo! her feet are on the mountains—the call of her clarions ring on every breeze; the banners of her dawning fret the sky! Who will hear her as she calleth; who will bid her come and welcome? Who will turn to her? who will speak for her? who will stand for her while she yet hath need?—Henry George.

✤ ✤

IF a friend of mine. . . gave a feast, and did not invite me to it, I should not mind a bit. . . . Buf if. . . a friend of mine had a sorrow and refused to allow me to share it, I should feel it most bitterly. If he shut the doors of the house of mourning against me, I would move back again and again and beg to be admitted, so that I might share in what I was entitled to share. If he thought me unworthy, unfit to weep with him, I should feel it as the most poignant humiliation, as the most terrible mode for which disgrace could be inflicted on me. . . he who can look on the loveliness of the world and share its sorrow, and realize something of the wonder of both, is in immediate contact with divine things, and has got as near to God's secret as any one can get.—Oscar Wilde.

IT has been thought a considerable advance towards establishing the principles of freedom to say, that government is a compact between those who govern and those who are governed: but this can not be true, because it is putting the effect before the cause; for as man must have existed before governments existed, there necessarily was a time when governments did not exist, and consequently there could originally exist no governors to form such a compact with.

The fact therefore must be that the individuals themselves, each in his own personal and sovereign right, entered into a compact with each other to produce a government: and this is the only mode in which governments have a right to arise, and the only principle on which they have a right to exist.

—Thomas Paine.

✤ ✤

Time to me is so precious that with great difficulty can I steal one hour in eight days, either to satisfy myself or to gratify my friends.—John Knox.

✤ ✤

THEY that love beyond the world can not be separated by it.

Death can not kill what never dies. ℂ Nor can spirits ever be divided, that love and live in the same divine principle, the root and record, of their friendship ✤ ✤

Death is but crossing the world, as friends do the seas; they live in one another still. . . .

This is the comfort of friends, that though they may be said to die, yet their friendship and society are, in the best sense, ever present because immortal.—William Penn.

✤ ✤

Man can not degrade woman without himself falling into degradation; he can not elevate her without at the same time elevating himself.

—Alexander Walker.

✤ ✤

However dull a woman may be, she will understand all there is in love; however intelligent a man may be, he will never know but half of it.—Madame Fée.

HAT Nature is always right, is an assertion, artistically, as untrue, as it is one whose truth is universally taken for granted. Nature is very rarely right, to such an extent even, that it might almost be said that Nature is usually wrong: that is to say, the condition of things that shall bring about the perfection of harmony worthy a picture is rare, and not common at all.

❡ This would seem, to even the most intelligent, a doctrine almost blasphemous. So incorporated with our education has the supposed aphorism become, that its belief is held to be part of our moral being, and the words themselves have, in our ear, the ring of religion. Still, seldom does Nature succeed in producing a picture ❧ ❧

* * * *

How little this is understood, and how dutifully the casual in Nature is accepted as sublime, may be gathered from the unlimited admiration daily produced by a very foolish sunset. * * * * * * ❡ And when the evening mist clothes the riverside with poetry, as with a veil, and the poor buildings lose themselves in the dim sky, and the tall chimneys become campanili, and the warehouses are palaces in the night, and the whole city hangs in the heavens, and fairy-land is before us—then the wayfarer hastens home; the

working man and the cultured one, the wise man and the one of pleasure, cease to understand, as they have ceased to see, and Nature, who, for once, has sung in tune, sings her exquisite song to the artist alone, her son and her master—her son in that he loves her, her master in that he knows her.

To him her secrets are unfolded, to him her lessons have become gradually clear.

* * * *

Through his brain, as through the last alembic, is distilled the refined essence of that thought which began with the Gods, and which they left him to carry out. Set apart by them to complete their works, he produces that wondrous thing called the masterpiece, which surpasses in perfection all that they have contrived in what is called Nature; and the Gods stand by and marvel, and perceive how far away more beautiful is the Venus of Melos than was their own Eve.—Whistler.

In the dark womb where I began
My mother's life made me a man.
Through all the months of human birth
Her beauty fed my common earth,
I can not see, nor breathe, nor stir,
But through the death of some of her.

Down in the darkness of the grave,
She can not see the life she gave.
For all her love, she can not tell
Whether I use it ill or well,
Nor knock at dusty doors to find
Her beauty dusty in the mind.

If the grave's gates could be undone,
She would not know her little son,
I am so grown. If we should meet,
She would pass by me in the street,
Unless my soul's face let her see
My sense of what she did for me.

What have I done to keep in mind
My debt to her and womankind?
What woman's happier life repays
Her for those months of wretched days?
For all my mouthless body leeched
Ere Birth's releasing hell was reached?

What have I done, or tried, or said
In thanks to that dear woman, dead?
Men triumph over woman still,
Men trample woman's rights at will,
And man's lust roves the world untamed.
O grave, keep shut lest I be shamed.

"C. L. M.," by John Masefield.

PASSION is a sort of fever in the mind, which ever leaves us weaker than it found us. . . ❡ It, more than any thing, deprives us of the use of our judgment; for it raises a dust very hard to see through . . . . . . ❡ It may not unfitly be termed the mob of the man, that commits a riot upon his reason.—William Penn.

❧ ❧

A man is an animal that writes.—Homer.

HE is fallen! ♠ We may now pause before that splendid prodigy, which towered among us like some ancient ruin, whose frown terrified the glance its magnificence attracted ♠

¶ Grand, gloomy, and peculiar, he sat upon the throne, a sceptered hermit, wrapped in the solitude of his own originality ♠ ♠

A mind, bold, independent, and decisive —a will, despotic in its dictates—an energy that distanced expedition, and a conscience pliable to every touch of interest, marked the outline of this extraordinary character—the most extraordinary, perhaps, that, in the annals of this world, ever rose, or reigned, or fell ♠ ♠

Flung into life, in the midst of a revolution that quickened every energy of a people who acknowledged no superior, he commenced his course, a stranger by birth, and a scholar by charity!

With no friend but his sword, and no fortune but his talents, he rushed into the lists where rank, and wealth, and genius had arrayed themselves, and competition fled from him as from the glance of destiny. He knew no motive but interest—he acknowledged no criterion but success—he worshiped no God but ambition, and with an Eastern devotion he knelt at the shrine of his idolatry. Subsidiary to this, there was no opinion that he did not promulgate: in the hope of a dynasty, he upheld the crescent; for the sake of a divorce, he bowed before the Cross: the orphan of St. Louis, he became the adopted child of the Republic; and with a paricidal ingratitude, on the ruins both of the throne and the tribune, he reared the throne of despotism.

A professed Catholic, he imprisoned the pope; a pretended patriot, he impoverished the country; and in the name of Brutus, he grasped without remorse, and wore without shame, the diadem of the Cæsars!

¶ Through this pantomime of his policy, fortune played the clown to his caprices. At his touch, crowns crumbled, beggars reigned, systems vanished, the wildest theories took the color of his whim, and all that was venerable, and all that was novel, changed places with the rapidity of a drama. Even apparent defeat assumed the appearance of victory—his flight from Egypt confirmed his destiny—ruin itself only elevated him to empire.

¶ But if this fortune was great, his genius was transcendent; decision flashed upon his counsels; and it was the same to decide and to perform. To inferior intellects, his combinations appeared perfectly impossible, his plans perfectly impracticable; but, in his hands, simplicity marked their development, and success vindicated their adoption.

His person partook the character of his mind—if the one never yielded in the cabinet, the other never bent in the field.

¶ Nature had no obstacles that he did not surmount—space no opposition that he did not spurn; and whether amid Alpine rocks, Arabian sands, or polar snows, he seemed proof against peril, and empowered with ubiquity! The whole continent of Europe trembled at beholding the audacity of his designs, and the miracle of their execution. Skepticism bowed to the prodigies of his performance; romance assumed the air of history; nor was there aught too incredible for belief, or too fanciful for expectation, when the world saw a subaltern of Corsica waving his imperial flag over her most ancient capitals. All the visions of antiquity became common places in his contemplation; kings were his people —nations were his outposts; and he disposed of courts, and crowns, and camps, and churches, and cabinets, as if they were the titular dignitaries of the chessboard! ♠ ♠

Amid all these changes he stood immutable as adamant. It mattered little whether in the field or the drawing-room —with the mob or the levee—wearing the jacobin bonnet or the iron crown—banishing a Braganza, or espousing a Hapsburg—dictating peace on a raft to the Czar of Russia, or contemplating defeat at the gallows of Leipsic—he was still the same military despot!

Cradled in the camp, he was to the last hour the darling of the army; and whether in the camp or the cabinet, he never forsook a friend or forgot a favor.

Of all his soldiers, not one abandoned him, till affection was useless; and their first stipulation was for the safety of their favorite ꙮ ꙮ

They knew well, if he was lavish of them, he was prodigal of himself; and that if he exposed them to peril, he repaid them with plunder. For the soldier, he subsidized every people; to the people he made even pride pay tribute ꙮ The victorious veteran glittered with his gains; and the capital, gorgeous with the spoils of art, became the miniature metropolis of the universe. In this wonderful combination, his affectation of literature must not be omitted ꙮ The jailer of the Press, he affected the patronage of letters—the proscriber of books, he encouraged philosophy—the persecutor of authors, and the murderer of printers, he yet pretended to the protection of learning!—the assassin of Palm, the silencer of De Stael, and the denouncer of Kotzebue, he was the friend of David, the benefactor of De Lille, and sent his academic prize to the philosopher of England ꙮ ꙮ

Such a medley of contradictions, and at the same time such an individual consistency, were never united in the same character. A Royalist—a Republican and an Emperor—a Mohammedan—a Catholic and a Patron of the Synagogue—a Subaltern and a Sovereign—a Traitor and a Tyrant—a Christian and an Infidel—he was, through all his vicissitudes, the same stern, impatient, inflexible original—the same mysterious, incomprehensible self—the man without a model, and without a shadow.

His fall, like his life, baffled all speculation. In short, his whole history was like a dream to the world, and no man can tell how or why he was awakened from the reverie. ❧ Such is a faint and feeble picture of Napoleon Bonaparte, the first (and it is to be hoped the last) emperor of the French.

That he has done much evil there is little doubt; that he has been the origin of much good there is just as little. Through his means, intentional or not, Spain, Portugal, and France have arisen to the blessings of a free constitution; superstition has found her grave in the ruins of the Inquisition and the feudal system, with its whole train of tyrannic satellites, has fled forever ꙮ Kings may learn from him that their safest study, as well as their noblest, is the interest of the people; the people are taught by him that there is no despotism, so stupendous against which they have not a resource; and to those who would rise upon the ruins of both, he is a living lesson, that if ambition can raise them from the lowest station, it can also prostrate them from the highest.—Charles Phillips.

I write. He sits beside my chair,
*   And scribbles, too, in hushed delight,*
He dips his pen, in charmed air:
*   What is it he pretends to write?*

He toils and toils; the paper gives
*   No clue to aught he thinks. What then?*
His little heart is glad; he lives
*   The poems that he can not pen.*

Strange fancies throng that baby brain,
*   What grave, sweet looks! What earnest eyes!*
He stops—reflects—and now again
*   His unrecording pen he plies.*

It seems a satire on myself,—
*   These dreamy nothings scrawled in air,*
This thought, this work! Oh, tricksy elf,
*   Wouldst drive the father to despair?*

Despair! Ah, no; the heart, the mind
*   Presists in hoping—schemes and strives*
That there may linger with our kind
*   Some memory of our little lives.*

Beneath his rock in the early world
*   Smiling the naked hunter lay,*
And sketched on horn the spear he hurled
*   The urus which he made his prey.*

Like him I strive in hope my rhymes
*   May keep my name a little while—*
O child, who knows how many times
*   We two have made the angels smile!*

        " A New Poet," *by William Canton*

AM inclined to believe that the intention of the Sacred Scriptures is to give to mankind the information necessary for their salvation. But I do not hold it necessary to believe that the same God who has endowed us with senses, with speech, with intellect, intended that we should neglect the use of these, and seek by other means for knowledge which these are sufficient to procure for us; especially in a science like astronomy, of which so little notice is taken by the Scriptures that none of the planets, except the sun and moon and once or twice only Venus, by the name of Lucifer, are so much as named at all. ¶ This therefore being granted, methinks that in the discussion of natural problems we ought not to begin at the authority of texts of Scriptures, but at sensible experiments and necessary demonstrations.—Galileo.

WHEREVER one goes one immediately comes upon this incorrigible mob of humanity. It exists everywhere in legions; crowding and soiling everything, like flies in summer. Hence the numberless bad books, those rank weeds of literature which extract nourishment from the corn, and choke it. They monopolize the time, money and attention which really belongs to good books and their noble aims; they are written merely with a view to making money or procuring places. They are not only useless, but they do positive harm. Nine-tenths of the whole of our present literature aims solely at taking a few shillings out of the public's pocket, and to accomplish this, author, publisher and reviewer have joined forces.—Schopenhauer.

I HAVE often tried to picture to myself what famine is, but the human mind is not capable of drawing any form, any scene, that will realize the horrors of starvation. The men who made the Corn Laws are totally ignorant of what it means. The agricultural laborers know something of it in some counties, and there are some hand-loom weavers in Lancashire who know what it is. I saw the other night, late at night, a light in a cottage-window, and heard the loom busily at work, the shuttle flying rapidly. It ought to have a cheerful sound, but it is at work near midnight, when there is care upon the brow of the workman— lest he should not be able to secure that which will maintain his wife and children —then there is a foretaste of what is meant by the word " famine." Oh, if these men who made the Corn Laws, if these men who step in between the Creator and His creatures, could for only one short twelvemonth—I would inflict upon them no harder punishment for their guilt—if they for one single twelvemonth might sit at the loom and throw the shuttle! I will not ask that they should have the rest of the evils; I will not ask that they shall be torn by the harrowing feelings which must exist when a beloved wife and helpless children are suffering the horrors which these Corn Laws have inflicted upon millions.
—John Bright.

TO know the mighty works of God; to comprehend His wisdom and majesty and power; to appreciate, in degree, the wonderful working of His laws, surely all this must be a pleasing and acceptable mode of worship to the Most High, to whom ignorance can not be more grateful than knowledge.
—Copernicus.

IF we wish to be just judges of all things, let us first persuade ourselves of this: that there is not one of us without fault; no man is found who can acquit himself; and he who calls himself innocent does so with reference to a witness, and not to his conscience.—Seneca.

WHEN a man of genius is in full swing, never contradict him, set him straight or try to reason with him. Give him a free field. A listener is sure to get a greater quantity of good, no matter how mixed, than if the man is thwarted ✒ Let Pegasus bolt—he will bring you up in a place you know nothing about!—Linnæus.

THERE are two great forces which seem sheer inspiration and nothing else—I mean Shakespeare and Burns. This is not the place or the time to speak of the miracle called Shakespeare, but one must say a word of the miracle called Burns ॐ ॐ

Try and reconstruct Burns as he was—a peasant born in a cottage that no sanitary inspector in these days would tolerate for a moment; struggling with desperate effort against pauperism, almost in vain; snatching at scraps of learning in the intervals of toil, as it were, with his teeth; a heavy, silent lad proud of his plow. ¶ All of a sudden, without preface or warning, he breaks out into exquisite song like a nightingale from the brushwood, and continues singing as sweetly, in nightingale pauses, till he dies. The nightingale sings because he can not help it; he can only sing exquisitely, because he knows no other ॐ So it was with Burns. What is this but inspiration? One can no more measure or reason about it than measure or reason about Niagara; and remember, the poetry is only a fragment of Burns. Amazing as it may seem, all contemporary testimony is unanimous that the man was far more wonderful than his works ॐ If his talents were universal, his sympathy was not less so. His tenderness was no

We are not sure of sorrow,
  And joy was never sure;
Today will die tomorrow;
  Time stoops to no man's lure;
And love, grown faint and fretful,
With lips but half regretful
Sighs, and with eyes forgetful
  Weeps that no loves endure.

From too much love of living,
  From hope and fear set free,
We thank with brief thanksgiving
  Whatever gods may be,
That no life lives forever;
That dead men rise up never;
That even the weariest river
  Winds somewhere safe to sea.

Here, where the world is quiet,
  Here, where all trouble seems
Dead winds' and spent waves' riot
  In doubtful dreams of dreams;
I watch the green field growing
For reaping folk and sowing,
For harvest-time and mowing,
  A sleepy world of streams.

I am tired of tears and laughter,
  And men that laugh and weep
Of what may come hereafter
  For men that sow to reap:
I am weary of days and hours,
Blown buds of barren flowers,
Desires and dreams and powers
  And everything but sleep.

" The Garden of Proserpine,"
       by A. C. Swinburne

mere selfish tenderness for his own family for he loved all mankind, except the cruel and base—nay, we may go further and say that he placed all creation, especially the suffering and depressed part of it, under his protection. The oppressor in every shape, even in the comparatively innocent embodiment of the factor and the sportsman, he regarded with direct and personal hostility ॐ But, above all, he saw the charm of the home. He recognized it as the basis of all society. He honored it in its humblest form, for he knew, as few know, how sincerely the family in the cottage is welded by mutual love and esteem. ¶ His verses, then, go straight to the heart of every home, they appeal to every father and mother; but that is only the beginning, perhaps the foundation, of his sympathy. There is something for everybody in Burns. He has a heart even for vermin; he has pity even for the arch-enemy of mankind. And his universality makes his poems a treasure-house in which all

may find what they want. Every wayfarer in the journey of life may pluck strength and courage from it as he pauses. The sore, the weary, the wounded will all find something to heal and soothe. For this great master is the universal Samaritan. Where the priest and the Levite may have passed by in vain this eternal heart will still afford resource. . . . . .

His was a soul bathed in crystal ❧ He hurried to avow everything. There was no reticence in him. The only obscure passage in his life is the love-passage with Highland Mary, and as to that he was silent not from shame, but because it was a sealed and sacred episode ❧ " What a flattering idea," he once wrote, " is a world to come. There shall I with speechless agony or rapture recognize my lost, my ever dear Mary, whose bosom was fraught with truth, honor, constancy and love." But he had, as the French say, the defects of his qualities. His imagination was a supreme and celestial gift, but his imagination often led him wrong and never more than with woman. The chivalry that made Don Quixote see the heroic in all the common events of life made Burns (as his brother tells us) see a goddess in every girl he approached; hence many love affairs, and some guilty ones, but even these must be judged with reference to time and circumstances. This much is certain: had he been devoid of genius they would not have attracted attention. It is Burn's pedestal that affords a target. And why, one may ask, is not the same treatment measured out to Burns as to others? ......

Mankind is helped in its progress almost as much by the study of imperfection as by the contemplation of perfection. Had we nothing before us in our futile and halting lives but saints and the ideal, we might well fail altogether. We grope blindly along the catacombs of the world, we climb the dark ladder of life, we feel our way to futurity, but we can scarcely see an inch around or before us ❧ We stumble and falter and fall, our hands and knees are bruised and sore, and we look up for light and guidance. Could we see nothing but distant, unapproachable impeccability we might well sink prostrate in the hopelessness of emulation, and the weariness of despair. Is it not then, when all seems blank and lightless, when strength and courage flag, and when perfection seems remote as a star, is it not then that imperfection helps us? When we see that the greatest and choicest images of God have had their weaknesses like ours, their temptations, their hour of darkness, their bloody sweat, are we not encouraged by their lapses and catastrophes to find energy for one more effort, one more struggle? Where they failed, we feel it a less dishonor to fail; their errors and sorrows make, as it were, an easier ascent from infinite imperfection to infinite perfection.

Man, after all, is not ripened by virtue alone. Were it so, this world were a paradise of angels. No. Like the growth of the earth, he is the fruit of all seasons, the accident of a thousand accidents, a living mystery moving through the seen to the unseen; he is sown in dishonor; he is matured under all the varieties of heat and cold, in mists and wrath, in snow and vapors, in the melancholy of autumn, in the torpor of winter as well as in the rapture and fragrance of summer, or the bamly affluence of spring, its breath, its sunshine; at the end he is reaped, the product not of one climate but of all, not of good alone but of sorrow, perhaps mellowed and ripened, perhaps stricken and withered and sour. How, then, shall we judge any one? How, at any rate, shall we judge a giant, great in gifts and great in temptation; great in strength, and great in weakness? Let us glory in his strength and be comforted in his weakness; and when we thank heaven for the inestimable gift of Burns, we do not need to remember wherein he was imperfect; we can not bring ourselves to regret that he was made of the same clay as ourselves.—Rosebery.

❧ ❧

THE country life is to be preferred, for there we see the works of God; but in cities, little else but the works of men; and the one makes a better subject for our contemplation than the other. ......
❧ The country is both the philosopher's garden and library, in which he reads and contemplates the power, wisdom, and goodness of God.—William Penn.

❧ ❧

I congratulate poor young men upon being born to that ancient and honorable degree which renders it necessary that they should devote themselves to hard work.—Andrew Carnegie.

HEN you come into any fresh company, observe their humours ✒ Suit your own carriage thereto, by which insinuation you will make their converse more free and open. Let your discours be more in querys and doubtings than peremptory assertions or disputings, it being the designe of travelers to learne, not to teach. Besides, it will persuade your acquaintance that you have the greater esteem of them, and soe make them more ready to communicate what they know to you; whereas nothing sooner occasions disrespect and quarrels than peremptorinesse. You will find little or no advantage in seeming wiser, or much more ignorant than your company. Seldom discommend anything though never so bad, or doe it but moderately, lest you bee unexpectedly forced to an unhansom retraction. It is safer to commend any thing more than is due, than to discommend a thing soe much as it deserves; for commendations meet not soe often with oppositions, or, at least, are not usually soe ill resented by men that think otherwise, as discommendations; and you will insinuate into men's favour by nothing sooner than seeming to approve and commend what they like; but beware of doing it by a comparison ✒ ✒

—Sir Isaac Newton to one of his pupils.

✒ ✒

WE are made for co-operation, like feet, like hands, like eyelids, like the rows of the upper and lower teeth. To act against one another then is contrary to Nature, and it is acting against one another to be vexed and turn away.

—Marcus Aurelius.

✒ ✒

NONE have fought better, and none have been more fortunate, than Charles Darwin. He found a great truth trodden underfoot, reviled by bigots, and rediculed by all the world; he lived long enough to see it, chiefly by his own efforts irrefragably established in science, inseparably incorporated into the common thoughts of men. What shall a man desire more than this?

—Thomas Huxley.

THE man who makes it the habit of his life to go to bed at nine o'clock, usually gets rich and is always reliable. Of course, going to bed does not make him rich—I merely mean that such a man will in all probability be up early in the morning and do a big day's work, so his weary bones put him to bed early. Rogues do their work at night. Honest men work by day. It 's all a matter of habit, and good habits in America make any man rich. Wealth is largely a result of habit.—John Jacob Astor.

✒ ✒

I FEEL most deeply that this whole question of Creation is too profound for human intellect. A dog might as well speculate on the mind of Newton! Let each man hope and believe what he can.—Charles Darwin.

✒ ✒

WE thank Thee for this place in which we dwell; for the love that unites us; for the peace accorded us this day; for the hope with which we expect the morrow; for the health, the work, the food, and the bright skies that make our lives delightful; for our friends in all parts of the earth, and our friendly helpers in this foreign isle ✒ Give us courage and gaiety and the quiet mind. Spare to us our friends, soften to us our enemies. Bless us, if it may be, in all our innocent endeavors. If it may not, give us the strength to encounter that which is to come, that we be brave in peril, constant in tribulation, temperate in wrath, and in all changes of fortune, and down to the gates of death, loyal and loving one to another.

—Robert Louis Stevenson.

✒ ✒

IN the name of the Past and of the Future, the servants of Humanity —both its philosophical and its practical servants—come forward to claim as their due the general direction of the world. Their object is to constitute at length a real Providence in all departments—moral, intellectual and material.—Auguste Comte.

✒ ✒

Education—A debt due from present to future generations.—George Peabody.

Y LORD: I have been informed by the proprietor of the *World* that two papers in which my Dictionary is recommended to the public, were written by your Lordship. To be so distinguished is an honor, which, being very little accustomed to favors from the great, I know not well how to receive, or in what terms to acknowledge ❧ ❧ When, upon some slight encouragement, I first visited your Lordship, I was overpowered, like the rest of mankind, by the enchantment of your address, and could not forbear to wish that I might boast myself *le vainqueur du vainqueur de la terre*—that I might obtain that regard for which I saw the world contending; but I found my attendance so little encouraged, that neither pride nor modesty would suffer me to continue it ❧ When I once addressed your Lordship in public, I had exhausted all the art of pleasing which a retired and uncourtly scholar can possess. I had done all that I could; and no man is well pleased to have his all neglected, be it ever so little.

Seven years, my lord, have now passed since I waited in your outward rooms, or was repulsed from your door; during which time I have been pushing on my work through difficulties of which it is useless to complain, and have brought it

I know not whether Laws be right,
　Or whether Laws be wrong;
All that we know who lie in gaol
　Is that the wall is strong;
And that each day is like a year,
　A year whose days are long.

But this I know, that every Law
　That men have made for Man,
Since first Man took his brother's life,
　And the sad world began,
But straws the wheat and saves the chaff
　With a most evil fan.

This too I know—and wise it were
　If each could know the same—
That every prison that men build
　Is built with bricks of shame,
And bound with bars lest Christ should see
　How men their brothers maim.

With bars they blur the gracious moon,
　And blind the goodly sun:
And they do well to hide their Hell,
　For in it things are done
That Son of God nor Son of Man
　Ever should look upon!

* * * * * *

The vilest deeds like poison words
　Bloom well in prison-air:
It is only what is good in Man
　That wastes and withers there:
Pale Anguish keeps the heavy gate,
　And the Warder is Despair.

(Concluded on next page)

at last to the verge of publication, without one act of assistance, one word of encouragement, or one smile of favor ❧ Such treatment I did not expect, for I never had a patron before.

The shepherd in Virgil grew at last acquainted with Love, and found him a native of the rocks. Is not a patron, my lord, one who looks with unconcern on a man struggling for life in the water and when he has reached ground, encumbers him with help? The notice which you have been pleased to take of my labors, had it been early had been kind: but it has been delayed till I am indifferent, and can not enjoy it; till I am solitary, and can not impart it; till I am known, and do not want it. I hope it is no very cynical asperity not to confess obligations where no benefit has been received, or to be unwilling that the public should consider me as owing that to a patron which Providence has enabled me to do for myself.

Having carried on my work thus far with so little obligation to any favorer of learning, I shall not be disappointed though I should conclude it, if less be possible, with less; for I have been long wakened from that dream of hope in which I once boasted myself with so much exultation, my lord,

Your Lordship's most humble, most obedient servant, Sam. Johnson.

R. ROGERS was complimented on his energy, his foresightedness and complimented in various ways, and he has deserved those compliments, although I say it myself; and I enjoy them all. There is one side of Mr. Rogers that has not been mentioned. If you will leave that to me I will touch upon that. There was a note in an editorial in one of the Norfolk papers this morning that touched upon that very thing, that hidden side of Mr. Rogers, where it spoke of Helen Keller and her affection for Mr. Rogers to whom she dedicated her life book. And she has a right to feel that way, because, without the public knowing anything about it, he rescued, if I may use that term, that marvelous girl, that wonderful Southern girl, that girl who was stone deaf, blind, and dumb from scarlet-fever when she was a baby eighteen months old; and who now is as well and thoroughly educated as any woman on this planet at twenty-nine years of age. She is the most marvelous person of her sex that has existed on this earth since Joan of Arc.

That is not all Mr. Rogers has done; but you never see that side of his chraacter, because it is never protruding; but he lends a helping hand daily out of that generous heart of his. You never hear of

For they starve the little frightened child
  Till it weeps both night and day:
And they scourge the weak, and flog the fool,
  And gibe the old and gray,
And some grow mad, and all grow bad,
  And none a word may say.

Each narrow cell in which we dwell
  Is a foul and dark latrine,
And the fetid breath of living Death
  Chokes up each grated screen.
And all, but Lust, is turned to dust
  In Humanity's machine.

The brackish water that we drink
  Creeps with a loathsome slime,
And the bitter bread they weigh in scales
  Is full of chalk and lime,
And sleep will not lie down, but walks
  Wild-eyed, and cries to Time.

* * * * * *

And every human heart that breaks,
  In prison-cell or yard,
Is as that broken box that gave
  Its treasure to the Lord,
And filled the unclean leper's house
  With the scent of costliest nard.

Ah! happy they whose hearts can break
  And peace of pardon win?
How else may man make straight his plan
  And cleanse his soul from Sin?
How else but through a broken heart
  May Lord Christ enter in?

"The Ballad of Reading Gaol," *by Oscar Wilde*

it. He is supposed to be a moon which has one side dark and the other bright. But the other side, though you don't see it, is not dark; it is bright, and its rays penetrate, and others do see it who are not God.

I would take this opportunity to tell something that I have never been allowed to tell by Mr. Rogers, either by my mouth or in print, and if I don't look at him I can tell it now.

In 1893, when the publishing company of Charles L. Webster, of which I was financial agent, failed, it left me heavily in debt. If you will remember what commerce was at that time you will recall that you could not sell anything, and could not buy anything, and I was on my back; my books were not worth anything at all, and I could not give away my copyrights. Mr. Rogers had long enough vision ahead to say, " Your books have supported you before, and after the panic is over they will support you again," and that was a correct proposition. He saved my copyrights, and saved me from financial ruin. He it was who arranged with my creditors to allow me to roam the face of the earth for four years and persecute the nations thereof with lectures, promising that at the end of four years I would pay dollar for dollar. That arrangement was made; otherwise I would now be living out-of-doors under an umbrella, and a borrowed one at that. ❡ You see his mustache and his head trying to get white (he is always trying to look like me—I don't blame him for that). These are only emblematic of his character, and that is all. I say, without exception, hair and all, he is the whitest man I have ever known.—Mark Twain. (From speech delivered at banquet to H. H. Rogers.)

WHEN a man's deeds are discovered after death, his angels, who are inquisitors, look into his face, and extend their examination over his whole body, beginning with the fingers of each hand. I was surprised at this, and the reason was thus explained to me:
Every volition and thought of man is inscribed on his brain; for volition and thought have their beginnings in the brain, thence they are conveyed to the bodily members, wherein they terminate. Whatever, therefore, is in the mind is in the brain, and from the brain in the body according to the order of its parts. So a man writes his life in his physique, and thus the angels discover his autobiography in his structure.

—Swedenborg.

IT takes a great deal of boldness mixed with a vast deal of caution, to acquire a great fortune; but then it takes ten times as much wit to keep it after you have got it as it took to make it.
—Mayer A. Rothschild.

TO the beloved and deplored memory of her who was the inspirer, and in part the author, of all that is best in my writings—the friend and wife whose exalted sense of truth and right was my strongest incitement, and whose approbation was my chief reward—I dedicate this volume. Like all that I have written for many years, it belongs as much to her as to me; but the work as it stands has had, in a very insufficient degree, the inestimable advantage of her revision; some of the most important portions having been reserved for a more careful examination, which they are now destined never to receive. Were I but capable of interpreting to the world one-half the great thoughts and noble feelings which are buried in her grave, I should be the medium of a greater benefit to it, than is ever likely to arise from anything that I can write, unprompted and unassisted by her all but unrivaled wisdom.—John Stuart Mill. (Dedication to " On Liberty.")

HAPPINESS itself is sufficient excuse. Beautiful things are right and true; so beautiful actions are those pleasing to the gods. Wise men have an inward sense of what is beautiful, and the highest wisdom is to trust this intuition and be guided by it. The answer to the last appeal of what is right lies within a man's own breast. Trust thyself.—Aristotle.

THE canons of scientific evidence justify us neither in accepting nor rejecting the ideas upon which morality and religion repose. Both parties to the dispute beat the air; they worry their own shadow; for they pass from Nature into the domain of speculation, where their dogmatic grips find nothing to lay hold upon. The shadows which they hew to pieces grow together in a moment like the heroes in Valhalla, to rejoice again in bloodless battles ✺ Metaphysics can no longer claim to be the cornerstone of religion and morality. But if she can not be the Atlas that bears the moral world she can furnish a magic defense. Around the ideas of religion she throws her bulwark of invisibility; and the sword of the skeptic and the battering-ram of the materialist fall harmless on vacuity.
—Immanuel Kant.

Let our schools teach the nobility of labor and the beauty of human service, but the superstitions of ages past—never!—Peter Cooper.

The ruin of most men dates from some idle moment.—George S. Hillard.

A great thing is a great book; but a greater thing than all is the talk of a great man.—Disraeli.

HAT knowledge is of most worth? The uniform reply is: Science. This is the verdict on all counts ✤ For direct self-preservation, or the maintenance of life and health, the all-important knowledge is—science. For that indirect self-preservation which we call gaining a livelihood, the knowledge of greatest value is—science. For the discharge of parental functions, the proper guidance is to be found only in science. For the interpretation of national life, past and present, without which the citizen can not rightly regulate his conduct, the indispensable key is—science. Alike for the most perfect production and present enjoyment of art in all its forms, the needful preparation is still—science. And for purposes of discipline—intellectual, moral, religious—the most efficient is, once more science.

—Herbert Spencer.

He is not only idle who does nothing, but he is idle who might be better employed.

—Socrates.

ONE comfort is that great men taken up in any way are profitable company. We can not look, however imperfectly, upon a great man without gaining something by it. He is the living fountain of life, which it is pleasant to be near. On any terms whatsoever you will not grudge to wander in his neighborhood for a while.—Carlyle.

Simplicity is an exact medium between too little and too much.

—Sir Joshua Reynolds.

WHEN I meet a laborer on the edge of a field, I stop and look at the man born amid the grain where he will be reaped, and turning up with his plow the ground of his tomb, mixing his burning sweat with the icy rain of Autumn. The furrow he has just turned is a monument that will outlive him. I have seen the pyramids of Egypt, and the forgotten furrows of our heather: both alike bear witness to the work of man and the shortness of his days.—Chateaubriand.

THE last moments which Nelson passed at Merton were employed in praying over his little daughter as she lay sleeping. A portrait of Lady Hamilton hung in his cabin; and no Catholic ever beheld the picture of his patron saint with more devout reverence. The undisguised and romantic passion with which he regarded it amounted almost to superstition; and when the portrait was now taken down, in clearing for action, he desired the man who removed it to "take care of his guardian angel." In this manner he frequently spoke of it, as if he believed there was a virtue in the image. He wore a miniature of her also next to his heart.—Robert Southey.

I am quite certain that there is nothing which draws so good, or at least so large a congregation as a fight in the pulpit.—Bolton Hall.

MY horse was very lame, and my head did ache exceedingly. Now what occurred I here avow is truth—let each man account for it as he will. Suddenly I thought, "Can not God heal man or beast as He will?" Immediately my weariness and headache passed; and my horse was no longer lame.

—John Wesley's Journal.

There is but one God—is it Allah or Jehovah? The palm-tree is sometimes called a date-tree, but there is only one tree.—Disraeli.

WE are intelligent beings; and intelligent beings can not have been formed by a blind brute, insensible being. There is certainly some difference, between a clod and the ideas of Newton. Newton's intelligence came from some greater Intelligence.—Voltaire.

Looking around on the noisy inanity of the world,—words with little meaning, actions with little worth,—one loves to reflect on the great Empire of Silence, higher than all stars; deeper than the Kingdom of Death! It alone is great; all else is small.—Carlyle.

Y DEAR SPENCER: Your telegram which reached me on Friday evening caused me great perplexity, inasmuch as I had just been talking to Morley, and agreeing with him that the proposal for a funeral in Westminster Abbey had a very questionable look to us, who desired nothing so much as that peace and honor should attend George Eliot to her grave *so so*

It can hardly be doubted that the proposal will be bitterly opposed, possibly (as happened in Mill's case with less provocation) with the raking up of past histories, about which the opinion even of those who have least the desire or the right to be pharisaical is strongly divided, and which had better be forgotten *so*

❡ With respect to putting pressure on the Dean of Westminster, I have to consider that he has some confidence in me, and before asking him to do something for which he is pretty sure to be violently assailed, I have to ask myself whether I really think it a right thing for a man in his position to do.

Now I can not say I do. However much I may lament the circumstance, Westminster Abbey is a Christian Church and not a Pantheon, and the Dean thereof is officially a Christian priest, and we ask him to bestow exceptional Christian honors by this burial in the Abbey *so* George Eliot is known not only as a great writer, but as a person whose life and opinions were in notorious antagonism

Oh, may I join the choir invisible
Of those immortal dead who live again
In minds made better by their presence; live
In pulses stirred to generosity,
In deeds of daring rectitude, in scorn
For miserable aims that end with self,
In thoughts sublime that pierce the night
   like stars,
And with their mild persistence urge man's
   search
To vaster issues.
       So to live is heaven:
To make undying music in the world,
Breathing as beauteous order, that
   controls
With growing sway the growing life of
   man.
So we inherit that sweet purity.
For which we struggled, failed and
   agonized,
With widening retrospect that bred despair,
Rebellious flesh that would not be sub-
   dued,
A vicious parent shaming still its child—
Poor anxious penitence—is quick dis-
   solved;
Its discords, quenched by meeting har-
   monies,

(Concluded on next page)

to Christian practice in regard to marriage, and Christian theory in regard to dogma. How am I to tell the Dean that I think he ought to read over the body of a person who did not repent of what the Church considers mortal sin, a service not one solitary proposition of which she would have accepted for truth while she was alive? How am I to urge him to do that which, if I were in his place, I should most emphatically refuse to do? You tell me that Mrs. Cross wished for the funeral in the Abbey. While I desire to entertain the greatest respect for her wishes, I am very sorry to hear it. I do not understand the feeling which could create such an unusual desire on any personal grounds save those of affection, and the natural yearning to be near, even in death, those whom we have loved. And on public grounds the wish is still less intelligible to me. One can not eat one's cake and have it too. Those who elect to be free in thought and deed must not hanker after the rewards, if they are to be so called, which the world offers to those who put up with its fetters.

Thus, however I look at the proposal, it seems to me to be a profound mistake, and I can have nothing to do with it. I shall be deeply grieved if this resolution is ascribed to any other motives than those which I have set forth at greater length than I intended.

Ever yours very faithfully, T. H. Huxley. (Letter to Herbert Spencer.)

LEONARDO painted souls whereof the features and the limbs are but an index. The charm of Michelangelo's ideal is like a flower upon a tree of rugged strength. Raphael aims at the loveliness which can not be disjoined from goodness. But Correggio is contented with bodies "delicate and desirable." ❧ His angels are genii disimprisoned from the perfumed chalices of flowers, houris of an erotic paradise, elemental spirits of nature wantoning in Eden in her prime. To accuse the painter of conscious immorality, or of what is stigmatized as sensuality, would be as ridiculous as to class his seraphic beings among the products of the Christian imagination. They belong to the generation of the fauns; like fauns, they combine a certain savage wildness a dithyrambic ecstasy of inspiration, a delight in rapid movements as they revel amid clouds or flowers, with the permanent and all-pervading sweetness of the master's style. ❡ When infantine or childlike, these celestial sylphs are scarcely to be distinguished for any noble quality of beauty from Murillo's cherubs, and are far less divine than the choir of children who attend the Madonna in Titian's "Assumption." But in their boyhood and their prime of youth they acquire a fullness of sensuous vitality and a radiance that are peculiar to Correggio . . . . .

As a consequence of the predilection for sensuous and voluptuous forms, Correggio had no power of imagining grandly or severely . . . . He could not, as it were, sustain a grave and solemn strain of music. He was forced by his temperament to overlay the melody with roulades. Gazing at his frescos, the thought came to me that Correggio was like a man listening to sweetest fluteplaying, and translating phrase after phrase as they passed through his fancy into laughing faces, breezy tresses, and rolling mists. Sometimes a grander cadence reached his ear; and then St. Peter with the keys, or St. Augustine of the mighty brow, or the inspired eyes of St. John took form beneath his pencil ❧ But the light airs returned, and rose, and lily faces bloomed again for him among the clouds. It is not therefore in dignity or sublimity that Correggio excels, but in artless grace and melodious tenderness.

* * * *

Now the mood which Correggio stimulates is one of natural and thoughtless pleasure. To feel his influence, and at the same moment to be the subject of strong passion, or fierce lust, or heroic resolve, or profound contemplation, or pensive melancholy, is impossible. Wantonness, innocent because unconscious of sin, immoral because incapable of any serious purpose, is the quality which prevails in all that he has painted.

It follows from this analysis that the Correggiosity of Correggio, that which sharply distinguished him from all previous artists, was the faculty of painting

Die in the large and charitable air;
And all our rarer, better, truer self,
That sobbed religiously in yearning song,
That watched to ease the burthen of the
*   world,*
Laboriously tracing what must be,
And what may yet be better—saw within
A worthier image for the sanctuary,
And shaped it forth before the multitude
Divinely human, raising worship so
To higher reverence more mixed with love—
That better self shall live till human Time
Shall fold its eyelids and the human sky
Be gathered like a scroll within the tomb
Unread forever.
*   This is life to come,*
Which martyred men have made more
*   glorious*
For us who strive to follow. May I reach
That purest heaven; be to other souls
The cup of strength in some great agony;
Enkindle generous ardor; feed pure love;
Beget the smiles that have no cruelty—
Be the sweet presence of a good diffused,
And in diffusion even more intense.
So shall I join the choir invisible
Whose music is the gladness of the world.

"Oh, May I Join the Choir Invisible,"
by George Eliot

a purely voluptuous dream of beautiful beings in perpetual movement, beneath the laughter of morning light, in a world of never-failing April hues.

When he attempts to depart from the fairyland of which he was the Prospero, and to match himself with the master of sublime thought or earnest passion, he proves his weakness. But within his own magic circle he reigns supreme, no other artist having blended the witcheries of coloring, chiaroscuro and faunlike loveliness of form into a harmony so perfect in its sensuous charm.

¶ Bewitched by the strains of the siren we pardon affectations of expression, emptiness of meaning, feebleness of composition, exaggerated and melodramatic attitudes ֍ In that which is truly his own—the delineation of a transient moment in the life of sensuous beauty, the painting of a smile on Nature's face, when light and color tremble in harmony with the movement of joyous living creatures—none can approach Correggio.—John Addington Symonds.

PRIESTS look backward, not forward ֍ They think that there were once men better and wiser than those who now live, therefore priests distrust the living and insist that we shall be governed by the dead. I believe this is an error, and hence I set myself against the Church and insist that men shall have the right to work out their lives in their own way, always allowing to others the right to work out their lives in their own way, too.
—Garibaldi.

Every war is a national calamity whether victorious or not.—Gen. Von. Moltke.

TITIAN by a few strokes of the brush knew how to make the general image and character of whatever object he attempted. His great care was to preserve the masses of light and of shade, and to give by opposition the idea of that solidity which is inseparable from natural objects. He was the greatest of the Venetians and deserves to rank with Raphael and Michelangelo.
—Sir Joshua Reynolds.

THE eyes and the mouth are the supremely significant features of the human face. In Rembrandt's portraits the eye is the center wherein life, in its infinity of aspect, is most manifest. Not only was his fidelity absolute, but there is a certain mysterious limpidity of gaze that reveals the soul of the sitter ֍ A " Rembrandt " does not give up its beauties to the casual observer—it takes time to know it, but once known, it is yours forever.
—Emile Michel.

The Vice of our Theology is seen in the claim that the Bible is a Closed Book and that the Age of Inspiration is Past.
—Emerson.

SOME have narrowed their minds, and so fettered them with the chains of antiquity that not only do they refuse to speak save as the ancients spake, but they refuse to think save as the ancients thought. God speaks to us, too, and the best thoughts are those now being vouchsafed to us. We will excel the ancients!—Savonarola.

The record of a generous life runs like a vine around the memory of our dead, and every sweet, unselfish act is now a perfumed flower.—Robert G. Ingersoll.

WIT is a happy and striking way of expressing a thought.
It is not often, though it be lively and mantling, that it carries a great body with it.
Wit, therefore, is fitter for diversion than business, being more grateful to fancy than judgment.
Less judgment than wit, is more sail than ballast.
Yet it must be confessed that wit gives an edge to sense, and recommends it extremely ֍ ֍
Where judgment has wit to express it, there is the best orator.
—William Penn.

You can never have a greater or a less dominion than that over yourself.
—Leonardo da Vinci.

FRIEND and Brother:—It was the will of the Great Spirit that we should meet together this day. He orders all things and has given us a fine day for our council. He has taken His garment from before the sun and caused it to shine with brightness upon us. Our eyes are opened that we see clearly; our ears are unstopped that we have been able to hear distinctly the words you have spoken. For all these favors we thank the Great Spirit, and Him only.

Brother, this council fire was kindled by you. It was at your request that we came together at this time. We have listened with attention to what you have said. You requested us to speak our minds freely. This gives us great joy; for we now consider that we stand upright before you and can speak what we think. All have heard your voice and all speak to you now as one man. Our minds are agreed

Brother, you say you want an answer to your talk before you leave this place. It is right you should have one, as you are a great distance from home and we do not wish to detain you. But first we will look back a little and tell you what our fathers have told us and what we have heard from the white people.

Brother, listen to what we say. There was a time when our forefathers owned this great island. Their seats extended from the rising to the setting sun. The Great Spirit had made it for the use of Indians. He had created the buffalo, the deer, and other animals for food. He had made the bear and the beaver. Their skins served us for clothing. He had scattered them over the country and taught us how to take them. He had caused the earth to produce corn for bread. All this He had done for His red children because He loved them. If we had some disputes about our hunting-ground they were generally settled without the shedding of much blood.

But an evil day came upon us Your forefathers crossed the great water and landed on this island. Their numbers were small. They found friends and not enemies. They told us they had fled from their own country for fear of wicked men and had come here to enjoy their religion. They asked for a small seat We took pity on them, granted their request, and they sat down among us. We gave them corn and meat; they gave us poison in return

The white people, brother, had now found our country. Tidings were carried back and more came among us. Yet we did not fear them We took them to be friends. They called us brothers. We believed them and gave them a larger seat. At length their numbers had greatly increased. They wanted more land; they wanted our country Our eyes were opened and our minds became uneasy. Wars took place, Indians were hired to fight against Indians, and many of our people were destroyed. They also brought strong liquor among us. It was strong and powerful, and has slain thousands.

Brother, our seats were once large and yours were small. You have now become a great people, and we have scarcely a place left to spread our blankets. You have got our country, but are not yet satisfied; you want to force your religion upon us.

Brother, continue to listen. You say that you are sent to instruct us how to worship the Great Spirit agreeably to His mind; and, if we do not take hold of the religion which you white people teach, we shall be unhappy hereafter. You say that you are right and we are lost. How do we know this to be true? We understand that your religion is written in a Book. If it was intended for us, as well as you, why has not the Great Spirit given to us, and not only to us, but why did He not give to our forefathers the knowledge of that Book, with the means of understanding it rightly? We only know what you tell us about it. How shall we know when to believe, being so often deceived by the white people?

Brother, you say there is but one way to worship and serve the Great Spirit. If there is but one religion, why do you white people differ so much about it? Why not all agreed, as you can all read the Book?

Brother, we do not understand these things. We are told that your religion was given to your forefathers and has been handed down from father to son. We also have a religion which was given our forefathers and has been handed down to us, their children. We worship in our way. It teaches us to be thankful for all the favors we receive, to love each other, and to be united. We never quarrel about religion.

Brother, the Great Spirit has made us all, but He has made a great difference between His white and His red children. He has given us different complexions and different customs. ❧ To you He has given the arts. To these He has not opened our eyes ❧ We know these things to be true. Since He has made so great a difference between us in other things, why may we not conclude that He has given us a different religion according to our understanding? ❧ The Great Spirit does right ❧ He knows what is best for His children; we are satisfied. ❧ Brother, we do not wish to destroy your religion or take it from you. We only want to enjoy our own.

Brother, you say you have not come to get our lands or our money, but to enlighten our minds. I will now tell you that I have been at your meetings and saw you collect money from the meeting. I can not tell what this money was intended for, but suppose that it was for your minister; and, if we should conform to your way of thinking, perhaps you may want some from us.

Brother, we are told that you have been preaching to the white people in this place ❧ These people are our neighbors. We are acquainted with them. We will wait a little while and see what effect your preaching has upon them. If we find it does them good, makes them honest, and less disposed to cheat Indians, we will consider again of what you have said.

Brother you have now heard our answer to your talk, and this is all we have to say at present. As we are going to part, we will come and take you by the hand, and hope the Great Spirit will protect you on your journey and return you safe to your friends.

—Red Jacket.
(Reply to a Missionary who had spoken about his Mission among the Seneca Indians.)

*They made the chamber sweet with
　flowers and leaves,
And the bed sweet with flowers on which
　I lay;
While my soul, love-bound, loitered on
　its way.
I did not hear the birds about the eaves,
Nor hear the reapers talk among the
　sheaves:
Only my soul kept watch from day to day,
My thirsty soul kept watch for one away:—
Perhaps he loves, I thought, remembers,
　grieves.
At length there came the step upon the
　stair,
Upon the lock the old familiar hand:
Then first my spirit seemed to scent the air
Of Paradise; then first the tardy sand
Of time ran golden; and I felt my hair
Put on a glory, and my soul expand.*

THE FIRST DAY

*I wish I could remember the first day,
First hour, first moment of your meeting
　me,
If bright or dim the season, it might be
Summer or Winter for aught I can say;
So unrecorded did it slip away,
So blind was I to see and to foresee,
So dull to mark the budding of my tree
That would not blossom yet for many a May.
If only I could recollect it, such
A day of days! I let it come and go
As traceless as a thaw of bygone snow;
It seemed to mean so little, meant so
　much;
If only now I could recall that touch,
First touch of hand in hand—Did one but
　know!*

(Concluded on next page)

❧ ❧

THE Public Health is the foundation upon which rests the happiness of the people and the welfare of the nation. The care of the Public Health is the first duty of the statesman.

—Disraeli.

OW many a man has dated a new era in his life from the reading of a book. The book exists for us perchance which will explain our miracles and reveal new ones ✍ The at present unutterable things we may find somewhere uttered. These same questions that disturb and puzzle and confound us have in their turn occurred to all the wise men; not one has been omitted; and each has answered them according to his ability, by his word and his life. Moreover, with wisdom we shall learn liberality. The solitary hired man on a farm in the outskirts of Concord, who has had his second birth and peculiar religious experience, and is driven as he believes into silent gravity and exclusiveness by his faith may think it is not true; but Zoroaster, thousands of years ago, traveled the same road and had the same experience; but he, being wise, knew it to be universal, and treated his neighbors accordingly, and is even said to have invented, and established worship among men. Let him humbly commune with Zoroaster then, and through the liberalizing influence of all the worthies, with Jesus Christ himself, and let " our church go by the board."

REMEMBER

Remember me when I am gone away,
Gone far into the silent land!
When you can no more hold me by the
*   hand,*
Nor I half turn to go, yet turning stay.
Remember me when no more, day by day,
You tell me of our future that you planned:
Only remember me; you understand
It will be late to counsel then or pray.
Yet if you should forget me for a while
And afterwards remember, do not grieve:
For if the darkness and corruption leave
A vestige of the thoughts that once I had,
Better by far you should forget and smile
Than that you should remember and be sad.

REST

O earth, lie heavily upon her eyes;
Seal her sweet eyes weary of watching,
*   Earth;*
Lie close around her; leave no room for
*   mirth*
With its harsh laughter, nor for sound of
*   sighs.*
She hath no questions, she hath no replies.
Hushed in and curtained with a blessed
*   dearth*
Of all that irked her from the hour of birth;
With stillness that is almost Paradise.
Darkness more clear than noonday holdeth
*   her,*
Silence more musical than any song;
Even her very heart has ceased to stir;
Until the morning of Eternity
Her rest shall not begin nor end, but be;
And when she wakes she will not think it
*   long.*

" Sonnets," *by Christina Georgina Rossetti*

We boast that we belong to the nineteenth century and are making the most rapid strides of any nation. But consider how little this village does for its own culture. I do not wish to flatter my townsmen, nor to be flattered by them, for that will not advance either of us. We need to be provoked goaded like oxen, as we are, into a trot ✍ We have a comparatively decent system of common schools, schools for infants only; but excepting the half-starved Lyceum in the winter, and latterly the puny beginning of a library suggested by the state, no school for ourselves ✍ We spend more on almost any article of bodily aliment or ailment than on our mental aliment. It is time that we had uncommon schools, that we did not leave off our education when we begin to be men and women. It is time that villages were universities, and their elder inhabitants the fellows of universities, with leisure—if they are indeed so well off— to pursue liberal studies the rest of their lives. Shall the world be confined to one Paris or one Oxford forever? Can not students be boarded here and get a liberal education under the skies of Concord? Can we not hire some Abelard to lecture to us? Alas! what with foddering the cattle and tending the store, we are kept from school too long, and our education is sadly neglected ✍ In this country, the village should in some respects take the place of the nobleman of Europe ✍ It should be the patron of fine arts. It is rich enough. It wants only the magnanimity and refinement. It can spend money enough on such things as farmers and traders value, but it is thought Utopian to propose spending money for things which more intelligent men know to be of far more worth.

—Henry David Thoreau.

✍ ✍

Ideals are like stars; you will not succeed in touching them with your hands, but like the seafaring man on the desert of waters, you choose them as your guides, and, following them, you reach your destiny.—Carl Schurz.

✍ ✍

Freedom is alone the unoriginated birthright of man; it belongs to him by force of his humanity, and is in dependence on the will and creation of every other, in so far as this consists with every other person's freedom.—Kant.

✍ ✍

IF any pilgrim monk come from distant parts, if with wish as a guest to dwell in the monastery, and will be content with the customs which he finds in the place, and do not perchance by his lavishness disturb the monastery, but is simply content with what he finds: he shall be received, for as long a time as he desires. If, indeed, he find fault with anything, or expose it, reasonably, and with the humility of charity, the Abbot shall discuss it prudently, lest perchance God had sent for this very thing. But, if he have been found gossipy and contumacious in the time of his sojourn as guest, not only ought he not to be joined to the body of the monastery, but also it shall be said to him, honestly, that he must depart. If he does not go, let two stout monks, in the name of God, explain the matter to him.—St. Benedict.

✍ ✍

Solitude is as needful to the imagination as society is wholesome for the character.

—James Russell Lowell.

AS to Vaucluse, I well know the beauties of that charming valley, and ten years' residence is proof of my affection for the place. I have shown my love of it by the house which I built there. There I began my article "Africa," there I wrote the greater part of my epistles in prose and verse. At Vaucluse I conceived the first idea of giving an epitome of the Lives of Illustrious Men, and there I wrote my treatise on a Solitary Life, as well as that on religious retirement ✍ It was there, also, that I sought to moderate my passion for Laura, which, alas, solitude only cherished. And so this lonely valley will be forever sacred to my recollections.

—Petrarch.

✍ ✍

No man is in true health who can not stand in the free air of heaven, with his feet on God's free turf, and thank his Creator for the simple luxury of physical existence.—T. W. Higginson.

✍ ✍

I love the man that can smile in trouble, that can gather strength from distress, and grow brave by reflection. 'T is the business of little minds to shrink, but he whose heart is firm, and whose conscience approves his conduct, will pursue his principles unto death.

—Thomas Paine.

✍ ✍

NEO-PLATONISM is a progressive philosophy, and does not expect to state final conditions to men whose minds are finite. Life is an unfoldment, and the further we travel the more truth we can comprehend. To understand the things that are at our door is the best preparation for understanding those that lie beyond.—Hypatia.

✍ ✍

There is one right which man is generally thought to possess, which I am confident he neither does nor can possess—the right to subsistence when his labor will not fairly purchase it.—Thomas R. Malthus.

✍ ✍

I do not value fortune. The love of labor is my sheet-anchor. I work that I may forget, and forgetting, I am happy.

—Stephen Girard.

THE enjoyment of my life has been greatly promoted by the undoubted love and untiring kindness of all with whom I have ever lived, and of a numerous association of disciples, from whom I have continually received the most pleasant attentions, in many cases amounting to a devotion to which I was in no way entitled; and I have quite often warned them against the injurious influence of *names* upon the independence of mind and of free thought on all subjects ♋ ♋

I have had much difficulty in convincing many that the authority given to names has been through all past ages most injurious to the human race, and that at this day their weakness of intellect was destructive of mental power and independence. That *truth* required no name for its support; it substantially supported itself ♋ But that falsehood and error always required the authority of names to maintain them in society, and to give them ready currency with those who never reflected or thought for themselves. ❡ Had it not been for the baneful influence of the authority given to names, this false, ignorant, unjust, extravagant, cruel and misery-producing system, of individual interest opposed to individual interest, and of national interests opposed to national interests, could not have been thus long maintained through the centuries that have passed ♋ The universe—the incalculable, superiority of the true, enlightened, just, economical, merciful, and happiness-producing system, of union between individuals, nations, and tribes, over the earth, would have been long since discovered and

Come, let me take thee to my breast,
  And pledge we ne'er shall sunder;
And I shall spurn, as vilest dust,
  The world's wealth and grandeur.

And do I hear my Jeannie own
  That equal transports move her?
I ask for dearest life, alone,
  That I may live to love her.

Thus in my arms, wi' a' thy charms,
  I clasp my countless treasure;
I 'll seek nae mair o' heaven to share
  Than sic a moment's pleasure.

And by thy een, sae bonnie blue,
  I swear I 'm thine for ever:
And on thy lips I seal my vow,
  And break it shall I never.
  " To Jeannie," *by Robert Burns*

practised, and the Millennial state of man upon the earth would have been now in full vigor and established for ever ♋ ♋

What divisions, hatreds, miseries, and dreadful physical and mental sufferings have been produced by the names of Confucius, Brahma, Juggernaut, Moses, Jesus, Mohammed, Penn, Joe Smith, Mother Lee, etc.! If any of these could have imagined that their names should cause the disunion, hatred and suffering which poor deluded followers and disciples have experienced, how these good or well-intentioned persons would have lamented that they had ever lived to implant such deadly hatred between man and man, and to cause so much error and false feeling between those whose happiness can arise only from universal union of mind and co-operation in practise, neither of which can any of the religions of the earth, as now taught and practised, ever produce.—Robert Owen.

♋ ♋

REMBRANDT'S domestic troubles served only to heighten and deepen his art and perhaps his best canvases were painted under stress of circumstances and in sadness of heart. His life is another proof, if needed, that the greatest truths and beauties are to be seen only through tears ♋ Too bad for the man! But the world—the same ungrateful, selfish world that has always lighted its torch at the funeral pyres of genius—is the gainer.
—John C. Van Dyke.

♋ ♋

To love and win is the best thing; to love and lose the next best.
—William Makepeace Thackeray.

IME was when slaves were exported like cattle from the British Coast and exposed for sale in the Roman market. These men and women who were thus sold were supposed to be guilty of witchcraft, debt, blasphemy or theft. Or else they were prisoners taken in war—they had forfeited their right to freedom, and we sold them. We said they were incapable of self-government and so must be looked after. Later we quit selling British slaves, but began to buy and trade in African humanity ❧ We silenced conscience by saying, "It's all right—they are incapable of self-government." We were once as obscure, as debased, as ignorant, as barbaric, as the African is now. I trust that the time will come when we are willing to give to Africa the opportunity, the hope, the right to attain to the same blessings that we ourselves enjoy.—William Pitt.

THE highest study of all is that which teaches us to develop those principles of purity and perfect virtue which Heaven bestowed upon us at our birth, in order that we may acquire the power of influencing for good those amongst whom we are placed, by our precepts and example; a study without an end—for our labors cease only when we have become perfect—an unattainable goal, but one that we must not the less set before us from the very first. It is true that we shall not be able to reach it, but in our struggle toward it we shall strengthen our characters and give stability to our ideas, so that, whilst ever advancing calmly in the same direction, we shall be rendered capable of applying the faculties with which we have been gifted to the best possible account.—Confucius

A great city, whose image dwells on the memory of man, is the type of some great idea ❧ Rome represents conquest; faith hovers over Jerusalem; and Athens embodies the preeminent quality of the antique world-art.—Disraeli.

Silence is a true friend who never betrays.
—Confucius.

WHAT makes a man noble? Not sacrifice, for the most extreme sensualist is capable of sacrifice. Not the following of a passion, for some passions are shameful. Not the serving of others without any self-seeking, for perhaps it is just the self-seeking of the noblest which brings forth the greatest results. No; but something in passion which is special though not conscious; a discernment which is rare and singular and akin to frenzy; a sense of heat in things which for others are cold; a perception of values for which no estimate has been established; a sacrificing on altars which are dedicated to an unknown God; a courage that claims no homage; a self-sufficiency which is super-abundant and unites men and things.—Nietzsche.

LACROIX told Gustave Doré one day, early in his life in Paris, that he should illustrate a new edition of his works in four volumes, and he sent them to him. In a week Lacroix said to Doré, who had called, "Well, have you begun to read my story?" ❧ "Oh! I mastered that in no time; the blocks are all ready;" and while Lacroix looked on stupefied, the boy dived into his pockets and piled many of them on the table, saying, "The others are in a basket at the door; there are three hundred in all!"
—Blanche Roosevelt.

When thee builds a prison, thee had better build with the thought ever in thy mind that thee and thy children may occupy the cells.—Elizabeth Fry. (Report on Paris Prisons. Addressed to the King of France.)

A man can know nothing of mankind without knowing something of himself. Self-knowledge is the property of that man whose passions have their full play, but who ponders over their results.
—Disraeli.

Love of truth will bless the lover all his days; yet when he brings her home, his fair-faced bride, she comes empty-handed to his door, herself her only dower.—Theodore Parker.

ELIX Mendelssohn was not a bit " sentimental," though he had so much sentiment. Nobody enjoyed fun more than he, and his company was the most joyous that could be.

One evening in hot summer we stayed in the wood above our house later than usual. We had been building a house of fir branches in Susan's garden up in the wood. We made a fire, a little way off it, in a thicket among the trees, Mendelssohn helping with the utmost zeal, dragging up more and more wood: we tired ourselves with our merry work; we sat down round our fire, the smoke went off, the ashes were glowing, it began to get dark, but we did not like to leave our bonfire.

" If we had some music!" Mendelssohn said, "Could any one get something to play on?" Then my brother recollected that we were near the gardener's cottage, and that the gardener had a fiddle. Off rushed our boys to get the fiddle. When it came it was the wretchedest thing in the world, and it had only one string.

Mendelssohn took the instrument in his hands and fell into fits of laughter over it when he heard the sounds it made. His laughter was very catching, he put us all into peals of merriment. But he, somehow, afterwards brought beautiful music out of the poor old fiddle, and we sat listening to one strain after another till the darkness sent us home.

—Reminiscences of Alice **Taylor.**

The wise man must remember that while he is a descendant of the past, he is a parent of the future; and that his thoughts are as children born to him, which he may not carelessly let die.

—Herbert Spencer.

A man is a great thing upon the earth and through eternity; but every jot of the greatness of man is unfolded out of woman.—Walt Whitman.

The Courage we desire and prize is not the Courage to die decently, but to live manfully.—Carlyle.

THO I am truly sensible of the high honor done me in this appointment, yet I feel great distress from a consciousness that my abilities and military experience may not be equal to the extensive and important trust. However, as the Congress desire it, I will enter upon the momentous duty, and exert every power I possess in their service and for the support of the glorious cause I beg they will accept my most cordial thanks for this distinguished testimony of their approbation

But lest some unlucky event should happen unfavorable to my reputation, I beg it may be remembered by every gentleman in the room that I this day declare, with the utmost sincerity, I do not think myself equal to the command I am honored with.

As to pay, sir, I beg leave to assure the Congress that as no pecuniary consideration could have tempted me to accept this arduous employment at the expense of my domestic ease and happiness, I do not wish to make any profit from it. I will keep an exact account of my expenses. Those, I doubt not, they will discharge, and that is all I desire.

—George Washington. On His Appointment as Commander-in-Chief.

Next to knowing when to seize an opportunity, the most important thing in life is to know when to forego an advantage.—Disraeli.

Given a government with a big surplus and a big majority and a weak opposition, and you would debauch a committee of archangels.—Sir John A. Macdonald.

Necessity reforms the poor, and satiety reforms the rich.—Tacitus.

Science, when she has accomplished all her triumphs in her order, will still have to go back, when the time comes, to assist in building up a new creed by which man can live.—John Morley.

That is a good book, it seems to me, which is opened with expectation and closed with profit.—Louisa M. Alcott.

MY piano is to me what his boat is to the seaman, what his horse is to the Arab: nay, more, it has been till now my eye, my speech, my life. Its strings have vibrated under my passions, and its yielding keys have obeyed my every caprice ✣ Perhaps the secret tie which holds me closely to it is a delusion; but I hold the piano very high ✣ ✣

In my view it takes the first place in the hierarchy of instruments; it is the oftenest used and the widest spread. . . . . In the circumference of its seven octaves it embraces the whole circumference of an orchestra; and a man's ten fingers are enough to render the harmonies which in an orchestra are only brought out by the combination of hundreds of musicians. . .

❡ We can give broken chords like the harp, long sustained notes like the wind, staccati and a thousand passages which before it seemed only possible to produce on this or that instrument . . . . The piano has on the one side the capacity of assimilation; the capacity of taking into itself the life of all instruments; on the other it has its own life, its own growth, its individual development ✣ It is a microcosm ✣ ✣

My highest ambition is to leave to piano-players after me some useful instructions, the footprints of attained advance, in fact, a work which may some day provide a worthy witness of the labor and study of my youth.

I remember the greedy dog in La Fontaine, which let the juicy bone fall from its mouth in order to grasp a shadow. Let me gnaw in peace at my bone. The hour will come, perhaps all too soon, in which I shall lose myself and hunt after a monstrous intangible shadow.

—Franz Liszt.

✣ ✣

The art of conversation is to be prompt without being stubborn, to refute without argument, and to clothe great matters in a motley garb.—Disraeli.

✣ ✣

Anybody can cut prices, but it takes brains to make a better article.

—Philip D. Armour.

THE first performance of the *Messiah* took place in the Neale's Music Hall in Dublin, on 18th April, 1742, at midday, and, apropos of the absurdities of fashion, it may be noted that the announcements contained the following request: " Ladies who honor this performance with their presence will be pleased to come *without hoops,* as it will greatly increase the charity by making room for more company."

The work was gloriously successful, and over £400 were obtained the first day for the Dublin charities. Handel seems always to have had a special feeling with regard to this masterpiece of his—as if it were too sacred to be merely used for making money, like his other works. . . . In this connection a fine saying of his may be repeated. Lord Kinnoul had complimented him on the noble " entertainment " which by the *Messiah* he had lately given the town.

" My lord," said Handel, " I should be sorry if I only entertained them—*I wish to make them better.*"

And when some one questioned him on his feelings when composing the Hallelujah Chorus, he replied in his peculiar English, " I did think I did see all heaven before me, and the great God Himself."

❡ What a fine saying that was of poor old George III, in describing the Pastoral Symphony in this oratorio—" I could see the stars shining through it! "

The now constant custom of the audience to rise and remain standing during the performance of this chorus, is said to have originated in the following manner: On the first production of the work in London, the audience were exceedingly struck and affected by the music in general; and when that chorus struck up, " For the Lord God Omnipotent " in the " Hallelujah," they were so transported that they all together, with the king (who happened to be present), started up and remained standing until the chorus ended. This anecdote I had from Lord Kinnoul.—Dr. James Beattie.

✣ ✣

It is much easier to be critical than to be correct.—Benjamin Disraeli.

THE Parnell I knew—and I may claim to have known him more intimately than anyone else on earth, both in public and private life— was incapable of motiveless brusqueries. That Parnell could crush utterly and without remorse I know; that he could deal harshly, even brutally, with anyone or anything that stood against him in the path he meant to tread, I admit, but that he would ever go out of his way to say a grossly rude thing or make an un-provoked attack, whether upon the personal appearance, morals, or character of another man, I absolutely deny. Par-nell was ruthless in all his dealings with those who thwarted his will, but—he was never petty.

Parnell had a most beautiful and har-monious voice when speaking in public. Very clear it was, even in moments of passion against his own and his coun-try's foes—passion modulated and sup-pressed until I have seen, from the Ladies' Gallery, his hand clenched until the " Orders of the Day " which he held were crushed into pulp, and only that prevented his nails piercing his hand. Often I have taken the "Orders " out of his pocket, twisted into shreds—a fate that also overtook the slips of notes and the occasional quotations he had got me to look out for him.

Sometimes when he was going to speak I could not leave my aunt long enough to be sure of getting to the Ladies' Gallery in time to hear him; or we might think it inexpedient that I should be seen to arrive so soon after him at the House. On these occasions, when I was able, I would arrive perhaps in the mid-dle of his speech and look down upon him, saying in my heart, " I have come! " and invariably I would see the answering signal—the lift of the head and lingering touch of the white rose in his coat, which told me, " I know, my Queen."

This telepathy of the soul, intuition, or what you will, was so strong between us that, whatever the business before the House, whether Parnell was speaking or not, in spite of the absolute impossi-bility of distinguishing any face or form behind the grille of the Ladies' Gallery, Parnell was aware of my presence, even though often he did not expect me, as soon as I came in, and answered my wordless message by the signal that I knew.—Katherine O'Shea (Mrs. Charles Stewart Parnell).

Rome endured as long as there were Romans. America will endure as long as we remain American in spirit and in thought.—David Starr Jordan.

If we had paid no more attention to our plants than we have to our children, we would now be living in a jungle of weeds.
—Luther Burbank.

The secret of happiness is not in doing what one likes, but in liking what one has to do.—James M. Barrie.

We no longer depend for Salvation upon either a man or a book. Men help us; books help us; but back of all stands our divine reason.—Charles W. Eliot.

You may depend upon it that there are as good hearts to serve men in palaces as in cottages.—Robert Owen.

It is only those who do not know how to work that do not love it. To those who do, it is better than play.—it is religion.
—J. H. Patterson.

Affection can withstand very severe storms of vigor, but not a long polar frost of indifference.—Sir Walter Scott.

Illusion and wisdom combined are the charm of life and art.—Joseph Joubert.

When one begins to turn in bed it is time to turn out.—Wellington.

Let us be thankful for the fools. But for them the rest of us could not succeed.
—Mark Twain.

Certain thoughts are prayers. There are moments when, whatever be the at-titude of the body, the soul is on its knees.—Victor Hugo.

IN my house you have met General Bonaparte. Well—he it is who would supply a father's place to the orphans of Alexander de Beauharnais, and a husband's to his widow. I admire the General's courage, the extent of his information, for on all subjects he talks equally well, and the quickness of his judgment, which enables him to seize the thoughts of others almost before they are expressed; but, I confess it, I shrink from the despotism he seems desirous of exercising over all who approach him ✒ His searching glance has something singular and inexplicable, which imposes even on our Directors; judge if it may not intimidate a woman. Even—what ought to please me —the force of a passion, described with an energy that leaves not a doubt of his sincerity, is precisely the cause which arrests the consent I am often on the point of pronouncing.

—Letters of Josephine.

You better live your best and act your best and think your best today; for today is the sure preparation for tomorrow and all the other tomorrows that follow.

—Harriet Martineau.

NOW wonderful is the human voice! It is indeed the organ of the soul! The intellect of man sits enthroned visibly upon his forehead and in his eye; and the heart of man is written upon his countenance. But the soul reveals itself in the voice only, as God revealed himself to the prophet of old,

Afoot and light-hearted I take to the
*   open road,*
Healthy, free, the world before me,
The long brown path before me leading
*   wherever I choose.*

Henceforth I ask not good fortune, I
*   myself am good-fortune;*
Henceforth I whimper no more, post-
*   pone no more, need nothing,*
Done with indoor complaints, libraries,
*   querulous criticisms,*
Strong and content I travel the open road

* * * * * *

All seems beautiful to me.
I can repeat over to men and women,
*   You have done such good to me I*
*   would do the same to you,*
I will recruit for myself and you as I go.
I will scatter myself among men and
*   women as I go,*
I will toss a new gladness and roughness
*   among them.*

" The Open Road," *by Walt Whitman*

in " the still, small voice," and in a voice from the burning bush. The soul of man is audible, not visible. A sound alone betrays the flowing of the eternal fountain, invisible to man!—Longfellow.

SOLDIERS, what I have to offer you is fatigue, danger, struggle and death; the chill of the cold night in the free air, and heat under the burning sun; no lodgings, no munitions, no provisions, but forced marches, dangerous watchposts and the continual struggle with the bayonet against batteries—those who love freedom and their country may follow me.

—Garibaldi to his Roman soldiers.

THE chief difference between a wise man and an ignorant one is, not that the first is acquainted with regions invisible to the second, away from common sight and interest, but that he understands the common things which the second only sees.

—Starr King.

We exaggerate misfortune and happiness alike. We are never either so wretched or so happy as we say we are.—Balzac.

That silence is one of the great arts of conversation is allowed by Cicero himself, who says there is not only an art, but an eloquence in it.—Hannah More.

Whether you be man or woman you will never do anything in this world without courage. It is the greatest quality of the mind next to honor.

—James L. Allen.

INDEXES

INDEX OF SUBJECTS

i

iii

INDEX OF AUTHORS

INDEX OF POETRY